THE ONE YEAR DEVOS FOR TEENS ②

Tyndale House Publishers, Inc., Carol Stream, IL

The ONE YEAR

DEVOS

Susie Shellenberger

for teens ❷

Visit Tyndale's exciting Web site at www.tyndale.com

TYNDALE and Tyndale's quill logo are registered trademarks of Tyndale House Publishers, Inc.

The One Year is a registered trademark of Tyndale House Publishers, Inc.

The One Year Devos for Teens 2

Copyright © 2005 by Susie Shellenberger. All rights reserved.

Cover photograph © by Photos.com. All rights reserved.

Designed by Jacqueline L. Noe

Published in association with the literary agency of Alive Communications, Inc., 7680 Goddard St., Suite 200, Colorado Springs, CO 80920.

Unless otherwise indicated, all Scripture quotations are taken from the *Holy Bible*, New International Version®. NIV®. Copyright © 1973, 1978, 1984 by International Bible Society. Used by permission of Zondervan. All rights reserved.

Scripture quotations marked NLT are taken from the *Holy Bible*, New Living Translation, copyright © 1996, 2004. Used by permission of Tyndale House Publishers, Inc., Carol Stream, Illinois 60188. All rights reserved.

Scripture quotations marked "NKJV™" are taken from the New King James Version®. Copyright © 1982 by Thomas Nelson, Inc. Used by permission. All rights reserved.

Scripture quotations marked TLB are taken from *The Living Bible*, copyright © 1971. Used by permission of Tyndale House Publishers, Inc., Carol Stream, Illinois 60188. All rights reserved.

Scripture quotations marked KJV are taken from the *Holy Bible,* King James Version.

Scriptures marked NCV are taken from the *Holy Bible*, New Century Version, copyright © 1987, 1988, 1991 by Word Publishing, Dallas, Texas 75039. Used by permission.

Scripture quotations marked TEV are taken from the *Good News Bible*, Today's English Version, copyright © 1976.

"Maria" on December 6 copyright © by Christina M. Turner. Used with permission.

"My Fiancée's Having Someone Else's Baby" on December 20–21 copyright © by Greg Asimakoupoulos. Used with permission.

"Names of God, Christ, and the Holy Spirit" on January 31, February 6, March 28, June 30, August 5, August 30, November 25, and November 30 adapted from *Experiencing God* teen study guide, copyright © 1994 by Henry Blackaby and Claude King. Used with permission.

Material on October 16, October 28, October 31, November 7, and December 7 adapted from Samaritan's Purse gift catalog. Used with permission.

Library of Congress Cataloging-in-Publication Data

Shellenberger, Susie
 One year devos for teens / Susie Shellenberger.
  p. cm.
 ISBN 978-0-8423-6202-3 Vol. 1 (Pbk.)
 ISBN 978-1-4143-0181-5 Vol. 2 (Pbk.)
 1. Teenagers—Prayer-books and devotions—English. 2. Devotional calendars. I. Title.
 BV4850 S47 2002
 242'.63—DC21   2002011517

Printed in the United States of America

15 14 13 12 11
10 9 8 7 6

Dedication

Imagine. You and your soul mate meeting together daily for a cup of java (or your favorite soft drink).

Smell the inviting aroma. Taste the rich flavor. Savor the intensity.

Enjoy the conversation. Grow from the stimulating challenge. Learn from the accountability.

It can happen.

You're holding the invitation in your hand.

That's right—this book.

You and God.

The King of kings fervently desires to be your soul mate, your Savior, your energizer, your life.

Go ahead—take the challenge. Meet with him every single day for one year.

I promise you'll savor the difference forever.

Your friend,

Susie Shellenberger

WHAT'S IMPORTANT TO GOD?

The Bible tells us that someday every knee will bow and every tongue will confess that Jesus Christ is Lord. We're also told that every single one of us will stand before God on a great Day of Judgment. Have you ever wondered what that will be like? What will God be concerned with? What will he ask? Let's think about that for a moment.

- God won't ask what kind of car you drove, but he might ask how many people you drove who didn't have transportation.
- God won't ask how big your house was, but he might ask how many people you welcomed into your home.
- God won't ask about your social status, but he might ask what kind of class you displayed.
- God won't ask what your highest salary was, but he might ask if you compromised your character or his will to obtain that salary.
- God won't ask how many promotions you received, but he might ask how you promoted others—how you encouraged them and considered them more important than yourself.
- God won't ask how many material possessions you had, but he might ask if they dictated your life.
- God won't ask what neighborhood you lived in, but he might ask you how you treated your neighbors.

God is concerned with the status of your heart. He's also concerned about your actions. And the truth is, our actions usually reflect our heart. Are your actions representative of Christ? It all starts with your heart. Is your heart totally dedicated to him? Are you more concerned about becoming all he wants you to be than seeing how much you can get? Let that be your goal this year. Instead of thinking, *How can I become more popular? How can I get so-and-so to notice me?* focus instead on, *Whom can I help who can't give back?*

Ask God to transform your thinking from *How can I make the most money? How can I be the most successful?* to *Dear Father, where I can serve you best? What can I do to help build your Kingdom?*

When your heart has that kind of focus, your actions will reflect Christ himself.

BREW IT!
God commands that we imitate him (see Ephesians 5:1). How's your imitation coming? Remember, it all begins in the heart. This week, do something for someone who can't return the favor. Is there an elderly shut-in from your church you can visit? Contact your pastor about someone in your church who has specific needs that you can meet: perhaps someone who's short of cash and needs groceries, a child from a single-parent home who needs some extra attention, or someone who's handicapped who needs help with chores.

POUR IT!
Drink in the flavor from the following Scriptures: 1 Corinthians 13; 2 Corinthians 5:10; Ephesians 5:1-2.

SAVOR IT!
Ask God to break you and reshape you in his image. Tell him you want to focus on making a difference for eternity.

BREW IT!

Spiritual discipline, like physical discipline, is a process. Your muscles don't take shape overnight. Consistency is the key! Determine to take your spiritual training seriously.

POUR IT!

Drink in the flavor from the following Scriptures:
1 Corinthians 9:24-27; Ephesians 3:14-21; 1 Timothy 4:8.

SAVOR IT!

Ask God to help you discipline yourself daily to his authority. Ask him to bring to light anything in your life that's hindering your spiritual fitness. And when he does, be willing to commit that area to him.

SPIRITUAL IRON

Maybe you're familiar with the Ironman Triathlon. It's a grueling athletic event held each fall in Hawaii that involves running, swimming, and biking. Here's how it began: In 1978 Navy commander John Collins wanted to settle an argument about who was more fit—runners or swimmers.

He combined the three toughest endurance races: a 2.4-mile rough-water swim, a 112-mile bike race, and 26.2-mile run. Competitors would start at 7 a.m., and the first to finish would win the title of Ironman.

Only fifteen participants showed up at the first triathlon. Commander Collins finished the course, but he didn't win. The Ironman title went to a Honolulu taxi driver.

Today more than 1,600 athletes compete in Hawaii's Ironman Triathlon each year, and more than 100 million people watch the event on TV. It takes 7,000 volunteers, 600 bottles of sunscreen, 100,000 gallons of fluids, and 12,825 bananas to make the annual competition a success.

God wants to mold you into a spiritual iron man. Think of him as a heavenly coach who wants to help you get into top spiritual shape. How can you develop spiritual muscles?

1. *Establish a routine*. Each triathlon competitor has a consistent physical workout schedule. Do you have a regular spiritual workout with God? Devour his Word and talk with him. This will strengthen you spiritually.
2. *Make yourself accountable*. Training—whether physical or spiritual—is always easier with a partner. Grab a friend and set some spiritual goals together. Hold one another accountable to having a quiet time with God each day. Connect with your friend in person, through e-mail, or over the phone and pray with each other. Ask questions about what God is teaching each of you.
3. *Memorize Scripture*. There will be days when Satan tempts you to throw in the towel. When he does, memorized Scripture will provide ample ammunition against the enemy.

INCREDIBLE PROMISE

Sixteen-year-old Rick Hoyt was watching the Ironman Triathlon on television with his dad. He was captivated by athletes with sculpted physiques biking 112 miles. Rick sat mesmerized as he watched the muscular competitors swim almost two and a half miles. He was glued to the screen as it displayed determined athletes running 26.2 miles.

Rick was so captivated by the entire event that he asked his dad, "Can I do that?"

His dad turned to him and said, "Yes. With my help, you can."

People who knew Dick Hoyt couldn't believe he'd make such an outrageous promise to his son. You see, Rick was a quadriplegic. He was born with cerebral palsy and couldn't walk or talk. The question he'd asked his dad wasn't verbal; his dad was reading his son's words on a computer screen. Rick had a special apparatus that allowed him to communicate via technology.

His dad had every reason to look at his son and say, "Rick, I'm so sorry. It's impossible for you to compete in a triathlon. You can't even speak. You can't control your tongue. When we feed you, the food falls out of your mouth. No. Son, you're handicapped. There's no way you can enter a triathlon."

Dick didn't say that. He was so full of love for his son that he determined to make the impossible possible. "Yes. With my help, you can. It's impossible on your own, but I'll make a way. I love you so much!"

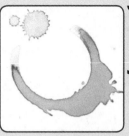

BREW IT!
God is crazy about you! Even though you're scarred and sinful, he has promised to make you whole. He loves you so much that he created a way for you to be forgiven of your sins. He gave his own Son to pay the price you couldn't afford.

POUR IT!
Drink in the flavor from the following Scriptures: Romans 3:22-28; 10:10-11.

SAVOR IT!
Thank God for loving you so much that he was willing to send his Son—God in human form—to die for your sins. Tell him you realize that you don't deserve that kind of love. Ask him to help you show your gratitude by a lifestyle of service and obedience to him.

BREW IT!

Regardless of whether you have an earthly dad who's willing to do whatever it takes to help you win, you have a heavenly Father who so desperately wants you to win that he's willing to pedal you, push you, carry you, pull you across the finish line into victory. He willingly died for you so that you can experience victory over sin. Are you living in that victory?

POUR IT!

Drink in the flavor from the following Scriptures: Romans 5:1-6; 1 Corinthians 1:8-9.

SAVOR IT!

Have you confessed your sins to Christ and accepted him as your personal Savior? If you've never done that, you can do it right now! Talk to God as you would your best friend—openly and honestly. You can commit your life to him right now and begin experiencing spiritual victory.

WHATEVER IT TAKES

Now that Dick Hoyt had promised his quadriplegic son entrance into the Ironman Triathlon, he had to figure out how to make it happen. It would be one thing to compete on his own, but how could he swim 2.4 miles, bike 112 miles, and run 26.2 miles carrying his son?

The first thing Dick had to do was learn how to swim! After completing his swimming lessons, he began running and training for the grueling triathlon. When he had readied himself for the challenge, he then had to figure out how to complete the event with his son, who couldn't move.

With the help of others, he was able to devise a special seat in front of the handlebars of his bicycle where Rick could sit while Dick pedaled. When he swam through rough waters, a rope was tied around his waist and attached to a raft in which Rick lay. And when he entered the marathon phase, Dick ran while pushing his son in a special wheelchair.

If you've ever seen the video clip of Dick and Rick's Ironman adventure, you've undoubtedly noticed the strain of muscles in Dick's legs, the bulging veins in his neck, and the determination on his face. It was an amazing feat!

The average finish time for the Ironman is eight hours. It took Dick and his son 16.4 hours to cross the finish line. But they made it! Rick experienced victory because he had a dad who was willing to do whatever it took to get him across the finish line.

NEW JEWELS AND A NEW NAME

None of us know exactly what heaven will be like, because no one reading this book has been there. But we do get a few snapshots of paradise in the book of Revelation. Do you like jewelry? When you get to heaven, you'll receive exquisite jewelry. In the second chapter of the last book in the Bible, we're told that each of us will receive a white stone.

A white stone? That doesn't sound like jewelry, you may be thinking.

Maybe. Maybe not.

But in Revelation 21, we're told what heaven is made of. Walls are made of jasper and built on twelve layers of foundation stones inlaid with these precious gems: jasper, sapphire, chalcedony, emerald, sardonyx, carnelian, chrysolite, beryl, topaz, chrysoprase, jacinth, and amethyst. The twelve gates are made of pearls. And the main street is pure transparent gold!

When the apostle John received his vision of heaven from God, he saw it in great detail. When he heard Jesus describe this white stone, he might have wondered what kind of stone it would be. Chances are, it was such an exquisite piece of jewelry, it was literally indescribable!

"No, it's not a diamond," he may have said. "And it's not pearl or emerald or jasper. Wow! I've never heard of anything like that before. It's sturdy like a rock. And it's so white and pure! I don't know what to call it. I guess the best I can do is simply describe it as a white stone."

But we don't simply get a cool piece of jewelry. God goes a step further. The Bible tells us that he will engrave a special name on the stone that no one knows except the giver and the receiver. In other words, God has a special nickname just for you! You won't know what it is until you get to heaven, and God can't wait to present you with this gift.

BREW IT!

God isn't a commander who rules from a distance. He's a loving creator who wants to be intimately involved in every single area of your life. And not only does he want to be personally involved with you right now, he'll continue that intimacy throughout all eternity! He's a God and Savior who has created a personal nickname just for you that only the two of you will know. That's intimate.

POUR IT!

Drink in the flavor from the following Scriptures: Revelation 2:17; Isaiah 45:3, 17.

SAVOR IT!

Do you simply know about God, or do you actually know him personally? Are you living intimately with him? Tell him that's the kind of relationship you desire. Ask him to reveal anything in your life that's not right with him, and be willing to surrender it to him.

BREW IT!
Your relationship with Christ—like heaven—should be holy, special, and indescribable. Are you ready to spend forever with him? Are you excited about your eternal home?

POUR IT!
Drink in the flavor from the following Scriptures: Revelation 4:5-6; 5:9; 7:9-10.

SAVOR IT!
Thank God for creating such an incredible eternal home for you. Ask him to help you look forward to spending forever with him in heaven.

HEAVEN: THE ULTIMATE DESTINATION

Not only will you receive new jewelry in heaven with a special nickname from God engraved on it, you'll also stand in amazement at the assortment of colors and sounds. God is the creator of all good things, and heaven will be saturated with everything good and perfect.

The fourth chapter of Revelation tells us that the apostle John saw lightning and thunder coming from the throne in heaven. He distinguished voices within the thunder. Heaven will be a sound-and-light show beyond imagination. The fascination we'll experience with color, sound, and rhythm will surpass the greatest of all technology!

John also saw a crystal sea. Who knows? Maybe there are water sports in heaven! If there's a crystal sea, it will be put to good use. Can you imagine windsurfing, jet-skiing, parasailing, snorkeling, and scuba diving in a sea that stretches for eternity and is as clear as crystal? Heaven is beyond our imagination!

In Revelation 5, John describes a concert deluxe. He says the inhabitants of heaven were singing a new song. If you enjoy concerts, you'll get the concert of a lifetime in heaven!

Do you like new clothes? In Revelation 7 we learn that believers get a new wardrobe. John saw a vast crowd of people from all nations and provinces standing in front of the throne clothed in white. No dirty T-shirts in heaven. You're getting brand-new white clothes.

John says the believers were shouting praises to God. Heaven is not a silent library. Heaven is a shout-fest of praise! There is so much going on, heaven is a multisensory experience.

Not only will you see heaven, you'll get to experience it in all its fullness. Every one of your senses will be expanded. You'll get to taste light and hear color. You'll hear the sweet fragrance of a perfect loving God, and you'll touch sound. Heaven is beyond description.

When you enter an intimate relationship with God, you're not simply gaining another buddy who happens to have a little extra power. When you enter into intimacy with Christ, you're entering something so magnificent and so sacred, it transcends your comprehension.

HEAVEN: THE PERFECT KINGDOM

Though it's obvious none of us know exactly what heaven will be like, we do have some insight into God's forever Kingdom because of the snapshots the apostle John has given us in the book of Revelation.

With these snapshots in mind—the crystal sea, the jeweled foundations, the walls of jasper, the sound-and-light shows, an eternal and holy atmosphere—imagine standing on the edge of heaven and peering inside. You're mesmerized by all you see. Jesus approaches you. You look at him longingly and say, "Jesus, can I live there?"

He'd have every right to look at you and say, "I'm sorry, but no. You're sinful. You're scarred. You've been deceptive, sexually intimate outside of marriage, and drunk; you've cursed, looked at porn, been in all the wrong chat rooms, taken drugs, manipulated others, gossiped, and lied. No. You can't live in my perfect Kingdom."

But Jesus doesn't say that. He looks at you and says, "Yes. With my help, you can!"

He reminds you that it's impossible to enter heaven on your own. You're sinful. But he loves you so very much, he's willing to do whatever it takes to get you across the finish line to experience eternal victory in heaven!

Remember the story about sixteen-year-old quadriplegic Rick Hoyt? (Flip back to January 3–4 for a quick recap.) Rick was unable to speak or walk on his own. So when he entered the Ironman with his dad, he couldn't contribute anything to their victory. Just as Rick was dependent on his dad, you, too, need to be totally dependent on your heavenly Father.

God wants you helpless—fully surrendered to his authority. When you're lying flat in the raft and have relinquished your rights and your will to the lordship of Christ, he's able to take you across the finish line into heaven.

BREW IT!

It's impossible for you to enter God's perfect Kingdom on your own. But with his help, you can! He transforms the impossible into reality. But it takes total surrender. Perhaps you've already asked Christ to forgive your sins, and you have a relationship with him. That's great! But are you still calling your own shots? Are you in charge of your life? Or have you totally surrendered to his lordship? He wants you flat in the boat!

POUR IT!

Drink in the flavor from the following Scriptures: Psalm 139:23-24; Isaiah 1:18; Joel 2:12-14.

SAVOR IT!

Tell God that you don't want simply to call yourself a Christian; you want to live a holy lifestyle! Pray that he will help you discern anything in your life that's keeping you from total surrender.

BREW IT!

Have you died to your rights? Have you relinquished the need to have your own way? Have you placed everything—your past, present, and future . . . your skills, relationships, fears, future spouse and career—into his hands? If you haven't, he's not Lord of your life.

POUR IT!

Drink in the flavor from the following Scriptures: Matthew 6:24; 16:24-28; Luke 14:25-33.

SAVOR IT!

If you haven't completely surrendered to the lordship of Jesus Christ, right now would be a perfect time to do so. Tell him you place it all—everything you are and everything you hope to be—in his hands.

DOES TOTAL SURRENDER REALLY MEAN EVERYTHING?

God is a jealous God. He's very clear throughout the Bible that he wants to be absolute Lord and ruler of your life. There aren't many gods to serve; there is one God. He will not share lordship with anyone or anything.

The church of Laodicea was scolded for being lukewarm (see Revelation 3:15-16). God tells us the same thing too: "Be hot or cold. Be really all-out for me or go ahead and admit I'm not Lord of your life, but don't ride the fence. Refuse to settle for middle ground. That won't cut it. I will spew the lukewarm out of my mouth."

Why is it so important to give God everything?

Because he gave everything for you!

And because he gave 100 percent, he commands you to do the same. When Christ went to the cross, he was thinking about you. And he gave everything he had!

He didn't hang on the cross with a lukewarm commitment to his Father. He wasn't crucified 65 percent. He didn't go to the cross simply to be uncomfortable or to lose a little blood. He was tortured beyond what we can imagine. He was beaten beyond recognition. Then he died. He didn't cling to his rights. He didn't demand his own way. He was submissive to his heavenly Father.

He demands the same of you.

"Want to follow me?" he asks. "First, consider the cost. It's expensive to follow me. It will cost you everything. Still want to come? Then pick up your cross and let's go. I'm calling you to come die with me."

Dying is hard. Real Christianity isn't easy. It demands a death to self. It's much more than a feel-good friendship of hanging out with a supernatural buddy. It's a relationship based on obedience and total commitment.

Salvation is free, but grace is not cheap.

God will forgive your sins when you confess with genuine repentance. But living a holy lifestyle will cost you everything.

IMAGINATION STATION

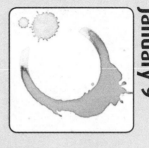

Act like a kid for second. Pretend you're five years old and living in an imaginary country called Ooomba-Puma. It's a land filled with concrete forests and cement parkways. Grass and vegetation are absent from OoombaPuma. Because the country consists mainly of roads, streets, and highways, the government has made it legal for five-year-olds to earn their driver's license.

You're five and ecstatic that today's the day you'll take your driving test. You're not old enough to read the written exam or write your answers to the questions, so the instructor presents it to you orally. You miss a few questions but get enough correct to take the driving portion of your test.

You climb behind the wheel of a special government car and sit on three phone books to enable you to see over the dashboard. Your feet can't reach the gas pedal of a normal car, so you're using a uniquely created vehicle with a gasoline button on the steering wheel. Another button controls the brakes.

The instructor gives you the go-ahead. You carefully fasten your seat belt, check your mirrors, turn the key, and proceed onto the street. You slow down and come to a complete stop at all red lights, and you make it a point to use your turn signal each time you change lanes or turn a corner.

Twenty minutes later, the instructor congratulates you with the news that you have passed your test. You're now a licensed driver! In OoombaPuma, the government gives each new driver a free car, and when you arrive home, a shiny red convertible is sitting in your driveway.

"Congratulations!" Dad says. "We're so proud of you. Unfortunately, the government only provided a small amount of gasoline in the tank. So let's drive to the station and fill her up. And as a special congratulations gift, I'm giving you twenty-five dollars to buy your first tank of gasoline."

"Thanks for the money," you say. "But I don't wanna spend it on gas. I've had my eye on a new toy at the mall. I'd rather buy that instead."

Dad begs you to reconsider, but you're intent on purchasing the new toy. So you climb behind the wheel of your new car and head toward the mall.

BREW IT!
Because God is God and you're not, it only makes sense to realize that he's all-knowing, all-powerful, and all-wise. Though you may desire something he knows isn't the best choice, he'll never force you to do his will. But if you're smart—and if you truly want his best for your life—you'll trust him, obey him, and let him guide you in all your decisions.

POUR IT!
Drink in the flavor from the following Scriptures: Proverbs 1:7-8; 2:1-6; 3:6.

SAVOR IT!
Ask God to help you relinquish your own desires and accept his leading, even when you don't understand.

USING THE RIGHT FUEL

You purchase the long-awaited toy and head home to play in the backyard with your neighborhood friends. After a few hours, the newness has worn off, and your friends suggest a picnic. "There's a great hiking trail about an hour from here. Let's pack some munchies and get going," they suggest.

Your dad overhears the conversation between you and your friends. "You used almost all your gas to get to the mall," he says. "You'll need to fill up soon or you'll never make it to the hiking trails."

"But, Dad, I spent the twenty-five dollars you gave me on my new toy."

"You still have your allowance," he reminds you. "That should be enough to fill your tank. You and your friends will still be able to have a fun time hiking, but you'll need to head straight for the gas station."

You quickly pack as many munchies as your five-year-old hands can grab and climb into your convertible with your friends. "There's the station," Angela says.

"Let's hurry and fill up so we can hit the hiking trails," Josh squeals.

You climb out of the car to fill the tank when Angela sees the price. "Wow! It's six dollars a gallon."

"Just put water in your tank instead," Josh suggests.

"That's a great idea," Angela says. "There's a little gift shop on the hiking trail, and we may want to spend your money on fun stuff instead of gas."

"Yeah," Josh continues. "If we spend it all on gas, we won't have money to buy anything else. So just use water—it's free!"

BREW IT!

The world is full of things that look and sound good. But guess what? As good as they may sound, if you're not filling your spiritual tank with the right fuel, it's only a matter of time until you encounter a spiritual breakdown.

POUR IT!

Drink in the flavor from the following Scriptures: Psalm 1; 15; 27:11.

SAVOR IT!

Ask God to give you his wisdom and discernment in the daily choices you make.

You think about it for a second and decide your friends are right. Why spend your allowance on gas when you can fill the tank with something that's free?

You pull away from the pump while Josh and Angela fill a few buckets with water. It doesn't take long to empty the contents into your tank, and the three of you head toward the mountains.

Let's interrupt this crazy story and make an obvious point, okay? You already know that it's simply a matter of time before your car sputters, stops, and refuses to start again. And while it seems absolutely ridiculous even to consider filling a gasoline tank with water, we do sometimes try to fill our spiritual tank with the wrong fuel.

MAKING THE RIGHT CHOICE

The past two days we've been living in an imaginary world called OoombaPuma. We've pretended it's legal for you to get your driver's license at age five.

It takes a little effort to picture filling a car's gas tank with water instead of gasoline, but we don't have to think too hard to imagine substituting for godly things to fill our spiritual tank. It happens all too easily, doesn't it?

Your car operates on many things, but gas and oil are two of the most important. Your spiritual life also operates on many things, but God's Word and prayer are the top two ingredients.

It would make sense to a five-year-old to substitute gasoline for water. After all, H_2O is less expensive. Using it doesn't require sacrificing other things. But even though water is convenient and free, it's not the right fuel!

You may find it easy to sacrifice reading the Bible for other things. It's much easier to absorb Christian music than to devour Scripture. You can even listen to music while you engage in several other activities. But reading your Bible requires sacrificing other activities and stopping long enough to absorb written words on the page. Though Christian music is great, it alone can't provide the spiritual fuel you need to have a strong relationship with Christ.

Instead of making time to pray and develop a strong bond with your Savior, it's much easier simply to hang out with Christian friends, go to youth group, and listen to your pastor talk about God. And though you'll receive wise instruction from people in the church, it's never the same as hearing from God himself. Nothing can substitute for your own personal prayer life with the King of kings.

So you have a choice to make. And it doesn't matter if you made a New Year's resolution on January 1. Today, on January 11, you can make a resolution, a pledge, a commitment to refuse any and all substitutes for keeping your spiritual tank full.

Are you willing to develop a strong prayer life this year? Do you desire to know God in a deeper way? It is possible! By reading the Bible consistently and praying daily, you can be much stronger spiritually at the end of this year than you are right now. If you'll do your part, God will certainly do his part. Will you make a conscious decision right now?

BREW IT!
God desires to draw you closer to himself.

POUR IT!
Drink in the flavor from the following Scriptures: 2 Timothy 3:16-17; James 4:8; 2 Peter 3:18.

SAVOR IT!
Father, I give you this year. I want to make wise choices and saturate my life with your Word and in prayer. I pledge to talk with you and read your Word consistently this year. I know you'll be faithful to bless my time with you and enable me to grow closer to you. Help me to be much stronger spiritually at the end of this year than I am right now. I trust you, Father, and I will meet with you daily throughout the year.

BREW IT!
Instead of trusting human nature, put your faith in God and his eternal Kingdom. Christ wants you to have friends, and he places great value on solid friendships. But friendships built on good intentions are only temporary at best. Godly friendships formed on the solid foundation of Christ will last eternally. Trust the eternal foundation.

POUR IT!
Drink in the flavor from the following Scriptures: 1 Kings 12:1-17; Romans 12:1-3; 1 Timothy 6:11-12.

SAVOR IT!
Tell God you want him to be more important to you than your friends. Ask him to help you make wise choices concerning your relationships.

GOOD INTENTIONS

Though your friends in the make-believe world of OoombaPuma had good intentions when they suggested filling your car's tank with water instead of gasoline, that was all they were—intentions.

Good intentions are never the same as God's perfect will. And no matter how dependable your friends are, they're still human. They'll blow it. God, on the other hand, will never disappoint you. He is perfect. Do you tend to put more trust in friends—whom you can see—rather than God, whom you can't see?

King Solomon ruled a successful and huge kingdom. God was pleased with him and told him to ask for anything he wanted. Solomon asked for wisdom, and God gladly granted it. Israel prospered under Solomon's wise rule. After Solomon's death, his son Rehoboam took the throne. Instead of listening to the godly advice of the wise elders who had guided his father, Rehoboam chose instead to listen to his friends. Though their intentions may have been good, their harsh advice caused the people to rebel against Rehoboam and eventually cost him the kingdom.

It pays to listen to God and those he chooses to speak through. Your friends may have good intentions, but if what they say goes against God's character, you'll have regrets. How would you handle the following situations where advice from friends contradicts advice from God?

- Your friends invite you to a party where alcohol will be served. They want you to have fun and remind you that you're not obligated to drink. Sound like good intentions? God encourages you to avoid even the appearance of evil. Whom do you listen to?
- Your friends offer to help you shoplift the MP3 player you've been wanting. They just want you to enjoy your fave tunes in a high-tech way. Sound like good intentions? God commands you not to steal. Whom do you listen to?
- You don't have a date for the winter dance. Your friends offer to set you up with Taylor—who's not a Christian. Hey, you're not actually starting a relationship, you're just spending an evening together. Sound like good intentions? God instructs you to choose your relationships wisely. Whom do you listen to?

WHAT'S LOVE GOT TO DO WITH IT?

Seminary professor Dr. Bracken was known for his elaborate object lessons, so the students weren't taken by surprise when they entered the classroom midsemester and saw a huge target attached to the front wall. Trisha knew something was up, however, when she noticed several darts carefully placed on a nearby table.

She took her seat and listened carefully to her professor's instructions. "Take out a sheet of paper and draw a sketch of someone you dislike; someone who has hurt you; someone who has angered you. When you're finished, I'll post each picture on the target and allow you to throw darts at the person's picture."

Toby drew a picture of his dad, who had struggled with alcohol and left the family when Toby was young. Emily drew a picture of a girl who had stolen her boyfriend. Darren drew a picture of his older brother. Trisha drew a picture of an ex-friend—one who had hurt her deeply. She delighted in drawing scars and acne on his face and tried to make him as ugly as she could.

The students posted their pictures over the huge target and one by one began throwing darts. Some threw with such force that their targets began ripping apart. Trisha couldn't wait for her turn. Her anger was growing with each passing minute.

"Okay, class. Return to your seats," Dr. Bracken said. "This exercise took a little longer than I expected, so we're going to have to cut it short because of time."

Trisha sat in anger, upset because she didn't get to throw even one dart at the picture she had placed on the target.

As she quietly fumed, Dr. Bracken began removing the target from the wall. Trish gasped. Underneath the target was a picture of Jesus. Silence fell over the room as each student viewed the mangled picture of Jesus. Holes and jagged marks covered his face, and his eyes were pierced.

Dr. Bracken then quoted Matthew 25:40 from the King James Bible: "Inasmuch as ye have done it unto one of the least of these my brethren, ye have done it unto me."

BREW IT!

It's easy to think that our grudges against others have nothing to do with our relationship with Christ. WRONG! When we harbor bitterness or an unforgiving spirit against someone else, our intimacy with Christ is greatly affected. If you're not feeling as close to God as you'd like to be, stop and think if there's anger, hate, or bitterness in your life toward someone else. With God's help, release that grudge and restore your spiritual intimacy with him!

POUR IT!

Drink in the flavor from the following Scriptures: Matthew 5:43-45; Luke 6:27-36; John 15:12-17.

SAVOR IT!

Ask God to bring to your attention anyone you're not loving as he wants you to love. Seek his forgiveness for any grudges or bitterness you may have toward someone. Ask him to help you love everyone the way he does.

BREW IT!

While it's your choice to love and forgive or to be angry and hold a grudge, God has already made it clear which choice a mature Christian should make. He commands us to love everyone—even those who criticize us and harm us. And he doesn't simply tell us to love others, he showed us by his very lifestyle on earth. Are you imitating his lifestyle? Or are you reflecting the attitudes of the world around you?

POUR IT!

Drink in the flavor from the following Scriptures: 1 Corinthians 13; 1 Corinthians 14:1; Ephesians 5:1-2.

SAVOR IT!

Tell your heavenly Father that you desire to love as he loves—freely and unconditionally. Thank him for loving you unconditionally, and thank the others in your life who love you consistently.

IS LOVE REALLY THAT IMPORTANT?

Remember the classroom situation we discussed yesterday? After Dr. Bracken quoted Matthew 25:40, no other words were necessary. The class understood. Tears filled the students' eyes as they focused only on the picture of Christ.

Imagine yourself in that classroom. How would you have reacted to Dr. Bracken's object lesson?

Would it have been easy for you to think of someone who has hurt you? Would you have drawn that person's picture with growing animosity, as Trisha did, or would you have simply sketched a basic outline?

We're all hurt by others at some point in our lives. Why? Because we're all human. We all make mistakes. We all fail. Every single one of us will hurt others, and we will be hurt. Even committed followers of Christ sometimes mess up and intentionally hurt someone else.

What will you do with the hurt you've experienced from others? You can either harbor a grudge and nurse your anger, or you can give your hurt to Christ and ask him to help you love as he loves.

How would you have scored on Dr. Bracken's test? It really comes down to a choice, doesn't it? The result is simple: you either score one hundred, or you score zero. It's up to you.

SOMETIMES LOVE HURTS

A little boy was wrestling with his dog. His mother was concerned that he was playing too roughly and said, "Eric, I know you love Rocket, but you're loving him too much. How would you feel if someone huge picked you up and squeezed you so hard you couldn't breathe?"

Eric thought for a moment and then said, "I guess I'd feel like it was my birthday and Aunt Martha was here!"

We may laugh at Eric's observation, but we also know the truth in loving someone so much that it hurts. It hurt so much for Jesus to love the world that it finally killed him. And though it hurt, it was still his choice. Jesus loved (and continues to love) each one of us so much that he chose to pay our death penalty for sin. But his love didn't end at the Cross. God raised him from the grave, and he lives in heaven right now, preparing your eternal home with him. And every person in the entire world who confesses his sins, accepts Christ as his Savior, and lives for him will spend forever in heaven.

Some people think that God planned to show the world his love through Jesus, but when people rebelled against him, sinned, and refused to follow him, his plan failed. Jesus was killed, and God simply did the best he could with Plan B.

But that's not the case. God doesn't make mistakes. He knows all, and he is all-powerful! He knew, even before he created people, that we would rebel and sin. When he sent his only Son to earth, he knew that Jesus would be the sacrifice for our sins.

BREW IT!
Jesus knew it would hurt, but he loved us so much that he was willing to pay the price. Don't take his immeasurable love for granted!

POUR IT!
Drink in the flavor from the following Scriptures: Deuteronomy 6:5; Psalm 32:10; 1 Corinthians 2:9.

SAVOR IT!
Ask God to help you show your gratitude for all he's done for you by your actions and your commitment to him.

BREW IT!
We don't dive into spiritual hypnosis. We take one small backward step at a time. And step by backward step, we walk farther from our Lord until we've reached a point of unfamiliarity. When that happens, don't sleepily rub your eyes and wonder what went wrong. Stop immediately and seek God's forgiveness for not paying attention to his Holy Spirit.

POUR IT!
Drink in the flavor from the following Scriptures: Ephesians 6:18; 1 Thessalonians 5:6; 1 Peter 5:8.

SAVOR IT!
Ask God to keep you spiritually alert. Tell him you want to grow as close to him as you possibly can and are willing to do whatever it takes to become the disciple he wants.

SPIRITUAL HYPNOSIS
Are you familiar with the term *highway hypnosis?* It's a frightening and extremely dangerous phenomenon. A person who experiences highway hypnosis can drive for hours at a time, yet not remember going from one city to the next. Her mind goes into a kind of "zombie" mode and doesn't take in the sights and sounds that accompany her travel. But a few hours later, she's in a different city.

You can imagine the danger a driver with highway hypnosis faces! Because she's not acutely tuned in to the details surrounding her, she could easily get in a wreck or even be the cause of a fatal accident.

Sadly, many Christians experience a similar phenomenon—spiritual hypnosis. We merely coast from Sunday to Sunday without paying any attention to the details God tries to make us aware of during the week. When a crisis hits, we suddenly wake up and can't figure out how we got from where we were to where are we now.

God used to be so close, we think. *What happened? Why does he seem so far away now? Why does it feel as though my prayers are bouncing off the ceiling?*

If we'd been paying attention to the details along the way, we would have felt God nudging our heart to spend more time reading the Bible. Or perhaps we would have realized our need to be more involved in church and Christian fellowship. Maybe we would have heard his still, small voice urging us to break a habit, release a grudge, or seek forgiveness from someone we hurt.

WHAT WILL YOU DO FOR A TROPHY?

We called it "Girls Getaway." It was a seven-day Caribbean cruise for six friends who simply wanted to laugh, pray, and fellowship with each other for a week without the daily stress of jobs, deadlines, and chores.

We swam with dolphins, dined on exquisite food, enjoyed the musical productions in the evening, and soaked in the sun during the day. Before we departed for our various cabins for the night, we gathered in one room to read the Bible, pray, and share together. It was an incredible vacation!

One evening, we heard there would be a hypnotist doing a show in one of the ship's theaters. We thought it would be fun to attend. When he asked the crowd of eight hundred for volunteers, I leaped out of my seat from the back of the auditorium and ran to the front. I was seated onstage with twenty other guests. Of course, I don't really believe in hypnosis, but I thought it would be fun to be part of the show. (The hypnotist had announced that a trophy would be given to the volunteer the audience selected as the most entertaining. I wanted that trophy!)

He gradually began to eliminate some of the guests on stage, as he told us to relax and imagine our left hand was holding a helium balloon. I raised my hand over my head. We were now down to fifteen volunteers.

He told us we were getting very sleepy. I really wasn't sleepy, but I acted like I was. I yawned, stretched, and placed my head on the lap of the person next to me. I guess the hypnotist thought he was doing a great job with me, because he sent some of the others offstage and kept me in the final six.

He spent the next several minutes suggesting a variety of activities for us to demonstrate while we were "hypnotized." I pretended to get shot, acted out the role of a nurse in a delivery room, rapped in Chinese, and danced my way across the stage to finally secure the vote of the audience and the coveted trophy.

When I think back on it, I'm amazed at all I did just to receive a trophy. It's now simply collecting dust somewhere in my basement.

BREW IT!
Are you placing too much emphasis on things that are only temporary? Five years from now, will that pair of jeans or that CD you just have to have right now be worth the money you spent? We live in a culture of instant gratification. We see what we want, and we think we have to get it now! God has a different plan. He wants to teach us discernment, patience, and wisdom.

POUR IT!
Drink in the flavor from the following Scriptures: 1 Corinthians 9:24-27; 10:23-24; 16:13-14.

SAVOR IT!
Ask God to give you a desire for things of eternal value instead of merely focusing on the temporary.

ARE YOU DELIVERING THE RIGHT MESSAGE?

When I returned to my seat in the back of the auditorium, my friends were doubled over in laughter. "Wow! You were so funny, Susie," Melany said.

"Do you remember anything you did?" Jennifer asked.

"Of course!" I replied. "I was awake the entire time."

"You knew what you were doing all along?" Kathy said.

"I knew hypnotic shows were fake!" Gaye announced.

"I just wanted the trophy," I explained. "I never went to sleep. I was never hypnotized. I was simply acting the whole time."

Throughout the remainder of the cruise, people approached me and asked me what it had been like to be hypnotized. They actually thought I had been under the hypnotist's control.

Even though my little game was just for fun, unfortunately many people play a similar spiritual game. They play the part of being a Christian by going to church, owning a Bible, and looking good on Sunday, but it's merely an act. If what you say in the locker room or on a crowded campus doesn't match what you say in church on Sunday, you're not living a genuine Christ-centered life. Anyone can play a game. Refuse to be part of the crowd. God calls you to a higher standard of living. He wants your lifestyle to deliver a message of holiness.

BREW IT!
Yes, I was acting, but I had delivered an untrue message to the audience. I had convinced them to believe I was hypnotized when I really wasn't. If you act one way at church and another way around non-Christians, you're delivering untrue messages too.

POUR IT!
Drink in the flavor from the following Scriptures: Proverbs 12:17; Ephesians 5:8-11; Jude 20.

SAVOR IT!
Ask God to show you any areas in which you may be delivering a false message to those around you.

He yearns to guide you into a consistent, stable relationship with him so you won't act one way on Sunday and another way during the week. There's no way you can become all he calls you to be by living in the middle. Get off the fence and commit your entire being to righteousness.

God wants us to develop such an intimate relationship with him that it affects every detail of our lives. What does that mean to you?

Read this out loud: God wants me to develop such an intimate relationship with him that it affects every detail of my life.

Are you living out a genuine relationship with Christ for others to see? Or are you simply playing the game? Are you for real spiritually? Or are you just acting? What kind of message do you send to those who are watching your life?

EVACUATE!

You may remember hearing about Hurricane Charley on the news in August 2004. It hit Florida with a wind force of 130 miles per hour. Hundreds of thousands of residents and tourists were urged to evacuate the Florida Keys, Tampa, St. Petersburg, and Clearwater. As the storm progressed, almost one million people were encouraged to leave the region. It was the biggest evacuation order since 1999, when Hurricane Floyd forced residents along the Atlantic coast to move to higher areas.

Can you imagine the fear that gripped those residents? They knew everything they had worked for (houses, cars, property, beachfront condos) could be wiped out in seconds. Gone forever! What a helpless feeling.

Though officials had planned for the very worst, fortunately the very worst didn't happen. Yes, Charley did some damage, but not at all what Florida residents expected.

We can learn a few things from this incident:

1. *Be prepared.* Just as Florida residents were expected to evacuate their homes, you too will be expected to vacate your home someday. Are you ready to leave your earthly home and enter heaven? Have you prepared? Is your relationship with Christ current, intimate, and growing?
2. *Build smart.* Those of us who don't live in a coastal area often wonder why people build expensive homes so close to the water, where they can quickly be destroyed in a tropical storm. The Bible urges us to build smart—to construct our homes on solid ground. What have you built your spiritual foundation on? Is it on solid ground—the Word of God, sound teaching, solid faith? Or have you built on trends, your parents' Christianity, or simply emotions?
3. *Build eternally.* Instead of emphasizing temporary things of the world, focus instead on what's eternal. Christ tells us to store things in heaven, because in his perfect Kingdom nothing will rot or be blown away. When we build spiritually, we're investing for eternity.
4. *Expect the best!* Florida officials planned for the worst because they expected the worst. If you're a Christian, you don't have to fear bad news about the future. You can expect the very best! You'll someday be "evacuated" to heaven, God's perfect paradise. Refuse to live in fear of what may happen around you. Instead, live in expectation of what will happen for you eternally.

BREW IT!
Regardless of the earthly storms, wars, and famine around you, you have God's eternal best waiting for you. Choose to pour your energy into your future with him.

POUR IT!
Drink in the flavor from the following Scriptures: Matthew 6:19-21; Luke 6:46-49; 1 Timothy 6:17-19.

SAVOR IT!
Ask God to help you rearrange your priorities to reflect your commitment to him.

BREW IT!

Some people would classify certain sins (like sexual intimacy outside of marriage or pirating music or making fun of someone) as "simple fun." But when we put fun and sin in the same category, we're breaking God's heart. We need to draw the line and walk away.

POUR IT!

Drink in the flavor from the following Scriptures: Proverbs 13:20; 14:16; Ecclesiastes 7:5.

SAVOR IT!

Thank God for being a fun and creative God. Thank him for giving you opportunities to have good, clean fun. Ask him to give you discernment to know when to draw the line between fun and something that would hurt him, yourself, or others.

THAT LOOKS FUN!

I was in New York City recently and wanted to purchase a ticket for a Broadway play. While I was waiting in line, I noticed a small crew with a video camera interviewing people. The more I watched, the more intrigued I became.

One guy got out of line, took off his shirt, and let someone smear peanut butter all over his back. Next came grape jelly. Then someone else actually licked it off him! The two participants were paid a nice sum of money while the film crew recorded the entire caper.

I watched a few more people leave the line and get filmed as they involved themselves in various pranks. Each time, they were paid with a wad of cash.

My curiosity got the best of me. I stepped out of line and approached the small crew. "What's going on? It looks like fun!"

"And you're just the person we're looking for," the guy with the microphone said. "Where are you from?"

"Colorado Springs," I replied.

"Perfect! You're up next."

"But what is this?" I asked innocently.

"It's an Internet show. We prove people will do really crazy things if you pay them enough money. The human sandwich guy just made five hundred dollars."

Wow! I thought. *Not bad for three minutes!*

Before I knew what was happening, he said, "I'll bet you have a lot of raccoons and chipmunks in Colorado, don't you?"

"Uh, yeah, I guess we do," I answered. I'd actually never really thought about it.

His assistant whipped out a huge animal costume that resembled a beaver or raccoon and handed it to me. Then the assistant placed a bowl of wood chips in front of me while the announcer continued. "And we all know what those critters like to munch on: wood!"

Everyone laughed. "We're going to give you $400 to wear this costume and eat wood chips." The crowd went wild. I hesitated—just for a second—and while I did, he raised the cash prize to $500! Everyone began to clap.

There's nothing wrong with being a little crazy, is there? We serve a creative God. He loves to see his children having fun, doesn't he?

Yes, God is creative. And yes, God wants us to have fun. But there are times when we need to draw the line. Have you thought about when and where the line should be drawn?

THE APPEARANCE OF EVIL

The New York City crowd swelled with excitement. The assistant on crew brought out several cans of beer and poured them over the wood chips. "Of course, we don't expect you to swallow all these chips dry," the announcer said. "We'll make sure they go down easy by drenching them for you."

"No, I can't do that," I said. "I don't drink beer."

He quickly raised the cash prize to $550 and showed me the cans. "This is nonalcoholic beer," he announced. "There's not one drop of alcohol in any of these cans. And we'll give you $600 to do it!" He waved six crisp one-hundred-dollar bills in front of me and in front of the camera.

I wanted the money. But even though the cans advertised nonalcoholic beer, they were still beer cans. "No," I said as I laughed. "I can't do that. It looks like beer."

The crowd began to chant, "Do it! Do it! Do it!" The crew had been filming the entire episode. The longer I stalled, the more the announcer increased the cash prize. He finally offered me $800. I couldn't help but think, *That's almost $1,000! I could do a lot with that much money!* But I knew in my heart it would be wrong. I speak and write against drinking. How would it look if just one person who knew me saw me eating wood chips soaked in beer? "No. I'm finished here."

I walked away from $800 with the crowd still screaming. Don't get me wrong. Christianity is fun, and God definitely wants his children to have fun! But, remember yesterday's devotional? There's a point where fun can cross the line. When and where is that line for you?

Is it when the fun goes against your conscience that you should draw the line and walk away? Is it when you're tempted to break the rules your parents have established? What about breaking God's heart?

The Bible tells us to avoid even the appearance of evil (1 Thessalonians 5:22, KJV). I knew if I ate wood chips soaked in beer—even though it was nonalcoholic beer—someone could have seen me who knew I was a Christian, and I could have blown my witness. Someone could have easily thought, *Hey, that's beer! If Susie's drinking beer, what's the big deal? I can, too!*

BREW IT!
When something advertised as fun can potentially damage your witness to others, it's time to draw the line and seek God's wisdom.

POUR IT!
Drink in the flavor from the following Scriptures: Proverbs 1:7; 2:6; 4:27.

SAVOR IT!
Ask God to help you develop a solid witness for him. Tell him you don't want anything to interfere with your witness to others.

THERMOSTAT OR THERMOMETER?

Ever thought about the difference between a thermostat and a thermometer? A thermometer measures temperature; a thermostat sets the temperature. You can choose to be a thermometer and merely reflect the environment around you. Or you can be a thermostat and choose to *determine* the temperature (environment) around you.

Time for a quick test. Read the following scenarios and decide whether the person involved is acting as a thermometer or a thermostat.

Conner walks into Justin's basement and approaches four of his buddies who are crowded around the computer. "Whoa!" Ryan says. "Conner! You gotta see this, dude! Justin's got porn." The guys laugh.

Conner pauses. "Come on, man. Get over here so you can see the screen," Justin says.

"No way," Conner counters. "I'm not even getting close. Don't you guys remember the pledge to sexual purity we made in youth group last month? I'm taking that pledge seriously. And we all committed to holding each other accountable, remember?"

"Yeah, he's right," Ryan admits.

"So come on, guys. Turn it off," Conner says. "We're held to a higher standard. And Justin—you gotta get a block, man! And we're all gonna ask you tomorrow if you've taken steps to block that, okay?"

Which was Conner being?

___ Thermometer ___ Thermostat

BREW IT!

How would you react in these situations? Would you, like Conner, be a thermostat and control the environment around you? Or, like Sarah, would you merely reflect and blend in with your environment?

POUR IT!

Drink in the flavor from the following Scriptures: Psalm 138:3; 2 Corinthians 3:18; Revelation 3:15-16.

SAVOR IT!

Ask God to help you take a stand when necessary and set the climate around you.

Sarah's parents were away for the weekend and allowed her to stay home because they trusted her with the house rule: No guests in the house while we're gone.

Sarah plugged in her favorite DVD and curled up on the couch with her cat. She quickly pushed the pause button when the doorbell rang. "Hey, girl! It's 9 p.m. and the night's just getting started!" Tina said. "We brought microwave popcorn, cookies, and Cokes. So what are we gonna watch?" she said as she rushed past Sarah with five of her girl pals.

"Uh . . . I'm not supposed to have any visitors while my parents are gone," Sarah said. "House rule. Sorry."

"When are they coming home?" Veronica asked.

"Tomorrow night."

"No prob, Sarah!" Tina said. "We'll be outta here by morning. They'll never know."

Why not? Sarah thought. *It's just my girlfriends having a good time together.*

Which was Sarah being? ___ Thermometer ___ Thermostat

WHAT'S HAPPENING?

In 2004, Typhoon Rananim killed 63 people and injured more than 1,800 when it slammed into China's southeastern coast. The typhoon had already killed one person in Taiwan and then came ashore south of Shanghai. People as far as 150 miles away from the typhoon experienced torrential rains and high winds.

The Bible tells us that strange and frightening things will happen in the sky and with the weather during the end times. We're told earthquakes will be common in all parts of the world, islands will be swallowed up by the sea, and many people will experience famine and sickness.

Though no one can predict exactly when the end times will come, we do have several signs from the Word of God. We're told to watch for these signs, to pay attention, and to realize when we see them that the end days are approaching.

How much do you know about the last days? Have you read the book of Revelation—the last book of the Bible? If not, determine to read it sometime this year. Not only does it give us a glimpse of the end times, but it also shows us snapshots of what heaven will be like.

We're told about the Antichrist and the Tribulation. We learn about the time of peace and the time of battle. We also get a peek into the future! By reading the entire book of Revelation, we learn that Christ (and his followers) come out on the winning side! Though the world will be full of devastating horrors, we also know that Christ has promised us eternal victory if we are faithful to him. (Revelation can be confusing at times, so when you read it, consider using a study Bible or another reference book that can help explain the significance of John's words.)

BREW IT!
You can't talk about what you don't know. Find out all you can about what God says will happen in the last days so you can talk intelligently with your friends about this important subject. And as you read through Revelation, thank God for the eternal future you have with him.

POUR IT!
Drink in the flavor from the following Scriptures: 1 Thessalonians 4:15-18; 5:1-8; Revelation 22:11-12.

SAVOR IT!
Ask God to give you a hunger for his Word. Ask him to help you understand what he wants to teach you through the book of Revelation.

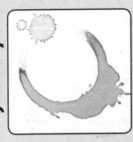

BREW IT!
There is such freedom in
placing God on the throne of
our lives! We tend to think
we'll become restricted and
won't have any fun when we
make Christ Lord. But the
reality is, once he's in charge
of everything in our lives, we
experience true freedom and
joy in a way we never
dreamed possible.

POUR IT!
Drink in the flavor from
the following Scriptures:
1 John 2:18-20, 22-23; 4:1-3.

SAVOR IT!
Ask God to reveal any area
where you're struggling with
following his lead. Confess
that area to him and ask him
to be absolute Lord.

WHO IS THE ANTICHRIST?

As you read about the end times, you'll become
aware of someone Satan will empower: the
Antichrist. Satan will give him the authority to heal
and do miraculous things. Many people will watch the
Antichrist in awe and be convinced that he is the
Messiah.

We halfway expect the world to be deceived, don't
we? After all, most people in the world don't claim to
have a personal, growing relationship with Jesus
Christ. So when they see someone promoting peace
and unity and performing miracles, it seems understandable that they'd be taken in by the deceit.

As Christians, we should know the Master so intimately that we're quickly able to spot the phony who
merely claims to be the Master. But the Bible tells us
that in the last days, even many Christians will turn
away from the truth and follow the world.

The Antichrist will be completely against God. But
even Christians can sometimes work against God in
the way they live. If you're not completely, 100 percent committed to the lordship of Jesus Christ, you
may be working against Christ in a specific area of
your life.

This is a dangerous place for a Christian to live.
Though God understands our humanness and knows
we make mistakes, he still expects us to allow him to
rule every area of our lives.

Is Jesus Lord of your devotional life but not Lord
of your money? Could it be you've given God control
of your friendships but not your dating life? Have you
committed your gifts and abilities to Christ yet still
hang on to your anger and hold grudges against
others? If so, you're battling an attitude of being
against Christ.

RESTORATION

The Parthenon is the most recognizable building on the Acropolis—a well-known hill in Athens, Greece. Greece is a country known for its ancient mythology, and the Parthenon began as a temple built to honor Athena, the goddess of the city. It was built in 438–437 BC and in its heyday was a vibrant religious center. Twenty-two tons of marble were used to build the Parthenon. A massive gold-and-ivory statue of Athena dominated the east side.

Over the years, however, time, weather, and war have taken their toll on this magnificent building. Restoration began in 1975 and is scheduled for completion in the near future. You can imagine that restoring a structure of this magnitude is quite an undertaking.

Each of the corner columns weighs sixty-five tons, and the middle columns weigh fifty-five tons. The uniformly straight columns appear as though they curve in. To counter that optical illusion, builders used entasis—an effect that slightly tapers the columns—to make them look straight. Twelve marble drums are built into the columns.

Areas that need repair are carefully measured before stonecutters chisel any pieces of marble. Diamond saws are first used to cut the marble, and the final cuts are made by hand. When the piece is a perfect fit, cement and epoxy affix the repair to the original.

Conservators calibrate the repair and chisel the new marble. Depending on the surface to be repaired, it can take fifteen days to chisel the piece by hand. In some instances, titanium rods are installed to join repairs. They're covered with a marble plug, then painted.

When the work is complete, the Parthenon will still be a ruin.

Restoration focuses on faithfully reconstructing existing parts, using new marble pieces where necessary for continuity. Despite the millions of dollars being spent, the years of work, and the careful attention to intricate detail, the completed and restored Parthenon will still be a ruin. After all this . . . still a ruin!

The Greeks aren't the only ones involved in restoration. God, too, is in the business of restoration. But when he completes his work in us, we are complete and whole. We're no longer seen as a ruin of sin.

BREW IT!

Whew! Aren't you glad God doesn't do halfhearted work? We can rejoice that he completes everything he begins. Praise God that Jesus didn't climb off the cross during the middle of the Crucifixion and pay for only part of our sins. He completed the job! And he continues to bring us to complete restoration each day as we faithfully walk in obedience to him.

POUR IT!

Drink in the flavor from the following Scriptures: Philippians 1:6; 1 Thessalonians 5:23-24; Revelation 21:5.

SAVOR IT!

Spend some time today simply thanking God for not quitting his work in you. Let him know how grateful you are that he has promised to completely restore you and remove all the ruins of sin from your life!

THE ULTIMATE THEME PARK

What do you enjoy most about theme parks? Is it riding a double-looped roller coaster? spinning around in circles on the Twister? munching on funnel cakes and cotton candy?

What if you could visit a theme park and do the things you're usually told not to do?

Well, now you can! Wannado City, located in the Sawgrass Mills shopping mall west of Fort Lauderdale, Florida, welcomes visitors into a metropolis the size of three football fields. To earn play money to spend in the city's shops and entertainment venues, attendees choose from hundreds of jobs and work at them in realistic surroundings.

Kiddie manicurists paint nails; teen fashion models strut a runway; child firefighters jump on a scaled-down version of a real fire truck and help extinguish a blaze. Teen doctors set a broken arm on a dummy and teen TV camera operators film the event.

All the things kids are told not to touch in real life are suddenly accessible to them. For approximately twenty-five dollars a day, visitors are exposed to a variety of interesting opportunities and activities.

Have you ever wished that finding God's will for your life could be that easy—and fun? If so, you're probably thinking that God's will for your life is synonymous with your future career. Your career, however, is only a portion of God's will for your life.

More important than which college you attend and what job you venture toward is who and what you become while doing those things! You see, God doesn't care as much if you attend your local city college or if you move away and enroll at a Christian university as he cares about what you become while you're in college.

His plan for your life is a process. It's something that's revealed every single day. He cares more about how you treated the gas station attendant this morning than whether you're going to enroll in zoology or calculus next semester.

His will for your life is that you surrender 100 percent to him every single day and live in obedience to him. That not only includes how you'll someday make a living; it also involves your decisions on how to dress, whom you hang out with, and how effectively you're being his hands and feet to those around you.

BREW IT!

Giving God complete control of every area of your life eliminates worry about your future. You'll learn that because he's faithful in guiding you with small decisions, he'll be faithful in helping you with the big ones. All choices should be made with the guidance of his Holy Spirit. That's God's will for your life!

POUR IT!

Drink in the flavor from the following Scriptures: Psalm 16:11; 119:35; Proverbs 3:5-6.

SAVOR IT!

Ask God to reveal his will for your life each and every day as you walk in obedience to him.

RELAX!

Lots of people pay big bucks to relax. Resorts and hotels offer massages. Cruise ships offer body wraps. Even some fitness centers provide reflexology for their members. For $165 you can get your colors balanced in an hour at the Enchantment Resort in Sedona, Arizona. You choose your favorite hues from bottles of colored oils, and the spa practitioner will supposedly assess your emotional and spiritual potential—all based on your color choices.

And if you want more options on how to relax, you can always search for one of the following:

- Aromatherapy: The use of plant oils in massage, facials, and body wraps. It supposedly enhances physical and psychological well-being.
- Body wrap: A treatment in which the body is wrapped in cloth strips soaked in herbal teas.
- Hot-stone massage: Massage done with river stones heated in water.
- Reflexology: The use of pressure-point massage on feet, hands, or ears to promote energy flow throughout the body.
- Watsu: An underwater massage using rhythmic movements, pressure-point massage, and stretches.

God is all for relaxation. The Bible tells us that he created the entire world in six days and rested on the seventh day. He wants his children to relax, but guess what! We don't have to use any of the above methods or pay any money to get the job done.

God wants us to relax and enjoy peace unlimited in him! How is that done? It's accomplished through an intimate, growing, totally surrendered relationship with him.

Here's how it works: As you surrender everything in your life to his care, you no longer have to worry about it! In fact, if you continue to worry, it proves one of two things: (1) you're not fully trusting Christ to take care of the things you've placed in his control, or (2) you haven't really given everything to him. When worries come to your mind, consciously ask God to take them away from you. Memorize a Scripture passage you can recite when you're anxious, such as Philippians 4:6-7.

An anxious spirit slows the work of God in your life. But the one who has learned to relax and trust the creator of the universe is the one who becomes spiritually stronger and more alert.

BREW IT!
God tells us to be still and know that he is God (see Psalm 46:10). It's in our quietness before him that we're able to see his sovereignty.

POUR IT!
Drink in the flavor from the following Scriptures: Psalm 37:7; 46:10; 1 Peter 5:7.

SAVOR IT!
Ask God to teach you total relaxation through trust in him.

SPORTS FANTASIES

Lance Armstrong, the world-class biking legend, had some unusual company as he pedaled to victory in the 2004 Tour de France. You'd expect reporters and photographers to be present. But sharing the course with Lance and other pro cyclists? Tourists from the United States! They were as close as they could be to the racers without being on the back of the bikes with them. Vacationing bicyclers shadowed the pros down the official route for the thrill of the ride.

Travel businesses have known for years that getting spectators to sports events was big business. But now there's a new twist. For the right price, you can get off the sidelines and onto the field with the pros!

If you've always fantasized about hitting a baseball out of a major league park, you can shell out five thousand dollars and the Chicago White Sox will let you take batting practice at U.S. Cellular Field.

If you admire basketball legend Michael Jordan and want to shoot hoops on his home court, the Chicago Bulls' new "Court of Dreams" program will let you do just that before the game begins.

If going faster pumps your adrenaline, you can experience the thrill of zipping around a NASCAR racetrack at 140 miles per hour. For $379 and up, the Lowe's Motor Speedway in Charlotte allows you to drive yourself in a real NASCAR racing car.

For fans who want more access—access to the players and access to the field—many professional sporting venues are turning customers' athletic fantasies into reality. Sports enthusiasts couldn't be happier!

Are you a Christian who wants more? If die-hard baseball fans are willing to shell out five thousand dollars for batting practice on Cellular Field, are you willing to pay the cost of living as Jesus did? While you can't actually live in the earthly home he did, you can live a holy life. But guess what! It will cost you.

Yes, forgiveness for sins is free. But to live as God calls you to live will cost you everything! Are you willing to pay the price? Do you want more out of your Christian life? A deeper relationship with your heavenly Father? The power to say no to temptation? The perseverance to maintain a consistent relationship with Christ? If you're a Christian who wants more, God is able to turn your spiritual fantasy into reality.

MORE SPORTS FANTASIES

As we discussed yesterday, many sports fantasies can become reality.

If your fantasy is to play skipper on an America's Cup yacht, you can turn your dream into reality for $1,980 for a four-hour charter aboard the *Stars & Stripes/USA 34.* It's available through San Diego's Next Level Sailing. The yacht is seventy-nine feet long and can go as fast as eighteen knots when heading downwind.

Admire tennis pro Serena Williams? The USTA National Tennis Center in Flushing, New York, home of the U.S. Open, will allow you access to the same court she plays on for $16 an hour (outdoor courts) or for $32 an hour (indoor courts) eleven months a year. You can't get access on the courts during the tournament itself. For $75 and up, you can even get private lessons—not from Serena but from one of the pros at the tennis center.

Or if golfing is your thing, you can start with a four-night package at $1,867 that includes tee times, lodging, and some meals at the Old Course at St. Andrews Links—frequent home of the British Open championship.

The Richard Petty Driving Experience, which oversees the tourist program at Lowe's Motor Speedway, has twenty-five raceways, four hundred employees, and one hundred cars for tourists. The advanced Racing Experience package sells for $2,999 and includes forty laps on the one-and-a-half-mile track.

Some people who shell out this kind of money are just out for a new experience, but a lot of them do it to feed their fantasies of fame. While many people fantasize about stardom in athletics, have you ever wondered how many fantasize about "stardom" in Christianity? Actually, "stardom" with Christ is opposite of the world's view of being a star. Whom does Christ see as stars? The servants. The ones giving and sacrificing. Disciples willing to put God first at any cost. Christians who are being persecuted for their faith, yet who remain steady in the midst of torture. These are the stars of Christianity. Not many people fantasize about this kind of stardom, yet this is the kind of spiritual fantasy God wants you to desire.

But why would I want to be tortured for my faith? you may be thinking. It's not that God wants you to desire pain; he wants the commitment level from you that is willing to endure pain if necessary to become all he calls you to be.

BREW IT!
Take stock of your dreams. Are you merely living out your own self-centered desires, or are you fulfilling God's dreams for your life?

POUR IT!
Drink in the flavor from the following Scriptures: Psalm 20:4; Romans 8:5-9; Philippians 2:14-16.

SAVOR IT!
Ask God to saturate you with the desire to become all he wants you to be. Ask him to place his dreams inside your heart.

BREW IT!
God can and will do incredible things with your life—if you're willing to pay the price. The cost is total surrender.

POUR IT!
Drink in the flavor from the following Scriptures:
Hosea 6:3; Joel 2:12;
Psalm 119:112.

SAVOR IT!
Ask God to give you a willing heart. Tell him you truly want to become all he desires for you. Ask him to bring anything to your mind that you need to commit to him; then do it.

NOT ALL FANTASIES = REALITY

Though your fantasies of driving on a NASCAR track, shooting hoops where Michael Jordan used to play, smashing tennis balls on the same court Serena Williams frequents, or getting batting practice where the White Sox play can all become reality, there are some sports fantasies that simply won't come true.

For instance, for fourteen dollars you can grab a guided tour of Yankee Stadium, but you won't be allowed on the field to smack any baseballs. Yankee Stadium is one of several famous sporting venues that have resisted the growing trend of offering access to enthusiasts willing to pay the price.

There are thousands of tennis fans in the world, but none will get to play at the All England Lawn Tennis Club unless they're actually competing in the Wimbledon tournament. You may enjoy playing eighteen holes of golf, but novice players and spectators aren't allowed on the greens at the Augusta National Golf Club (the Masters).

Nearly everyone loves an exciting game of football, and fans often cheer wildly for their favorite team. But even if they have the money, fans aren't allowed on the FedEx Field (Washington Redskins). You may enjoy watching the Kentucky Derby on television, but you'll have to settle for watching from a distance, because you won't be allowed on Churchill Downs—the track where the actual race is held. All sports fantasies don't come true.

Your spiritual fantasies, however, can come true. You can become all you dream—and all God desires—if you'll let him do the guiding, training, and molding. Want to have a spiritual depth that's an inspiration to others? You can . . . if you're willing to be a student of the Bible. Do you desire to love others as Jesus loved? You can . . . if you're willing to reach out as he did. Dreaming of being a great spiritual leader? It's possible . . . if you're willing to serve. But if you're intent on being first, if you always have to be right, and if washing feet disgusts you, your spiritual fantasies will never become reality.

THINKING ABOUT GOD

Spend some time today simply thinking about God and who he is.

Sovereign Lord
The compassionate and gracious God
The eternal God
The consuming fire
The exalted God
The faithful God
The glorious Father
The Glory of Israel
The God who saves me
The God who sees me
The living Father
The Majestic Glory
The Majesty in heaven
The One who sustains me
The only God
The Potter
The Rock in whom I take refuge
The spring of living water
The strength of my heart
The true God
He who hears prayer
He who tests the heart and mind
He who keeps his covenant of love

BREW IT!
What can you do to help others see the many facets of God Almighty?

POUR IT!
Drink in the flavor from the following Scriptures: Isaiah 25:1, 4-5; 26:8.

SAVOR IT!
Ask God to help you fall in love with him more and more every single day of your life.

CAN YOU SMELL HIM?

Zach and his family grew up near the water because his dad was in the fishing business. One afternoon ten-year-old Zach accompanied his dad and some coworkers in their small fishing boat. After they'd been out for some time, a storm came out of nowhere. It was so violent that it caught the men off guard.

They were tossed back and forth, and they struggled to gain a firm standing while they reeled in their lines and sails. Huge torrents of water rushed over the boat's rails, knocking some of the men to the floor. Zach's dad screamed his instructions over the roar of the waves.

Young Zach gained his composure and followed the sound of his dad's voice. The water grew so violent, however, that soon Zach couldn't hear his dad's voice any longer. "But I wasn't scared," Zach said, "because I could smell him. I knew my dad was nearby. I couldn't see him, hear him, or touch him, but he was so close, I could smell him. That's how I knew he was nearby, and I wasn't afraid."

You can experience the same closeness with God. When you're battling tough times, determine to live so close to God in the midst of heartache that you can smell him. Learn his sweet fragrance. How is that possible? By developing an intimacy with him that stands strong when you can't hear his voice, see his face, or feel his touch.

And how is that intimacy developed? By allowing him to sift out the things in your life that don't reflect his character. Are you willing to rid yourself of anything and everything that doesn't echo Jesus? Will you ask him to cleanse you of the clutter in your life that blocks your intimacy with him?

There's a huge difference between being a casual Christian and living so close to Jesus that you can smell him. Get in his face. Allow him to get in your face. He yearns for that kind of closeness with you. Instead of simply reading a quick devotional and shooting up a sentence prayer, spend time with him! Get to know him. Develop an actual growing relationship with him.

BREW IT!
As you grow close to God, it won't matter how many storms you face or if you can feel God's presence. When you develop this kind of intimacy with Christ, you'll be living so close to him that you'll be able to smell him even when you can't hear him.

POUR IT!
Drink in the flavor from the following Scriptures: Psalm 1:2; 15; 25:14.

SAVOR IT!
Ask God to start sifting—to begin the process of getting rid of all the clutter in your life that doesn't reflect his character.

BREW IT!
Do you need surgery for spiritual vision?

POUR IT!
Drink in the flavor from the following Scriptures: Matthew 15:14; 23:16; John 9:25.

SAVOR IT!
Ask God to give you new spiritual eyes.

SPIRITUAL EYES

I've worn glasses since the fourth grade, and I grew to hate feeling my specs slide down my nose during a game of tennis, taking them off and putting them on again at swimming events, and constantly having to push them up my nose during a sweaty game of hoops.

By my senior year of college, I had finally saved up enough money to purchase contact lenses. I thought I was in heaven! No more glasses seemed too good to be true. I wore contacts for several years, but I finally got tired of having to clean them, rinse them, and disinfect them.

So when I heard about a new surgery called LASIK that could correct my nearsightedness, I jumped at the opportunity. The doctor explained that he'd work on my right eye first, then the left one. He propped my eye open with a little contraption that prevented me from blinking. Then, using the precision of a laser, he actually changed the shape of my cornea to improve the way light is focused or refracted by my eye.

After the doctor reshaped the tissue, the outer flap of my cornea was laid back in its original position. Because of the cornea's extraordinary natural bonding qualities, healing was fast and didn't require stitches. The physician removed the wire contraption and asked me to blink, and then he began the same routine with my left eye. The entire procedure took less than thirty minutes, and I was awake the entire time!

Since my eye surgery, I can't even count how many times I've awoken in the night and thought, *Wow, I can actually see the clock! I know what time it is!* Because I'd been wearing corrective eyewear since I was ten, I felt as though I had a brand-new pair of eyes.

I can't help but think about the time when I accepted a brand-new life from God—when I truly allowed Jesus to become *Lord.* It was different from simply asking him to forgive my sins. There came a time when I realized that I couldn't live a godly life in my own power. I wasn't good enough or intelligent enough. I needed the supernatural power of the Holy Spirit.

When we allow God to release the power of his Spirit within us—through total surrender on our part—we begin to see through new eyes. We begin to see through the eyes of God. We see others as he sees them, and it makes all the difference in the world.

My eyes will still age. They'll grow weaker the older I get, but for several years I'll have perfect vision. As much as I love my new eyesight, I cherish my spiritual eyesight even more. It will never fade. My spiritual eyesight will last for eternity.

RALLYING TOGETHER

Hosting the Olympics is a major task. Today we're all too familiar with the threat of terrorism at any large event that draws millions of people. Back in 1984, terrorism wasn't as high profile as it is today, but the Los Angeles Olympic organizers still feared enemy attacks, boycotts, and financial ruin.

The result? People rallied together. The desire to make the 1984 Olympics an overwhelming success brought in the largest peacetime volunteer force in U.S. history! The 1984 Olympics also netted a $225 million profit. Wow! When people decide to accomplish something—and unite to do it—big things happen.

What would be the result if those in your church truly united? If you decided not to focus on the disagreement about what kind of coffee should be served between services or how much time should be spent singing choruses, and united instead? If you became a harmonious and obedient body of believers committed to living out the gospel, people would notice! They'd be drawn to your church. People want to be part of something that's united and happy and contagious.

Unity. That's one of the ingredients that helped a little ragtag team of disciples change the world. Many of them were from different backgrounds—an accountant, fishermen, a political zealot—yet they banded together because of their love for Christ and their obedience to his call.

It certainly wasn't their skills that turned the world upside down. The disciples were ordinary men. They probably had dirt under their fingernails and teeth that needed whitening. Chances are they didn't use perfect grammar when they spoke, and they probably never sat down to a dinner table with more than one fork at a place setting.

BREW IT!
Guess what! God is still looking for disciples who are willing to unite together for his greater purpose. If you're willing . . . he can use you to change the world!

POUR IT!
Drink in the flavor from the following Scriptures: Psalm 133:1; John 17:23; Colossians 3:14.

SAVOR IT!
Ask God to bring to your mind someone with whom you need to become more unified. Seek his help in putting your selfish desires aside and focusing on establishing harmony in that relationship.

They were persecuted. Laughed at. Frightened at times. Confused. Doubtful. Yet they changed the world. How? Again, unity was one of the most important ingredients in their strategy. In the days after Jesus' death until after Pentecost, we're told that the disciples stayed together and worshipped together. They prayed for each other. They made decisions together.

The disciples probably did have some personality clashes and differences of opinion. But they learned to put those things aside, unite together, and focus on something and Someone much greater than their own desires: their Lord and Master, Jesus.

INTERESTING CUSTOMS

You may have learned about ancient Greece in your history class. But here are some interesting food customs your teacher may not have told you about.

- The ancient philosopher Plato, though born into a wealthy family, lived very simply and ate only one meal a day.
- The Athenians, who were seen as the master bakers of classical times, created breads flavored with olives, cumin, honey, garlic, coriander, fennel, sage, or capers.
- All food that fell to the floor during a meal was believed to belong to the gods. The Greeks refused to sweep it up during dinner, because they believed to do so would bring bad luck.
- Ancient Greeks didn't often eat beef. They ate more goat, rabbit, deer, and pork, because the rocky Mediterranean region made it difficult to raise cattle.
- Honey was not only valued as one of the most important sweeteners to ancient Greeks; it was also valued for its ability to preserve foods.

Just as the above tidbits were important to Greeks in past years, it's important for you to develop some customs right now. Do you have any spiritual customs?

Have you made church attendance a good habit, or is it something you do every now and then—when nothing else interferes? What about church involvement? Do you have a custom of ministry? Are you giving, serving, and helping?

BREW IT!

It's foolish to assume you can deepen your spiritual life without the necessary disciplines. Determine to draw as close to Christ as you can.

POUR IT!

Drink in the flavor from the following Scriptures: 1 Corinthians 15:58; Ephesians 3:20; 4:22-24.

SAVOR IT!

Tell God that you want to be a strong Christian. Then back it up by developing spiritual accountability and a consistent prayer life topped with Bible reading.

Have you made reading your Bible an important, customary part of your daily routine? Do you read it every morning or every evening? Or only when you have nothing else to do?

What about sharing your faith? Is that one of your customs? Or is it something you shy away from for fear of what others will think?

The spiritual customs (or disciplines) you develop now will not only deepen your relationship with Christ today; they'll put you on a consistent track for your adult spiritual life as well. Begin by committing to daily Bible reading. Do you have a Bible you understand and enjoy? If not, seriously consider purchasing a new one, or request one for a birthday or Christmas gift. There are many easy-to-understand study Bibles filled with eye-grabbing graphics and Scripture helps for young adults. It's crazy to use the "I don't understand what I read" excuse. There really isn't an excuse.

Get a Bible you can understand and be proud to carry it. Next, develop the custom of accountability. Making yourself accountable to someone who's spiritually mature will help you develop the other necessary spiritual disciplines in your life.

NUTRITION: A NECESSITY

For the original Olympians, good nutrition was essential. The big winner of the Olympics in 480 BC said his diet consisted only of meat for ten months prior to the Games. Ancient Greek athletes also ate a lot of figs, because they were believed to build muscle and stamina. Hercules—a mythical athlete of grand and heroic proportions—reportedly ate fresh figs for dessert.

Athletes avoided sugar because it reduced energy, and bread was a definite no during training. Hippocrates wrote that if you want to lose weight, you should consume more meat and protein because you'll end up craving less food. The low-carb diets we know today actually began with the ancient Greeks.

That's not the only thing the Greeks started; they also came up with vegetarianism. Pliny the Elder believed that people were physically and mentally sharper without meat. The Mediterranean diet was modeled after the Greek way of eating.

Food was a major part of early Greek life and discussions. The Greeks believed that man should be connected to what he ate to maximize his health and personality. They believed that mood and health were related and that food could actually change one's personality. If you were stressed or hot-tempered, for example, you were advised to eat less meat. If you didn't have much energy, you were encouraged to consume more meat.

While it's important that we find proper nutrition through the food we consume, it's also essential that we seek spiritual nourishment. What's the point of being physically fit if we're not in good spiritual shape? Our physical fitness is merely temporary; it will only last during our lifetime on earth. But our spiritual fitness will last for eternity.

BREW IT!
Just as an Olympian would stay away from chips and cupcakes, you too have a responsibility to refuse spiritual fluff. Seek out solid spiritual nutrition. Determine to feed on spiritual meat.

POUR IT!
Drink in the flavor from the following Scriptures: Psalm 119:47; 1 Corinthians 3:1-3; 6:19-20.

SAVOR IT!
Ask God to help you read his Holy Word, understand what you read, chew on it, and digest it so that it shows up in your lifestyle.

How spiritually fit are you? Do you desire to get into spiritual shape? If so, you've made a good start by reading this book! Because by doing so, you're disciplining yourself to a daily quiet time with God. But determine not to simply read the devotional part. Make it a point to read the Scriptures listed and to pray daily. While there are hundreds of good devotional books on the market, the ultimate devotional book is the Holy Word of God. And a good devotional will always direct you right back to Scripture.

BREW IT!
Choose one of these names and focus on this specific facet of God all day.

POUR IT!
Drink in the flavor from the following Scriptures: Isaiah 2:12-18; 6:3; 9:6-7.

SAVOR IT!
Ask God to help you know him better and better.

WHO GOD IS
Spend some time today simply thinking about God and who he is.

Lord my Banner
Lord my Rock
Lord of heaven and earth
Lord of lords
Lord our God
Lord our Maker
Lord our Shield
Lord who heals me
Lord who is there
Lord who makes me holy
Lord who provides
Maker of all things
Maker of heaven and earth
Most High
My comforter in sorrow
My confidence
My helper
My hiding place
My hope
My light
My song
My strong deliverer
My support
One to be feared
Only wise God
Our dwelling place
Our judge
Our lawgiver
Our leader
Our Redeemer
Righteous Father
Righteous judge
Rock of our salvation
Shepherd
Sovereign Lord

ORDINARY PEOPLE

On February 3, you read about the disciples changing the world. Again, they were simply ordinary men. They hadn't received an expensive education at a prestigious university. They didn't have fancy certificates hanging on their office walls. They didn't even have office walls!

Yet God used these very ordinary people to impact the world with Christianity. We discussed one of the ingredients that helped make that possible: unity.

But there were other factors involved in helping these ordinary men turn the world upside down. Facing opposition, experiencing persecution, and establishing brand-new churches would require more than simple unity. The disciples needed boldness. They needed power!

Think about it: After Jesus had been falsely accused and arrested, the disciples were seen as a weak group of men easily intimidated and frightened. Where were they when Christ was crucified? They were scared to death! They fled for their lives. Only one disciple, John, stayed and watched his Lord being nailed to the cross.

Bible scholars say that Judas hung himself. Peter, the one whom Jesus called "the Rock," denied he even knew Christ . . . not once but three times! Thomas lost hope. The others were confused and may have been thinking, *We gave the last three years of our lives for the Messiah and for his message. What happens now?*

After Christ's resurrection, he appeared to the disciples. He told them he'd go on to heaven to prepare their eternal home, but he would leave them with a precious gift: his very Spirit—the Holy Spirit. He announced that with his Spirit, they'd receive the boldness and courage they needed to build churches, spread the gospel, and influence the world.

BREW IT!
You can't become all that God wants you to be in your own strength. You need his power. Do you have it?

POUR IT!
Drink in the flavor from the following Scriptures: Romans 6:19; 12:1; Hebrews 12:14.

SAVOR IT!
Thank God for making his power available to you so that you can fulfill his will for your life.

God says the same thing to you! When you find yourself huddled in your room wondering how you're going to face tomorrow, tired of being made fun of and misunderstood, God is with you—right there in your room—and he's promising you power to fulfill the call he has placed on your life.

You, like the disciples, may find that hard to believe. But take God at his word. He's never failed you yet, and he has promised that he never will! He's a God you can trust with your life!

BREW IT!
Just like the disciples, you too need the indwelling power of the Holy Spirit to fill you, energize you, and saturate you. It's in his power that you can become all he calls you to be.

POUR IT!
Drink in the flavor from the following Scriptures: John 14:26; 20:22; Acts 1:8.

SAVOR IT!
Tell God that you desire to live a holy life in the power of his Spirit. Ask him to bring anything to your mind that keeps you from doing that. Seek forgiveness for what he brings to your mind, and commit that area to him.

CHANGING THE WORLD

You can imagine the disciples huddled together in the upper room, waiting for God to act. Though Jesus had told them God would release his power on them, it may have seemed hard for those eleven men to believe. And it may seem tough for you to believe that God wants to empower you to impact your campus, share Christ with your boss, speak out boldly against sin, and live a holy life. Recognize that he doesn't expect you to do any of this in your own power. Like the disciples, you're only human. It would take supernatural power for you to become all that God calls you to be.

Has the lightbulb clicked on inside your head yet? That supernatural power is the power of the Holy Spirit. And just as God filled the disciples with his power, he also wants to saturate *you* with his power.

The disciples waited, just as Jesus had instructed them. Crowded together in an upper room, wondering how in the world they could go on, they began praying and worshipping. (When we pray and worship in a genuine way, big things happen!)

Throughout the Bible, we read about numerous times God's presence was felt and enjoyed by his people when they put aside their selfish agendas and simply worshipped him. God responds to that. One example is when King Solomon led the Israelites in building a beautiful temple for God. It took years of effort and lots of coordinated, painstaking work from many, many people. When the temple was dedicated, the Bible says "the glory of the LORD filled the temple," and the people were awed. (See 2 Chronicles 7:1-3.)

And God responded to the disciples in the upper room. Just as Jesus said it would happen—it happened! The Holy Spirit descended on them in fullness. Completeness. Wholeness. And ordinary people received the power and boldness they needed to accomplish what God was directing them to do.

When you're discouraged, take time to worship and praise God, even though you may not feel like it. Doing so will take your mind off yourself and will focus your thoughts on Christ. As you worship and praise him, your fear, confusion, and apprehension will subside.

BUT HOW DO I GET HIS POWER?

Talking about the power of the Holy Spirit and actually experiencing it are two different things. Living in his power requires total surrender on your part.

Let's back up. Imagine one of your friends approached you and said something like this: "You know, I really want to do what God tells me to. I want to follow him and do what's right, but it seems like every time I decide to do the right thing, I end up doing what's wrong. It's like there's a battle going on inside of me. My head says, 'Follow God. Do what he tells you to do.' And that's what I want. But when I start in that direction, the struggle rages inside of me, and I feel myself being pulled toward sin. And you guessed it—I end up doing what I know God doesn't want me to do."

How would you respond to your friend? What kind of advice would you give him? You might be thinking, *I'd tell him to become a Christian.*

Oh. Guess I forgot to give you all the details. You see, he's already a Christian. In fact, your friend is the apostle Paul. That's right. You can read about his struggle in Romans 7:15-25. So Paul doesn't need to become a Christian all over again—he's already been saved from his sin. Now he needs to be *sanctified.* (He shares his discovery of that in Romans 8.)

God commands us to live holy lives. *But how can I do that?* you may be thinking. *I'm only human. It would take some supernatural kind of power for me to live a holy lifestyle.*

The exciting thing about God is that he will never command you to do something and then frustrate you by not equipping you with everything you need to fulfill his command.

He tells you to live a holy life. Then he provides his supernatural power—the power of his Holy Spirit—which enables you to fulfill that command. In the power of his Holy Spirit, you can live a holy life.

So if you're a Christian (as Paul was), you don't have to start all over again by praying, "Okay, God. Make me a Christian again. This fourteenth time maybe I can make it work."

Recognize that you can't make it work. That's the problem. That's the struggle Paul displayed in Romans 7. Only God can live a holy life through you, but it requires a willing and surrendered lifestyle.

BREW IT!
Imagine trying to pour a can of Coca-Cola into a glass filled with Silly Putty. You wouldn't get much Coke in there, would you? You need an empty glass to pour your liquid into. In the same way, God needs a willing life emptied of self in which to pour his Spirit.

POUR IT!
Drink in the flavor from the following Scriptures: Romans 7:15-25; 1 Peter 1:16; Hebrews 12:10.

SAVOR IT!
Go ahead. Give God everything. Let him have complete control.

BREW IT!

Do you recognize the difference between this kind of commitment and the commitment of a casual Christian? Leave casual Christianity behind. Determine to live in radical obedience to the lordship of Jesus Christ!

POUR IT!

Drink in the flavor from the following Scriptures: Romans 6:6-8, 11-14, 22.

SAVOR IT!

Are you ready to pray the prayer in today's devotional and mean it?

TOTAL SURRENDER

If you desire to live in the power of the Holy Spirit, tell God. He loves it when his children talk to him with an open heart. Tell him you understand his command that you live a holy life. And go ahead—share your frustration (as Paul did in Romans 7) about the struggle that takes place within you when you try to live a holy life and can't cut it.

He wants to unleash the power of his Spirit within you, which will enable you to live in holiness. But, as we discussed yesterday, you don't have to become a Christian all over again to make that happen. If you are already a Christian, have repented of your sins, have accepted Christ's forgiveness, and are living in obedience to him, you can come to him just as you are—in frustration, in confusion, and with the desire to live a holy life.

You can say something like, "Father, thank you for granting me forgiveness. Thanks that you've saved me from sin. But I want to live a holy life. And when I try to do what's right, I often end up experiencing the same struggle Paul did, and I give in to sin. I don't want that. I realize when I accepted you as my Savior, I didn't get just a little bit of you. I got you (Jesus), your Holy Spirit, and Father God. But the thing is . . . you didn't get all of me. Yes, I confessed my sins and asked you to be my Savior, but now I want to ask you to be my Lord.

"So I give you every single detail of my life. My past, my present, and my future. I give you my relationships, my future spouse, my future children, my career, my rights, my possessions, my fears, my hurts, my talents, everything. And I ask that you sanctify me wholly. Give me a spiritual bubble bath in the depths of my soul.

"I yield all control of my life to you. Break me and remold me in your image. Release the power of your Holy Spirit within me. I realize the Holy Spirit has been here since I accepted you as Savior, but I want to live in your Spirit's power. So I surrender to you. I'm becoming an empty glass. Saturate and fill me with your Spirit's power. I give you my will. My self. My entire life! I no longer have any claim to myself. I belong totally, completely to you."

DO I HAVE TO BE PERFECT?

But doesn't living a holy life mean being perfect?
you may be thinking. Yes and no. You're not perfect,
and you won't become perfect until you're in heaven
with God for eternity. But when you yield 100 percent to his authority (when you die to your rights,
your self, your dreams, your own way), he can perfect your heart.

You see, when you allow God to wholly sanctify
you, you're in essence saying, "Dear Jesus, I want
your will above my own. I want your way. Your
dreams. Your life. My heart now belongs to you."

And God perfects your heart. In other words, you're
still human, and yes, you'll still blow it. You're not
perfect—but your heart is made perfect. The difference is that when you blow it, you can come to Christ
and say, "Oh, Lord, I blew it. I'm so sorry. I realize
what I did was wrong. I broke your heart. Will you
forgive me? You know my heart's desire. You know
that my heart yearns to do only what you want me
to do. You know that my heart's cry is 'your will, your
way.' Thank you for giving me that desire deep within
my heart. Thank you for perfecting my heart.

"Now, please help me set up safeguards, accountability, and boundaries so I don't blow it in this same
area again. Thanks that you've taken over my heart.
My deepest desire is truly to do what you command.
Help me to fall in love with obeying you."

No, you won't become perfect. You still have to
live in a fleshly human body that's weak and faulty as
long as you're on earth. But when you totally surrender to his authority, he will perfect your heart. And
when he does, his Holy Spirit will prompt you and
nudge you when you've done something wrong.

Let's go over that again: his Holy Spirit will
prompt you and nudge you when you've done
something wrong.

BREW IT!

That's Christian growth. It
doesn't do any good to
throw in the towel and start
all over; that becomes a
vicious cycle. Continue walking with Christ. Continue
growing! Learn through his
forgiveness and grace, and
allow him to mold you into
his likeness. And remem-
ber—this is a process.

POUR IT!

Drink in the flavor from
the following Scriptures:
1 Corinthians 1:30-31;
1 Peter 1:15; 2 Peter 3:11.

SAVOR IT!

Ask God to cleanse you,
sanctify you, and perfect
your heart.

And when you feel the Holy Spirit nudging you, go to Christ and seek forgiveness for
that specific area in your life. Guess what! God will always forgive a genuinely repentant
heart. And when he has forgiven you, you don't have to start all over again thinking,
Okay, this fifteenth time of becoming a Christian it will finally click. You simply accept
his forgiveness, thank him for the faithfulness of his Holy Spirit working within you
(helping you recognize that you did something wrong), and continue walking in obedience with him.

BREW IT!
Remember, this is a process, and the Holy Spirit is in charge of it.

POUR IT!
Drink in the flavor from the following Scriptures: John 8:34-36; Romans 6:22-23; Galatians 4:7.

SAVOR IT!
Thank God for his desire to perfect your heart.

BUT WHAT ABOUT SIN?

But because I'm human I'm doomed to keep sinning the rest of my life, right? you may be wondering.

Well . . . don't assume that. You see, when God sanctifies you, releases his supernatural power within you, and perfects your heart, it's possible for you to live within that power. Now think about that for a second.

That's a lot of power! The same mighty power that raised a dead man to life, set the stars in the sky, and put the whole world in motion is now filling, saturating, and ruling your life. If you actually have that kind of power within you, why wouldn't you be able to say no to sin?

Again, think about it: If you're living with the same power that raised a dead man to life, made blind people see and lame people walk, why wouldn't you be able to use that same mighty power to say no to sin?

You can.

But wait a sec! you may be thinking. *I'm still human.*

Yes, but you've asked God to empower you to live a holy life, remember?

Oh, yeah.

So when you're tempted to sin, you don't have to. Sanctification releases you from the power of sin . . . meaning you no longer have to live as a slave to sin. You no longer have to be under sin's control. You're now under the control of the Holy Spirit. You relinquished control to him, didn't you?

Yeah. That's right. I did! So I'll never be tempted again?

Yes, you'll be tempted. You're still human, and you're still living in a sinful world. But the difference is now you're living in a sinful world with a holy, supernatural power to enable you to live above sin. You don't have to give in!

But what if I sin without even knowing it?

Okay. Two important things we need to talk about: (1) The Holy Spirit will nudge you when you've done something wrong. It's his responsibility to let you know that you've sinned, so you can seek forgiveness. He's in the process of making your heart tender. He's also in the process of making sin look worse and worse to you and perfecting your heart so that your deepest desire is no longer to jump into sin but instead to do the will of your Father.

We'll chat about the second important thing we need to discuss tomorrow.

CAN I LIVE ABOVE SIN?

Let's continue our conversation from yesterday. We were talking about what happens if we sin without knowing it, and we mentioned that the Holy Spirit will let us know if we sin. Here's the second important thing: (2) We need to define sin. If you're calling sin something that happens whenever you make a mistake in math or sneeze without remembering to say, "Excuse me," you're right: You'll keep sinning all the time every single day.

But think back to Christ's death. He not only paid the penalty for your sins, but he died so you wouldn't have to keep living in sin. In other words, his death set you free from being enslaved to sin's power. So let's look at another definition of sin: *going against the known will of God.*

God created you, and he understands the way you're wired. He understands when you're suffering with a migraine and you're short with your little brother. According to the true definition of sin, have you deliberately gone against God's known will?

But when you sense God saying, "I don't want you listening to that CD anymore because the lyrics are filled with obscenities and the group sings about things that break my heart" and you deliberately continue to listen to it, you're going against God's will.

BREW IT!
Do you continue to live as a slave to sin? You don't have to!

POUR IT!
Drink in the flavor from the following Scriptures: 1 John 2:1, 15-17, 27.

SAVOR IT!
Thank God for his desire to fill you with his very self— the Holy Spirit.

At this point, the Holy Spirit will nudge you and convict you (make you feel guilty) and remind you that you're living in disobedience. Then it's your responsibility to confess your sin to God, accept his forgiveness, and set a plan in motion to help you not repeat that sin. (Throw away the CD, replace it with a Christian CD that has the same musical style but positive lyrics, etc.)

Let's back up to when you first realized that God was telling you not to listen to that CD anymore. Right then—at that very moment—you had a choice. Either you deliberately disobey him (and sin), or you rely on the supernatural power of his Holy Spirit that's flooding your life and you use that power to resist the temptation to listen to the CD.

You'll still face temptation, but with the Holy Spirit's power ruling your life, you no longer have to give in to temptation. In other words, it is possible to live above sin. Not in your own strength, but by his supernatural power within you.

We know this is true because the apostle John tells us it is in 1 John 2:1. But in the very next sentence, he also tells us that if we do sin, there is always someone we can go to for forgiveness. In other words, in God's power we can resist the temptation to sin. We don't have to give in. But sometimes we will. We're human. We'll blow it. And when we do, God will always forgive a genuinely repentant heart.

BREW IT!
Today—on Valentine's Day—love as Jesus loves!

POUR IT!
Drink in the flavor from the following Scripture: 1 Corinthians 13.

SAVOR IT!
Think of someone you're having a difficult time loving. Give that person to God, and ask him to help you see the person through his eyes and to love as he does.

DO I HAVE TO LOVE WILLIAM?

When I was a high school teacher, I had a student in my class who sat near the back of the room and made animal noises all hour. William didn't have many friends (would you wanna sit next to someone who sounded like he was emitting a moose mating signal?), and he was dying for attention. But I didn't want to love him.

When I was a youth minister, there was a girl in our group who smelled bad. Always. And her hair was oily. Very oily. When we took trips, none of the kids wanted to sit next to her on the bus. And on retreats? No one wanted to bunk with Elizabeth. She was dying for friends. But I didn't want to love her.

When I started speaking and traveling a lot, I noticed there was usually one kid at each conference who just sort of claimed me. This one kid would run to the cafeteria to sit with me, seek me out during free time, and hang on to my arm or hand as I walked from area to area. And this one kid never had any friends, needed some deodorant, hadn't brushed her teeth, and was picked on by everyone else. This one kid was always dying to be loved. But I didn't want to love her.

Then there was this adult. She didn't always say or do the right things. She was impulsive and spontaneous—which resulted many times in doing before thinking. She was impatient with people and held unreal expectations of others. Though she had friends, she was still dying to be loved—intimately. And you know what? Even though she was far less than perfect, someone loved her anyway. And not just a little bit. He loved her as if she were the only one in all the world to love. He treated her like a queen—even died for her. And because *Jesus* cared enough to love *me* (and I'm still impulsive), I in turn must love others.

Not just when it's convenient and easy. Not just when they smell good and look great. Not just the popular people and the funny, outgoing, creative ones. It means if I'm going to call myself a disciple, I will love others, period. William. Elizabeth. The lonely kid at camp. And not just on Valentine's Day, but every single day of the year.

GIVE YOUR HEART AWAY

Giving our hearts away—by loving others as Jesus himself loves them—is actually a pretty good idea, isn't it? And not just on Valentine's Day when people expect us to be nice. We should strive to love as Jesus loves every single day of the year!

It's comforting to know that he never asks us to do anything he hasn't done first. In other words, when our Father commands us to reach out to those who are tough to love (the Williams and Elizabeths), he himself enables us to do that by filling us with his love. That's how Christians can genuinely love and make a difference. And again, not just on Valentine's Day, but the day after and every day of the year. And not just when we're loved back, but even when we're overlooked or treated wrongly.

That's why I baked bread for my grouchy, hard-to-love next-door neighbor. She's never happy and complains about everything. When she complained about my dog, I was furious. I wanted to yell at her. Instead, I took her some homemade bread.

When she yelled at me for parking my car in the street instead of my driveway, I wanted to send my dog over on an attack mission! Instead, I delivered her mail that was accidentally sent to me.

When Karen, a new employee with a loud voice, was given an office close to mine, I wanted to bang on the wall between our offices and say, "Hey! Quit talking so loud. I'm trying to write in here." And when I could hear her obnoxious laugh clear down the hallway, I wanted to scream, "Put a cork in it!" Instead, I invited her out to lunch. Got to know her. Found out she was struggling and needed a friend. She felt insecure about her new position.

How will the world know we're Christians? If we tote our new leather-bound Bibles? (Not hardly.) If we wear a cool gold-plated cross around our neck? (Even Madonna has been known to do that!) If we quote Scripture? (Satan did that.)

They'll know we are Christians by our love. And here's the hard part. Ready? They'll know we are Christians not by our love for *God.* That's the simple part. It's easy to love God, because he's perfect and he already loves us. Instead, others will know we are Christians by our love for *each other.* (Oooh, that's tough!)

BREW IT!
It's a lot easier for me to love God than for me to love people. But that's where our true colors show. The mark of a mature disciple is his love for those around him.

POUR IT!
Drink in the flavor from the following Scriptures: John 13:34; Romans 13:10; 1 John 3:18.

SAVOR IT!
Ask God to give you ideas of specific ways you can show love to those around you.

BREW IT!
Love and spiritual growth go together. It's impossible to become a mature, strong Christian without learning how to love as Jesus does.

POUR IT!
Drink in the flavor from the following Scriptures: John 15:9-13; Philippians 1:9-11; 1 Thessalonians 3:12-13.

SAVOR IT!
Tell God that you're serious about becoming all he wants you to be and that you're willing to allow him to teach you to love, even when it's tough.

LOVING WHEN IT'S TOUGH

Jeremy is saying unkind things about you behind your back. Should you love him? Yes. It seems as though Mrs. Thompson always picks on you during class. Should you love her? You bet.

God has already made this "loving thing" explicitly clear . . . with his life. No one ever said loving others would be easy. It's not. According to Webster's dictionary, love is "unselfish, loyal, and benevolent concern for the good of another." That's hard work. It requires conscious action. So let's create a strategy that will help you love those who bug you.

- *Strive not to argue.* Yeah, sometimes it's tempting to get into a heated argument, but remember, God is not calling you to win fights; he's calling you to love others! And when you get the urge to jump into an argument? Check out what 1 Thessalonians 5:13 and Ephesians 4:31-32 have to say about quarreling. If you'll look closely, you'll find that the apostle Paul gives a great suggestion for what to do instead of arguing!
- *Ask God for a deep, growing love.* Since Jesus displayed intimate love for us when he gave his life, we should also seek to love others beyond a surface, halfhearted commitment. Want others to see Christ's love in you? Then develop a deep, solid, genuine love for others.
- *Develop a lifestyle of love.* Yes, love is action. It's something you do. But it's also something you are. In other words, God wants his love to become more than your reaction to circumstances you encounter. He wants it to flow through your veins. To move you forward. To become your lifestyle.
- *Pray for strength to love others.* Even when it's the last thing you want to do, God still calls you to love. Obviously you can't do this in your own strength, so pray for his. And when you doubt that's possible, check out Colossians 1:11 for a clue about what Christ's strength will enable you to do.

OWN A LIGHTHOUSE

Years ago, seafarers were guided by whale-oil fires burning in waterside towers called lighthouses. Today, with radar and global positioning on ships, lighthouses aren't necessary. They're beautiful structures, but they're no longer needed.

A few years ago, the government wondered what to do with the unused lighthouses still standing in America. Demolish them? Sell them? Because they're such a part of our history, it seemed a good idea to restore them and allow tourists to visit the towering structures around the country.

But instead of selling the lighthouses, the Department of the Interior and the coast guard announced that many of them would be given away to people who promised to take good care of them. Excitement quickly spread. Many people wanted to own a piece of our nation's history by having their own lighthouse.

One national newspaper even showed photographs of the lighthouses that were up for grabs. One lighthouse in Virginia had a three-story keeper's quarters. Talk about a creative place to host a party! How fun would it be to say to all your friends, "Movies, popcorn, and all the munchies you can eat tonight at the lighthouse!"

Many people wanted a lighthouse at first. But when they found out everything that would be required to own such a historical novelty, the excitement quickly faded. You see, even though the lighthouse was free for the taking, a lot of responsibility went with the gift. There was the tremendous expense of restoring the lighthouse; simply getting a lighthouse ready for the public to visit and view can cost tens of thousands of dollars.

All applicants had to pass a grueling acceptance process to prove they could maintain the structures according to specific restoration guidelines. The new owners also had to be willing to open their lighthouses to the public. So those dreaming of a quiet retirement in a free lighthouse realized they didn't even need to apply!

At first glance, owning a lighthouse sounded intriguing. It would be fun to own something that so few others had. But we can't always get the full scope of things simply by looking at the surface. It's only when we dig deeper that we get the full story.

BREW IT!
Don't be one who simply accepts everything you hear. Be willing to do some research. Dare to go beneath the surface.

POUR IT!
Drink in the flavor from the following Scriptures: 1 John 4:1-3, 5-6; 2 John 1:9-11.

SAVOR IT!
Ask God to help you become a disciple of depth—someone who's willing to go beneath the surface.

BREW IT!

Think about yourself for a moment. Are you into Christianity for the "stuff"? The feel-good emotions of being in a youth group, the fun of attending church camp, the activities with your friends at church? Or are you a Christian because you love Christ and realize all he has done for you? In gratitude to him, you will want to live a life that's pleasing to your heavenly Father.

POUR IT!

Drink in the flavor from the following Scriptures: Matthew 16:13-18; 1 John 2:4-6, 15-17.

SAVOR IT!

Ask God what specific responsibilities he wants to give you within the body of Christ.

LIGHTHOUSES AND CHRISTIANITY

Learning not to accept something simply because others say it's a good idea is one lesson we can learn from the great lighthouse giveaway. But there's something else we can take away from this event.

Yes, the lighthouses were free. Many wanted them. But when they realized the cost and responsibility involved in owning one of the towering structures, many walked away. Does this remind you of Christianity? Forgiveness of sins is free for the taking. Salvation is an incredible gift! Everyone wants something free—especially eternal life when we know we don't deserve it, can't earn it, and won't ever be able to purchase it.

But with salvation comes the responsibility of living a Christ-centered life. We can't simply say, "Yahoo! I believe in Jesus, so I'm a Christian and will end up in heaven someday" and yet continue to do our own thing apart from Christ. Even Satan believes in Jesus. Head knowledge has never been enough to receive eternal life. God wants our hearts, our love, and our lifestyle.

Think back to Jesus' ministry. While he was healing the sick and multiplying food, crowds rushed to see and hear him. But when the teaching got tough, many walked away. (See John 6:60 for one example.) It was as if they wanted a free lighthouse but refused to accept the responsibility that went along with it.

At one point Jesus turned to his disciples and asked if they, too, wanted to leave. Peter boldly blurted out, "No way! You're the Messiah." Jesus affirmed him and told him he would be a rock of the church.

DIFFERENT FOR A REASON

In the 2002 WNBA play-offs, Indiana Fever star Tamika Catchings wore a face mask that looked . . . well, frightening! Even though it was plastic and see-through, it pressed against her nose and cheekbones, slightly distorting her facial features.

People criticized her and wondered why she would walk out on the court wearing such a monstrosity. There was a simple and logical explanation: In July, she had accidentally been elbowed in the face by the Miami Sol's Ruth Riley.

Twenty-three-year-old Tamika had a broken nose.

She was wearing a customized plastic mask to protect her nose as it continued to heal. Even though the mask was hot, cumbersome, and looked funny, it didn't affect her stats. Tamika Catchings, the WNBA Rookie of the Year and former University of Tennessee star, averaged 18.6 points and 8.6 rebounds and led the league with 594 points! Looking different and being uncomfortable was a small price to pay to be able to play the game she loved.

What about you? Are you so in love with Jesus that you're willing to look a little different and be uncomfortable at times to serve your Master? Face it: If you're dressing modestly, you definitely look different from the world. If you dare to carry your Bible on campus, you (and your backpack) are standing apart from the others.

And if you're refusing to attend parties where alcohol is being served, you're definitely going to feel a little uneasy when others make fun of you. Though refusing to cheat on a test when everyone else is may feel uncomfortable, it's the right thing to do.

Tamika wore a customized face mask to protect her nose. Wouldn't it be cool if you could get some customized gear that would protect you from the slams Satan and his followers toss your way? Wait a sec! There is such a thing! It's the armor of God.

BREW IT!
When you walk out on the court of life and face your opponents, are you wearing God's protective gear? Are you willing to look and act different because you love him?

POUR IT!
Drink in the flavor from the following Scripture: Ephesians 6:10-18.

SAVOR IT!
Ask God to help you fall in love with him more and more each day.

BREW IT!

Don't even consider going another day without accepting God's free gift of salvation. You need that helmet to protect you from Satan's schemes.

POUR IT!

Drink in the flavor from the following Scriptures:
2 Corinthians 4:8-9;
Colossians 1:11-12;
1 Peter 1:3-7.

SAVOR IT!

If you've never accepted God's free gift of salvation, tell him you want it right now. See tomorrow's devotional for a guide on how to pray for salvation.

WEARING THE RIGHT ARMOR

What if WNBA star Tamika Catchings had simply worn a fun mask she grabbed at the local Wal-Mart to protect her broken nose? After all, it would have been much less expensive than having a mask customized for her face. But it wouldn't have protected her nose. Obviously, just any mask wouldn't do. Because she was serious about protecting her face, she was willing to pay the price for the best mask.

Why is it that so many Christians leave their homes each morning and walk onto their campuses or career sites with less than the best spiritual protection? God has provided spiritual armor to protect our relationship with him, yet many of us don't take the time to put it on, or we try to make do with a cheap substitute.

In yesterday's Bible reading (Ephesians 6:10-18), you read about the armor of God. To resist Satan, we're told to use every piece of God's armor. We're not told to grab something that looks like God's armor or something we feel is adequate enough. We're even given the specifics of his armor: a helmet, belt, breastplate, shield, sword, and shoes.

The helmet of salvation is the foundational piece of God's armor. Why would Christians need a helmet? Because Satan hates you with a passion! He wants to get to your mind through movies and TV shows that portray sexual intimacy outside of marriage as not only okay but expected. He wants to entice your mind with all that's available through the Internet—going to the wrong chat rooms, giving away too much information on a blog, getting sucked into cyber relationships.

Does this mean you should never turn on the television or a computer? No, but it does mean you have to be extremely careful. You need a guard. You need the helmet of God's salvation to protect you from the evil that Satan so desperately wants to put in your head. If you've received God's gift of salvation, you're no longer under sin's—or Satan's—power.

Can you imagine watching a Super Bowl in which none of the players are wearing helmets? Any pro football player knows he's in the game to be as dangerous as the rules allow. He knows what he's up against. He realizes his opponents want him down hard. It would be absolutely stupid to play the game without head protection.

You face an opponent who's much more powerful than any pro football player. Satan not only wants to knock you down; he wants you to be tormented for all eternity!

SALVATION: A FREE GIFT!

If you've never asked Christ to come into your life and forgive your sins, you're not a Christian. You may be a good person doing good things who's involved in church and reading your Bible. But if you don't have a personal relationship with Jesus Christ, you're not a Christian.

But the good news is that you can be! The helmet of salvation is a free gift. God not only has the power to forgive your sins, but he wants to forgive your sins. In fact, he gave his only Son, Jesus Christ, to die an excruciating death on a cross so the penalty for your sins would be paid. Wow! That's love.

And it doesn't stop there. Christ not only died for your sins, he was also raised from the dead and is preparing your future home with him in heaven right now. Would you like to receive this precious gift of forgiveness and salvation? Let's pray.

Dear Jesus, I believe you are the Son of God. I believe you died for my sins. Thank you, Jesus! If you hadn't been willing to do that, I would have no hope of eternal life. Thank you for loving me so much!

I realize I was born a sinner. There's nothing I can do to earn forgiveness for my sins, and I can't do enough good things to overcome my sins. But I understand you're willing to forgive me.

Dear Jesus, I confess my sins right now. I repent. I'm turning the direction of my life over to you. I want you to be in charge. Will you forgive me? I'm so sorry I've sinned. I'm so sorry I've broken your heart. I trust you with my life. I trust you with eternity. Right now I place my faith in you.

I thank you for the Bible, which contains your true words and can help me get to know you. Dear Jesus, help me to live a life that's pleasing to you. Help me to grow stronger in you and to obey you in every area of my life.

Jesus, thank you so much for forgiving my sins and granting me eternal life. Thank you for this wonderful gift of salvation. I don't deserve it, Jesus, but I am so glad you've given it to me! Now help me become all you want me to be and use me to build your Kingdom.

I love you, Jesus.

In your holy name I pray this. Amen.

BREW IT!
If you prayed that prayer and meant it, you now belong to the body of Christ! But this is just the beginning. Now it's important to get involved in a church and a youth group, as well as to read your Bible. This will help you grow stronger in your faith.

POUR IT!
Drink in the flavor from the following Scriptures: John 3:16; Romans 3:22-24; 5:1-2.

SAVOR IT!
Spend a few minutes thanking Christ for his incredible love for you. Tell him how excited you are to be a Christian. If you've already made this commitment, thank God for giving you his salvation! Is there someone in your life who needs to understand God's love and forgiveness? Pray for that person right now.

WEARING THE BELT

Christians who are serious about living for God know how important it is to know his truth and to know why they believe it. Being able to articulate why you believe as you do is called *apologetics*. There are several quality Christian books on the market that can help you with this. I recommend the student version of *The Case for Christ* by Lee Strobel for explaining the reality of Christ, and Lee's student version of *The Case for Faith* for articulating logical reasons to believe in a loving God. Lee has also written a powerful book, *The Case for a Creator*, that presents striking evidence from all aspects of science for God's role as creator of the universe.

It's important not only to say, "I don't believe that," but also to be able to explain why—based on God's truth—you believe as you do. Now let's get to this special piece of God's armor, the belt of truth.

When soldiers fought, they were decked out in full armor. The belt was the important piece that held everything together. What good is a shield if it doesn't stay on? The belt was the connecting point for the other important pieces of armor.

God needs disciples who will not only accept him as Savior, but who will also dig and study and articulate with confidence and boldness why Jesus Christ is the only way to heaven. That truth is what connects everything else in your relationship with him.

The belt worn by ancient soldiers wasn't simply a fashion accessory like we wear today. It was a larger garment that also protected the groin. Let's stretch this for a moment.

BREW IT!
Have you accepted God's truth in every area of your life? In believing that the Bible is his Holy Word and is absolute truth? In believing that a relationship with him is the only way to spend eternity with God? In lifestyle and morals?

POUR IT!
Drink in the flavor from the following Scriptures: Ephesians 5:3-7; Colossians 3:5-8; 1 Thessalonians 4:3-5.

SAVOR IT!
Seek God's forgiveness for any sexual sins you have committed. If you're sexually pure, thank God for that, and tell him you need his continued help to stay pure.

The Bible warns against sexual intimacy outside of marriage. That's not because God wants to rob you of fun; it's because he wants to protect you from hurt, and because he doesn't want you experiencing the intimacy sex brings until you're married.

Sex works like cement. It bonds two people together more tightly than anything else in the world. When you experience sexual intimacy (not just intercourse, but all sexual intimacy) outside of marriage, you're bonding with someone outside of God's will. You're setting yourself up for hurt. You're also sinning.

When you've accepted God's absolute truth on this, you're able to use this truth to protect your most private areas—just as a belt would protect ancient soldiers.

DO YOU HAVE GOD'S APPROVAL?

The apostle Paul tells us that to resist Satan, our great enemy, we need the helmet of God's salvation, the belt of God's truth, and the breastplate of God's righteousness. When we act righteously—do the right thing—God approves. Why is his approval so important?

Athletes who are committed to their coach not only want to win the game, they also want to win in a way that makes their coach proud. It's not simply winning that's of ultimate importance; it's how we win.

For example, let's say you're a basketball player and you tackle your opponent during the state championship. You grab the ball while he's down, tuck it underneath your arm like a football, and make a mad dash to your team's hoop. When you reach the end of the court, you quickly pass, and your friend makes the basket.

Now, even though this is really hard to believe, let's also imagine the refs didn't see what you did. People in the stands would probably complain, wouldn't they? The opposing team's coach would approach the refs and ask what in the world was happening. And though you may have fooled the officials, chances are you wouldn't get by your coach. He knows the rules. Yes, he desperately wants to win, but he also wants you to play by the rules. No good coach would ever approve of your antics on the court.

In the same way, God also wants you to play by his rules. It's not simply filling up a church building with huge numbers of people he's concerned about; he wants you to invite them because you genuinely care about where they'll spend eternity. It's not just memorizing Scripture, it's believing it and living out the words through your actions. It's not simply saying you love your neighbor, it's offering to shovel her driveway when it snows.

In other words, it's not just doing that's important; it's how it's done that determines if God approves. A solid Christian is one who seeks God's approval. A solid Christian is one who knows God's approval is much more important than the approval of coaches, friends, teachers, or whomever you're dating.

BREW IT!
Do you have God's approval in every single area of your life? Let this be your goal!

POUR IT!
Drink in the flavor from the following Scriptures: Philippians 4:7; Colossians 2:6-7; 1 Thessalonians 1:4.

SAVOR IT!
Tell God you desperately want his approval. Ask him to bring to your mind anything in your life that doesn't meet his approval. Seek his forgiveness, and be willing to commit that area to him.

There's no better ammunition against Satan's attacks than a strong, deep, intimate, growing faith in Christ Jesus. Use it as your protective shield.

POUR IT!

Drink in the flavor from the following Scriptures: Hebrews 11:1-4, 24-27.

SAVOR IT!

Ask God to deepen your faith. Let him help you activate it as an important piece of your armor.

THE SHIELD OF FAITH

The apostle Paul says we need the shield of faith to stop the fiery arrows shot at us by Satan. That makes sense, doesn't it? It would be silly to go into battle without a strong shield. A shield of faith is the strongest shield you can have.

Enemies can imprison you, torture you, and take away your rights and privileges. But no one can steal your faith! You can continue to believe strongly in God and all he's doing in your life even in the midst of darkness, solitude, confusion, and persecution.

By faith you accepted Christ as your personal Savior. By faith you believe he forgave your sins. And by faith you're trusting him to care for you and guide you to heaven for all eternity. Without faith, you wouldn't have anything.

Wait a sec! you may be thinking. *What about billionaires? Many of them don't have faith in God, but they sure have a lot!*

Yes, they do—materially speaking. But material things can be taken away in an instant. You may remember the violent hurricanes that swept through Florida in 2004: Charley, Ivan, Jeanne, and others. Many rich people lost their beautiful homes.

You may also remember the story of Job in the Old Testament. He was the wealthiest man in the land of Uz. Yet in a short amount of time, his houses, his livestock, his servants, and his family were all destroyed. His faith, however, remained.

Take a good look at your own life. If your home, your friends, your family, your clothes, your achievements, your car, your job, your school, and your money were all taken away, what would you have left? If you've placed your trust in Christ, you'd still have a strong faith in him.

If your faith in him is shallow or wavering, you may be tempted to walk away from the Lord. You may have known people who, when faced with trials, shake their fist at God and walk away. That's not the mark of a mature Christian.

Thousands of Christians today are being persecuted for their faith. Many are beaten, others imprisoned, others killed. Those in prison quote memorized Scripture and continue to pray. As they do, God strengthens their faith.

DO YOUR SHOES FIT?

I have to admit something: I'm a shoe freak. I absolutely love shoes. One of the first things I notice when I meet people is their shoes. I love to try shoes on, I love to buy them, I love to wear them, I love to give them away, and I even love the smell of new shoes!

I'm especially drawn to unique shoes—shoes that are extremely colorful or bizarre but still have no heel. This is important to keep me from falling over when walking. I've been tempted several times to purchase a pair of shoes because of how they look instead of how they feel. I know in my head this isn't smart, but my heart says maybe it won't matter. Maybe I can get used to them. Perhaps I can make them fit.

There's nothing better than a pair of comfy shoes, is there? Shoes that are too small rub the tops of your toes and the back of the your heel in that weird, painful way that produces blisters. And shoes that are too big sort of let your feet get lost, don't they? It's as if the shoe, instead of your foot, is suddenly in charge of where you're headed.

But the perfect pair of shoes . . . ahhh! That's life!

The apostle Paul mentions shoes as part of God's armor and tells us to wear shoes that can speed us on as we tell others the Good News about God. It's obvious that too-tight shoes and shoes that are too big can't speed us on. And can you imagine trying to run a race in heavy shoes or combat boots? Or what if your shoes had several textbooks on top of them and you had to balance that stack of books while running?

To run the race God has called you to run, you don't need extra weight on your shoes. Yet many of us carry all kinds of heavy equipment in our walk with Christ. Maybe we're afraid of what others might think of us or we're worried that we don't know the right thing to say.

BREW IT!
Do your spiritual shoes fit? Or are you carrying extra baggage on your feet that's hindering you from being all God wants?

POUR IT!
Drink in the flavor from the following Scriptures: 1 Corinthians 9:24-27; Hebrews 12:1-2.

SAVOR IT!
Give God anything in your life that's weighing you down, tripping you up, or slowing you in the process of sharing his Good News.

When we carry this baggage, we're not able to give God our best. We're not able to run at top speed as we share his plan with those around us. The apostle Paul also tells us in the book of Hebrews that we should strip off anything that hinders our race, or anything that slows us down from becoming all God calls us to be.

HOW SHARP IS YOUR SWORD?

You've seen them—the plastic or rubber swords in the toy section at the store. And you've probably also seen kids in the toy aisle, waiting for their moms to finish shopping, pick up a sword and fight an imaginary battle by swinging it vigorously against an invisible opponent.

We smile at the thought of anyone actually trying to defeat a real enemy with a sword made of plastic or rubber.

Yet when we try to fight Satan with any sword other than the Word of God, we're merely fighting with a toy. God's Holy Word is our sword. In the book of Hebrews, the apostle Paul tells us exactly how sharp it is. He says it's double-edged and cuts deep into our innermost thoughts. In other words, it slices way past the bone.

Wow! That's a sharp sword. And when we're fighting temptation we need something just that sharp. Oftentimes, however, we leave the Bible on our nightstand and grab for something much less powerful. Instead of taking the time and effort to study the Scriptures, we rationalize that something we read in a good book or something we heard a smart person say will be just as good at fighting temptation.

When it comes to God's Holy Word, there is no substitute! Take time to read the Bible, memorize Scripture, and study God's truth. Be proud of your sword, the Bible. Carry it with you. Dive into it on a daily basis. This is where your spiritual nourishment will come from.

BREW IT!

If you don't have a Bible you can understand, it's time to go shopping! Search for a student Bible filled with Scripture explanations and fun graphics that keep you wanting to read each page.

POUR IT!

Drink in the flavor from the following Scriptures: 2 Timothy 3:16-17; Hebrews 4:12-13; 2 John 9.

SAVOR IT!

Ask God to give you an unquenchable thirst for his Holy Word and the discipline to keep your sword used and sharpened daily.

If you're not used to having a daily quiet time with God, pledge now to start. And don't begin with a huge goal such as, "For the rest of my life, I'm going to read my Bible two hours a day." You might do that a few days, but you'll get discouraged and be tempted to quit when you aren't consistent with it.

Instead, pledge something like this, "For the rest of my life, I'm going to read my Bible at least one minute every day." You can do that! You've set a goal that will be easily attainable. And once you've spent a month or so reading your Bible for a minute each day, you'll find yourself reading far more than a minute without even realizing it!

The cool thing about your Bible is that unlike most swords, it doesn't become dull with use. In fact, just the opposite happens! The more you use it, the sharper it becomes in your life.

WHY PRAY?

As we conclude our wardrobe of God's armor, you'll notice that the apostle Paul wraps up the list by telling us to pray all the time. But because God knows everything, you may be thinking, *Why bother praying? He already knows what I'm going to say.*

Prayer is communication with the creator of the universe. It's talking with—and listening to—the King of kings and Lord of lords. And true communication isn't just about conveying information. It's the process that's important. Think about it this way.

Your best friend, Jody, is competing in high jump at the state track meet. You aren't able to attend the event because you have to work all day Saturday. But your thoughts and prayers are certainly with your friend.

You get off work Saturday evening and swing through the drive-through at Hamburger Hut. Your friend Justin takes your order and then says, "Hey! Did you hear about Jody? First place! Can you believe it?"

You thank God for Jody's success, grab your burger, and head home. Later that night, Jody calls, excited to share the news. Your mom hands the phone to you and says, "It's Jody."

Chances are you won't say, "Yeah, yeah, yeah. I already heard about it, so I don't even need to talk with Jody. I'm going to bed. I'm really tired."

Even though you already know what Jody is going to say, you still want to hear it! You want to share the excitement. In fact, your friendship with Jody deepens as the two of you communicate.

Prayer works the same way. Yes, God already knows what you're going to tell him, but he still wants to hear you voice your heart to him. And not only that . . . he wants to talk back to you! Prayer is a two-way thing. And the more you talk to God and listen to what he has to say, the deeper your relationship with him grows. You'll get to the point where you can't wait to tell him something, so you start praying throughout your entire day.

This is what "praying without ceasing" means. Not that you're a prayer warrior 24/7, but that you're in a consistent attitude of prayer. Throughout your day, you constantly shoot up sentence prayers about everything: "God, thanks for the sunshine today." "Help me smile at someone who needs it." "Show me what to do about that guy in the chat room." "Should I try out for the team?" "Who do you want me to invite to church?" "Ugh! I forgot to study for this test. Be close."

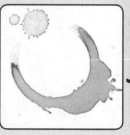

BREW IT!
How's your prayer life? Do you see prayer as a tedious task—something you have to do? Or has it become an exciting avenue of communication between you the King of kings?

POUR IT!
Drink in the flavor from the following Scriptures: Ephesians 6:18-19; James 5:15-16; 1 Peter 3:12.

SAVOR IT!
If you find it difficult to pray, ask God to help you write your prayers—by hand or on the computer. Think of it as simply having a conversation with your best friend.

BREW IT!
Strive to make prayer an exciting part of your daily walk with Christ.

POUR IT!
Drink in the flavor from the following Scriptures: Philippians 4:6-7; Colossians 4:2; 1 Timothy 2:8.

SAVOR IT!
Ask God to give you excitement about talking to him.

WHAT SHOULD YOU PRAY ABOUT?

Okay. You know prayer is important. But what should you pray about? Everything that comes to your mind! If it concerns you, it concerns your heavenly Father. There's nothing too small to pray about. Having trouble finding the perfect birthday gift for your best friend? Pray about it. Feeling uneasy about Friday night's band concert? Talk with God about it.

There's nothing too small to pray about, and there's also nothing too big to pray about. Worried about how to pay college bills? Pray about it. Don't know how you're going to make your next car payment? Talk with God about it. Wondering how much you should give in the missions offering at church? Pray. Want to grow closer to Christ? Prayer is the key.

Let's make a list of things you can start praying about right now. I'll get you started, and you fill in the rest.

- Pray about your relationships.
- Pray for your future spouse.
- Pray for your parents.
- Pray for your brothers and sisters.
- Pray for your pastor.
- Pray about your future career.
- Pray about school.
- Pray about having more confidence.
- Pray about how to show others you care about them.
- Pray for our government.
- Pray that God will use your life to make a positive difference in the world.

- _____
- _____
- _____
- _____

STUFF YOU *DON'T* HAVE TO PRAY ABOUT

Did you know there are some things we don't need to spend time praying about? For instance, God has commanded us to love everyone. So you don't need to pray about whether God wants you to love Chester. If Chester is tough to love, pray instead that God will love him through you.

God has made it clear that we're to tithe at least 10 percent of our income. So don't spend time asking God if you should tithe. Pray instead about not only tithing your money but also tithing your talents and your time.

Let's make a list of other things you don't need to pray about. I'll get you started, and you complete the list.

- Being kind. (Pray for opportunities to show kindness instead.)
- Not speeding. (But you can ask for patience.)
- Respecting those in authority whether you agree with them or not. (Try asking God for humility.)
- Being a man/woman of your word. (Instead, ask God for help in following through on your commitments.)
- Sharing with those in need. (Ask God to show you which organizations to support.)
- Being faithful in church attendance. (Pray for someone to keep you accountable—and get a good alarm!)
- Taking your schoolwork seriously. (But you can ask God for perseverance—and maybe even a tutor!)
- Taking a stand against sin. (Try asking him for strength to do what's right.)
- Reaching out to new students. (Why not pray for courage to invite them to your lunch table?)
- Loving the elderly. (Instead, ask him to open your eyes to opportunities around you.)
- Monitoring what you watch on TV. (But God will honor your request for wisdom.)
- Using your money wisely. (Try praying about your attitude on cash instead.)
- Valuing people. (Try asking him to help you see others through his eyes.)
- Monitoring your use of the Internet. (Pray for a friend who will keep you honest.)
- Reading your Bible. (But you can ask him to show you stuff when you read it.)

- _____
- _____
- _____
- _____

BREW IT!
Consider asking someone to be a prayer partner with you. It helps to have a friend praying for us and about the things that concern us.

POUR IT!
Drink in the flavor from the following Scriptures: Luke 6:28; 22:40; Romans 8:26.

SAVOR IT!
Ask God to give you a growing excitement about talking with him, and ask him to help you recognize the sound of his voice when he talks to you.

DON'T TALK TO THE PARROT

Mrs. Harrison phoned the repairman because her dryer quit working. He couldn't accommodate her with an after-hours appointment, and because she had to go to work, she said, "I'll leave the key under the mat. Fix the dryer, leave the bill on the kitchen table, and I'll mail you a check. By the way, I have a large Great Dane inside named Killer. He won't bother you. I also have a parrot, and whatever you do, don't talk to that bird!"

The repairman came by and began working on Mrs. Harrison's dryer, and sure enough the big dog, Killer, totally ignored him and lay peacefully in the living room. But the whole time the repairman was working, the parrot yelled, screamed, and screeched at him. It just about drove the poor repairman nuts.

As he was ready to leave, he couldn't resist saying, "You're an awful bird! Can't you behave and be quiet?"

To which the bird replied, "Killer, get him!"

Things often aren't as they appear, are they? Let's transition this thought to temptation. It's not likely you'll be tempted to hijack an airplane or rob a bank. Satan probably won't try to make sins such as these look enticing. It would be tough to convince you to forsake everything you know is right and dive into obvious sins most of the world would consider wrong. To trip up Christians, Satan has to be more clever. He has to take evil and somehow sugarcoat it so it doesn't look so bad. When he can get you thinking, *I'm not sure that would really be sin. After all everyone else is . . .*, then he's won a partial battle in your life, because he's getting you to question sin.

Satan is no dummy. He's extremely clever, cunning, and sly. He'll do anything he can think of to catch you off guard. Now that you know this, be prepared. In other words, don't talk to the parrot. Don't assume something is harmless because it doesn't appear to be "that bad." Satan is working overtime to make sin look "not that bad" to you. If he can make evil appear harmless, he knows you may be curious enough to take a closer look.

BREW IT!
Talked with any "parrots" lately? Have you recently flirted with sin because it didn't appear that bad? Christians can't afford to get comfortable; we always need to be prepared!

POUR IT!
Drink in the flavor from the following Scriptures: Mark 14:38; Luke 4:13-14; James 1:13-16.

SAVOR IT!
Tell God you don't want to fall for Satan's schemes. Thank him for the power he has given you to say no to the tempter.

BREW IT!

Are you concerned about Satan's attacks? If not, you should be. Frightened? No. You're living in God's power. Concerned and aware? Yes. As an intelligent Christian, you need to be on guard.

POUR IT!

Drink in the flavor from the following Scriptures: Mark 4:15; Luke 10:18-20; 22:3-4.

SAVOR IT!

Ask God to give you discernment to recognize when Satan is tempting you.

CONCERNED? YES. SCARED? NO.

Because you know Satan is willing to do anything to trip you, push you flat on your face, and eventually kill you, you should be really scared, right? Yes and no.

If you have an active, growing relationship with Jesus Christ and have placed your faith in him, you can rest assured that he lives inside of you and is way more powerful than your enemy, the devil. The apostle John reminds you that God in you is much greater than the enemy (see 1 John 4:4). You can live within the strength and power of your heavenly Father.

But that doesn't mean you shouldn't be concerned about Satan and how much he hates you. Peter tells us to live on the defensive and to be on guard (see 1 Peter 5:8-9). If you're playing a soccer game against a rival school that you've always beaten, you probably aren't frightened to compete against them, but if you're a smart athlete, you won't go onto the field unconcerned or with your guard down. You'll still do your best; you'll still fight to win.

It works the same way spiritually. Yes, as a Christian, you have God's mighty power within you that is and always will be stronger than Satan. You can be bold in this knowledge, and you can live a confident Christian life because of it. But you can't afford to let down your guard or be unconcerned about Satan. He's just waiting for you to take off your spiritual armor so he can attack. Keep your armor on!

Be concerned—very concerned—about Satan's strategies to entice you to give sin a second look by making it appear harmless. Thousands of teens are experimenting with Wicca today because Satan has convinced them it doesn't have anything to do with him. "It's harmless," he has them believing. "You're not worshipping me. Hey, I don't even exist!"

Wiccans are quick to say their religion doesn't have anything to do with Satan, because they don't even believe in Satan. Bingo! He's already won the battle by convincing them he doesn't exist.

Do you see the danger in becoming comfortable around Satan? He's the master deceiver, manipulator, and killer. He'll do whatever he needs to do to convince people it's not really him they're involved with; that it's simply a new way of thinking (New Age), looking to the stars for guidance (astrology), playing harmless games (Ouija boards), or believing there are alternate paths to heaven (any religion other than Christianity).

BACKWARD STEPS

The last Scripture you read in yesterday's devotional talked about Satan entering Judas Iscariot. Have you ever thought seriously about that? Take a quick peek at Judas's life. He was a follower of Jesus: a disciple, one of the special twelve whom Christ had specifically chosen to advance his Kingdom.

Judas didn't simply wake up one morning and think, *Christ has been good to me. He's forgiven my sins, explained the Scriptures to me, given me truth from God himself . . . but I think I'll toss it all away and betray him. Yep. I'll turn him over to the chief priests and maybe even make a little money off of him.*

Betrayal probably wasn't a decision that came quickly for Judas. Again, he was a follower of Jesus. As a disciple, he started out excitedly spreading the gospel. But remember, Satan is the master deceiver, and he was working overtime to plant ideas in Judas's mind that Judas could have resisted if he'd used Christ's power.

How did it start? We can imagine it was a slow, gradual process of backward steps that led Judas away from intimacy with Jesus. Maybe he was annoyed with all the children who approached Christ. *I've had it up to here with these bratty kids,* he may have thought. Perhaps he was weary of the sick and diseased who wanted to be near Jesus. Did he think, *What is it with these lepers? I'm really tired of this.*

Maybe he took his job as treasurer of the group selfishly. *We'd better not spend money on buying food for the poor again,* he may have thought, *or we won't have enough for ourselves next week.* The apostle John reveals in his Gospel that the disciples later discovered that Judas had been stealing from the treasury. When he objected to money being spent, it wasn't out of concern for the poor or for God's Kingdom; it was selfish motivation. Judas wanted more for himself.

Slowly, surely, he began taking backward steps—steps that would lead him away from Jesus. Did he begin to tune him out as Christ preached to the multitudes? Was he dreaming about self-gain or his political pursuits?

Did he allow Satan to plant seeds of doubt in his mind and then fixate on them? It's clear that Judas wasn't wearing spiritual armor. He allowed himself to believe the lies of his enemy. When he should have and could have been walking forward with the King of kings, he began walking backward with Satan himself.

BREW IT!
Don't allow yourself to play with thoughts Satan plants in your head. You can't help who knocks on the door of your mind, but you can decide if you'll invite him in. Keep your mind tuned to Christ. Don't entertain thoughts that will lead you away from intimacy with him.

POUR IT!
Drink in the flavor from the following Scriptures: John 12:4-6; Philippians 4:8; Colossians 2:6-7.

SAVOR IT!
Ask God to convict you with his Holy Spirit when you begin to walk in the opposite direction from your Lord.

BREW IT!
You serve a God of grace, mercy, and forgiveness. God will always forgive genuine repentance.

POUR IT!
Drink in the flavor from the following Scriptures: Numbers 14:17-19; Psalm 32:1-2; James 5:15.

SAVOR IT!
Determine to be honest with God. Start now by telling him about your struggles.

WHAT IF?

What if? Just what if Judas had been honest with Jesus when he took his first backward step away from the Master? What if Judas had said, "Lord, I . . . I'm embarrassed to tell you this, but um . . . well, I love being treasurer of the group, but I'm tempted. This money is looking good to me! I find myself wondering if anyone would know if I took some of it for myself. I don't like admitting this to you. But I'm scared of what could happen if I don't allow myself to be open, honest, and accountable to you. Please help me! I want to remain close to you. I want my heart to be in your control. I'm struggling, Jesus."

And what if? Just what if you were honest with Jesus at the very moment you're being tempted? What if you'd say, "Lord, I . . . I'm embarrassed to tell you this, but um . . . well, I got this e-mail yesterday on my computer. I didn't ask for it. I didn't even know what it was—at first. I clicked on it and found out it was, well you know . . . a little bit of porn. Not much. But out of curiosity, I clicked on the site and whoa! I don't really want you to know this, Jesus, but well . . . it kind of set stuff off in my brain and it was hard to pull away.

"And, Lord, I'm sorry. I really am. I realize that looking at stuff like that is sin. And now I've sinned against you. Will you forgive me? I don't wanna go there again. But I'm being honest with you, Jesus, I keep thinking about what I saw. And I kind of want to go there again. I'm being tempted. I'm really struggling with this.

"But I don't want to jeopardize my relationship with you. So help me, Jesus. Give me the strength to tell my parents so we can get some kind of block on the computer. Help me set up accountability with my friends or my youth pastor or someone who will help me through this struggle. I love you, Jesus. I want you to control my heart and my thoughts."

Maybe it's not computer porn you're struggling with. Maybe it's gossip. Or jealousy. Or bitterness, anger, drinking, or lying. Whatever you're battling, instead of taking backward steps that lead you away from intimacy with the Father, go to him. That's right— walk toward him and tell him exactly what's going on. He can't wait to help you!

PREPARE TO FIGHT

Satan isn't too concerned with the nonbelievers. It's the Christians he's after. The devil would love nothing more than to mess you up and plant doubts in your mind. He hates it that you're following Christ. He wants you to be ineffective in your faith so you can't share it with others. He'll do anything within his power to cause you to stumble.

How much power does Satan have? The devil is tremendously powerful. But he isn't—and never will be—as powerful as Jesus Christ. He is powerful enough, however, to perform miracles. He is a supernatural being with supernatural power. Don't underestimate his power, but never forget that God is always more powerful. In fact, the book of Revelation tells us that there will come a time when God will chain Satan, strip him of power, and condemn him to eternal darkness. So keep focused on the fact—and it is fact—that Christ has won the battle. As a Christian, you're on the winning team!

When you're in the midst of persecution, temptation, or satanic attack, it may not seem as though you're on the winning team, but you are. Place your faith in what God has proclaimed in his Holy Word and live expectantly for the day when he will rule and every knee will bow before him.

Knowing that Satan will do anything in his power to mess you up, it's no wonder that the apostle Peter told us to stand guard. Think of Peter as your coach. He wants to give you a winning strategy against your opponent. It's as if he's cupping his hands around his mouth and lovingly yelling out his instructions to you across the court: "On your toes! Stay on your toes. Watch out! Be careful. Don't fall asleep during the game. Come on; wake up! Be on the defensive."

Great advice, huh? So let's look at a strategy that will help you win when your enemy is actively opposing you.

Prepare to fight. We're talking about spiritual battles. So . . . how can you prepare to fight spiritually? Your first piece of ammunition is simply knowing that there's a battle going on! Christians who think they're exempt from temptation are the ones at greatest risk. Realizing that God is for you and Satan is against you will help you prepare for spiritual battle.

Your second piece of ammo is reading the letter from God—your general. In his Holy Word he's already given you everything you need to win the battle. So read it. Memorize sections of it. Believe it. Absorb it. Digest it. Let it show up in your lifestyle.

BREW IT!
How's your spiritual preparation coming? Are you reading the game plan? Are you applying it to your life? Without relying on the Word of God, you can't adequately prepare for battle.

POUR IT!
Drink in the flavor from the following Scriptures:
1 Peter 1:24-25; 4:1-2; 5:8-9.

SAVOR IT!
Tell God you always want to be ready for spiritual battle. Ask him to help you prepare.

BREW IT!
Know that as you learn and practice your spiritual battle strategy, you'll become more confident in God's power inside you.

POUR IT!
Drink in the flavor from the following Scriptures: Matthew 13:37-39; Luke 4:1-13; James 1:12.

SAVOR IT!
Thank God that he is—and always will be—more powerful than Satan.

WATCH OUT!

As a Christian, you're engaged in a spiritual battle. Yes, Satan wants to give you much more than a hard time, but don't become discouraged. God gives you his power—which is far mightier than the devil's—to win the battle.

So *prepare to fight* by recognizing that you really are involved in a spiritual battle. Take the Word of God seriously. Read it. Study it. Believe it. Memorize it. Live it!

And continuing with our strategy:

Be spiritually defensive. If you're a basketball player, you know this means not standing still on the court. Keep moving. Be on guard. If you're a baseball or softball player, you know this translates into not daydreaming in the outfield. If you do, you'll miss that fly ball you could have caught. Don't fall asleep while guarding second; your opponent might steal third.

Being spiritually defensive means you can't fall asleep in your relationship with Christ. It's impossible to "watch out" if your eyes are closed. Stay spiritually awake. You can't afford to take your relationship with him for granted. Be grateful that he has forgiven your sins, and be actively growing toward a deeper, more intimate walk with him.

Stand firm in your faith. When you're being made fun of because of your decisions, when you're looked down on for standing against sin and following Christ, don't give up! Stand firm in your faith. Christ didn't give up for you. In fact, during his final hours on earth, he prayed so hard, he began sweating blood. He knew he was under great satanic opposition, but he didn't waver. He remained strong in his faith, and he'll empower you to do the same.

How can you stand firm in your faith? Your first piece of ammunition is your faith. If you have any doubts, admit them and give them to Jesus. Christ can handle your questions and doubts. So when you're questioning, take it to the Lord. Then consider talking to your youth pastor or reading books that can address your doubts.

Your second piece of ammo is to clothe yourself in God's armor. For a refresher on this, review the devotionals from February 22–27. Don't leave your house in the morning without first putting on his armor. Just as you wouldn't consider entering a boxing match without gloves, don't consider walking into an ungodly society without protection.

RECOGNIZE YOUR ENEMY

Let's review your spiritual strategy:

- Prepare to fight.
- Be spiritually defensive.
- Stand firm in your faith.

The next piece of strategy is:

Recognize your enemy. Opposing teams wear different colored uniforms because that enables the athletes, the refs, and the spectators to quickly recognize who is on what side. Imagine fighting a war in which millions of soldiers were engaged, and each combatant was wearing the exact same uniform. You wouldn't know who you were up against.

Fighting Satan can be similar to this. Sometimes it can be difficult to recognize him because he's able to disguise himself. In other words, sometimes he wears the same uniform you're wearing.

The Bible warns us that Satan can masquerade as an angel of light. We're also told that false prophets and false teachers exist. If Satan has disguised himself as an angel of light or is hiding behind the mask of a pastor or teacher, how will you recognize him?

Again, we go back to the Bible. Knowing that the Bible warns you about this is important ammunition. Just because someone is articulate, says positive things, appears to do good deeds, and claims to be a Christian doesn't mean he actually is.

You see, Satan is extremely intelligent. When he's trying to make you crash, he'll disguise himself so you won't recognize him. And what better way to disguise himself than appearing to be good!

Know this. Believe it. Watch out for it.

How can you learn to recognize Satan? First, ask God for discernment. In fact, ask God about everything. This is why it's so important to be praying consistently (review the devotional from February 27). If you're always asking God about your friends, your relationships, those in direct authority over you, and the people you work with and learn from, he'll give you the discernment you need to see them as he does: as a true Christian, as a nonbeliever, as a deceived person who thinks he's teaching the right thing, or as one who is masquerading as a Christian but trying to mess you up.

Over and over again, the apostle Paul talks about specific people in his day who acted as good teachers but discouraged the believers, confused them, and taught false things. Again, know your Bible. Know your God!

BREW IT!
When you're not sure about something you've heard preached or something you've read, take it to God and seek his wisdom.

POUR IT!
Drink in the flavor from the following Scriptures: Psalm 26:12; 27:11; Proverbs 1:7.

SAVOR IT!
Ask God to help you recognize false teaching and prayerfully address it.

BREW IT!

Make sure there are no holes in your spiritual armor. Be prayed up! Grow stronger in your faith. Keep running toward Christ, deepening your relationship with him each day.

POUR IT!

Drink in the flavor from the following Scriptures: 2 Timothy 3:1; 4:3; 1 John 4:1-3.

SAVOR IT!

Tell God you don't want to be gullible—believing everything you hear that simply sounds good. Ask him to help you learn and remember what the Bible says so you'll know his absolute truth.

STACKIN' IT AGAINST THE WORD

Let's go over our strategy for fighting spiritual battles:

- Prepare to fight.
- Be spiritually defensive.
- Stand firm in your faith.
- Recognize your enemy.

The next piece of strategy is:

Stack your spiritual attack against the Bible. In other words, if you're hearing things being preached that are positive but don't really add up spiritually, see what the Bible has to say. The way you can tell if it's a message from God is if you can back it up with Scripture. If what you're hearing goes against God's Holy Word—even though it may sound good, and though it may come from a "spiritual leader"—don't believe it.

Paul warned Timothy, his young pastor friend, that it would be very difficult to be a Christian in the last days. He also told Timothy that people would come to the point of not wanting to hear God's actual truth; they would simply want to hear positive teaching—whatever would make them feel good. I hope going to church sometimes makes you feel good, but I also hope that's not the reason you're going.

Going to church is about hearing God's truth, genuinely worshipping him, fellowshipping and growing with other believers, and bringing people who are unsaved into God's family. So when we go to church, we need to hear solid teaching and preaching that makes us uncomfortable sometimes and gives us something to think about.

Why is this important? So we'll keep growing spiritually and not become stagnant. If all you hear are positive feel-good messages, you'll never be challenged to sacrifice, to serve, or to sweat.

Again, Satan is too intelligent to put someone in a spiritual leadership position who's going to say, "Okay, everyone! Follow me. We're all going to sin." He'll work through someone who's charming, smart, and articulate. Someone who's friendly, popular, and plays to your ego. And that's why it's important to be clothed in God's armor.

You see, Satan is in the process of creating cleverly and carefully designed schemes to knock you off track. Be very aware.

PLAYING WITH THE MASTER MAKES THE DIFFERENCE

A mother took her young son to a concert featuring renowned pianist Ignacy Paderewski. After they were seated, the mother spotted a friend in the audience and walked down the aisle to greet her.

Seizing the opportunity to explore the wonders of the concert hall, the boy got up and eventually went through a door marked "No Admittance."

When the house lights dimmed, the mother returned to her seat and discovered that her son was missing. Suddenly, the curtains parted and spotlights focused on the impressive Steinway piano onstage.

In horror, the mother saw her little boy sitting at the keyboard, innocently picking out "Twinkle, Twinkle Little Star." At that moment, the great piano master made his entrance, quickly moved to the piano, and whispered in the boy's ear, "Don't quit. Just keep playing."

Then, leaning over him, Paderewski reached down with his left hand and began filling in a bass part. Soon his right arm reached around to the other side of the child, and he added a running accompaniment. Together, the old master and the young beginner transformed a frightening situation into a wonderfully creative experience. The audience was mesmerized.

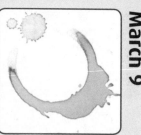

BREW IT!
Are you using what God has blessed you with to bring glory to his name?

POUR IT!
Drink in the flavor from the following Scripture: Matthew 25:14-30.

SAVOR IT!
Ask God to help you use your gifts to build his Kingdom.

Let's translate this to our spiritual life. What we can accomplish on our own is hardly noteworthy compared to what heaven turns out. We try our best, but the results aren't exactly graceful, flowing music. But with the help of the Master, what we do can be magnificent. He is able to create beautiful music from our haphazard plucking. It's playing with the Master that makes all the difference!

God has given each of his children special gifts, such as leadership, hospitality, teaching, evangelism, and service. If you haven't yet realized what your spiritual gifts are, ask your pastor if your church has a spiritual gifts test you can take or a class you can attend. If you're in the process of learning what your spiritual gifts are, recognize that they are from God himself. Don't become prideful of your gifts, because they're not something you earned or deserved in the first place.

Remember the parable about the wealthy master who gave three of his servants a specific number of talents (a form of money) to invest during his absence? The first and second servants invested aggressively, and because of that, they doubled what they started with.

The third servant simply buried his talents.

The master returned and blessed the first and second servants more than the third, because they used what they'd been given to the maximum. The third servant was stripped of all he'd been given.

SPIRITUAL GROWTH

A family of three tomatoes was walking downtown one day when the little baby tomato started lagging behind. The big father tomato walked back to the baby tomato, stomped on her, and squashed her into a red paste.

"Ketchup!" he said.

There's actually something to learn from this corny joke! The baby tomato wasn't moving as quickly as her father knew she could. He wasn't asking her to outrun the other tomatoes; he simply wanted her to keep up.

The apostle Paul has referred to our relationship with Christ as a race. It may be like a race in some ways, but it's not about crossing the finish line first. You don't have to have more Bible verses memorized than whoever sits next to you in youth group for God to love you. He already loves you! But he does want you to keep growing spiritually. He doesn't want you lagging behind.

His desire for you is consistent spiritual growth. That doesn't mean you'll live on a spiritual high every day. Some days you may actually feel as though you're living in a spiritual desert. There will be times you don't move forward by leaps and bounds; you may find yourself only taking baby steps some days. Other days you may not be walking at all; you might simply be crawling. But the key is to keep moving forward. Continue to grow closer to your heavenly Father.

If you're not moving forward, there's a good chance you'll start moving backward. It's hard to remain stagnant—in neutral—for long. You'll eventually have to go forward or backward. If, however, you determine (with God's help) to simply keep moving closer to him (even though some days it's baby steps), it will become tougher and tougher to backslide.

The secrets to spiritual growth? The keys to moving forward spiritually? Read Scripture daily. Talk with Christ daily. If you'll take these two things seriously and invest your life into these two elements, it will be very difficult for you to backslide.

Back to the corny joke. If the baby tomato had been clinging to the father tomato, she wouldn't have lagged behind. But she quit holding his hand. She was walking on her own, and that's when it became evident that she couldn't keep pace with the others without holding the hand of the one leading.

BREW IT!
God's not going to smash you into a pile of ketchup, but it is important that you cling to him, hold his hand, and walk with him in order to be where he wants you spiritually.

POUR IT!
Drink in the flavor from the following Scriptures:
1 Corinthians 9:24-27;
2 Corinthians 8:10-11;
Philippians 2:12-13.

SAVOR IT!
Tell God you don't want to lag behind spiritually. Ask him to lead you at his pace.

FREECYCLING

It's relatively new—this concept of freecycling—and it sounds almost too good to be true. If you're a pack rat and you find it really tough to throw things away, or if you love to get free stuff, you may want to consider freecycling.

If you have a closet full of stuff that's too good to throw away and you don't want to mess with trying to sell it, you can freecycle it. Or if you're willing to take another person's old stuff off his hands, you can freecycle it.

Here's how it works: There are approximately a million givers and takers of everything from dining-room sets to cars to beds to Ping-Pong tables to guitars. You simply go onto the Web site www.free cycle.org to offer what you want to give and take what you want to have.

One man from Missouri gave more than one thousand books to a church sale. After he had cleared that huge space in his garage, he then had room for a freecycled lawn mower and leaf blower he got from the Web site. The grassroots movement began in May 2003 in Tucson, Arizona, and now is in more than 2,300 cities worldwide.

If you actually have a garage full of stuff you can't seem to get rid of, freecycling seems to be the answer. Let's stretch this concept a bit.

You may not have a garage full of stuff, but it's possible you've collected some things in your heart that you need to clear away. Or perhaps your mind is filled with thoughts and fantasies you really wish you could get rid of.

Good news! Jesus Christ doesn't simply freecycle, he completely removes! He doesn't simply want to clean up your heart, he wants to purify it. Yes, he could give your mind a bubble bath, but he'd much rather allow his Holy Spirit to permeate your thinking.

BREW IT!
Forgiveness for sins and purity of mind and heart didn't start in Tucson, Arizona. It began in a stable with the King of kings taking on human form. Have you taken advantage of the offer that makes an eternal difference? If not, now would be a great time to confess your sins and receive Jesus as your personal Savior.

POUR IT!
Drink in the flavor from the following Scriptures: Luke 1:68-79; 19:9.

SAVOR IT!
Thank God for his power not only to cleanse you but also to make you holy.

You don't need a spiritual garage sale to get rid of the sin in your life that hinders you from becoming all God calls you to be. You don't need to freecycle, and you don't even need a Web site. All you need is a repentant heart and trust in Jesus.

He, and he alone, can get rid of the excess junk that's crowding your heart and beginning to rust your mind. Almost sounds too good to be true, doesn't it?

BREW IT!
Take a close look at your life
. . . and your sleep. Are you
living with a clear conscience?
Do you sleep well at night? (Of
course, there are other factors
that determine restful and
restless nights, but a clear
conscience is one of them.)
Are you truly experiencing
God's great peace?

POUR IT!
Drink in the flavor from
the following Scriptures:
1 Timothy 1:5, 19; 4:12.

SAVOR IT!
Ask God to reveal to you anything that's keeping your conscience from being clear.
Confess that to him. Ask him
to give you solid sleep.

FUN + ZZZZS = NO SLEEPLESS NIGHTS

Minneapolis has been named the "Most Fun City" in America by Bert Sperling—an author known for his "best places" lists. The game Cranium also names Minneapolis as the "Most Fun City." Interestingly, Minneapolis has also been named the "Best City for Sleep" in America.

The best cities for sleep?
1. Minneapolis, Minnesota
2. Anaheim, California
3. San Diego, California
4. Raleigh-Durham, North Carolina
5. Washington, DC

The worst cities for sleep?
1. Detroit, Michigan
2. Cleveland, Ohio
3. Nashville, Tennessee
4. Cincinnati, Ohio
5. New Orleans, Louisiana

Is there a connection between Minneapolis being the "Most Fun City" and the "Best City for Sleep"? The city's mayor thinks so. "We have a lot of fun, but it's good clean fun, so we can go to sleep with a good, clean conscience," says Mayor R. T. Rybak.

That makes a lot of sense, doesn't it? When you're weighed down with a guilty conscience, it's tough to nod off at night. When you've spent the day sitting around the house watching movies and crunching munchies, it's also hard to get to sleep at night. But when you have put in a full day of classes, have worked hard, have done your best, and are living with a clean conscience, it's usually pretty easy to sleep. It's as though your body and mind are in sync with each other and both know you need a good night's rest.

Having a clear conscience goes a long way. Remember the Old Testament story about Daniel in the lions' den? (See Daniel 6.) King Darius, who signed the law that caused Daniel to be thrown into the lions' den, couldn't sleep all night because he knew he'd done the wrong thing. Daniel, on the other hand, had a clear conscience and his faith in God was strong.

THE PEACE THAT PASSES UNDERSTANDING

A clear conscience and a life that's permeated with God's peace go hand in hand. You can't have one without the other. The Bible has a lot to say about peace. We're told in the book of Matthew to be peacemakers. The apostle John records Jesus telling his disciples that the peace he gives is much different from the fragile peace the world offers.

It makes sense that to reap peace, we need to sow peace. If you want peace but you're not willing to be a peacemaker, chances are you're not living a peaceful life. "Ugh! I'm so tired of all the hassles in my life," Sarah says. "I just wish things would be peaceful."

Nice desire. But if Sarah is a complainer, loves to argue, and is constantly picking on someone about something, she's not going to experience the full realm of God's peace.

In yesterday's devotional, we mentioned Daniel of the Old Testament, who was thrown in a den of lions because he continued to worship God instead of the king. Do you know who Daniel's best friends were? Shadrach, Meshach, and Abednego. And you probably remember their story as well (see Daniel 3).

These three young men were thrown into a fiery furnace; the king literally wanted to burn them alive! Yet they were able to maintain calm because they experienced God's genuine peace. They knew God was with them.

You're not locked in a lions' den or peering out of a fiery furnace, but no doubt you're facing some trials that seem just as big. Are you panicked? Are you worried?

BREW IT!
You don't need to lose sleep over your troubles. God wants you to experience his deep, solid peace.

POUR IT!
Drink in the flavor from the following Scriptures: Micah 5:4-5; Matthew 5:9; John 14:27.

SAVOR IT!
Ask God to fill you with his everlasting peace.

BREW IT!

If you're not experiencing God's peace, you can be! Why live a life with a twisted stomach and a tense mind from worrying about your struggles? Give them to God, and accept his peace.

POUR IT!

Drink in the flavor from the following Scriptures: Nahum 1:15; Haggai 2:9; Zechariah 8:19.

SAVOR IT!

Tell God you don't simply want to know about his peace; you want to fully experience it.

A PIECE OF GOD'S PEACE

When you're filled with anxiety . . . when you're struggling with a problem that doesn't seem to have an answer . . . when you can't see the light at the end of the tunnel . . . meditate on Scriptures of God's peace. Pray these Scriptures. Write them on index cards and carry them with you or place them on the visor of your car. Memorize them. Make them part of your lifestyle.

- "The LORD gives strength to his people; the LORD blesses his people with peace" (Psalm 29:11).
- "Since we have been made right with God by our faith, we have peace with God" (Romans 5:1, NCV).
- "A heart at peace gives life to the body" (Proverbs 14:30).
- "You will keep in perfect peace all who trust in you, all whose thoughts are fixed on you!" (Isaiah 26:3, NLT).
- "How beautiful on the mountains are the feet of the messenger who brings good news, the good news of peace and salvation, the news that the God of Israel reigns!" (Isaiah 52:7, NLT).
- "Christ himself is our peace" (Ephesians 2:14, NCV).
- "The peace of God, which transcends all understanding, will guard your hearts and your minds in Christ Jesus" (Philippians 4:7).
- "Let the peace of Christ rule in your hearts, since as members of one body you were called to peace" (Colossians 3:15).

FUNKY-LOOKING CAT

A woman in Santa Cruz, California, thought she was being a Good Samaritan to an injured kitty she saw on Highway 1. She spotted the cat, which had been hit by a car, and loaded it into her vehicle to take it to the animal shelter. Fortunately for her, the cat was too out of it to move. It turned out to be a bobcat with extremely sharp claws and three-quarter-inch fangs. The rescuer was surprised to find out what kind of cat she'd picked up. "I thought it looked kind of strange," she said.

Though the woman was doing a good deed, she did so in danger. She acted zealously. In other words, she was so intent on doing something good, she didn't stop and think through the possible results before she acted. That can be good and bad.

Yes, the Lord wants you to do good, to be kind, and to reach out. But he also wants you to be smart about it. Jehu—from the Old Testament—also acted zealously. (See 2 Kings 9–10 for the complete story.) He had a good idea: He wanted to wipe out Baal worship in Israel. But he didn't completely think things through first. And he didn't always consult the Lord.

He acted impulsively, and he didn't follow God's commands all the way. He stopped short. He did destroy much of Baal worship throughout the country—a huge task and a worthy accomplishment. But he left a few golden calves standing. He did an incomplete job. He didn't follow God with all of his heart, and his lack of total obedience is recorded forever in Old Testament history.

Christ wants us to be willing to make a difference in the lives of others, but he never wants us to act outside of his will. *But wait a second,* you may be thinking. *If there's an opportunity to do something good, why not just go ahead and do it? Should I really pray about it first?*

Yes. God wants you to seek him before you act. Even though it may look like you're doing a good deed, you may actually be reaching out to a "bobcat." Things aren't always as they seem!

BREW IT!
Christ wants you to be his ambassador. But he doesn't want you stomping on top of others to do it. Slow down. Seek his will. Listen for his voice. Follow his leading.

POUR IT!
Drink in the flavor from the following Scriptures: Matthew 6:33; 7:7; Luke 12:31.

SAVOR IT!
Ask God to help you pray about everything and not to act impulsively or out of his holy will.

BREW IT!
You may never know until heaven the powerful effect your kindness had on someone.

POUR IT!
Drink in the flavor from the following Scriptures: Luke 10:30-37; Ephesians 4:32.

SAVOR IT!
Ask God to help you notice someone who needs you to be a Good Samaritan. Then take the risk and reach out.

TAKING A RISK

Remember the story of the Good Samaritan in the New Testament? He went out of his way to help a victim who had been beaten and robbed. He not only cared for the injured man's wounds, he paid for his lodging and offered to come back later and pay more if the bills escalated.

What if word had gotten out to the men who robbed this poor guy? Perhaps they would have been so angered, they would have come after the Good Samaritan and beaten him, too. Yet this man was willing to take the risk. Jesus wants all of us to dare to be kind to one another. He wants us to be willing to go out of our way.

There's always a risk in being a Good Samaritan. There's the risk of receiving no gratitude from the person you've helped. What if she's not thankful? There's the risk of being made fun of by others who don't understand why you're going out of your way for someone else. Whatever the risk, it's always worth it.

Why? you may be thinking. Because Jesus took the risk for you. He knew you might not be grateful for his death on the cross. He knew you might not accept his kindness and his gift. He was made fun of by those who crucified him. "You're the King, are you?" they yelled. "Then save yourself and come down from that cross" (see Matthew 27:40).

But it was worth it, because he loves you. And because Jesus went the extra mile for you, he expects you to go the extra mile for others.

Go ahead.

Take the risk.

Reach out to someone who can't pay you back.

What about the one who's always alone on campus? Dare to start a conversation. The car that's trying to cut in front of you? Why not go ahead and let him in? That girl who never smiles? Smile at her first, and keep smiling at her every day. The teacher who always seems to be in a bad mood? Compliment him on something after class.

What about giving up a Saturday night and serving at the local soup kitchen? Raking leaves, shoveling snow, or mowing the lawn for an elderly person? Writing a note of encouragement to someone who seems down?

DO IT GOD'S WAY—
NOT YOUR OWN

Simon, one of Jesus' disciples, was a member of an anti-Roman political sect called the Zealots. Judas, the disciple who turned Jesus in to the authorities, may have been a Zealot as well. And just like the name of the group, he acted zealously. Some Bible scholars believe that Judas didn't realize that by turning Jesus in, the Lord would be killed. They believe Judas was only trying to hurry up Jesus' political takeover. Judas was impatient.

Jesus kept talking about being king and setting up his Kingdom. It sounded good, and Judas wanted in on the action. But Jesus was sure taking his time. *Maybe I can force his hand,* Judas may have thought. *Maybe I can speed things up by allowing the authorities to pour on the pressure. Then Jesus will rebel, rise against the authorities, and set up his Kingdom. Then finally we'll be in charge!*

Of course, Jesus wasn't talking about a political kingdom. He was talking about an eternal Kingdom. Judas acted zealously, impulsively. He was determined to do things his way instead of seeking direction from Christ. It eventually cost him his life.

When we act stubbornly and assume we know what's best for us, we're in danger. How can the created ever know more than the Creator? We can't. The wise Christian will always seek God's will and do things the Lord's way instead of his or her own.

In the Old Testament book of Isaiah, the prophet warns anyone who dares to fight with his Creator. He compares each of us to a dish created by a potter. We'd never hear the pot criticize the maker for what he's doing. A beautiful pot is merely clay in the hands of its master.

God is our Potter, and we are his clay. Are you willing to be molded and shaped in his holy image instead of demanding to do things your way? We often think we know ourselves better than God; after all, we're the ones living in our skin. But never underestimate your Creator. He knows you and loves you much more than you'll ever comprehend. You can trust him!

BREW IT!
It's tempting to act impulsively and do things on your own—especially if you're impatient by nature. But doing so may cost you greatly. Determine to seek God first in all you do.

POUR IT!
Drink in the flavor from the following Scriptures: Isaiah 45:9-11; Jeremiah 29:13; Hosea 10:12.

SAVOR IT!
Give God your impatience and ask him to help you seek his will in every area of your life.

BREW IT!
Make time to stay spiritually sharp as you go about building God's Kingdom.

POUR IT!
Drink in the flavor from the following Scriptures: Psalm 62:1-2; 73:28; 86:11-13.

SAVOR IT!
Tell God you're willing to adjust your schedule to spend the time necessary with him to make you the disciple he calls you to be.

HOW SHARP IS YOUR AX?

Nineteen-year-old Conner was home for the summer and needed to earn money for his next year in college. He loved the Oregon summer weather and desperately wanted to work outdoors. He noticed an ad in the local paper for a logging crew that was hiring.

Conner, who was well built, muscular, and a hard worker, felt confident he could land the job. He introduced himself to Mr. Wilson, the foreman, and explained that he was home for the summer and needed work. "I'm willing to work long hours, and I'm very dependable," Conner stated.

Mr. Wilson led him to a row of trees and handed him an ax. "Let's see if you can take this first one down," he said.

Conner took the axe and skillfully felled the huge tree. Mr. Wilson was impressed. "You can start on Monday," he said.

Conner worked hard Monday, Tuesday, and Wednesday. Thursday morning, Mr. Wilson approached him and said, "Conner, you can pick up your paycheck at lunchtime today."

"I don't understand," Conner said. "I thought you paid only on Fridays."

"That's right," Mr. Wilson responded. "But I'm letting you go. You're finished at noon today. Our records show that you've consistently fallen behind. You were in first place on Monday. You dropped on Tuesday, and on Wednesday you were in last place."

"I still don't get it," Conner said. "I work really hard. I'm always the first one here and the last one to leave. I've even worked through my breaks."

Mr. Wilson knew Conner was a young man of integrity and that he wouldn't sluff off on the job. He thought for a moment then asked, "Have you been sharpening your ax?"

"No," Conner said. "I've been working too hard to take the time."

Can you relate to Conner? Maybe you're a good Christian doing a lot of good things. But if you're not taking time to pray daily and read your Bible consistently, you're not keeping your ax sharp. In other words, your spiritual life will soon become dull like a blade that's been worn down.

The more you pray and spend time with your heavenly Father, the sharper you become and the more he's able to develop the fruit of the Spirit within you. Good intentions are wonderful, but they'll never make you the disciple God calls you to be. Without consistent time with the Lord, you'll eventually become spiritually dull.

ARE YOU TRUSTWORTHY?

Rev. Albright and a member of his church, Mr. Thompson, made a visit to a rich man in their congregation. "Hello, Edward," Pastor Albright greeted him. "May we come in?"

Edward graciously invited the men in. "We need to get right down to business," the pastor said. "I'll be blunt. There's a very sick woman in our congregation. She desperately needs financial help. I'm here to ask you to make a generous monetary gift."

"Who's the sick woman?" Edward asked.

"I can't tell you that," Rev. Albright replied. "It's really hard for her to admit that she needs help. She has tried and tried to secure funds many other ways, but she has been unsuccessful. She's embarrassed, and I promised I'd keep her identity a secret."

Edward was persistent. "I'd like to help," he said. "But I need to know whom I'm helping."

"I won't betray her confidence," the pastor replied.

"I was going to give you $600, but if you'll let me know whom I'm helping, I'll double the amount to $1,200."

"I can't reveal her name," the pastor said.

"I want to help her, but I need to know whom I'm helping. I'll gladly give you $2,500 if you'll reveal her name."

The pastor remained firm. "I won't break her confidence," he said.

BREW IT!
What about you? Are you a person of integrity? Can others trust you to keep your word? We can't always trust humans, but we can always trust God with our deepest needs!

POUR IT!
Drink in the flavor from the following Scriptures: Proverbs 11:13; Daniel 6:4; Luke 16:10-12.

SAVOR IT!
Ask God to help you develop integrity and trustworthiness for his glory.

Mr. Thompson leaned toward Rev. Albright's ear. "Pastor! That would almost cover her hospital bills. Please reveal who it is and get the money."

Before the pastor could respond, Edward increased his amount to $5,000.

Rev. Albright stood. "Under no circumstances will I reveal the name of the woman who trusts me."

As the pastor was leaving, Edward pulled him back inside his home. "I need to speak with you privately," he said. Mr. Thompson waited on the porch as Edward and the pastor went inside the kitchen. When they were alone, Edward began crying. "My stocks have crashed, my investments have gone sour, and I've lost everything. I'm in danger of losing my home if I can't make payments. I've wanted to seek help, but I couldn't risk the embarrassment of people finding out how badly I've managed my money."

"Edward, I understand," Rev. Albright said. "You were testing me. You needed to know that I could be trusted with your problem. Don't worry. I'll keep what you told me in confidence, and I'll seek financial help for you as well as the sick woman in our church."

March 20

BREW IT!

Where are your priorities? Are you doing what God has called you to do, or have you lost his vision for your life?

POUR IT!

Drink in the flavor from the following Scriptures: Haggai 1:1-13; 2:1-5.

SAVOR IT!

Ask God to give you his vision for your life.

WHERE ARE YOUR PRIORITIES?

He had a funny name: Haggai (pronounced "Hey, Guy!"). And he had a unique career: prophet. (His job was to tell people about God and warn them what would happen if they didn't follow his leading.) Surprisingly, people listened to his message. Maybe they listened because everything was messed up. We have a tendency to do that, don't we? When things get really bad, we're finally ready to listen to someone tell us how to get back on track again.

The time: 520 BC.

The place: Jerusalem.

The situation: God's Temple was in ruins.

The background: Babylonian armies had destroyed the Temple—God's house. Several years later, the Jews were granted permission to return to their homeland to rebuild the Temple. They excitedly made the journey and began the construction process. But it was hot outside. And they wanted to work on building their own homes, too. Some of them decided to plant gardens and join the JCC (Jerusalem Country Club)—it offered a terrific price to families joining during the summer months. Others enlisted in summer softball leagues and went camping. (Okay, I'm having a little creative fun with the way I'm telling this story.)

The result? Their priorities shifted. What once was their purpose now became only a past hobby. Apparently no one minded going to services in a Temple that was falling apart. It didn't seem to bother anyone that the air conditioner squeaked, the back wall was missing, and only twenty-three of the five hundred pews were left standing (and those had lots of splinters). No one cared that the heater pumped out rust instead of heat, mice had taken over the carpet, the altar had only one leg, and no one was doing anything for missions.

In short, this church was pitiful. And what's really sad is that it was God's house—a symbol of his presence with them. He was the one who had freed them from captivity and allowed them to go back to their homeland. Wouldn't you think they'd be grateful?

God had kept them safe during the journey, provided good leaders for them, and met their every need. Wouldn't you think after all God had given them, they'd want to give back to him?

Well, you'd think so. But again, we have to remember their priorities were out of whack. Even though God had given them the specific assignment of building his Temple, they had put it on the back burner. They'd lost his vision. They weren't taking him seriously.

GIVE GOD WHAT'S HIS

When the people lost God's vision, the prophet Haggai entered the scene. And even though this happened twenty-five centuries ago, his message still rings clear today. Haggai told the people exactly what they needed to hear, which wasn't necessarily what they *wanted* to hear. He knew most of the population gathered around the city square for pizza on Friday nights, so he borrowed one of the megaphones from a Jerusalem Community College cheerleader, and around 7 p.m., he let them have it.

"Why is everyone saying it's not the right time to rebuild the Temple?" he asked.

One guy choked on his extra-cheese pizza. Someone else raised his hand and asked for more Parmesan. Another man shouted, "Hey, Guy! While you're up front, mind getting me a refill on this Coke?"

Haggai ignored them and repeated the question with more force. "Why are you all saying this isn't the right time to rebuild the Temple?"

"It's Friday night," moaned Dave. "This is the only time I have to relax and eat pizza and forget about finals."

"Too much work," said another.

"I'd get dirty."

Well, Haggai had had it! But he didn't let up. He was a prophet, and he took his responsibility seriously. He reminded them of how bad things were. It was easy to forget their problems while munching on pizza and downing bread sticks, but Haggai brought them back to reality.

"Too bad you never have enough money," he said. "And too bad your clothes are old and worn out. And too bad you work so hard to get back so little."

Coach Mueller sighed. He had a family to support and a new baby on the way. He worked hard, but he never could make ends meet. "You probably feel as though you're living in a rut, don't you?" Haggai continued. "You get up. You go to school or work. You put in a full day. You come home. No purpose. No real happiness. You don't have what you need, and you can't have what you want."

By now most people had wiped the tomato paste off their chins. A few were chewing on ice from the bottom of their Coke glasses, but they were listening. So Haggai continued. "God has commanded that we build the Temple, yet you sit around week after week and say it's not the right time. Well, when will it be the right time? If you'll simply give God what is his (obedience, and at least 10 percent of your time to rebuilding the Temple), he'll give back to you more than you can imagine!"

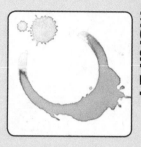

BREW IT!
Are you giving God what's rightfully his?

POUR IT!
Drink in the flavor from the following Scripture: Haggai 2:6-13.

SAVOR IT!
Ask God to help you rearrange your priorities to ensure you're giving him what's his.

BREW IT!
You don't always desire to brush your teeth, but you do so because you know you need to. You may not always desire to do what God tells you, but dedicate yourself to obedience because you know it's right.

POUR IT!
Drink in the flavor from the following Scripture: Haggai 2:14-23.

SAVOR IT!
Tell God you're willing to obey him regardless of how you feel about the situation.

OBEYING GOD

We can't outgive God. He has given us far more than we'll ever be able to give him. We often forget that fact, don't we? Have you ever found yourself thinking, *I've really been doing a lot for God. It's okay for me to slack off now. I deserve to take it easy for a while.*

Haggai continued to address the crowd. "So what is it the right time for? Is it the right time for stuffing yourselves with pizza when God's Temple lies in ruin? Is it the right time for adding on to your home, planting gardens, planning expensive vacations, or buying a car when the Temple needs repairing? Get your priorities straight!"

Andrew raised his hand. "Okay, we hear you, Haggai. We'll start praying for God to give us the desire to rebuild his Temple."

"Why do you have to pray about it?" Haggai asked. "God has already commanded that you do it."

"Yeah, but we have to want to," piped Brooke.

"I don't think so," Haggai said. "Whether you want to has absolutely nothing to do with God's command. Just do it!"

Well, it was late. People were restless. Many of them left, deciding to pray for the desire to rebuild the Temple. "When God gives us the desire to do it, we'll obey," someone said.

But some of the people—the ones who were really listening—heard God's voice through Haggai. And they obeyed. Even though they didn't have a burning desire to rebuild the Temple, they did anyway because God had commanded them.

Guess what! After they started putting the Temple together, God blessed them with the desire.

TITHE? WHAT'S THAT?

We often have it backward when it comes to doing God's will, don't we? How often do you catch yourself thinking, *I'll pray for the desire to invite Ashley to church or the desire to get more involved in my youth group or the desire to read my Bible more. And when God gives me the desire, I'll do it.*

That's backward thinking. Desire isn't part of the command. The issue is this: Will you obey God even when you don't feel like it? If so, just do it! And as you obey him, God will bless you with the desire to continue doing his will after you've started.

What are we really talking about here? Repainting the walls in your youth room at church? Could be. But there's a much deeper issue I want you to focus on. And that's the issue of tithing.

It's clear that God has commanded you to build his temple. How do you do that? One way is by support-ing his work through your tithes and offerings. This is how his temple—the church—is built and enabled to grow.

Well, just how much money are we talking about when we talk tithe? you may be thinking. And that's a good question. If you're a Christian, then God really owns everything you have, doesn't he? But he only asks that you give a minimum of 10 percent back to him. Ten percent out of 100. Not bad, considering he owns it all.

BREW IT!
Are you tithing? If so, great! If not, why aren't you?

POUR IT!
Drink in the flavor from the following Scriptures: 1 Samuel 15:22; Psalm 103:17-18; Matthew 19:17.

SAVOR IT!
Ask God to help you trust him with your money. Pledge to begin tithing con-sistently on everything you earn.

You don't need to spend time praying about whether God wants you to tithe. He's already made it clear: "Build my temple!" And again, one of the most important ways you can do that is by giving tithes and offerings. (See Malachi 3:10 for another encour-agement to tithe.) So instead of praying about what he's already told you to do, pray instead about:

1. *Giving more than money.* Instead of simply giving 10 percent of all you earn, why not consider giving away a few other things as well?

Your time: Volunteer to babysit free for a couple in your neighborhood who would love to have an evening out. Or offer to walk the neighbor's dog.

Your skills: Could you offer to redecorate a few of the bulletin boards at church? clean an elderly person's house?

Your creativity: Purchase a child's lunch box at the mall and pack it full of surprises (microwave popcorn, a fun gel pen, wacky stickers, licorice sticks, bubble gum) and mail it to someone who's lonely, a college student who's away from home, or a child who's from a dysfunctional family.

We'll talk about some other ways to give tomorrow.

BREW IT!
Think of a time when someone gave unselfishly to you. Make time to write that person a note of gratitude this week.

POUR IT!
Drink in the flavor from the following Scriptures: Mark 10:21-23; Philippians 2:3-7; Colossians 3:23-24.

SAVOR IT!
Tell God that you're willing—from this day forward—to give at least 10 percent of all you earn to him. Tell him you want to do your part in building his Kingdom.

GIVING DOESN'T END WITH MONEY

Tithing involves giving at least 10 percent of what you earn back to the Lord. When you fail to do this, you're robbing God of what's really his. Tithing is an important issue of obedience. If Christ isn't Lord of your money, he's not Lord. Pray about:

1. *Giving more than money.* Consider being generous with your time. How about walking a dog in your neighborhood or baking cookies for a shut-in? Or send your pastor a fun note with a two-dollar bill inside (yes, they are available at the bank) and don't tell him who it's from.
2. *Gaining a proper perspective on your money.* Who's really in charge of your finances? Don't cling to something that's only temporary. Though we tend to place great importance on money, we can't take it with us when we die.
3. *Giving to someone less fortunate.* Compassion International has a wonderful child sponsorship program. For less than thirty dollars a month, you (or you and your youth group) can give a child in a third world country an education, school supplies, a school uniform, and a hot meal once a day. Your sponsored child will write you letters, send you her report card, and let you know how you can pray specifically for her. Call 1-800-336-7676 for an information packet, or go to www.compassion.com.
4. *Giving to someone in trouble.* Mercy Ministries is a Christian organization that takes in unwed teen moms, girls struggling with eating disorders, and girls who have been abused. You can make a huge difference in the life of someone who desperately needs it by going to www.mercyministries.org or calling 615-831-6987.

Are you generous or selfish with what you have? Think for a moment about how generous God is with you. He gave his life! Will you pray seriously about giving yourself to those around you? Jesus wants you to be his hands and feet. A few ways you can do that are by tithing and then giving extra to those in need.

GIVING SACRIFICIALLY

Years ago a woman named Edie Ogan related a true story about giving that I'll never forget. Let's eavesdrop on Edie as she recalls the story. . . .

I'll never forget Easter 1946. I was fourteen years old. My little sister, Ocy, was twelve, and my older sister, Darlene, was sixteen. We lived at home with our mother, and the four of us knew what it was to do without many things.

My dad had died five years before, leaving Mom with seven schoolkids to raise and no money. By 1946 my older sisters were married, and my brothers had left home.

A month before Easter, the pastor of our church announced that a special Easter offering would be taken to help a poor family. He asked everyone to save and give sacrificially.

When we got home, we talked about what we could do. We decided to buy fifty pounds of potatoes and live on them for a month. This would allow us to save twenty dollars of our grocery money for the offering.

Then we thought that if we kept our electric lights turned out as much as possible and didn't listen to the radio, we'd save money on that month's electric bill. Darlene got as many housecleaning and yard jobs as possible, and both of us babysat for everyone we could. For fifteen cents, we could buy enough cotton loops to make three pot holders to sell for one dollar. We made twenty dollars on pot holders.

That month was one of the best of our lives. Every day we counted the money to see how much we had saved. At night we'd sit in the dark and talk about how the poor family was going to enjoy having the money the church would give them. We had about eighty people in church, so we figured that whatever amount of money we had to give, the offering would surely be twenty times that much. After all, every Sunday the pastor had reminded everyone to save for the sacrificial offering.

The day before Easter, Ocy and I walked to the grocery store and got the manager to give us three crisp twenty-dollar bills and one ten-dollar bill for all our change. We ran all the way home to show Mom and Darlene. We had never had so much money before!

That night we were so excited we could hardly sleep. We didn't care that we wouldn't have new clothes for Easter; we had seventy dollars for the sacrificial offering. We could hardly wait to get to church!

BREW IT!
This family knew the meaning of giving sacrificially. It's one thing to give; it's another thing to give sacrificially. Have you ever given sacrificially?

POUR IT!
Drink in the flavor from the following Scriptures: John 13:34; Acts 3:6; Romans 12:8.

SAVOR IT!
Ask God to help you learn the joy of giving sacrificially.

BREW IT!

Have you participated in an offering at church to help a family less fortunate than yours? If not, ask your pastor about organizing such an offering. Or pray about filling shoe boxes next December for Operation Christmas Child, sponsored by Samaritan's Purse. There are many ways you and your church family can help others.

POUR IT!

Drink in the flavor from the following Scriptures: Proverbs 28:27; Matthew 10:42; 2 Corinthians 9:7.

SAVOR IT!

Ask God to bring specific people and needs to your mind that you can help.

THE POOR FAMILY

Edie Ogan continues her story on giving. . . .

On Sunday morning, rain was pouring. We didn't own an umbrella, and the church was more than a mile from our home, but it didn't seem to matter how wet we got. Darlene had cardboard in her shoes to fill the holes. The cardboard came apart, and her feet got wet, but we sat in church proudly. I heard some teenagers talking about us having on old dresses. I looked at them in their new clothes, and I felt so rich.

When the sacrificial offering was taken, we were sitting on the second row from the front. Mom put in the ten-dollar bill, and each of us girls put in a twenty-dollar bill. As we walked home after church, we sang all the way. At lunch Mom had a surprise for us. She had bought a dozen eggs, and we had boiled Easter eggs with our fried potatoes!

Late that afternoon the minister drove up in his car. Mom went to the door, talked with him for a moment, and then came back with an envelope in her hand. We asked what it was, but she didn't say a word. She opened the envelope and out fell a bunch of money. There were three crisp twenty-dollar bills, one ten-dollar bill, and seventeen one-dollar bills.

Mom put the money back in the envelope. We didn't talk, just sat and stared at the floor. We had gone from feeling like millionaires to feeling like poor white trash.

We kids had had such a happy life that we felt sorry for anyone who didn't have our mom plus a house full of brothers and sisters and other kids visiting constantly. We thought it was fun to share silverware and see whether we got the fork or the spoon that night. We had two knives that we passed around to whoever needed them.

I knew we didn't have a lot of things that other people had, but I'd never thought that we were poor. That Easter Day I found we were. The minister had brought us the money for the poor family, so we must be poor.

THE RICH FAMILY

Edie Ogan continues her story on giving. . . .

I didn't like being poor. I looked at my dress and worn-out shoes and felt so ashamed that I didn't want to go back to church. Everyone there probably already knew we were poor! I thought about school. I was in the ninth grade and at the top of my class of more than one hundred students. I wondered if the kids at school knew we were poor. I decided I could quit school since I had finished the eighth grade. That was all the law required at that time.

We sat in silence for a long time. Then it got dark, and we went to bed. All that week, we girls went to school and came home, and no one talked much. Finally on Saturday, Mom asked us what we wanted to do with the money. What did poor people do with money? We didn't know. We'd never known we were poor.

We didn't want to go to church on Sunday, but Mom said we had to. Although it was a sunny day, we didn't talk on the way. Mom started to sing, but no one joined in, and she only sang one verse.

At church we had a missionary speaker. He talked about how churches in Africa made buildings out of sun-dried bricks, but they needed money to buy roofs. He said one hundred dollars would put a roof on a church.

BREW IT!

Money really doesn't have anything to do with being rich, does it? If Jesus is truly Lord of your finances, and if you're serving him with all your heart, you are rich. Don't take your relationship with him for granted.

POUR IT!

Drink in the flavor from the following Scriptures: Psalm 19:8; Matthew 6:3-4; James 1:25.

SAVOR IT!

Thank God for making you rich in Christ Jesus.

The minister said, "Can't we all sacrifice to help these poor people?"

We looked at each other and smiled for the first time in a week. Mom reached into her purse and pulled out the envelope. She passed it to Darlene. Darlene gave it to me, and I handed it to Ocy. Ocy put it in the offering plate.

When the offering was counted, the minister announced that it was a little over one hundred dollars. The missionary was excited. He hadn't expected such a large offering from our small church. He said, "You must have some rich people in this church."

Suddenly it struck us! We had given eighty-seven dollars of the "little over one hundred dollars." We were the rich family in the church! Hadn't the missionary said so?

From that day on I've never been poor again. I've always remembered how rich I am because I have Jesus.

BREW IT!
We don't often think about the various facets of our heavenly Father. Strive to think about him more often. Meditate on his Word.

POUR IT!
Drink in the flavor from the following Scriptures: Isaiah 61:1-3; Hosea 6:2-3.

SAVOR IT!
Go over the list again and thank God for being all that he is in your life.

REFLECTIONS ON WHO GOD IS

Spend some time today simply thinking about God and who he is.

Your heavenly Father
A faithful God who does no wrong
A forgiving God
A fortress of salvation
A glorious crown
A jealous and avenging God
A Master in heaven
A refuge for his people
A refuge for the oppressed
A refuge for the poor
A sanctuary
A shade from the heat
A shelter from the storm
A source of strength
A stronghold in times of trouble
An ever-present help in trouble
Commander of the Lord's army
Creator of heaven and earth
Defender of widows and orphans
Eternal King
Father of compassion
Father of our spirit
Father of the heavenly lights
Father to the fatherless
God
God Almighty
God and Father of our Lord Jesus Christ
God Most High
God my Maker
God my Rock
God my Savior
God my Stronghold
God of Abraham, Isaac, and Jacob
God of all mankind

BUT IT TASTES SO SWEET!

Five-year-old Timmy's mother went next door to the neighbor's house for a few minutes. While she was gone, Timmy grabbed a chair and climbed on the kitchen counter to see if there was anything good to eat inside the cupboard. He saw a small paper bag with white powder inside.

Timmy stuck his finger inside the bag and tasted the contents. *Mmmm, that's good!* he thought. He scooped out several handfuls and put the bag back on the shelf. It wasn't long after his mother came home that Timmy began to feel extremely sick.

When she asked if he had eaten anything while she was away, he said, "Yeah, I ate some of that sweet white sugar stuff."

"Timmy! That's poison! It'll kill you," she screamed. She immediately rushed him to the hospital, and because he arrived soon after swallowing the poison, doctors were able to save his life. Timmy never forgot, though, that even though something may taste sweet, it may actually be poisonous.

It's the same way with sin. The Bible tells us that sin is pleasurable for a season. In other words, the fun is temporary. It won't last forever. It may seem cool to drink, but too much alcohol can eventually kill a person. Your friends may try to convince you it's okay to smoke a few cigarettes, but thousands of people die of lung cancer each year. It may seem fun to gossip about others, but those harsh words will eventually kill your reputation and your witness.

BREW IT!
Make a list of other things in life that seem okay but are actually dangerous. Take heed to refrain from these things.

POUR IT!
Drink in the flavor from the following Scriptures: Proverbs 12:15; 14:12; 22:3.

SAVOR IT!
Ask God to give you discernment to know sin when you see it. Ask for the discipline to run away from it.

Sin may taste sweet. But it's poison and will eventually result in spiritual death. Is it worth risking eternity for something that tastes sweet only temporarily?

We often think if we can rationalize our actions and make sin seem to make sense, then it's okay. That's a lie! At one point in the Old Testament, the prophet Samuel told King Saul to destroy all the animals in a specific city. Saul rationalized and thought, *It would be wasteful to kill the fattest calves. And I won't kill the best sheep.*

When Samuel asked Saul why he had disobeyed, Saul made excuses. He thought he could rationalize his sin because it seemed okay at the time. But as a result of his sin, God rejected Saul as Israel's king. (See 1 Samuel 15 for the full story.) Again, sin may seem fun for a season, but sin is never right. Sin is *always* disobedience in God's eyes.

Take stock of your media choices. Be careful which movies you watch. They may contain sweet poison that can injure your character, your mind, and your life. A steady diet of poison will eventually kill you.

BREW IT!

God is your ultimate best friend! Make it your top priority to spend time with him, read the letter he wrote you, and strive to get as much of him as you can. He wants that.

POUR IT!

Drink in the flavor from the following Scriptures: James 4:8; 1 Peter 1:15-16; 2 Peter 1:2-4.

SAVOR IT!

Tell God you want to be saturated with him!

TOO MUCH?

I was excited! I'd heard that Starbucks had created a new drink and was going to test-market it in a few select cities. And my city, Colorado Springs, Colorado, had been chosen! I'm not a coffee drinker. Never have been. I love the smell, but I've never been able to enjoy the taste. I just can't make myself like it.

So when I go to Starbucks with friends, I grab a hot chocolate or a caramel apple cider. But word was out! It had been advertised that Starbucks had created a brand-new drink for chocolate lovers: Chocofina! I couldn't wait to try it. An entire cup of exquisite solid chocolate literally melted into liquid. What could be better?

I stood in line, waited my turn, and placed my order. After letting my drink cool a bit, I anxiously lifted it to my lips and let the gooey brown liquid slide down my throat. *Wow! This is unbelievable,* I thought. I quickly took two more sips.

Then I took the cup—still filled with Chocofina—and tossed it in the trash. What happened?

It was too much chocolate! It was too rich. Too sweet. Too sugary. Too chocolaty! Even though I hadn't even consumed half the drink, I couldn't take any more. I absolutely love chocolate, but this was just too much of it.

Fortunately, you'll never get too much of God. But why not go ahead and try? As you seek to get as much of God as you possibly can, you'll deepen your intimacy with him (as we talked about on February 1). Make it your goal to get so much of God that you gasp in wonder.

It happened with Moses. When God appeared to him in the form of a burning bush, Moses couldn't even look up. And when he came off the mountain to join the children of Israel, his face was blazing with glory—God's glory.

Can you imagine getting that much of God? Make it your goal. Strive to get as much of God as you possibly can. The Bible assures us that as we draw close to him, he'll draw close to us. That's quite a promise. Grab it and get in his presence!

How does one grow close to God? you may be thinking. Well, how do you grow close to anyone? Think about a close friend. You spend time with him. You talk with him. You share your heart. You enjoy being together. And the more time you spend together, the deeper your friendship grows.

SCRAMBLED EGGS
SHUT DOWN HIGHWAY

If you've visited Houston, you may be familiar with the Interstate 610 loop. But you may not be familiar with the accident that closed the highway one day. It happened like this: A truck carrying thirty thousand pounds of eggs spilled the entire load, shutting down the highway for several hours and leaving a smelly mess for cleanup crews.

Police suspect the truck's driver may have fallen asleep. He crashed his 18-wheeler into some plastic barrels along the interstate. As the trailer went up onto the rails of the overpass, the eggs were sent tumbling onto an unoccupied transportation department truck below.

Other than breaking his nose and losing thirty thousand pounds of eggs, the driver suffered no major injuries. Environmental workers spent fourteen hours cleaning up the mess while trying not to slip on egg yolks as they worked. They used a special substance to fight the smell and soak up the fuel.

It's hard to imagine exactly how smelly thirty thousand pounds of dumped eggs would be. But obviously, it's not a mess many people would be drawn to.

Our sense of smell is important. We don't have to taste milk to know it's sour. We can tell it's bad simply by its smell. And fortunately, we can smell escaping gas in our home in time to do something about it. If not, the gas could kill us.

Not only do we possess the sense of smell, we

BREW IT!
Your scent (your lifestyle, your actions, your reputation) can be a powerful witness. Are you giving off a positive, Christlike scent, or by your scent are you conveying a damaging, negative witness?

POUR IT!
Drink in the flavor from the following Scriptures: Psalm 90:12; 112:1-2; 2 Corinthians 2:14-16.

SAVOR IT!
Ask God to help you live so closely to him that you give off his holy scent.

also have a smell about us. In other words, we carry a scent. Dogs know the scent of their owners. I have a 150-pound Saint Bernard, and even if I blindfolded him and approached him from behind, he'd still know it was me, because he knows my scent.

What kind of scent does your lifestyle carry? Through your actions, do you carry a scent of kindness and a gentle spirit? Does your character reflect a scent of honesty and integrity? Do you have a reputation that smells of high morals and standards?

The apostle Paul tells us in 2 Corinthians that Christians have a sweet, wholesome fragrance. He says that's the "smell" of Christ within us. To unbelievers, we're a scent of death, but to other Christians, we're an exquisite perfume. Unbelievers sense the smell of death from us because unless they place their trust in Christ, they'll spend eternity in hell. But other Christians sense the eternal, sweet smell of their forever home in heaven through our lifestyle.

JUST AS YOU ARE

Everyone has something he wishes were different about his physique or facial features. The trick is learning to accept those things about yourself, then working them to your advantage. Sylvester Stallone, Michael J. Fox, and Dustin Hoffman are all movie stars who are fairly short. But they've overcome. Instead of wishing they could be something they're not, they've used their lack of height to their advantage.

What if Barbra Streisand had said, "I might as well forget a singing and acting career. My nose is too big. No one would want to see *me* perform!" Former top model Cindy Crawford could have said, "I'll only model in my dreams. I've got this mole by my lip that's just wrecking everything."

Talk-show hostess Oprah Winfrey has been open about her struggle with weight. The issue really isn't how much she weighed or currently weighs, how she took it off, or the marathons she has run. The real issue is that she became successful in spite of what she didn't like about herself.

Though I've never heard any of the above celebrities mention a personal relationship with Jesus Christ, we can still admire their determination to overcome things they might not like about themselves.

What is it about *you* that you're struggling with right now? Will you take the challenge to simply accept yourself? love yourself? Why is this so important? Because your Creator accepts and loves you right now . . . *just as you are!* And if the King of kings calls you beautiful, who are you to argue?

Former U.S. president Abraham Lincoln is said to have been homely. His nose was huge and his ears stood out. Yet he was a confident, determined man, and though he experienced many difficulties in life, he overcame them. I like to think it was because of the strong relationship he had with his heavenly Father.

When you develop a growing intimacy with Jesus Christ, *he* becomes your security. You don't need to look for popularity or positions to make you feel good about yourself, because your relationship with Christ fills that need.

The closer you become with Jesus, the better you like yourself, the more confidence you have, and the more secure you become. Others are drawn to well-balanced people, and a deep, growing relationship with the Lord provides that.

BREW IT!
What is it that you don't like about yourself? Are you allowing that to hold you back from becoming all God wants you to be? Are you allowing it to cripple you?

POUR IT!
Drink in the flavor from the following Scripture: Psalm 139:1-18.

SAVOR IT!
Ask God to help you accept yourself just as you are. And take a moment to thank him for loving you and seeing you as beautiful just the way you are.

BREW IT!
God is totally, absolutely, incredibly in love with you! Isn't it about time you started loving yourself?

POUR IT!
Drink in the flavor from the following Scriptures: Psalm 145:17-19; 148:14; 150:6.

SAVOR IT!
Ask God to teach you to see yourself through his eyes rather than your own.

IT DOESN'T HAVE TO BE AN EXPENSIVE LESSON

Many people *never* learn to accept their weaknesses or flaws. And because they're unhappy, they tend to make everyone around them unhappy as well. Others go through life spending a fortune trying to create the perfect body, as if chasing a dream.

A few years ago, I watched a talk-show host introduce a panel of guests who had gone through extensive surgeries to change the parts of their bodies they weren't satisfied with. One guest was nicknamed Barbie, because she had spent more than fifty thousand dollars trying to look just like a Barbie doll!

It was eerie. The camera focused on a Barbie doll, then threw a freeze-frame of the Barbie look-alike right next to it. They sported the same clothes, same hair color, and same body shape.

But when the talk-show host began taking questions from the studio audience, one woman stood and addressed Barbie. She said, "Haven't you stopped to think about what you'll look like in ten years? I mean, you're a duplicate right now, but your body, like every body, will eventually start to sag and wear. What will you do then? Spend even more money trying to stay caught up with the perfect look?"

It was sad that an entire panel of people were willing to go on national television to share what they didn't like about themselves and talk freely about the huge sum of money they had willingly spent to become "perfect."

No matter how much money we can offer, we'll never have the perfect body. Still, people line up by the hundreds to get bags removed from underneath their eyes, liposuction, dimples put in or taken out, tummy tucks . . . you name it, and you can get it done with the right amount of money. But as soon as you do, you'll probably notice something else you'd like to have changed. When does it end?

Liking yourself and accepting how you were created doesn't have to be an expensive lesson! When God created you, he made you in his image. The Bible tells us that you are "fearfully and wonderfully made" (Psalm 139:14). In other words, he created you in awe. He gasped in delight at your uniqueness. And he calls your appearance good and beautiful.

He loves the way you sometimes snort when you laugh really hard. He adores your ears, your nose, and your hair. He thinks you're the perfect height, and he even enjoys looking at your feet.

MAKE THE BEST OF WHO YOU ARE

Because the One who created you accepts you just as you are, he wants you to love and accept yourself as well. Years ago when Arnold Schwarzenegger was only a bodybuilder trying to break into acting, he was turned down for three reasons.

He was first told that his body was too muscular and big for him to be a successful actor. Next, he was told that he was too hard to understand; his foreign accent was too thick. It was then suggested that he change his name. Arnold? Sounds like a nerd. And Schwarzenegger? Doesn't quite flow easily.

But you know what happened, don't you? He didn't give up. He could have. It probably would have been easier simply to quit and conclude, *I guess they're right.*

But he began working to trim down his muscular body. He was still muscular but a lot lighter. He also began working to improve his speech and enunciation. He took time to study the English language.

He *didn't*, however, change his name. And I'm glad he didn't. It serves to remind us that if we work hard enough we can turn our "flaws" (or the things we don't like about ourselves) into our assets. Arnold even went on to become the governor of California—the state's first foreign-born governor in more than one hundred years.

In the Gospel of John, Jesus warns us to watch out for thieves who will manipulate and strive to steal what God has for us. Those who put you down, criticize you, and constantly try to get you to doubt yourself, your abilities, and your looks can be considered thieves. They're trying to rob you of the healthy self-esteem God wants you to have. Your heavenly Father wants to help you love and accept yourself. Anyone who tries to focus your attention in the opposite direction can be considered a robber.

It comes down to attitude. You can become bitter about those who make fun of whatever it is you don't like about yourself and cave in and agree with them. Or you can accept yourself and determine to become the best you can be with God's help.

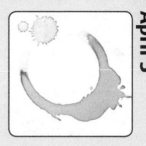

BREW IT!
If your friends are consistently putting you down and making you feel bad about yourself, it's time to get new friends!

POUR IT!
Drink in the flavor from the following Scriptures: Proverbs 4:14-15; 12:5; John 10:10.

SAVOR IT!
Thank God for making you just as you are.

BREW IT!
God is in the process right now of preparing your eternal home!

POUR IT!
Drink in the flavor from the following Scriptures: Acts 7:55; Revelation 21:18, 21.

SAVOR IT!
Spend some time thanking God for the home-beyond-your-imagination he's preparing for you.

MORE LIFE

I've heard that the world's tallest mountains are underwater. It's incredible to know there's another world below sea level. It's hard to believe, because most of us haven't experienced the depths of the ocean. We haven't seen the underwater mountains or the variety of life underneath the sea. I've snorkeled the Great Barrier Reef in Australia, and though I saw a lot, I still don't have a clue about life inside the ocean.

Marine scientists recently discovered 178 new species of fish and hundreds more species of plants and other animals in the world's oceans. This brings the number of species in the world's waters to 230,000. The Census of Marine Life is involved in a ten-year count, and approximately one thousand scientists in seventy countries are involved. Thus far in the count, scientists have described 15,482 species of fish alone.

Does this information stretch your imagination even further? What does your mind's eye see when you try to imagine the depths of the ocean and the world that exists underneath sea level?

My mind doesn't have the capacity to imagine how exciting that world must be. Even in my wildest dreams, I can't project a mental image of what that underwater world is truly like. I can't imagine the deep hues of color, the funny-looking fish I've never even seen, the incredibly tall mountains, or the amazing plant and animal life.

Guess what? As incredible as the underwater world is, there's another world that's even more indescribable. And *that* world is where you'll get to spend eternity if you've placed your trust in Jesus Christ. You've already guessed it—that other world is heaven.

We've heard there are streets of gold, gates made of pure pearl, and a crystal sea. But I have a feeling even descriptive words will pale next to what we'll actually see when we enter God's eternal home. I can't imagine it—but I'm sure excited about getting to live there forever!

How do you feel about heaven? Does the thought of living there frighten you or excite you? Of course, it's natural to be a little anxious about the unknown, and much about heaven is unknown. None of us have seen it or experienced it yet. So though you may feel a little apprehension, you don't have to struggle with doubt. You can know for sure that heaven is your eternal home. If you're not sure—if you've never placed your faith in Jesus Christ and made him Lord of your life, you can do that right now! (Consider praying the prayer of salvation in the devotional on February 21.)

PAID IN FULL!

Ben had admired a beautiful sports car in a dealer's showroom for months, and knowing his dad could easily afford it, he told him that was all he wanted for his approaching college graduation. On the morning of Ben's graduation, his dad called him into his private study. "I'm proud of you, Son," he said. "I love you more than I can express. Congratulations on your college graduation today." He then handed Ben a beautifully wrapped gift box.

Disappointed yet curious, Ben opened the box and found a handsome leather-bound Bible with his name imprinted on the cover in gold. He was angry and snarled, "With all your money, you give me a Bible?" He stormed out of the house.

Years passed and Ben became successful in his business. He lived in a beautiful custom-built home with his wife and children and had just about everything money could buy. But he realized his dad was very old and thought maybe he should visit him after all these years. They hadn't seen each other since graduation day.

Before Ben could make his flight arrangements, he received a phone call informing him that his dad had passed away and had willed all his possessions to his son. Ben would need to go home immediately and take care of things.

When Ben arrived at his dad's house, sudden sadness and regret filled his heart. He began searching through his dad's important papers and saw the still gift-wrapped Bible, just as he had left it years ago. With tears streaming down his face, he opened the Bible and began to turn the pages. His dad had carefully underlined some special verses.

As Ben read the words on the pages, a car key dropped from the back of the Bible. It had a tag with the dealer's name—the same dealer who had the sports car Ben had so desperately wanted. On the tag were the date of his graduation and the words "Paid in full."

BREW IT!
How many times have you missed God's blessings because you haven't seen past your own desires?

POUR IT!
Drink in the flavor from the following Scriptures: Jeremiah 31:34; Amos 9:15; Matthew 7:11.

SAVOR IT!
Take a moment to thank God for paying your debt of sin in full!

BREW IT!

God has a high calling for your life. Don't fall for the pressure from those who don't know him to do things that would break his heart.

POUR IT!

Drink in the flavor from the following Scriptures: Proverbs 15:1; 21:2; Matthew 5:14-16.

SAVOR IT!

Ask God to shine clearly through your life, no matter who surrounds you.

PEER PRESSURE . . . A *GOOD* THING?

You may think peer pressure ends when you get out of college, but it doesn't. I was recently part of an expedition cruise to Antarctica. It was a small ship that held approximately one hundred passengers. After our ship pulled out of Ushuaia, Argentina, we headed for the Drake Passage—commonly referred to as "Shaky Draky" because of the extremely turbulent waters. It took us forty-four hours to get through Drake Passage, and a few days later we were on the white continent.

Because this was an expedition cruise, it hosted guest lecturers from Ivy League universities, scientists, researchers, and biologists. It was obvious I was out of my league. I didn't have any scientific reason for being part of this expedition. I simply wanted to fulfill a lifelong dream of mine to go to Antarctica.

I was hoping I'd find a few other Christians on board, but if they were present, they kept their relationship with Christ a secret. I was surrounded by affluent professors and biologists who drank freely and used four-letter words like they were oxygen. At one dinner, the wife of one of the lecturers sat next to me. She watched as I drank my water, then turned to me and sarcastically asked, "Why don't you drink?" She was actually offended because I wasn't joining in with everyone else.

In casual conversation throughout this two-week adventure, people next to me on the ship or exploring on the land would ask what my profession was. I explained that I was editor of a magazine for Christian girls, was involved in annual international mission trips, and wrote Christian books.

Word got around, and people actually began avoiding me. They didn't like it that I bowed my head and silently prayed before eating. Though I made an effort to be kind to all and engaged openly in conversation with them, they were uncomfortable being around a Christian who was confident in her faith.

I continued to enjoy the expedition and prayed that God would use me to make a difference. He did! Before the end of the cruise, some of the participants were asking me to pray at their tables before dinner! God had taken peer pressure and turned it around to something positive.

You may be facing a tremendous amount of peer pressure right now on your campus, with your friends, or at your part-time job. Have you considered striving to turn negative peer pressure into positive peer pressure? Instead of allowing people to intimidate you with negative things, put a spin on the pressure and strive to influence them for the good.

DISCOVERING GOD'S WILL

My grandma was an excellent nurse who lovingly cared for hundreds of patients over the course of several years. Hearing her recount stories of how she helped sick people made such an impression on my six-year-old mind that I determined that's what *I* would be. . . until I decided the guy who drove the neighborhood ice cream truck had a much more exciting profession.

Then, when I was in the fifth grade, I wanted to be an explorer. (We had just finished studying Lewis and Clark and I was ready to carve some trails.) By the seventh grade I knew I was going to be an oceanographer, but by my junior year in high school, I had switched to wanting to become a tennis pro. But to be honest, I still wasn't satisfied. I had spent a lot of time in prayer seeking God's will for my life and had told the Lord I wanted his best plan—not my own.

By my senior year in high school, when I still didn't know what God's will was, I gave the Lord an ultimatum. After all, we're told in James 1:5 to expect an answer when we ask God what to do. So I expected. I told God I wanted to know his exact will for my life in one week. (I figured if he could whip up a couple of humans out of dust, set the world in motion, and hang the stars in place all in a good six days, giving me a hint about my future would be no big deal.)

As I waited for his answer, I also spent more time in prayer and reading the Bible. Toward the end of the week, a funny thing happened. God began to talk to me, but not in a thundering voice. Sometimes he used my thoughts as I read his Word. Verses took on new meaning; things seemed clearer in my mind. I began to realize this was God's voice; his special way of helping me understand and communicate with him.

BREW IT!
Discovering God's will for your future can sometimes be a process. Instead of becoming impatient, expectantly await what he will reveal to you!

POUR IT!
Drink in the flavor from the following Scriptures: Habakkuk 2:3; Hebrews 6:12; James 1:5.

SAVOR IT!
Ask God to replace your impatience with a genuine excitement as you wait for him to reveal his future for you.

BREW IT!
Don't miss the opportunity to influence your world for God right now because you're too concerned about your future career.

POUR IT!
Drink in the flavor from the following Scriptures: Proverbs 14:6; 15:14; 17:24.

SAVOR IT!
Ask God to help you become his hands and feet to those around you.

GOD'S WILL ISN'T A JOB

The more I prayed about knowing God's will for my life (including the fact that I had told him I wanted to know in one week), the more I began to think, *Who am I to put a time limit on the creator of the universe?* He showed me that because I was so concerned about his will for my future, I was missing out on his will for *today*!

My prayer changed. Instead of worrying about what I would do for a career, I began to pray, "Lord, help me to be all you want me to be *right now*."

Guess what? As I concentrated on being in the center of his will *one day at a time*, he began to reveal (in bits and pieces) his dreams for my future. Maybe you, too, are interested in a variety of things and are struggling with narrowing down your future goals. Your friends may already know what they want to do and how they're going to achieve it. That's okay. Don't get stressed out just because you don't. Instead, ask God to help you become all he wants you to be right now.

My big mistake was thinking "God's will" meant my career. Actually, our vocation is only a small part of God's will for our lives. God's will also includes:

- your impact on those around you
- the people you date
- how you treat your family
- if you'll marry or remain single
- whom you'll marry
- where you'll live
- the type of person you'll become
- how you'll raise your children
- _____

(You fill in the blank. There are a whole lot more!)

Do you know what the apostle Paul's vocation was? He was a tent maker. Do you think he spent time praying about whether God wanted him to live a holy life? No. Living like Christ does not depend on our job title. Reflecting Jesus is our number one, absolute, most important major reason to live. Our career—no matter what it is—is merely something we do on the side. Our main focus is to be Jesus to the world around us. *That's* God's will for our lives.

GOD'S WILL IS A TREASURE!

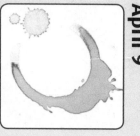

When it comes to knowing and following God's will, you may be thinking, *What if I miss what he has in store for my future because I take a wrong turn?*

Remember this: Christ paid a mighty big price for you. Think he's going to let you miss out on his best that easily? No way.

Imagine that your dad lost his job, and your mom's part-time position at the local bank isn't enough to support your entire family. You receive a phone call informing you that you've just won a million dollars from some off-the-wall contest you entered about six months ago. The money is being given away by an eccentric billionaire. He explains that he's going to deliver the money—in cash. There are a couple of weird things about this contest, though. First, you can't actually *keep* the money but must give it to your family. Second, you can't just *give* it to them, you have to hide it and give them clues as to where it can be found.

No problem. You would have given the money to your dad anyway. Your family needs it right now, and you're excited to help out. So you carefully wrap the money in a metal box and hide it near the sandbox in the backyard.

You write a poem filled with clues about where the treasure can be found. Your family ventures into the backyard. If you see them heading toward the old oak tree in the corner, you'll probably steer them away from that and toward the sandbox. And if they meander into the garage, you'll coax them out and in the direction of the sandbox. When they saunter over to the swing set, you'll gently guide them back to the sand. And as they rush to the garden, you'll probably take their hands and pull them toward the money.

BREW IT!
God has even given you a map that points to his treasure for your life. It's called the Bible: his Holy Word. Follow it closely, and you won't easily miss his will for your life.

POUR IT!
Drink in the flavor from the following Scriptures: Isaiah 12:2; 26:4; 30:15.

SAVOR IT!
Ask God to help you understand the treasure map (Bible) he's given you. Read it with excitement and expectancy!

You'll do everything you can to make sure they know exactly where the treasure is. It works the same way with God's will. When he wants you to do something, he'll give you a million and one clues to head you in the right direction. And when you start to veer off to the side, he may shut the door in your face. Don't panic. Simply realize it's his way of turning you around. Change direction and notice that he's opened a window for you to climb through.

He'll even take your hand and guide you . . . if you'll ask him. He has way too much invested in his plan for your life to let you just "not get it."

BREW IT!
Sometimes God leads us in a specific direction, then changes our course at a later date. The issue isn't where you're going; it's who you're going with.

POUR IT!
Drink in the flavor from the following Scriptures: Isaiah 50:10; Jeremiah 39:18; Nahum 1:7.

SAVOR IT!
Thank God for holding your future in his hands.

PRAYING GOD'S WILL

Settled. You don't have to:

- plead with God about where your life is going to be ten years from now. Christ wants you to focus on being all he wants right now!
- worry about whom you'll marry. God is big enough to bring just the right person along at just the right time.
- beg God to lead you in a specific direction. Trust him to fulfill your heart's desires.

Why use your creative energy worrying about the future when instead you can throw yourself into making the most out of your present? Spend time praying about:

1. *Using the gifts and abilities God has blessed you with.* Feel as though he's leading you into some kind of music ministry? Then instead of becoming obsessed with being the hottest new contemporary Christian artist on the scene, focus on being the best soprano (or bass) your church choir or worship team has.

   You're sensing Christ is calling you into preaching? Instead of becoming a loud-mouthed, in-your-face know-it-all to students around you, simply speak the truth in love. And make yourself available for praying before football games and track meets and sharing your testimony at before-school Bible studies.

   In other words, allow God to make you the best you can be right where you are! It's not being in the spotlight or making money carrying out God's will that makes the Father smile. It's being all you can be in the center of his will right now that makes him proud.

2. *Believing in his dreams for your life.* You serve a God who wants your fulfillment even more than you do. Therefore, he dreams bigger dreams for you than you would ever dare to create for yourself. You serve a GIANT of a God; therefore, learn to think BIG.

   But what if you think God is calling you to the mission field? Again, the most important thing in your life is to be 100 percent sold-out for him right now! If he's really Lord, it won't matter *where* he wants to send you next year or ten years from now. It may be he *will* send you to the mission field. Or it might be that he simply wants to know that your answer is "Yes, Lord" to anything he asks.

DID GOD CREATE EVERYTHING?

A university professor challenged his class with this question: "Did God create everything that exists?"

One student bravely answered, "Yes, he did."

The professor continued, "If God created everything, then God created evil, since evil exists. And according to the principle that our works define who we are, then God is evil."

No one in the entire class spoke. The professor boasted to his class that he had proven once more that faith in God is only a myth.

Another student stood and said, "May I ask you a question, Professor?" The professor agreed. "Does cold exist?" the student asked.

"What kind of question is that?" the professor said. "Of course it exists. Have you never been cold?" The students laughed.

But the young man continued. "The fact is, sir, that cold does *not* exist. According to the laws of physics, what we consider cold is, in reality, the absence of heat. Absolute zero (–460 degrees Fahrenheit) is the total absence of heat. All matter becomes inert and incapable of reaction at that temperature. Cold doesn't exist. We have created this word to describe how we feel if we have no heat."

BREW IT!
Throughout your life, you will face people who question your faith. Are you prepared?

POUR IT!
Drink in the flavor from the following Scriptures: Proverbs 17:10; 28:11; Philippians 1:10.

SAVOR IT!
Ask God to help you discern his truth.

The student continued. "Professor, does darkness exist?"

The professor responded, "Of course it does."

"Once again you are wrong, sir. Darkness doesn't exist either. Darkness is, in reality, the absence of light. We can study light, but we can't study darkness. In fact, we can use Newton's prism to break white light into many colors and study the various wave lengths of each color. You can't measure darkness. A simple ray of light can break into a world of darkness and illuminate it. Darkness is a term we use to describe what happens when there's no light present."

Then the student asked the professor, "Sir, does evil exist?"

The professor responded, "Of course. We see it every day. It's in the daily example of human injustices and abuse. It's in the rampant cases of crime and violence everywhere in the world. These manifestations are nothing else but evil."

To this the student said, "Evil doesn't exist, sir. Or at least it doesn't exist unto itself. Evil is simply the absence of God. It's just like darkness and cold—a word that man has created to describe the absence of God. God didn't create evil. Evil isn't like faith or love that exist as light and heat do. Evil is the result of what happens when man doesn't have God's love present in his heart. It's like the cold that comes when there's no heat or the darkness that's a result of no light."

BREW IT!
Be willing to ask questions. Speak out when you hear something that doesn't sound right.

POUR IT!
Drink in the flavor from the following Scriptures: 1 John 4:1-3: 2 John 1:9-11; Jude 3.

SAVOR IT!
Ask God for the confidence to speak out when you hear something that's not right.

KNOW THE TRUTH!

I'm not 100 percent certain the story I shared with you in yesterday's devotional actually happened, but I love the story. We can learn a lot from it, whether or not it actually happened. I admire the student's boldness to confront the professor when he heard something he knew wasn't true.

Too many colleges and universities are filled with professors who sound good, speak articulately, and can easily verbalize their opinions in persuasive ways, but who are not speaking the truth. It's okay to question what you hear. A big part of college *is* questioning what you've believed through the years. It's learning to make your faith your own instead of relying on your parents' faith to get you into heaven.

Christianity can take your questions. It can handle every single doubt you toss its way . . . or it wouldn't have lasted more than two thousand years. Doubting becomes wrong, however, when we keep it smashed inside and allow it to fester and grow. If you're taking your doubts to the Word of God, Christ will turn those doubts into solid faith.

If you'll ask your questions and honestly seek for Christ's response through his Holy Word, he'll transform these questions into answers grounded in truth. So when you hear something you're not sure about from a classmate, or even a teacher, don't be afraid to challenge the statement. Ask the questions. Just make sure you go to the Lord for your answers.

Just because someone sounds good doesn't mean he's right. And simply because a professor can easily articulate his opinions about religion and make them sound like proven truth doesn't make them acceptable to Christians. You may be listening to someone who's extremely positive, someone whose message is clear and feels good. If you can't back it up with the Bible, it's not the message you need to be listening to.

As you continue with your education, and as you plunge into the career world, you'll be surrounded by decent people spouting "good" things. But again, if what they're saying can't be supported by Scripture, they're not the people you should listen to.

Open your ears and your mind to those who speak God's truth. The apostle John tells us in 1 John 4 that we're not to believe everything we hear. He challenges us to test what we hear and see if it is supported by what God has said. If not? It's not truth.

WHERE'S YOUR HEAD?

Twelve people changed the world. They altered the course of history and shattered the face of reality as people knew it. These twelve people were Christ's disciples. They were just like you and me. They worried. They were scared. They struggled with peer pressure. They were insecure. Sometimes they worried about their looks. But they changed the world.

They were guys you could've bumped into at the mall. You might have seen them trying on a pair of Nikes or buying a baked potato with the works at the food court. They were just like us. Yet they changed the world!

How did twelve ordinary men who made tons of mistakes accomplish such an incredible task? They didn't have a youth group to support them. They'd never been on a mission trip or had experience standing at their school flagpole in prayer (see the devotional on September 16). They'd never been involved in a campus Bible study and didn't own the latest cool student edition of the Bible. Yet they changed the world.

I'm convinced twelve ordinary people like you and me were able to turn the world upside down—no, right side up—because they had a solid mind-set. They refused to be deterred. They realized that what went into their minds would determine what they set their minds on. When Peter and John were threatened by the Pharisees and told to quit preaching, for example, they shut out those words and stayed focused on Jesus. (See Acts 4:1-22.)

Because God created our minds, he knows what a powerful thing the mind is. Proverbs 4:23 says, "Be careful how you think; your life is shaped by your thoughts" (TEV).

My *life* is shaped by my thoughts? Whew. That's quite a statement. If that's true (and I choose to believe God's Word is true), then my thinking affects everything I do. The way I dress, the friends I hang out with, the things I do to get a laugh, how I spend my time, what I do with my money . . . everything is influenced and determined by what goes on in my head.

Ralph Waldo Emerson (he's that guy you were supposed to study in English class) said, "A man is what he thinks about all day long."

Marcus Aurelius (he's that guy you were supposed to study in history class) said, "Our life is what our thoughts make it."

Again, if this is true, then the mind has a lot of power. What we *think* about is going to make a difference in how we live our lives. That's why the apostle Paul said, "Fix your thoughts on what is true and good and right" (Philippians 4:8, TLB).

BREW IT!
According to Proverbs 4:23, our lifestyle is shaped by our thoughts. Psychologists tell us that our thoughts produce behavior. So . . . what are you thinking about?

POUR IT!
Drink in the flavor from the following Scriptures: Psalm 26:2-3; Isaiah 26:3-4; Jeremiah 17:10.

SAVOR IT!
Ask God to saturate your mind with his Holy Spirit.

BREW IT!
The human mind is a powerful thing! What is your mind set on?

POUR IT!
Drink in the flavor from the following Scriptures: Romans 8:6; 12:2; 1 Corinthians 2:16.

SAVOR IT!
Diligently set your focus, your mind, your attention, on Jesus Christ.

THE MIND IS A POWERFUL THING

To a degree, we can say that our thinking makes us who and what we are. What is your mind focused on? God is searching for disciples who will set their minds on Christ. He's looking for disciples who refuse to be swayed by the world's opinions and beliefs.

Even though my college tennis coach encouraged us to attend every practice, she knew we would miss a few. One day she said, "If you have to miss, at least practice your serve in your mind. See yourself tossing the ball at just the right height. Picture bringing back your racket and coming in with a perfect follow-through."

We all realized, of course, that we had to pour a lot more than thoughts into developing a good serve, but we also learned that thinking about doing it right actually helped our performance.

Many years ago, I read a story about a prisoner of war who had been held captive in Vietnam for several years. He was held in an extremely small cell—if you could even call it a cell. After his long-awaited release, one of the many things on his want-to-do list was playing golf. He finally got the opportunity, and his score was almost even par.

"This is the first time you've played since your release, right?" his friends asked.

"Yes, it is. And it felt great," he replied.

"How in the world did you do so well after missing so many years on the greens?"

"I played every single day of my captivity," he explained.

"You're kidding! There was a golf course at your POW camp?" They couldn't believe what they were hearing.

"No. In fact, I was rarely allowed the privilege of getting out of my cell," he replied.

"We don't understand," his friends said.

"Every single day of my captivity," the former POW explained, "I imagined myself getting out of the cell, picking up a set of golf clubs, and heading toward the greens. And every single day, I played an absolutely perfect game of golf . . . in my mind!"

I'm not talking about a "name it and claim it" strategy, but rather a time of working something out in your mind and striving to match your behavior to the picture in your thoughts.

DON'T BE SWAYED BY THE WORLD

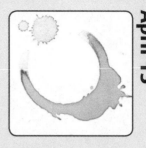

Christ wants to saturate our minds with himself. If our thoughts are filled with him and with positive, holy, good things, our behavior will be affected. Why is this so important? Because it is disciples with a godly mind-set who will continue to change the world. And if we have a solid, godly mind-set, we'll be less swayed by the world's views.

New Agers know how important our thinking is. Some of them say all you have to do is think about something long enough, and it's yours. Want a new car? Visualize it. In a matter of time, you'll be in the driver's seat. Want more power? Imagine it's yours, and you'll have it. This line of thinking is not scriptural. But a Christian whose mind is not settled is easy prey for the New Age roundup.

One day when I was teaching speech class, a student gave an informative oral presentation on his personal beliefs. Kyle stood confidently in front of the class and claimed that Jesus Christ was no more the Son of God than he was.

He went on to say that all of us are on a spiritual journey. "There are actually several ways to reach heaven," he said. "Some of you have chosen Christianity. That's one way. Others have chosen Buddha. I'm on a personal journey to becoming my own god. It's simply a matter of time before I have more power."

BREW IT!
You can guard your mind from the things of the world by saturating it with the Bible. Make time to read God's Word consistently.

POUR IT!
Drink in the flavor from the following Scriptures: Deuteronomy 11:18; Luke 24:45; 1 Peter 4:7.

SAVOR IT!
Ask God to give you wisdom and discernment to recognize false beliefs.

Then he talked about how God was everywhere. "He doesn't just live inside you," Kyle said. "He's in the floor I stand on and inside my note cards—even in your desks. So, in a sense, all these things are god."

He explained his crystal. "I draw and receive energy from it," he said. "Because God is a part of this crystal—and because God is power and energy—I have access to that when I have my crystal."

Kyle was an intelligent young man. Good-looking. Popular. Sharp. Confident. Articulate. Even convincing. I wondered if the few Christians I had in class were being swayed or if their minds were set solidly on Jesus Christ.

Students listened intently as he continued . . . many of them never knowing Kyle was presenting them with New Age propaganda. New Age thinking is not to be taken lightly. It's sweeping our nation like a wildfire and is one of the fastest growing belief systems in the world right now.

New Age merchandising is slick. The vocabulary is seductive with phrases such as "cosmic harmony" and "self-realization." Don't be taken in by this false belief system!

BREW IT!

Can you verbalize your faith in Christ Jesus? Be ready to explain to those around you why you've placed your trust in him.

POUR IT!

Drink in the flavor from the following Scriptures: Romans 3:23, 27-28; 5:1-2.

SAVOR IT!

Thank God for wanting to live in your life and make you holy in his precious sight.

THAT'S NOT ALL!

We need to pierce through all the glamour of the New Age belief system and realize through the Word of God that this is a counterfeit, false religion. It's nothing more than hungry people searching for God's truth. We expect those who don't know Christ to fall for that stuff. But sadly enough, they're not the only ones who are being swept up in New Age philosophies. Christians whose minds are not focused completely on Christ—whose thoughts aren't saturated with God himself—are prime targets for the world's false belief systems.

The dangerous part of New Age thinking is that if we're all on the pathway to becoming gods, then it really doesn't matter if we sin. Kyle stood in front of my speech class and said, "I'm not concerned with what you would label right and wrong. If I do something wrong, it's simply because I need awareness of that action during this lifetime. For instance, if I kill someone, I'm not going to worry about it. It simply means that, for a reason I'll probably never understand, I needed to know what it would feel like to take a life or spend years behind bars."

Kyle believed he was a god. And he's not the only one. Many other New Agers believe they have gained an awareness of their goodness and are gods. But that goes directly against the Bible! God's Holy Word claims that there's only one true God—and it's Jesus Christ. The Bible also tells us that we're not innately good; we're all born with sin. We *need* God, but we'll never become God.

The frightening thing about rationalizing yourself into believing you're God is that you'll also rationalize yourself into believing that you can call your own shots, create your own logic, plan your own life, make your own rules, save your own soul, determine your own destiny, do your own thing, and create your own eternity.

New Age is full of dangerous philosophies and frightening beliefs. Quite bluntly, its doctrine will lead you straight to hell. It's nothing more than sugarcoated satanism.

So again . . . what's your mind set on? If it's not planted firmly on God and his Word, you're easy prey for New Age beliefs or other false religions. Know *what* you believe and *why.* Practice articulating your faith. God not only wants to live in your heart—he wants to saturate your thinking. He wants to possess your entire life with his love and his absolute truth.

THE AUTHOR OF NEW AGE

The one who's at the heart of the New Age movement is the same one who's at the heart of witchcraft and the same one who wants your mind to be set on the world instead of Christ. You guessed it—the author of all this deceit and confusion is Satan.

I met Jill at a retreat where I was speaking. She told me she was involved in a few New Age teachings. She was also into drugs, witchcraft, sexual relationships, and had gotten an abortion just hours before coming on this church retreat.

After talking and praying with Jill but not getting through, one of the youth pastors praying with us realized that demons were hindering her prayers. Satan had literally blocked her prayer line to God.

Eight youth ministers and I prayed with Jill from 10 p.m. to 6 a.m. and watched in amazement as Christ's holy power was demonstrated over the demons that were cast out of her. During those long hours, we consistently led her in a prayer of salvation.

It was the most frightening experience I've ever encountered. I watched in horror as Satan threw her to the ground and screamed through her voice. Her body twisted and convulsed with hatred from hell. Satan glared through her eyes and hissed, "She's mine!"

Why? How did this happen to a girl raised in a Christian home? Her dad had even been a pastor for a short while. What went wrong? Though Jill had never verbally invited Satan to invade her life, by her sinful lifestyle she had willingly opened the doorway to accepting the beliefs of the world.

At one time she had made a halfhearted commitment to God. But she'd never *set her mind* firmly on Jesus Christ. She'd never allowed him to possess her thinking or to take complete control of her heart and her life. She was uncommitted and wishy-washy. Her thoughts and beliefs vacillated back and forth from church to the world to God to friends to the world to church to . . .

Get the picture? God is looking for disciples with their minds set firmly on him. Disciples who refuse to be swayed or influenced by what's going on around them. Disciples who are grounded in their thinking and who are living out God's Word.

BREW IT!
If your friends don't have a personal relationship with Jesus Christ, they're easy game for false religions. Be ready and willing to share your faith with them.

POUR IT!
Drink in the flavor from the following Scriptures: Isaiah 53:12; 1 John 1:7-8; 3:6-9.

SAVOR IT!
Ask God to help you reach your unsaved friends with the gospel.

BREW IT!
Is your thought life centered around your heavenly Father?

POUR IT!
Drink in the flavor from the following Scriptures: Proverbs 14:15; 21:29; 2 Corinthians 10:5.

SAVOR IT!
When your thoughts begin to stray to things that go against the nature of God, stop and pray immediately.

EVALUATE YOUR COMMITMENT

So what happened to Jill? Her new "commitment" lasted almost six months before she fell right back into her old, sinful lifestyle. Why? Because the mind is a powerful thing. If we're filling our thoughts with the ideas, philosophies, and ways of the world, our lifestyle will eventually reflect our thinking. We need a serious commitment to Christ in our hearts and in our minds to be his dedicated disciple. And we need to follow up our commitment with action—imitating our heavenly Father. He won't impose himself on us. He has given us the freedom to turn away, so we need to choose to turn toward him.

And what happened to Kyle? (Flip back to the devotionals on April 15–16.) The same Kyle who so eloquently presented his New Age beliefs in speech class wasn't even old enough to drive a car. Two months earlier, he had gotten a fourteen-year-old girl pregnant, and two weeks after his speech class debut, he was married.

The marriage lasted three weeks. He dropped out of our school and enrolled in another—still searching for something to fill his mind, still desperately hunting for answers to happiness, meaning, and fulfillment.

God wants to fill your mind with himself. When you're totally saturated with him, your desire for the things of the world will diminish. Your interest in other religions will wane because you'll have an authentic relationship with the one true God. Set your mind on him!

What does it mean to have a godly mind-set? It means you're dedicated to one thing—committed 100 percent. Sold out. Firmly attached. Completely devoted. But *that one thing has to be Jesus Christ*.

If our minds are set 100 percent on Jesus Christ, our actions will reflect our thoughts. If our hearts are totally dedicated to God, our lifestyle will echo that commitment. Your heavenly Father is calling you to set your mind firmly on him—just like the first disciples who were chosen to follow him. God is searching for young men and women with a godly mind-set—disciples who will commit even their thoughts to him.

THINKING = BEHAVIOR

Several years ago there was a minister in the South whose actions finally caught up with his thoughts. He pastored a successful church. Everything looked great on the outside. But on the inside, his thoughts were far from being planted firmly on God.

He employed a janitor with a physique similar to his own. The janitor had several tattoos, and of course his facial features were different, but other than that, the two men were very similar in size and appearance.

The minister took out a $100,000 life insurance policy and decided he wanted to cash in. So he *set his mind* on evil. He decided to get rid of the janitor while making it look like he was the one who had been killed.

He stabbed the janitor to death, shaved off his tattoos, beheaded him, and finally put his own clothes on the body of the dead employee. It looked as if the minister had been murdered. When his wife tried to cash the insurance policy a few months later, the police put a few clues together, found the minister, and eventually arrested him for the crime.

The Bible tells us that our sins will find us out. In other words, whatever is on the inside will eventually come out. King David knew the power of the mind. That's why he prayed, "Search me, O God, and know my heart." (Read the entire prayer in Psalm 139.) King David knew that the heart and mind are connected. He realized that what went on in his mind would eventually seep into his heart. He knew that God could see inside his heart and his mind, so he pleaded with the Lord to correct his wrong thinking.

BREW IT!
Do what Randy did. For the next month, try giving yourself a constant reminder about your thought life.

POUR IT!
Drink in the flavor from the following Scriptures: Matthew 15:19; Hebrews 3:1; 4:12.

SAVOR IT!
Ask God to help you memorize Scripture to keep your thoughts focused on him.

King David knew from experience (his affair with Bathsheba) that thoughts eventually lead to actions. Thinking = behavior. That's why he fervently and consistently asked God to monitor his thought life. He wanted his thoughts to be godly.

Randy and I were youth ministers at the same church. He worked with the junior high group, and I had the senior high. One day we were riding in his Jeep and his watch beeped. "What's that, Randy?" I asked. "Do you have an appointment?"

"No," he replied. "I've set my watch to go off every hour, Susie. I use it as a constant reminder. Every time the alarm sounds, I ask myself, *What are you thinking about, Randy? What's going on in your mind right now?*"

Godly disciples intent on changing the world care about their minds. They determine to set their thoughts on God and *saturate* their thinking with him.

BREW IT!
Dare to be a Daniel! Determine—with God's help—to live a life of integrity in the midst of those who don't. Set your mind on him and him alone.

POUR IT!
Drink in the flavor from the following Scriptures: Isaiah 59:15-16; Daniel 6:3; Acts 6:8-15; 7:54-60; 1 Peter 1:13-15.

SAVOR IT!
Ask God to help others notice that your mind is set on things above instead of things of the world. When they ask you about it, be ready to share your faith.

ESTABLISHING A GODLY MIND-SET

Developing a mind set on Christ is something you can decide to do and, with God's help, can accomplish. Here are a few tips to get you headed in the right direction. Pray about:

1. *Being a godly disciple among those* who aren't. Sometimes it's tough to do what's right when everyone around you is doing the opposite. Again, the key is to have a godly mind-set. In other words, set your mind on Jesus Christ and refuse to allow other junk to sway you.

    Daniel had a godly mind-set. And because of that, he was able to live a godly lifestyle—even among those who weren't. Not only did he live a godly life . . . he maintained his integrity in the midst of a heathen court. What set Daniel apart from the others in the king's court? Daniel had an intimate, no-compromise relationship with his heavenly Father.

2. *Looking past those around you and focusing on God.* If your attention is on what everyone else is doing, your thoughts won't be centered on Christ. Remember the New Testament story of Stephen? He was stoned for his faith, yet he looked right past his murderers and focused his attention on Christ instead. He had a godly mind-set. His mind was set on God and God alone. What effect do you think his actions and reactions had on those around him? If you started focusing *your* attention on God instead of people, what kind of impact could you make?

3. *Developing a godly mind-set.* Establishing yourself in holy ways and as a reflection of Christ himself requires the Holy Spirit living through you, as well as a commitment on your part to set your mind on God and God alone. Memorize this verse—I like the way it sounds in *The Living Bible:* "Happy is the man who delights in doing [God's] commands. . . . For he is *settled in his mind* that Jehovah will take care of him" (Psalm 112:1, 7, italics mine).

WHERE ARE THE TOMATOES?

In 2004, because of several hurricanes in Florida and severe rain in California, the United States suffered one of the worst tomato shortages in decades. In California alone, 1,500 acres of tomatoes were lost due to the rains. Tomato prices in some parts of the nation tripled to thirty dollars for a twenty-five-pound box.

The shortage really hurt America's tomato-loving fast-food chains. Subway and Wendy's felt the pinch, and even the Olive Garden restaurant noticed the shortage. How did they respond?

Well, Wendy's had to change their marketing. They promoted only items that didn't feature tomatoes. They postponed their planned push for Chicken Temptations sandwiches until the tomato shortage declined. Burger King posted signs in their restaurants when they didn't have tomatoes. The Olive Garden had to change some of its recipes. And the Mexican restaurant Chipotle began using salsas that required fewer tomatoes.

It's fascinating how the weather in California and Florida can have such a tremendous effect on what we eat and how we eat it all around the nation! You, too, can have a huge impact on your own world by how deep, steady, and authentic your relationship with Christ is. The closer you are to the creator of the universe, the easier it is for the people of the universe to notice him working in your life. How's your influence? Are you running a shortage on impact? Or are you moving full speed ahead . . . living out a vibrant faith to those around you?

April 21

BREW IT!
There's a shortage of missionaries. Will you rise to the occasion, change your priorities, and make sharing your faith the most important thing in your life?

POUR IT!
Drink in the flavor from the following Scriptures: Mark 16:15; Acts 1:8; Romans 1:16.

SAVOR IT!
Ask God to mold you into the flexible, teachable disciple he desires you to be.

It's also fascinating how some fast-food chains and restaurants compensated to address the lack of tomatoes. Many did everything possible to keep their customers happy, including changing their menus. Those who were inflexible lost customers and money.

Are you willing to make a difference for those who are experiencing a "shortage" of the gospel? Would you be willing to change your summer schedule and consider going on a short-term mission trip instead of making money for your own interests?

Are your plans—like some restaurant menus—so set in stone that you're unable to be flexible when a need arises? People who don't have a personal relationship with Jesus Christ are lost. They're living in darkness. The exciting thing, however, is that many of those people would love to place their faith in Christ if they truly understood the gospel. That's where you come in. You may or may not be able to go overseas on a mission trip, but you can be a missionary right where you are.

OBSESSED

Lloyd Ostendorf was obsessed with images of Abraham Lincoln and collected memorabilia of him for almost seventy years. He tracked down rare photos and even strands of the sixteenth president's hair. He also managed to get a piece of the bloody coat Abraham Lincoln was wearing when he was shot. Lloyd had more than two hundred photos and objects in his collection before he died.

He began searching for Lincoln items when he was thirteen years old and didn't stop until he passed away at age seventy-nine. His intensive search led him to find rare photos the experts never knew existed. He even wrote the authoritative book on the subject, *Lincoln's Photographs.*

Imagine . . . what if you became a "collector" of Jesus Christ? What if you were so in love with the Lord that you wanted everything you could get your hands on that would help you know him better?

Having one Bible wouldn't be enough. You'd want a few different translations. You wouldn't want to miss church and Bible study. You'd be excited to open the pages of his Holy Word each day and refresh your mind with his truth. You wouldn't simply pray when you needed something; you'd pray throughout the day. And you wouldn't be concerned with praying simply to "get" from him. You'd also want to *give* to him, to worship and praise him.

BREW IT!
What would it take for you to become totally obsessed with Jesus Christ?

POUR IT!
Drink in the flavor from the following Scriptures: Psalm 1:1-3; 5:7; 16:3.

SAVOR IT!
Tell God that you don't want to settle for him simply living in your heart; you want him living in your mind, your daydreams, your conversations, and your free time.

He'd be as real to you as your fingers and your hands. You'd enjoy talking with others about him and sharing what he was doing in your life. He'd be the last thought on your mind at night and the first thought on your mind in the morning.

That's obsession, isn't it?

Guess what—God *wants* you to become obsessed with him! He's obsessed with *you!* Psalm 139 says that he thinks about you all the time. He knows when you stand and when you sit. The Gospel of Matthew tells us he even knows the exact number of hairs on your head. That's obsession, isn't it?

Why is it so easy to become obsessed with professional athletes, political figures, and celebrities? We collect their posters, buy their books, and seek their autographs and photos. But these are mere humans; they'll eventually pass away, along with their fame. Jesus Christ, however, is eternal. And he's so obsessed with you that he gave his very life for you. That should make you want to become a collector of everything that will help you know him better.

REVELATION

Many Christians love the last book of the Bible, Revelation. But many other Christians purposely stay away from it because it seems hard to understand. Though much of it is written in symbolic language and imagery, it's an important book and contains extremely relevant messages for us today.

It's the sixty-sixth book in the Bible, and we need some knowledge of the previous sixty-five books before we can truly understand this last book. Many people don't want to take the time to study the other books. They've heard Revelation talks about the end times, and they simply jump into it, become confused, and decide the Bible is a waste of time.

The book of Revelation is a powerful read. It's the only prophetic book in the New Testament, compared to seventeen prophetic books in the Old Testament. In the Gospels (Matthew, Mark, Luke, and John), we see Jesus in the flesh, but we don't have the full revelation of him. For the most part, we see him as humble, meek, and lowly. He made himself subject to his enemies. He willingly died on the cross.

But we get an entirely different picture of him in the book of Revelation. The Lamb has become the Lion, and he's in absolute control. This last book of the Bible is the unveiling, or the revelation, of Jesus Christ.

Revelation was written by the apostle John, and it was actually given to him *as* a revelation. Let's set the scene: The year is AD 95, and the evil ruler Domitian is on the throne of Rome. Like Nero, an earlier emperor, Domitian is an egomaniac. He claims that he is God and commands that everyone worship him.

BREW IT!
Do you need a fresh revelation of Jesus Christ? Ask him for it!

POUR IT!
Drink in the flavor from the following Scriptures: Romans 5:6; 8:28; 10:10-11.

SAVOR IT!
Thank God for always knowing exactly where you are and what you're experiencing. Tell him how grateful you are for his strength and comfort.

The Christians refuse to worship this madman, and a wave of persecution breaks loose. Among the Christians being persecuted is the apostle whom Jesus loved, John. He's very old, and Domitian hates him. The evil ruler tries to boil him alive and is unsuccessful, so he banishes John to the island of Patmos. It's a rocky, barren, volcanic, seemingly God-forsaken place off the coast of Asia Minor. It's ten miles long and six miles wide.

And it's there on that harsh, rocky island that God gives John the revelation of the glorified Christ. Isn't it interesting how God is willing to meet us exactly where we are? John didn't have to escape his terrible situation, clean himself up, and head to church to find God. The Lord knew exactly where John was and showed up when the apostle desperately needed to hear from his heavenly Father.

YOUR OWN PATMOS

You may experience times when you feel as though you might as well have been banished to some far-off barren island. Maybe your friends aren't who you thought they were. Unkind words were said about you. Perhaps rumors spread. Your heart was broken. Someone you trusted deserted you. You feel alone, and you're hurting. You're experiencing your own island of Patmos.

The good news is that you're *not* alone! And God hurts with you. He feels the pain you feel, and he's ready to reveal himself to you in a fresh and brand-new way if you'll let him. The Bible is full of others who had their own "Patmos" experiences. Remember Abraham? (Flip forward to October 26 for a quick snapshot.) Abraham had prayed for years that God would bless him with a son. But some time after God answered Abraham's prayer, he commanded Abraham to give his son, Isaac, to him.

As Abraham climbed Mount Moriah with his son, tears streaming down his face, he probably wondered, *Why would you do this, Father? I don't understand.* Just as he was ready to plunge a knife into his only son's chest, God stopped him. It was as if the Lord was saying, "Stop, Abraham! I see that you love me. You're willing to obey my every command. That's what I wanted to know. Set your son free. I've provided a ram over there for you to sacrifice to me. I am Jehovah-jireh, the God who provides" (see Genesis 22:1-13).

Because Abraham was obedient, he received a fresh revelation of God. He revealed an aspect of his character to Abraham in an unforgettable way—God would forever be the provider.

God also appeared to Jacob during his "Patmos" moment (see Genesis 32:22-32). Jacob was probably thinking, *I'm sure I've been forgotten. I've ripped off my brother, Esau, all his life, and now God has turned his back on me.* God appeared to Jacob even in the barren spot where he confronted his faults and shortcomings—and God blessed him.

And as Moses was leading the children of Israel out of Pharaoh's grip toward the Promised Land, he took his frustrations to the Lord. "The people have been without water for three days. They want to kill me!" He was certainly having a "Patmos" moment in the desert. But God met him there.

"See that tree, Moses? Chop it down and throw it into the water, and I'll transform the bitter water into clean water. I am Jehovah-rophi, the God who heals." When did this revelation come? When Moses was in trouble (see Exodus 15:22-26).

Have you ever considered that the trouble you're experiencing right now might bring you to a fuller revelation of Jesus Christ?

A SPECIAL BLESSING

Did you know that a special blessing is promised to everyone who reads the book of Revelation or hears it read? The Bible is powerful no matter how we consume it, because it's the Holy Word of God. But it seems there's sometimes something extra special about hearing it read out loud. In John's day, it's likely many people weren't able to read or weren't able to get their hands on an individual copy of his letter of Revelation. But whether they read it or heard it, they were blessed.

The same holds true for us. Some people enjoy listening to an audio version of the Bible while they drive or exercise. Others enjoy curling up in bed and diving into the Bible. One method isn't better than another. It's just important that we spend time in the Word.

To whom was John directing this letter? He wrote it to the seven churches in Asia Minor, which is now Turkey. When Jesus revealed himself to John through a vision, he identified himself as the Alpha and the Omega, the beginning and the end. Alpha and omega are the first and last letters in the Greek alphabet. We make words from the letters in the alphabet, and Jesus is called the Word of God. He's the only alphabet you can use to reach God. The only language God speaks and understands is the language where Jesus is the Alpha and the Omega and all the letters in between. If you're going to get to God the Father, you're going to have to go through the Son, Jesus Christ.

In the original Greek manuscripts, we can see that John wrote out the word "alpha," the first letter of the Greek alphabet. But when it came to "omega," he only used the letter. Why? Maybe it's because Jesus is the beginning and the end without end. In other words, Omega is never written out fully because Christ never ends. We'll spend eternity getting the full revelation of our Lord.

BREW IT!

There will be times when you, too, will experience persecution for your faith in God. Stand strong and remember that God is with you.

POUR IT!

Drink in the flavor from the following Scriptures: Jude 24-25; Revelation 1:3, 8-9.

SAVOR IT!

Ask God to help you center your life around him as the beginning, the middle, and the end without an ending.

John had been pastoring the church in Ephesus and supervised the other churches in the region. He'd been actively preaching the Word of God. And now he was in trouble—banished to the barren island of Patmos. John understood persecution; he was right in the middle of it. And he was writing to Christians who were also being persecuted for their faith.

BREW IT!
Have you "turned to see" recently? If not, make it a habit to start turning toward the voice of God.

POUR IT!
Drink in the flavor from the following Scriptures: Exodus 3:1-7; Revelation 1:10-11.

SAVOR IT!
Ask God to help you always turn and listen to his voice when he speaks to you.

SHARE IT!

The Lord told the apostle John to write what he saw in the vision given him by God and share it with others. John received a brand-new revelation of Christ, and he obediently wrote it down and shared it with the other Christians.

How has God revealed himself to you this week? Has he shown you a quality of himself you haven't experienced before? What are you doing with what he's teaching you? Are you writing it down? Do you keep a journal? Do you have a prayer list? Do you e-mail friends and share what you're learning from the Lord? Do you share in youth group or Bible study what God is teaching you?

If you don't have any accountability in your life, make it your goal to establish some with someone of the same sex. Determine to meet with this person on a regular basis for coffee, a Coke, or breakfast and share your struggles and your answers to prayer. If you're not involved in a small group such as a Sunday school class or a Bible study, join one. Sharing with others what God is teaching you sparks continued growth in your relationship with him. By sharing what you're learning from Christ, you're also being obedient. God has made it clear that we are to tell others what he teaches us.

After God told John to write down what he saw and send it to the seven churches in Asia Minor, the Bible tells us that the apostle turned to see who was speaking to him. Whenever God speaks to you, it's important to turn around and listen. Many Christians assume they can keep doing whatever they're doing and still listen to God. They're into multitasking, and God's voice is simply one more among many others in their hectic schedules.

When God Almighty speaks to us, he deserves our full attention and our reverence. John was wise to "turn and see." We read about others in the Bible who cared enough to turn and see and were blessed because of it.

Moses was tending his father-in-law's sheep when he turned to see a bush burning nearby. When the Lord saw that Moses was willing to turn and listen to him, he commissioned Moses for a spectacular ministry.

THE POWER OF TURNING

In the same way the apostle John and Moses turned to the Lord, the shepherds in the fields outside Bethlehem were also obedient in turning. They were simply watching and caring for their sheep when suddenly an angel appeared to them and told them to travel to Bethlehem. The shepherds could have easily said, "Nah. We don't want to make that trip. We've got all these sheep to care for. Let's just stay put." But they turned. And went. And ended up rejoicing in the birth of the long-awaited Messiah.

It's important to turn toward God when he speaks to us or reveals himself to us. The wise men in the East were diligently studying the stars when they noticed one star they'd never seen before. They could have rationalized, "Ah, that's not really a star; it just looks like a star." But they dared to turn and follow the star and made a two-year journey on their camels across the desert to meet and worship the King of kings.

There's a group of folks in the Bible, however, who refused to turn. They were the Bible scholars. When the wise men finally made it to Jerusalem, they asked where the Scriptures prophesied the Messiah would be born. The scholars were quick to answer: "He will be born in Bethlehem." They knew the prophecies. They had memorized the Scripture. They knew all about the Virgin Birth, and they must have realized the wise men were on to something.

Yet they never made the five-mile walk from Jerusalem to Bethlehem to have a personal, genuine encounter with God in the form of a baby. If we're not careful, we can fall into the same trap. We can know a lot *about* God. We can read the Bible and memorize Scripture and be actively involved in youth group. But if we never make the effort to turn and get to know Jesus Christ intimately, we're lost. If we never turn our lives over to his authority, we're just like the Bible scholars in Jesus' day who were unwilling to make the effort to have a personal relationship with Christ.

John knew the value of turning toward God. And even Jesus himself knew the importance of turning toward his Father. "I do exactly what I see my Father doing," Jesus told those around him. He literally turned and imitated God himself. What God said, Jesus repeated. What God did, Jesus copied.

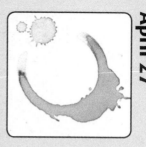

BREW IT!
Do you know a lot about God without knowing God personally? If so, consider praying the prayer of salvation in the devotional on February 21.

POUR IT!
Drink in the flavor from the following Scriptures: Proverbs 2:6; 3:13; John 5:19.

SAVOR IT!
Thank God for his willingness to reveal himself to you.

BREW IT!
Think of ways you can help others this week. Actively do things that will reflect God's character to those around you.

POUR IT!
Drink in the flavor from the following Scriptures: Psalm 34:14; 37:3; Revelation 2:2-3.

SAVOR IT!
Ask God to help you notice how you can help others. Tell him you want to live a life worthy of his commendation.

THE FIRST LETTER

The apostle John was instructed to write what he saw to the seven churches in Asia Minor (now known as Turkey). The messages he wrote to the churches aren't outdated or hard to understand; they're timeless. They're relevant to us right now, right here. They're also extremely practical. We'll look at all seven letters over the course of this year.

John wrote his first letter to the church in Ephesus. Let's take a quick visual tour of the city. It was beautiful, huge, and the chief city of the entire province of Asia. If you landed at the harbor in Ephesus, you would have climbed out of your boat and headed down the main street of the city. This wasn't just any street; this boulevard was paved in pure, white marble.

As you headed toward the center of town, you would have noticed numerous temples, beautiful buildings, and lots of shops. Even further toward the center of the city, you would have seen a large market. A little further, and you'd see a theater actually built into the side of a mountain. This theater held about twenty thousand people. As you continued down the white-marbled boulevard, you would soon arrive at the great amphitheater, which held more than one hundred thousand people.

Ephesus was a large, heavily populated city filled with activity. It was here in Ephesus that Paul had his most effective ministry, and it was also here that the apostle John became pastor of the Ephesian church.

As we take a quick peek at John's first letter in the book of Revelation—his letter to the church in Ephesus—we hear Jesus speaking while John writes what he sees and hears. Jesus is dictating what he wants John to share with the churches—and with us today.

First he affirms the church in Ephesus. He encourages them and commends them. God loves to affirm his children when he sees them doing their best to follow him.

Are you actively doing things that are worthy of commendation? Do you consistently look for ways to help others, talk about your faith, or go the extra mile? God wants to affirm you, but you need to live a lifestyle worthy of commendation.

JESUS KNOWS AND SEES

In his first letter to the church of Ephesus, John shares with the believers that Jesus wants to commend them. He has noticed their good works. He has seen the positive things they're involved in, and he affirms them for it.

Because we're saved by grace and not by our works, Christians often lose sight of the importance of works. The apostle James tells us that faith without works is dead. Yes, our salvation is a gift from God. But once we become Christians, he expects us to do good things. God wants his children involved in good works, because by doing them we reflect his character and express his love to others. Jesus spent his lifetime doing good while he walked the dirt roads in our world.

It's important to remember that Jesus is talking to Christians in this letter. He expects good works from his children; he doesn't ask nonbelievers for good works. First you come to know Christ as your Savior, then he'll talk to you about doing good works.

Is there an area of ministry where you could get involved at your church? Could the nursery use another helper? What about volunteering to fold bulletins or set up chairs or mow the lawn in the summer? Would you consider writing a few notes each week to people who are absent or joining the visitation team?

BREW IT!
You may grow weary, but God continually offers renewed strength for his children.

POUR IT!
Drink in the flavor from the following Scriptures: Romans 4:5; Titus 3:5; James 2:17-20.

SAVOR IT!
Be honest with God. When you're weary, tell him. When you need his strength, ask for it.

John also tells the Ephesians that God is aware of their labor. He not only sees the good works they're accomplishing, but he's fully aware that they're weary. Again, these were persecuted Christians. They were suffering for their faith and for their labor in Christ. They needed to hear God's commendation. They desperately needed affirmation.

Have you ever felt as though your back was against a wall or there wasn't a light at the end of the tunnel? Remember, God is with you right in the midst of your weariness. He sees the tunnel you're in, and he comes to take your hand. Continue to trust in his faithfulness even when you feel weary, weak, and alone.

Daniel must have been weary in his labor for the Lord. He was being persecuted by the king's court, yet he continued to pray three times each day. He remained consistent in his relationship with God, even though he probably grew weary of the taunting and the threats. And when he was finally tossed into a den of hungry lions, he certainly felt alone.

Yet in his aloneness, he remained faithful to God. And sure enough, God showed up right in the midst of the dark, cold den and delivered his servant. God is faithful! You can trust him!

BREW IT!
Don't be afraid to stand for truth simply because a non-Christian may call you judgmental.

POUR IT!
Drink in the flavor from the following Scriptures: Matthew 7:1, 15-16; Romans 2:1-4.

SAVOR IT!
Ask God to give you the discernment needed to recognize spiritual lies.

WHAT'S THE DEAL WITH JUDGING?

Jesus told the Ephesian Christians that he was proud of them for carefully examining those who came to their church claiming to be apostles. The Christians in Ephesus tested everyone who came to their church claiming to know God. "Have you seen the resurrected Christ?" they might have asked. "Do you have a personal, genuine, growing relationship with Jesus?" By asking tough questions, the Christians found out quickly who was real and who was fake. If they were real, they welcomed them into the church, had fellowship with them, and learned from them.

If they were phonies, the Christians asked them to leave their fellowship. They didn't want false doctrine creeping inside the body of believers who were paying such a high price for serving the Lord. Remember, this group of Christians was being persecuted for their faith. They wanted to make sure they spent their time with genuine believers instead of phonies who would try to dissuade them from worshipping the one true God. And Jesus affirmed them for this.

You may have friends who aren't Christians, and one of the most popular things they like to say is, "Don't judge me. Christians aren't supposed to judge. Even Jesus said not to judge people."

They're *partly* right. In Matthew 7:1 we're told not to judge. But fifteen verses later we're told we'll know someone by his fruit. Is Jesus contradicting himself? Not at all. We're told not to judge for condemnation in Matthew 7:1. Only God has the authority and wisdom to condemn someone. We don't have that right, and we never will.

But in Matthew 7:15-16 we're instructed to judge for identification. Jesus tells us to beware of people who try to look and sound like Christians but who really aren't believers. He calls them wolves in sheep's clothing. And we're given permission to judge in the sense of identifying them.

If we only talk about the Bible but don't take it personally, we're not experiencing the fullness of God's Holy Word. In the same way, if we don't warn fellow Christians about false doctrine and false teachers, we're simply fattening each other up for the kill. God *wants* his children to be wise and to recognize those who belong to the flock and those who simply claim to know him but really don't.

He wants to give us discernment to recognize a spiritual lie when we hear it. These false teachers were trying to inch their way into the church of Ephesus, and the Christians were smart enough to ask the tough questions, stand their ground, and politely ask them to leave their midst. And God smiled at them for their wisdom.

REAL . . . OR FAKE?

Time for a little fun. Try to guess which of the following holidays in the month of May are real and which ones are fake. Write an *R* by those you think are real, and write an *F* by those you believe are fake.

___ Better Sleep Month
___ Learn More about Japan Month
___ Cinco de "Mayo"—Mayonnaise Month
___ National Egg Month
___ National Hamburger Month
___ National Physical Fitness and Sports Month
___ Lizards Make Pets Too Month
___ World Soupfest Day
___ International Pickle Week
___ Taller Is Beautiful Day
___ No Socks Day
___ Knee Safety Awareness Month
___ Totally Chipotle Day
___ Lumpy Rug Day
___ National "Denim Days" Month
___ Go Solar Month
___ National Salad Month
___ National Senior Travel Month
___ Celebrate Sardines Month

It's really not important to know all the holidays in a given month. But it is important to know the Word of God. When someone says something and attributes it to the Bible, a mature Christian should know if it's true or be willing to research the Word and find out if it's true.

Try to go a step further than simply reading your Bible. Strive to memorize a verse each week. You may even want to choose one of the Scriptures listed in this devotional book.

BREW IT!
How well do you know the Word of God? Make it your personal goal to study and understand the Bible.

POUR IT!
Drink in the flavor from the following Scriptures: Psalm 119:1-5, 89-91, 105-106.

SAVOR IT!
Ask God to help you understand what you read in his Holy Word, and ask him to speak to you through the Bible.

Real: Better Sleep Month, National Egg Month, National Hamburger Month, National Physical Fitness and Sports Month, International Pickle Week, No Socks Day, Totally Chipotle Day, Lumpy Rug Day, National Salad Month, National Senior Travel Month. (All the others are fake.)

BREW IT!

Reading God's Word takes time. Are you willing to make the investment? You'll never regret what you learn from the Bible.

POUR IT!

Drink in the flavor from the following Scriptures: Hosea 14:9; James 2:12-13; 1 John 4:1-3.

SAVOR IT!

Ask God to help you discipline yourself daily to spending time with him and reading his Word.

IN THE BIBLE . . . OR NOT?

Continuing along the same lines as our "real or fake" quiz, take a few minutes to decide which of the following statements are found in the Bible and which aren't. Write a *B* by the ones you believe are in the Bible, and write an *N* by those that are not.

___ "A penny saved is a penny earned."

___ "Our courts oppose the righteous man."

___ "Cleanliness is next to godliness."

___ "Charity suffereth long, and is kind."

___ "Selfishness bequeaths unrighteousness."

___ "Listen to your father, who gave you life, and do not despise your mother when she is old."

___ "He who dwelleth on the mountain can provide adequately for the downtrodden."

___ "Rome wasn't built in a day."

___ "Ask not what your country can do for you; ask what you can do for your country."

___ "One if by land, and two if by sea."

___ "Blessed is the man who fears the Lord."

___ "Blessed are those who give much offering."

___ "Blessed are the peacemakers."

___ "You are the honey of the world."

___ "You are a candle in the forest."

___ "To strengthen your promise with a vow shows that something is wrong."

___ "Give me liberty or give me death."

___ "Read my lips: No more taxes."

___ "Don't do your good deeds publicly, to be admired."

It's important to know the Word of God so you can recognize false statements made by false teachers. The apostle John tells us not to believe everything we hear, but to test it and see if it's actually found in the Bible. You'll hear a lot of "good" things from nice people, but don't assume it's from the Lord unless you can back it up with Scripture.

In the Bible: "Our courts oppose the righteous man" (Isaiah 59:14, TLB). "Charity suffereth long, and is kind" (1 Corinthians 13:4, KJV). "Listen to your father, who gave you life, and do not despise your mother when she is old" (Proverbs 23:22). "Blessed is the man who fears the LORD" (Psalm 112:1). "Blessed are the peacemakers" (Matthew 5:9). "To strengthen your promise with a vow shows that something is wrong" (Matthew 5:37, TLB). "Don't do your good deeds publicly, to be admired" (Matthew 6:1, NLT).

ABUNDANT LIFE

Jesus makes his purpose clear in John 10:10: "I am come that they might have life, and that they might have it more abundantly" (KJV).

Jesus always goes the extra mile and then some. He could have simply said, "I am come" and we would have been able to rejoice. *Thank you, Lord, for coming!* Simply coming was a huge sacrifice for him. He left the glory and splendor of his perfect Kingdom and chose to invade our sinful, corrupted world with love. What a sacrifice!

Thank you, Lord, for coming! He chose to be born in a cave and to encounter what humans battle. Though he had all the power of God in human form, he still faced the same things you encounter. He probably suffered headaches, scraped his knees, and felt the awkwardness of going through puberty.

Thank you, Lord, for coming! Thanks for loving us so much that you cared enough to enter our messed-up world with the very presence of God in human flesh. That's going the extra mile! But Jesus didn't stop there. He went the extra mile and then some.

"I am come that they might have life." *Oh, thank you, Jesus, not only for invading our world with your very self and giving us your presence, but for offering us* life *as well!* We don't have to settle for a mundane, purposeless existence. Jesus came to give us *life*. He came so that our lives could be fulfilling, forgiven, meaningful, and purposeful. He could have stopped right there, and we would have rejoiced. But he went the extra mile and then some.

BREW IT!
Are you living abundantly, or are you merely living?

POUR IT!
Drink in the flavor from the following Scriptures: Psalm 145:7; John 10:10; Romans 5:17.

SAVOR IT!
Ask God to forgive you for settling for less than he wants you to be.

"I am come that they might have life, and that they might have it more abundantly." God wants to give you even more than you can imagine. Not only has he come (by leaving his perfect paradise and entering your world), but he's come to give you life (filled with meaning and forgiveness), and he's come so that you won't merely have an average life. He's come so you can live life all out. In abundance! His desire is that you live the life he has given you in all its totality. Wow! What a God.

So . . . are you living life to the fullest? Or have you settled for an average existence? Yes, you may be a Christian who is grateful for God's forgiveness of your sins. You may be involved in a vibrant church, youth group, or Bible study. But are you falling more and more in love with your heavenly Father every day of your life? Are you growing and solidifying your relationship with him every day? Or have you become static? lukewarm?

BREW IT!
Don't settle for living in the mundane when God wants you to live abundantly!

POUR IT!
Drink in the flavor from the following Scriptures: John 14:26; 15:26; 16:13.

SAVOR IT!
Ask God to deepen your love for him and your commitment to him every day.

DON'T SETTLE!

Imagine settling for a piece of half-cooked chicken when you *could* be eating a succulent, juicy, prime piece of steak. Can you imagine someone saying, "Hey, really, it's okay. I'll just stick with this piece of chicken, even though it's not fully cooked. It's partly cooked, so it's all right."

Why would anyone want to settle for a below-average meal when he could have the very best? And why would anyone want to settle for being a sleeping Christian who's grown lukewarm when God wants to fill him with power, enthusiasm, confidence, and abundant life?

Christianity doesn't stop with forgiveness for sins; it begins there! Many people receive Christ's forgiveness and think that's it. *Okay, now I'm ready for heaven,* they think. No! God wants to give you a fulfilling life right here, right now, right where you are. How can you experience abundant life?

1. *Realize there's always room for more.* Don't ever allow yourself to stop growing spiritually. Many older saints in your church will testify that even at eighty years of age, they're still learning new things and growing spiritually. Continue to meet with God and ask him to show you specific areas in your life where you need help.

2. *Keep reading the Bible.* Much of your spiritual growth will come from God's Holy Word. Strive to read the entire Bible once every year. It's not as big of a task as it seems. If you read three chapters six days a week and five chapters every Sunday, you'll get through the entire Bible in a year. And each year, God will show you brand-new things and give you more spiritual insight.

3. *Realize God wants 100 percent.* Total surrender is a continuing process. You can tell him that you give him your entire life right now, but two months down the road you'll encounter something you haven't dealt with before. At that point he'll say, "I need that, too. Remember, you gave me everything." Continue to surrender everything to his authority as you keep walking with the Lord.

4. *Don't let your spiritual life become routine.* If you usually have your quiet time every morning, try some variety. Have devotions in the evenings on Monday, Wednesday and Friday. Or read the Bible on your knees. Try writing your prayers on a computer. Keep a prayer journal and record the answers you receive.

FAST FOOD FAST!

When you think of fast food, burgers and fries might immediately come to mind. But a few years ago, many fast-food restaurants began offering salads. Now fast food is embracing fast fruit.

Get this: McDonald's buys more apples than any other restaurant chain. Wendy's is rolling out a fruit bowl entrée. They also offer mandarin oranges in kids' meals. Arby's chops apples into their chicken salad. Chick-fil-A began selling fresh fruit sides in the summer of 2004. Jack in the Box puts applesauce cups into their kids' meals, and Burger King sells strawberry-flavored applesauce as kids' meal substitutes. About one in ten customers chose applesauce instead of fries when it was test-marketed.

Now almost every fast-food chain has a new fruit salad or fruit side in the planning or testing stage. In a society where people are health conscious yet still want their food quickly, many are opting for fruit and salads. Fresh-cut fruit has exploded into a $3.8 million business at grocery stores.

But there are problems with cut fresh fruit. It doesn't last long on the shelf, it costs a lot to store, and it has to be refrigerated. On top of that, special packaging is needed to let nitrogen out but keep air from getting in. In other words, it requires a lot of expense, planning, and extra care for fast-food chains to offer fruit. So why do it? Because people want it and need it.

Switch your thoughts from physical nutrition to spiritual nutrition. The fact that you're reading this book proves you want spiritual food, and no doubt you realize you need it to grow into the strong Christian God desires. But just like fruit, spiritual nutrition has its own set of requirements.

BREW IT!
Find a variety of spiritual growth foods: reading the Bible, devotional books, and Christian biographies; listening to the Bible on CD; and participating in Bible studies with others.

POUR IT!
Drink in the flavor from the following Scriptures: Mark 1:35; Luke 4:14, 32.

SAVOR IT!
Ask God to help you develop into a spiritually strong disciple.

- *It requires a long shelf life.* Fruit has an extremely short shelf life, but it's the opposite with spiritual nutrition. Spiritual growth is a process. You need to chew on what you've digested. Let it simmer inside you. Think about it. Pray over it. Allow the Holy Spirit to work it into every area of your life.
- *It requires discipline.* You may crave fries, but if you take the fruit instead, you'll be better off in the long run. You may crave cranking up your MP3 player, but if you first make time to meditate on God's Word, you'll draw closer to him. In other words, do the right thing even when you crave the opposite.

BREW IT!
You can learn to know God's voice so well that you don't have to doubt when you hear it.

POUR IT!
Drink in the flavor from the following Scriptures: Exodus 19:19; Deuteronomy 30:20; 1 Samuel 15:22.

SAVOR IT!
Ask God to help you recognize the sound of his voice.

TUNING IN TO THE RIGHT STATION

"I've been a Christian a long time," Samantha told me. "But I still haven't gotten to know God as my personal friend and Father. What can I do? I want to be close to him."

How do you get close to *any* friend? By spending time together, talking, and doing things together. What happens as you do these things? You deepen your friendship. You grow closer.

It works the same way with God. The more you read his letters to you (the Bible), the better you'll understand what he has in store for you. The more time you spend talking with him, the more time you'll *want* to spend talking with him. And as you bring him into every area of your life (by shooting quick sentence prayers to him throughout the day), you'll begin to depend on him more and more.

Let's pretend you have a pager, and you've assigned a special signal or code to your mom. As soon as she pages you, you know immediately who it is. You recognize that signal. You probably recognize her handwriting, too. And her shoes, her perfume, her voice inflection. You *know* her.

You can know God's voice that clearly, too! He speaks to us in a variety of ways:

- Through his Word.
- In your mind and in your heart. (This is done through the Holy Spirit who lives within you, guiding you in the right direction, helping you to know his will.)
- Sometimes through trusted adults who are close to him (like your pastor, youth leader, parents, and relatives).

But you know what? It takes *discipline* to learn what his voice sounds like. It means making time daily to shut out everything else to focus on his "still, small voice" that comes from *within*. In other words, make sure you're tuning in to the right station.

How do you accomplish this? Through devotions—reading your Bible and praying. And as you pray—talk with him—don't forget to *listen*.

When you know the voice of God, BIG things happen. The Bible is filled with believers who did incredible things simply because they knew God's voice. When God spoke, they responded!

Imagine how much more effective your witness could be if you were confident of God's voice. If you knew beyond doubt that he was talking to you, you'd probably be more apt to respond in obedience. But so often we doubt. *Was that God?* we wonder. *Or was it just me? Or maybe it was even Satan. How do I know?*

THE OBEDIENT MAN

Let's talk about Elijah—the Old Testament prophet who challenged King Ahab to a fiery duel over a dead bull. If you've ever been discouraged because your youth group isn't as big as you wish it was, Elijah could relate . . . in a major way! You see, whenever his youth group had a pizza fling, he was the only one who showed up.

When they organized money-raising projects such as car washes or tickets sales for the church chili supper, he was the only one who participated. That's because Elijah was from a reeeeeeally small church. We're talkin' itsy-bitsy-teeny-weeny-yellow-polka-dot-bikini-sized church. It was so small, he was the only member.

In fact, it *seemed* as though he was the only follower of God in the land. (There were really more, but he couldn't find them. Kind of like *you* feeling as if you're the only Christian on your campus.)

But Elijah's strength was in *knowing the voice of God*. When God spoke, Elijah acted! Well, God spoke. He told Elijah to tell King Ahab that he was doing a lousy job of running the country, and that if he didn't shape up, God would punish the people by withholding the rain. (Bad news, 'cause the crops would wither and die and everyone's stomach would growl and no one would be able to buy Honeycombs or Trix or even Pop-Tarts. So, yeah, it was pretty serious.)

Now, I don't know how *you'd* react if God spoke to you and told you to run to the White House and

BREW IT!
Elijah didn't hesitate, because he knew God's voice.

POUR IT!
Drink in the flavor from the following Scriptures: Exodus 24:7; Numbers 7:89; Deuteronomy 28:1.

SAVOR IT!
Tell God you want to be confident in knowing his voice.

tell our president a few things, but I'm guessing you'd tend to wonder, *Was that* God *telling me that? Or was it Satan trying to mess me up and get me to do something really stupid? Or are those just my own thoughts wanting to do something important?*

Elijah didn't have to wonder if it was God speaking to him. Why? Because he knew the voice of God. And he responded immediately. This mountain man walked right into the king's quarters and told him what a twit he was. (Okay, he may not have used the word *twit*. He probably told him he was evil.) He said that God wasn't pleased with the way things were going, and if Ahab didn't make a turn for the better and get the people to start worshipping God instead of that stupid little statue of Baal, he'd be mighty sorry because a famine would sweep the country and there wouldn't be any rain—which not only meant no crops but also put a damper on summer fun. How can you go water-skiing, swimming, tubing, or rafting without *water*? Pretty basic.

Well, other than talking in run-on sentences, Elijah did a good job delivering the message. But King Ahab didn't listen. Next move? God told Elijah to head to the mountains.

THE MOUNTAIN MAN

We don't know for sure the location of the mountain Elijah fled to, but I live in Colorado Springs, Colorado, and I like to think that if God were going to send anyone to the mountains for a few years, it would probably be the Colorado Rockies. So let's just assume that's where Elijah went, okay?

I know what you're thinking: *Even the Colorado Rockies can get boring after a few years . . . all alone . . . no food . . . nothing to do.* Wrongo. The Bible tells us (see 1 Kings 17:2-4) that God provided for Elijah's needs. We read that the Lord sent ravens to bring him food every day. (Not bad room service, huh? I wouldn't mind a few birds flocking by *my* house every morning to drop off Egg McMuffins, a few cans of Coca-Cola, and a double-thick cheese pizza with pepperoni on top.)

He had it made! Okay . . . he *was* alone. But do you know what I think probably happened? I can imagine God tampering with the power system on the ski lifts—setting the whole thing on automatic—and I can see Elijah popping moguls, doing jumps, and having the time of his life on a snowboard!

A few years passed. And just about the time when his parallels were almost perfect (ski term for making reeeeally quick, sharp turns left and right and left and right and . . . well, you get the picture), God spoke. Know what he said? No need to guess—I'll tell you.

God told Elijah to go back down the mountain and talk to King Ahab again. (Can't stay on a spiritual mountaintop forever, can we?)

Again, I don't know what *you'd* think if God told you that. But I might wonder or question. *Nah, that can't be God, because he's the one who sent me here! Hmmm. Must be Satan trying to get me away from being where God wants me. Or maybe it's just me wanting to go back home and see my friends and family.*

Elijah had no questions. He didn't doubt for a second. He *knew* it was God. How? Because *he knew the voice of the Lord.* And when God spoke, he responded!

Wouldn't you like to know God's voice that well? Wouldn't it be great to hear God's voice, recognize it, and be so confident in it that you respond in immediate obedience? Good news! You *can* know God's voice. It doesn't take a degree or an Ivy League education or a special certificate. If a mountain man can learn the sound of God's voice, you can too.

MOUNTAIN MAN GOES TO TOWN

You can probably imagine how King Ahab reacted when he saw Elijah heading for his presidential suite. He pointed his bony finger at God's man and screamed, "You!" (Man of great verbiage, that Ahab.) "You're the one who's responsible for this mess!"

And it really was a mess. Just as Elijah had predicted, God had withheld the rains for several years. People were dying, the crops had withered, the country was a disaster.

But Elijah stood his ground. "Back off, Jack!" (Or something similar.) "I'm not the reason for this famine; you are! I told you this would happen. God has allowed our country to suffer because of the way you have chosen to rule."

"But . . . but . . . but, I . . ." (Be glad Ahab never spoke at one of your school assemblies. It would've taken him forever to get his point across!)

"Listen up, Ahab!" Elijah continued. "Almost the entire country is worshipping Baal. That's not right. God wants to turn the hearts of his people back to him."

"Well, I, ah . . ."

"Quit stammering, Ahab, and pay attention!" (Elijah was pretty confident, wasn't he? Would you talk to the president that way? Maybe you would if you knew beyond all doubt that God told you to do so. Again—the key is *knowing the voice of God*.)

"If there's one thing God can't stand, it's a lukewarm commitment," Elijah announced. "Be hot or cold, Ahab, but don't stand in the middle." He thought maybe he should make this part reeeeeally simple in case Ahab was having trouble understanding it. After all, Ahab wasn't the sharpest tool in the shed. If he was, he would've been serving God, right?) "In other words, decide to serve Jehovah or decide not to. You can't remain neutral."

"Neutral? But, I, ah . . ." (Yo, Ahab, get a life! Or at least a language.)

"You can't ride the fence, Ahab," Elijah warned. "Time to make a decision. What's it going to be? Serve God? Or worship your silly idols?"

That's a powerful message! And it still rings true today. God calls his children to be hot: sold-out, 100 percent committed, totally dvevoted to his lordship. What a radical way to live! If your lifestyle truly reflected this kind of dedication to Christ, people around you would be drawn to your boldness, your confidence, and your Christlikeness. Have you made the decision to quit riding the fence?

BREW IT!
Which side of the fence do you live on? Hot or cold?

POUR IT!
Drink in the flavor from the following Scriptures: Matthew 6:24; Colossians 3:2.

SAVOR IT!
Tell God you don't want to settle for being lukewarm. Ask him to help you become hot—100 percent dedicated to him.

BREW IT!

God wants you to be confident in your relationship with him. You don't have to prove anything. He's fully capable of proving himself!

POUR IT!

Drink in the flavor from the following Scripture: 1 Kings 18:21-27.

SAVOR IT!

Ask God to increase your confidence in his existence.

MOUNTAIN MAN ACCEPTS CHALLENGE

"Wait a second, Elijah!" King Ahab said. "Maybe I wouldn't mind serving your God if I knew he was really God. But I need to be sure."

"Tell you what," Elijah said. "Let's have a contest. You get the 450 prophets of Baal, and we'll have a showdown between you and your god and me and my God."

Sounded like an idea. (Not necessarily a *great* idea—why should we ask for proof of God's existence? Isn't that where faith comes in? But, it was an *idea* nonetheless.)

So, being the creative men they were, they decided on a terrific name. They called it "The Contest." (Wowsers!)

First Church of Baal got majorly excited. They had a humongous youth group. Like over five thousand teens. They decided this would be a great way to earn money for their surf 'n' swim trip to Jamaica. So they had special T-shirts printed that read "The Contest" and sold them for twenty-five dollars apiece.

The big day arrived and the Houston Astrodome was packed out. (Okay, maybe it wasn't the Astrodome but someplace kind of like that.)

John Madden—who usually only announced football stuff—was hired to commentate. He went through the rules: "Elijah has graciously let the Baal team go first. They'll drag their dead bull out here and pray to their god to burn it up. And guys, you're aware that you can't use kerosene or charcoal bits, aren't you? Okay, good.

"Then, after they've had a chance to prove the existence of their god, we'll give Elijah a shot with his dead bull. Let the games begin!"

The team of Baal pulled their carcass onstage while the First Church of Baal youth group sold popcorn, hot dogs, and those giant pretzels. The Baal team members danced around their bull and prayed loudly to their god. People watched closely. Reporters were crouched on the edge of their seats in the press box. Cameras zoomed in extra-close.

But nothing happened. The crowd grew restless. They wanted to see some action!

Finally, Elijah grew impatient. And being the good sport that he was (tee hee), here's what he said. (And this is straight from *The Living Bible*. I promise. Look it up yourself!) "You'll have to shout louder than that," he scoffed, "to catch the attention of your god! Perhaps he is talking to someone, or is out sitting on the toilet, or maybe he is away on a trip, or is asleep and needs to be wakened!" (1 Kings 18:27).

MOUNTAIN MAN TAKES CENTER STAGE

After Elijah had scoffed at the Baal team for failing to produce results, they began shouting and cutting themselves. They danced around the bull and prayed to Baal for hours. They were serious, weren't they? They were slashing themselves and causing blood to gush from their own bodies to show their false god how determined they were.

Aren't you glad you don't have to use drastic measures to get Jehovah's attention? He's as close as the whisper of his name. When you call on him, he's there. And do you realize there's absolutely nothing you can do to make him love you any more than he already does? There's also nothing you can do to make him love you any less! Cutting yourself, starving yourself, isolating yourself—it's all useless. God is crazy about you exactly as you are. He's in love with you right now!

Back to the story. The Baal team had been messing around all day long. Now it was evening, and still nothing had happened. So Elijah stepped forward and told the contest helpers to clear the stage. They had to hose it down because of all the blood. As they dragged Elijah's dead bull to center stage, he gave them some interesting instructions.

"Dig a trench all the way around the stage and fill it with water," he said. So they did. "Fill it again," he instructed. So they did. "And again," he continued. (Hmmm. You may think filling trenches with water wasn't the best strategy for starting a fire . . . but Elijah was plugged into a mighty power source, remember?)

Finally, they had thrown so much water onstage, the bull was literally lying in a pool of H2O. Then I can imagine Elijah stepping *away* from the microphone so no one could hear him. I think he probably prayed something like this:

"God, I *know* you're God. I have no doubt that you created this entire universe and you have more power than anything anywhere. I'm not asking you to burn this bull to prove your power to me, because—like I said—I'm already convinced of your power.

"I *am* asking you to burn my bull, though, so these thousands of doubting, questioning, lost people can be convinced that you are the only true God."

Then I imagine a hush fell across the stadium. And taking the microphone center stage, Elijah probably boomed in his deepest and loudest voice, "Father God of heaven and earth, *burn this bull!*"

BREW IT!
Are you still struggling with the same doubts you had when you first came to Christ? Those need to be settled so you can move forward in your walk with him.

POUR IT!
Drink in the flavor from the following Scripture: 1 Kings 18:28-37.

SAVOR IT!
Ask God to show you any doubts you have that are prohibiting solid spiritual growth. Nail those down.

BREW IT!

Again, it takes discipline to get to know the voice of your heavenly Father. Are you willing to make the effort necessary to learn his voice?

POUR IT!

Drink in the flavor from the following Scriptures: 1 Kings 19:11-15; Jeremiah 11:4; 1 Peter 1:13-16.

SAVOR IT!

Ask God to show you anything that's keeping you from hearing his voice. Commit that area to him.

MOUNTAIN MAN PLAYS WITH FIRE

After Elijah prayed, the dead animal was suddenly wrapped in flames. It was incredible! People all over the arena began to realize they'd been duped into believing a false god. They saw this power, and they wanted what they saw.

It was really pretty cool. Kind of like a giant evangelistic crusade. People got up from where they were seated and went forward to give their lives to God.

Elijah wasted no time. Microphone still in hand, he exclaimed, "If you came on a bus, it'll wait. If you came with friends, they'll wait. There's nothing more important right now than where you stand with the creator of the universe!"

Then he grabbed some of the new converts and convinced them to help him slaughter the prophets of Baal. (I know, I know. It sounds terrible and gross. But before Jesus came to die for our sins, God had no choice but to abolish evil through death. Elijah knew he *had* to wipe out the Baal gang, or they'd travel to the next town and start the same old thing all over again.)

After all the prophets of Baal were killed, God spoke to Elijah and told him to head back to the mountains. (Back to the mountains? You're kidding! With all *this* action going on? Why? Because God wanted to talk with him, that's why.)

And again, Elijah didn't question whether it was God's voice or the voice of Satan or his own thinking. He responded immediately because (you already know this part, so read it out loud) *he knew the voice of the Lord.*

Remember on May 6 when we started talking about God speaking to you and how it takes daily discipline to learn to tune in to his voice and shut out everything else?

Here's what happened. When Elijah got to the mountain, he waited for God to speak to him. All of a sudden there was a terrible blast (tornado material)—so strong that the mountain started splitting. And there was an earthquake. And a fire.

Wouldn't you think all these spectacular events meant God had spoken? But Elijah waited. He hadn't heard God's voice in any of the commotion. After all that, there was the sound of a soft whisper. And when Elijah heard it, he knew it was the Lord.

Do you get it? Most of the time when God speaks to you, it won't come in a thundering voice or an e-mail from heaven. We wish it would happen that way. Things would seem a lot easier. But most of the time when God speaks to you, his voice will come in a gentle whisper. And guess what—that whisper is going to come from *within*.

GOD'S VOICE

If God's voice comes as a whisper, and if it comes from within your heart, do you know what that means? It means when you learn to tune everything else out (TV, music, computer, friends) and tune in to *his* voice, you're going to deepen your relationship with him.

Why? Because the more you know his voice, the more you'll respond to his voice. The better you know God, the more confident a Christian you'll be.

A disciple who knows God's voice = a disciple who responds when God speaks = God working through your life to impact those around you!

A Christian who knows God's voice = a Christian who is *confident*. A confident Christian = one who will dare to take a stand in school, at work, and at home.

So the bottom line is learning to recognize God's voice and then responding in obedience to his voice. Remember, God can speak in a soft whisper from your heart or your mind. He can speak through your pastor or other spiritual leaders. He can speak through your parents and even your friends. He *is* speaking. Are you hearing him?

Tell God that you want to be able to hear his voice no matter what's going on around you! So when you're driving downtown, amidst the blaring of horns and screeching of brakes, if he speaks you'll hear him. Or if he speaks to you during the shouting, clapping, and whooping of a football game, you'll hear his voice. Or between classes, if God should choose to speak to you, you'll hear his voice above the ringing of bells, the scuffling of feet, and the chitchat of fellow students.

So back to the question posed by Samantha on May 6: How can you grow closer to God? How can you truly know him as your Friend *and* Father? Spend time with him. Talk to him. Tell him everything that's going on in your life. Converse with him. Read the Bible. Study the Scriptures. As you do this, you'll fall in love with Jesus Christ more and more every single day.

And finally . . . listen to the sound of his voice!

BREW IT!

How close are you and God? I hope he's as real to you as your fingers. I hope he's as close as your breath. Strive to make him the first thing on your mind when you get up in the morning and the last thing on your mind when you go to bed at night.

POUR IT!

Drink in the flavor from the following Scriptures: Psalm 66:19; 69:9-15; 73:1.

SAVOR IT!

Spend some time today simply listening to God's voice.

STRATEGIZING VICTORY

I love children's books, and one of my favorites is *Alexander, Who Used to Be Rich Last Sunday* by Judith Viorst. It's the story of a boy who received one dollar from his grandparents one Sunday and over the course of a week spent it frivolously on a variety of things.

Though it's really just a fun book for kids, after I read it I couldn't help thinking about finances. If we want to be financially successful, we have to plan for it, don't we? We seek financial advice; invest in stocks, bonds, or other moneymaking projects; and watch for opportunities that promise consistent and good returns.

What many of us don't realize is that to some degree, this principle also holds true in our spiritual lives. If we want to be spiritually successful (live victoriously), there are certain truths that need to be set in motion. In other words, we need to plan for spiritual consistency instead of just expecting to evolve into mature, godly giants.

The apostle Paul asks a penetrating question in Galatians. He recognized that the people he was writing to had been doing well spiritually. In the past tense. And the question he asked was right to the point: "Who interfered with you? You were doing great! Who's been holding you back? It can't be God. It takes only one person who's off course to knock the rest of you off" (my paraphrase of Galatians 5:7-9).

Place yourself into that scenario. Where are you right now, spiritually? Doing well? Or used to be doing well? Are you living in a spiritual past tense or present tense?

What's your strategy? How do you plan to do well spiritually? How can you live consistently with victory in your life? In other words, how can you triumph over sin and live the way God wants you to live?

Again, you need a good strategy to win. A solid game plan. The apostle Peter presents a winning combination in 2 Peter 1. It almost reads like a recipe, and if we follow this specific strategy, we're making plans to live victoriously on a daily basis. I'll list these verses at the end of today's devotional so you can take a peek at what he says. And as you read it, notice the victory ingredients as well as the strategy to obtain them.

BREW IT!
In 1 Corinthians 9, the apostle Paul compares the Christian life to a race. Keep that image in mind, and let's just pretend that the apostle Peter is our coach. We're headed out for a track meet, and he's in the locker room with us going over our strategy. Think in those terms as you read the following Scriptures and pray.

POUR IT!
Drink in the flavor from the following Scriptures:
1 Corinthians 9:24-27;
Galatians 5:7-9; 2 Peter 1:2-8.

SAVOR IT!
Ask God to help you develop a winning strategy—based on his Word—to live a victorious Christian life.

A WINNING STRATEGY

Let's take a look at a strategy that will help you maintain your spiritual victory:

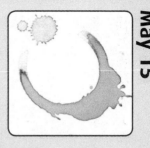

1. *Learn to know him better and better.*

To run fast and consistent on the track, you have to know your event. If you're a sprinter, you'll run differently than a long-distance runner. The more times you practice your event and the better you know all the ins and outs, the better you'll be able to pace yourself.

To be victorious in the race of Christianity, you must find out all you can about your Creator (because he, in turn will guide and mold you to be the best "runner"—or disciple—you can be).

I used to be a public high school teacher. I taught speech, drama, and English. Each year my students would go through the process of getting to know me. They realized that the better they knew me the more they knew what to expect for tests, homework assignments, and class environment. Being successful in class, to a degree, depends on how well you learn what's expected—or, in other words, how well you learn the teacher's style.

Peter tells us to get to know the Lord better and better. It's not just a once-in-a-while get-together. It's a process. It's continually getting to know him. And as we know him better, we begin to understand him more. That's when we reap the benefits of his friendship (power, joy, and security).

Makes sense, but how does that work? you may be thinking.

Getting to know someone takes action and effort on your part, doesn't it? When you establish a friendship with someone, you're anxious to talk with her, and you look forward to spending time with her.

It works the same way in your relationship with Christ. To know the Lord intimately requires some action and work on your part. So the first part of your strategy in a victorious Christian life is to know your Creator as well as you can. The apostle Paul tells us in his letter to the Ephesians to imitate Christ. In other words, it's okay to be a copycat when you're copying the Master. The more you imitate the lifestyle of Jesus, the more you get to know him and start becoming like him.

You see, the goal of a mature disciple is not living close to Christ. Rather, the mature Christian wants to live inside of Christ. Not just next to him, but a part of him. The Holy Spirit has the power to make that happen, but it requires total surrender on your part. And the Holy Spirit is the one who will help you imitate your Father.

BREW IT!
As you copycat the Master, you'll become more like him. And as you become more like him, you'll experience spiritual victory.

POUR IT!
Drink in the flavor from the following Scriptures: Psalm 86:11-13; 119:47-48; Ephesians 5:1

SAVOR IT!
Ask God to help you imitate him in every area of your life.

BREW IT!

Do you tend to be stubborn when God tries to change something in your life? Be honest. Change can be hard, but when God is the author of change, it's always for your best! You can trust him.

POUR IT!

Drink in the flavor from the following Scriptures: Deuteronomy 30:15-20; 31:6.

SAVOR IT!

Ask God to give you a teachable spirit. Tell him you're willing to let him change whatever he wants in your life to give you spiritual victory.

CONTINUING THE WINNING STRATEGY

The next step in your strategy to experience spiritual victory is to:

2. *Follow his strategy—not your own.*

If you're competing in a track meet, one of your top priorities is to carry out the instructions your coach has given you. One runner told me her coach had suggested that she hold her fingers a certain way when she ran. "He told me to run as if I'm holding a dime between my thumb and first finger. I hold both hands this way the entire time I'm running."

"Why?" I said. "What does that accomplish?"

"If I don't hold my fingers this way," she explained, "my hands just sort of flop around when I run. This gives me a specific thing to do with them and helps me focus more intently on what I'm doing."

Hmmm. Makes sense. It also made sense that she didn't argue with her coach or try to talk him into a plan she had created.

To live a victorious Christian life, you have to have a strategy for doing so. It's important that you adopt God's strategy for winning instead of stubbornly demanding to live out your own plan. After all, your Creator knows far better than you do what you're up against, what your future holds, and how you can be victorious.

How does it work? Just like the key to getting to know God better, the key to adopting his strategy is to spend time in prayer and reading his personal letter to you (the Bible). The more time you spend with your heavenly Father, the clearer his strategy for your life becomes. As you get to know him better and better, his Holy Spirit will reveal his truth to you on a daily basis.

By working out consistently with your track coach, you learn his strategy. You meet with him daily at practice. You listen to his instructions. And because you know he wants you to win, you're willing to change the way you start the race; you're willing to shift your strategy to his. God, too, wants you to be a winner. The most victorious Christians are those who are willing to be flexible, moldable, and teachable. They don't say, "But, God, I don't want to do it that way! I think I can make it work my way." They simply say, "I trust you, Father. Help me obey. I want your will."

YOU CAN ENCOURAGE OTHERS!

The next step in your strategy for spiritual victory is to:

3. Be an encourager.

When you're competing in a track meet, it always helps to see and hear people on the sidelines (and in the stands) cheering you on. Many times that little extra encouragement can affect the outcome of a race.

In our walk with God, too, we need to be cheered on by our Christian friends. It makes a difference to know someone is praying for you, doesn't it? The apostle Paul mentions a huge grandstand of saints who are cheering you on right now!

Likewise, to be consistently victorious in your relationship with God, you need to be an encourager. Plan to cheer others on. Affirm those around you. Find the good things in others and focus your attention on those positive qualities. Build others up. Put your arm around someone. Make a phone call. Sit with a visitor at your church. All these things add up to making a difference in someone's life. That, in turn, helps you maintain your own spiritual consistency.

And if you're thinking, *Makes sense, but how does it work?* we'll unpack this strategy. Again, like (1) getting to know God, and (2) following his strategy for your life, (3) being an encourager requires action! It's hard work, but it's a necessary part of becoming all God wants you to be.

BREW IT!
Who are two people you can encourage today? And what, specifically, can you do to encourage them?

POUR IT!
Drink in the flavor from the following Scriptures: Hebrews 3:13; 10:25; 12:1.

SAVOR IT!
Ask God to make you aware of people who need encouragement.

We live in a world that encourages sarcasm. Every sitcom is filled with dialogue laced with fast comebacks, sarcastic one-liners, and quick put-downs. It has become not only accepted but expected for us to be sarcastic and short with others.

Breaking that mold will require active thinking, doing, and being on your part. It's often easier to put someone down in a joking manner than to build him up.

But guess who the victorious people are? They're the ones who have made a habit of affirming those around them. Think about it: Whom do you absolutely love being around? People who make you feel good about yourself, right?

Every time you help someone else feel worthwhile, the encouragement comes back to you. God, in turn, affirms you and sets you on that streak of spiritual victory we're talking about. Again, we're talking about imitating the Father. Jesus was an amazing encourager. He encouraged little children to come to him—in spite of all the adults who wanted "front-row seats" at his public speaking sessions.

And Jesus encourages you. His greatest desire is for you to experience spiritual victory. He wants to make you a winner. But as he encourages you, he expects you, in turn, to encourage others.

MAKE ENCOURAGEMENT A HABIT

Encouraging others requires conscious action. Several years ago, Christian contemporary singer Steven Curtis Chapman cut a music video called *The Great Adventure*. I was invited to join the cast and crew for the making of the video while I was interviewing Steven for a magazine cover story.

We shot in the Teton Range in Jackson Hole, Wyoming. I had a bit part as an extra in the video. It was my job to sit on a fence and toss a cowboy hat in the air. I'm in the video three times, but if you blink, you'll miss me.

Now, granted that was really a teeny-tiny role. Steven, of course, had the major part. After all, it was his video! He obviously had a lot on his mind—cues to remember, camera angles, words to the song, etc. Yet he still took the time to stop and encourage me—an extra in a bit role.

As I watched him throughout the shoot, I saw him doing the same thing with other crew members. The stylist who applied his makeup. The one who cut his hair. The wardrobe personnel. I began to realize that for Steven, being an encourager was a way of life. He had developed a healthy habit of affirming those around him, until it had almost become second nature.

That's part of being "Jesus" to our world, isn't it? And as we reflect him . . . again, we're planning for spiritual victory. What did you do yesterday to encourage someone? It takes a conscious effort, doesn't it? Are you willing to do that?

The greatest encouragement Jesus gave you was to go to the cross and give up his life. Is it really that tough to verbally encourage those around you? As you do, you're imitating your Father. And as you become more like him, you're reaping spiritual victory.

BREW IT!
Wouldn't it be great if people thought of you as an encourager? What if that was part of your reputation? When you genuinely learn to encourage others, everyone wants to be with you. We all love hanging around someone who affirms us and makes us feel good—if it's done genuinely. Strive to make encouragement part of your lifestyle.

POUR IT!
Drink in the flavor from the following Scriptures: Romans 1:11-12; Colossians 2:2; Hebrews 6:18.

SAVOR IT!
Ask God to help you develop a lifestyle of encouraging others.

SPIRITUAL SUCCESS

God wants you to be spiritually successful even more than you do! He died for your spiritual victory. But it won't happen if you run the Christian race carelessly, without aim or purpose. To be successful, we have to plan.

Do you need to spend time praying about how you can attain spiritual victory? Nope. God has already outlined his plan. He's already given you a specific strategy to follow. Let's recap:

1. *Learn to know him better and better.*
2. *Follow his strategy—not your own.*
3. *Be an encourager.*

Instead of praying about how to live victoriously, focus your prayers on *being an infector*. Remember the verses in Galatians 5:7-9 we talked about on May 14? The apostle Paul pointed out that it took just one person to infect an entire group. He was talking about a negative action. But infection doesn't need to be negative; it can actually be a positive thing!

You're either infected (affected by others), or you're an infector (affecting others). If you're infected negatively, seek God's forgiveness and move forward.

If you're an infector, you're either infecting others positively or negatively. If you're the one who's always complaining, bringing disharmony to your youth group, being negative, or exhibiting pride or selfishness, then it doesn't take a genius to figure out that you're infecting those around you in an extremely harmful way. (It only takes one, remember?)

BREW IT!
Ready to infect your world in a positive way? Think of three positive bits of gossip you can spread tomorrow; then think of three people whom you can positively infect.

POUR IT!
Drink in the flavor from the following Scriptures: Isaiah 1:17; Acts 14:21-22; Romans 12:8.

SAVOR IT!
Ask God to help you infect those around you in a positive way!

But if you're infecting in a positive manner, then you're spreading love and affirmation to those around you. Determine to be a positive infector. (It only takes one, remember?) What a huge difference you can make on your campus and in your church!

Being an infector is like spreading gossip. When you gossip negatively about someone, you're hurting him; you're destroying his reputation. But it's possible to be a positive gossip by spreading genuine and kind things about others. For example: "Hey, Jessica, have you noticed how Matt always tries to include others? That's pretty cool!"

That's spreading positive gossip. That's being a positive infector.

"Pastor Steve, I really appreciate the time and energy you invest in our Bible study. In fact, I was bragging about you yesterday to some other students on my campus."

Again, you're being a positive infector. Imagine . . . if you always went around infecting people with positive affirmation, what an incredible difference it would make!

BREW IT!
We're talking about total surrender again, aren't we? That's the key to victory in Christ! It's also the key to living a holy life and fulfilling God's personal plan for you. God doesn't call you to victory and walk away without helping you become victorious. He'll never ask you to do what he's not willing to accomplish through you.

POUR IT!
Drink in the flavor from the following Scriptures: Isaiah 66:9; Jeremiah 18:2-6; 2 Peter 1:2-8.

SAVOR IT!
Ask God to bring to your mind anything in your life that's stopping you from experiencing spiritual victory.

FOLLOWING THE STRATEGY
Remember the children's story about Alexander that we chatted about on May 14? Alexander wasn't financially stable because he didn't plan how he was going to spend his money. If you're not spiritually victorious, it's because you're not actively following God's plan for spiritual victory. Again, let's review our game plan:

1. *Learn to know him better and better.*
2. *Follow his strategy—not your own.*
3. *Be an encourager.*

Your strategy is specifically explained in 2 Peter 1:2-8. Like a detailed recipe, follow each step for attaining and maintaining spiritual victory. Again, you don't need to spend time praying about whether God wants to give you spiritual victory. Instead, spend time praying about becoming a positive infector.

Also, pray about following the strategy he's given you. It's obvious he wants you to be victorious; he paid the highest price imaginable for your victory. He's even outlined your strategy through his Holy Word. Now, like the old Nike commercial: JUST DO IT!

Of course, you're not expected to do this on your own. That's where the precious and powerful Holy Spirit comes in. He wants to empower you to live out this strategy. He can empower you to live a victorious Christian life. He can help you become consistent and rock-solid in your relationship with the Father.

So don't even attempt this on your own. Admit to God that you need his help to live a victorious Christian life. Tell him you want to follow his game plan. Surrender your way to his way. Give up your strategy for his. Relinquish the dream of winning on your own, and submit to winning on his terms.

INTO SPACE

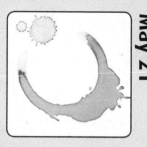

In June 2004, a privately built rocket plane soared into space, giving everyone who has ever dreamed of being an astronaut hopes of making it off the planet someday. The world's first space tourism company, founded by Richard Branson, wants to ferry passengers through space starting within the next couple of years.

Many engineers and scientists don't think it can be done by then. It took three years to build *Mercury*, the first U.S. manned vehicle to fly in space. It took seven years to build *Apollo*, the ship that took astronauts to the moon. And *SpaceShipOne*, the first privately developed manned spaceship, took five years to develop.

SpaceShipOne seats just three people, and its designer, Burt Rutan, has said it won't be used for commercial flights. He vows to make his new ships one hundred times safer than any vehicle that has ever flown in space. That's good, because *SpaceShipOne* doesn't have a great track record so far. On its first spaceflight, June 21, 2004, a control system failed. During a September 29, 2004, flight, it rolled rapidly forty times as it shot toward space.

If designers like Burt Rutan and entrepreneurs like Richard Branson can overcome the technological problems and government restrictions, they can make a lot of money. More than 7,500 people have asked for more information on spaceflights. And more than one hundred people have put down 10 percent of a $100,000 payment with Space Adventures, a company that connects would-be astronauts with companies building spaceships.

If it's new, wild, adventurous, and extreme, people want it. We want to fly through the frontier of space, zip through time, and experience the utmost. And while all that is perfectly okay, we still need to remember that often it's the tried and true that offers security, foundation, and peace. In our quest for adventure, we often lose sight of what's around us and who is right here next to us.

You may not get the chance to shuttle through space, but you do have the opportunity to focus on some people who have been around for a while: your family. No, they may not be as extreme and exciting as you desire, but they've seen you through the good and bad times. They loved you when you were throwing up with the flu, when you lost the track meet, when you failed the test, and even when you wrecked the car.

Make it a point to spend some quality time with them this week. Focus on them today. Hug your parents. Compliment your brother and sister. Tell your mom and dad you love them. Don't be so quick to go after the newest fad or adventure if it means overlooking those around you.

BREW IT!
We'll never appreciate the possibility of soaring into space until we truly value the relationships we have right here on earth.

POUR IT!
Drink in the flavor from the following Scriptures: Psalm 73:21-26; 77:13-14; 91:1-6.

SAVOR IT!
Thank God for your family. Pray for them daily.

BREW IT!
Try a few random acts of kindness this week: Clean the house without being asked; make dinner for your family; help a younger brother or sister with homework; do something for a neighbor—pick up their newspaper and take it to the door, mow the lawn, deliver some cookies; write your pastor a note of appreciation.

POUR IT!
Drink in the flavor from the following Scriptures:
Luke 6:35; 1 Corinthians 13:4; Ephesians 4:32.

SAVOR IT!
Ask God to teach you to be kind regardless of how you're treated.

WHAT'S GOING ON?

A few years ago, Washington Wizards basketball center Brendan Haywood was suspended for the first three games of the season for fighting with Chicago Bulls player Antonio Davis, who was suspended for two games. Antonio lost about $267,000 because of the suspensions. Brendan's suspensions cost him about $58,000. Before he threw punches at Antonio, Brendan fought with Bulls guard Kirk Hinrich. Kirk was fined $10,000.

What's going on? Why all the fighting? Healthy competition is one thing, but when it ends up in anger-induced fighting, it's not healthy anymore. If we can't compete without fighting, we shouldn't be competing.

Wouldn't you think with such a high price tag on suspension, professional athletes would learn to control their tempers? Something's gone terribly wrong with our society. We're too quick to fight. We get angry too fast. And we often act as though there aren't any consequences.

Jesus commanded us to love one another. How can we follow that command if we're always angry? He also commanded us to show kindness to others. Love and kindness actually go hand in hand, don't they? When you love someone, kindness comes more easily.

But Jesus was even kind to those who *didn't* love him. To the soldiers who arrested him, the ones who cursed him, and even Judas, who betrayed him, Jesus continued to show kindness. He even asked his Father to forgive them for crucifying him.

Are you familiar with the book *In the Presence of My Enemies* by Gracia Burnham with Dean Merrill? Gracia and her husband, Martin, were missionaries in the Philippines when they were kidnapped by terrorists and held as prisoners in the jungle for more than a year.

Though they were always respectful to their captors, after several months, Martin told his wife that God had told him to go a step further. He felt compelled to serve their captors—to be kind to them. Martin died in the jungle, but Gracia lived to tell how his actions had a positive influence on her attitude.

Can you imagine how professional sports would change if opponents went out of their way to show respect and kindness to the other team? Can you imagine how much faster Christianity would spread if you and I went out of our way for others? If we truly started treating people with kindness?

THE REAL THING . . . OR A SUBSTITUTE?

If you've always dreamed of sleeping in the Lincoln bed at the White House but knew you'd never get to, you're in luck. The History Company in Ithaca, New York, builds reproductions of the famous bed. They take great care in creating the grapevine design and the eight-foot-high mahogany headboard.

Because the Lincoln bed is considered one of the most prized possessions in the White House, people are automatically drawn to it. But the replica isn't cheap. It sells for $6,900. The History Company also builds reproductions of the Resolute desk in the Oval Office. You can see the replica in the Clinton Presidential Library.

Even if someone is a die-hard American history buff, it's still hard to imagine why he'd be willing to shell out almost $7,000 for a replica. I can understand paying $7,000 for the actual Lincoln bed. That would be quite a historical souvenir. But $6,900 for a bed that's not even the real thing? It's clearly a substitute.

In a sense, millions of people are using substitutes to persuade themselves that they have the real thing when it comes to fulfillment. That's why drugs, alcohol, and smokes are so popular; they provide a temporary buzz or a phony happiness. But it's only a matter of time until the fake fulfillment wears off.

BREW IT!
Take a close look at yourself. Have you fallen in love with the genuineness of Jesus Christ, or are you making do with false substitutes?

POUR IT!
Drink in the flavor from the following Scriptures: Galatians 5:22-23; Ephesians 4:22-24; Philippians 2:9-11.

SAVOR IT!
Seek God's forgiveness for allowing anything to take the place of Christ in your life.

People who are desperately seeking love often search for it in sexual relationships outside of marriage. Yet they, too, are soon unfulfilled and realize their deep emptiness. There's an old, old song called "Only Jesus Can Satisfy Your Soul." Another song—not quite as old, but still dated—is "Jesus Is the Answer." Both represent absolute truth.

As Christians we should know this. Yet we, too, sometimes turn in the wrong direction to something we hope will bring fulfillment but is only a substitute at best.

Every person in the world longs to be fulfilled, loved, and feel their life has meaning. And everyone who's experiencing an intimate, growing relationship with Christ *is* loved, fulfilled, and has purpose in life. But if we don't allow God to be all he wants in our lives, we'll be tempted to turn to substitutes.

We get a taste of what God wants to produce in our lives when we read the list of the fruit of the Spirit in Galatians 5. If you place real fruit next to finely crafted artificial fruit, it can be difficult to discern the difference. They can look extremely similar. The telling sign comes in the taste. Once you bite into a genuine strawberry, you fall in love with the sweetness. Once you bite into an artificial strawberry, you're disgusted with the plastic in your mouth. Don't settle for cheap artificial substitutes when you can have the real thing.

BREW IT!
Do you care enough about others to risk your job and your well-being to help?

POUR IT!
Drink in the flavor from the following Scriptures: Nehemiah 1:1-11; 2:1-5.

SAVOR IT!
Ask God to create a genuine tenderness in your heart.

THE WALL

Nehemiah was an outstanding basketball player. In fact, he was on a full athletic scholarship at Susa Community College. He was also a strong leader on campus and was enjoying his junior year as student body president.

One of his friends, a high school senior from his hometown of Jerusalem, came to visit him and look over the campus during spring break. Nehemiah was ecstatic to see his old pal, and over a caramel latte at Starbucks, he casually asked how things were "back home."

Putting down the coffee and straightening his chair, the friend replied, "Well, things are not good. The wall of Jerusalem is still torn down, and the gates are burned."

The Bible tells us that Nehemiah was so disturbed by the shocking news that he cried. During the next several days, he refused to eat. Instead, he poured out his heart in prayer to God.

Maybe you've been in a crisis situation similar to Nehemiah's. You know what it feels like to be so bothered about something that even to consider eating seems absurd, because food is the last thing on your mind.

Nehemiah was concerned about his hometown. I can imagine what that feels like. I live in Colorado Springs, Colorado, but my hometown is Oklahoma City. When my mom called in tears just moments after the bombing of the Murrah Building on April 19, 1995, I wanted to fly home and make sure my friends and loved ones were okay.

That's exactly what Nehemiah wanted to do when his high school buddy informed him that the walls surrounding the city were down.

The city wall was important. As long as a strong, sturdy wall was intact, the people inside were safe from enemy attacks. When the wall stood high, the spiritual condition of the people was sturdy as well. The wall symbolized not only *physical* strength and protection but also *righteousness*. That wall was important!

Nehemiah had a great off-campus job. He worked part-time for the king. Most kings would kill for a worker like him. He always punched in on time, never took more than fifteen minutes for a coffee break, and gave terrific visitor tours around the palace.

No wonder his employer took a special liking to him. Noticing that the collegian was a little down, the king asked if anything was wrong. Nehemiah came right to the point. "My hometown is a wreck! The gates have been burned and the wall that surrounds the city is down. Sir, that's my city—my family and my friends! Could I have an indefinite leave of absence to go home and help restore the city wall?"

ACME CONSTRUCTION CREW: NOW HIRING

It's obvious that Nehemiah had a tender heart. He loved the people in his hometown enough to do something about their dire situation. It's also obvious that he was a bold man. Do those two traits seem opposite—tenderness and boldness? When used for God, they actually complement each other!

The king responded cheerfully and quickly granted Nehemiah's request to go home and rebuild Jerusalem's walls. The collegian packed his bags and walked away from his basketball scholarship, his great-paying job, and his student council position to reconstruct the needed walls in his hometown.

He hit the radio stations for publicity and even put flyers on cars in shopping mall parking lots. Nehemiah finally recruited a good group of volunteer workers and set them to the task.

Meanwhile, the neighboring governors Sanballat and Tobiah heard about what was going on and began making plans to thwart the construction. With the wall down, Sanballat and Tobiah had free rein to walk in and out of the city, flaunting their wickedness and working to sway the citizens to their twisted political views. They knew that if the wall was rebuilt, their influence over the people within the city would end. So they tried to distract and discourage the workers by hurling verbal insults at them.

"Hey, Nehemiah! Where'd you get your construction license—out of a Cracker Jack box?"

"You call *that* thing a wall? I've seen stronger stuff built out of LEGOS!"

"Nehemiah, my *grandmother* could build stronger walls than that!"

Nehemiah warned his men not to stop working. "Don't pay any attention to Sanballat and Tobiah. We are doing the most important thing in the world—rebuilding the wall of righteousness. We will *not* stop!"

It's obvious Nehemiah was committed to what God had called him to do. He was determined to fulfill his purpose. Do you have purpose for your life? Are you making time to seek God's will on a daily basis? Are you asking, "Lord, what is it you want me to do?"

Knowing God's will means actively pursuing God. If you're in consistent pursuit of your heavenly Father, he'll make his will clear to you. If you're unsure of God's will, seek him more intently.

Nehemiah's heart was in line with his heavenly Father's. His greatest desire was to rebuild the wall around Jerusalem, because he knew that's exactly what God had called him to do.

BREW IT!
When you know God's will and throw yourself into it, you find fulfillment and purpose. When you know God's will and run from it (as Jonah the Old Testament prophet did), you're miserable. (See the devotionals on September 22–23.)

POUR IT!
Drink in the flavor from the following Scriptures: Nehemiah 2:18-20; 4:1-3; James 1:5-8.

SAVOR IT!
Tell God you want to pursue him more actively.

BREW IT!
When you're doing God's will, there will always be people who try to thwart your work.

POUR IT!
Drink in the flavor from the following Scriptures: Isaiah 59:21; 62:6-7; 66:9.

SAVOR IT!
Tell God you want to be more focused on doing his will.

STICKS AND STONES

When Sanballat and Tobiah realized the insults weren't going to distract Nehemiah and his workers, they decided to use an all-out physical attack. They began firing arrows and hurling stones at the crew. Nehemiah, calmly downing a Twinkie, instructed half of the men to deck themselves in the armor of God while standing guard against the enemy's attacks, and the other half to continue building the wall. (For more information on the armor of God, see devotionals on February 20–26.)

When you read about the armor of God in Ephesians 6:13-17, you'll notice there's no armor for our backs. The front is amply covered from our head down to our shoes, but the fact that there's no armor for the back tells us we're unprotected if we turn and run from God's assignment. Nehemiah wasn't about to run. Neither was he going to quit. He was determined to complete the task God had given him.

It didn't take Sanballat and Tobiah long to realize that God's armor couldn't be penetrated, so they put their heads together and came up with master plans A, B, C, and D.

The next morning they implemented Plan A. As the men were arriving for work, Sanballat and Tobiah set up a lemonade stand right across the street from the construction site. Glowing with all the fake charm they could gather, they tried to entice the men with cold drinks.

"Listen, guys, I know we gave you a hard time the other day, but we realize now what a super job you're doing for your city. And to show our admiration, we're offering you complimentary glasses of lemonade anytime you want it during this hot, scorching, humid day."

Nehemiah quickly instructed his men not to stop for *anything*. So they worked consistently, and the two neighboring governors got waterlogged from trying to drink twenty-five gallons of hot, pink lemonade. Sanballat and Tobiah were forced to move to Plan B. The next morning, after Acme Brick Company delivered a fresh supply of bricks for the wall, the two governors invited Nehemiah and his men to a "special dinner."

"Look, Nehemiah, we admire the work you're doing; we really do. And to show our appreciation for a job well done, we want you and your entire crew to be our guests of honor at a barbecued rib party tonight right after you punch out for the day."

A TEMPTING OFFER

A barbecue party sounded great! The construction crew was always tired and hungry at the end of the day, and the thought of barbecued ribs tickled their taste buds. Nehemiah's instructions to his men, however, were firm. "Men, we will *not* be side-tracked. We will *not* stop."

No problem. Sanballat and Tobiah pulled out Plan C. They did their homework. They sent some FBI agents to SCC (Susa Community College) and found out that Nehemiah had walked away from a full basketball scholarship to rebuild the wall. They knew athletics were important to him and could possibly be his weak spot.

"Nehemiah," Sanballat said, "we realize we've given you a hard time about rebuilding the wall. But the past is over, and we'd like to do our part to help bridge the gap between our cities."

Tobiah piped in. "We've decided to sponsor an inter-city basketball tournament. We'll coach the teams from our cities, and we want you to coach the Jerusalem team."

Nehemiah's interest was rising high. He knew he'd make a terrific coach.

"Of course," Sanballat said, "this means you'll need to take a little time off from the construction site to recruit your players, teach them strategy, and get them into shape."

BREW IT!
Make it a habit to seek God's direction and wisdom in your choices.

POUR IT!
Drink in the flavor from the following Scriptures: Proverbs 2:6; 3:13; 4:7.

SAVOR IT!
Ask God to forgive you for sometimes ignoring his leading and plunging ahead on your own. Tell him you want his guidance and wisdom.

That sounded great! If there was one thing Nehemiah loved, it was sports. The sweat of competition and the thrill of victory raced through his imagination. *I could take our men all the way to first place,* he thought. So that night he talked to the Lord about it.

"Father, this would be a great way to bridge the gap between the neighboring cities, and I know that's important to you."

"Yes, Nehemiah, that *is* important. But at this particular time, what's *more* important?"

"I guess rebuilding the wall. But God, this is such a *good* thing."

"What's the *better* thing?"

"Rebuilding the wall."

"Right."

The next morning, Nehemiah turned down the basketball challenge and didn't even miss a day of construction work.

If he *had* accepted the offer, Sanballat and Tobiah would have quickly moved forward and demolished the wall Nehemiah and his crew had been so diligently building. Even though something may sound good, it doesn't mean it's of God. The world is full of wicked people who know how to talk smoothly, persuasively, and articulately.

BREW IT!

Think about the decisions you've made during the past year. How would your circumstances be different if you had sought God's direction in each of those decisions?

POUR IT!

Drink in the flavor from the following Scriptures: Nehemiah 5:9; Proverbs 3:7; 8:11.

SAVOR IT!

Ask God to use his Holy Spirit to convict you when you fail to seek his guidance regarding the decisions you make.

TAKE IT TO GOD

When Nehemiah turned down Sanballat and Tobiah's basketball offer, the wicked governors moved to their final strategy: Plan D.

This time Sanballat and Tobiah forged a letter to Nehemiah from the king. The letter expressed gratitude and admiration for the work Nehemiah had done on the wall. It also stated that the government thought he was an excellent role model for the youth of the nation. And because of Nehemiah's excellent leadership abilities, the king was honoring him with a special seat in Congress. Of course, this meant that Nehemiah would have to take some time off to accept the award and fulfill some publicity obligations.

Nehemiah was ecstatic. He realized this would be a fantastic witness to all students everywhere. Because of his new platform, people would certainly listen to him when he talked about the Lord.

That night, he talked with God about the situation.

"Lord, this is fantastic! Think of the witness I'll be."

"Yes, Nehemiah. A good witness is important. But at this particular time in your life, what's the *most* important?"

"Rebuilding the wall of righteousness that guards our land?"

"That's right."

"But Lord, this is such a good thing!"

"Yes, being a witness in the public eye is good. But right now, what's the *best* thing?

"Doing your will for my life. Rebuilding the wall of righteousness."

"Exactly."

Through discussing the matter with God, Nehemiah began to realize that the letter was a forgery and that the two governors were secretly planning on killing him.

When we take our questions to God, as Nehemiah did, he quickly helps us to distinguish right from wrong, better from good, best from better, and what's the very most important. When you question God's will, it's comforting to know that he's ready to give you direction and discernment.

Nehemiah showed great wisdom in going to the Father. Too often we try to figure things out for ourselves, or we simply plunge ahead without first consulting God. Nehemiah would have lost a great deal if he hadn't sought guidance from the Lord.

WANTED: WALL BUILDERS

The next day Nehemiah sent a reply to Sanballat and Tobiah. Check out his response: "I am doing a great work! Why should I stop to come and visit with you?" (Nehemiah 6:3, TLB). In other words, "What I am doing is the most important thing in the world, because I'm doing the will of God. Why should anything sidetrack me from accomplishing what my Father has called me to do?"

Just fifty-two days after they had started, the construction crew completed rebuilding the wall around the entire city of Jerusalem. Wow! Less than two months—that's incredible! How did they do it?

They were consistent. Day after day, they placed brick upon brick. They refused to allow *anything* to sidetrack them from doing God's will. Just as God commissioned Nehemiah to rebuild the wall of righteousness, he also commissions *you* to build a wall of righteousness. The place? Your life.

Nehemiah continued to complete the work God had called him to, even though it was clearly unpopular with unbelievers. Following God's job description for your life may not be applauded by unbelievers. Do you quit? No way! You continue building God's Kingdom by doing what he instructs you to do.

Just what is this wall of righteousness? It's a strong, rock-solid relationship with Jesus Christ. And yes, he wants you to build one. He's already made it clear. *Wanted: Construction workers . . . disciples who will invest time and commitment into building a strong, steady, solid wall of righteousness around their lives.*

How can you build a strong wall of righteousness?

1. *Check your foundation.* Make sure you're building on the right basics. If you're using anything other than Jesus Christ as your foundation, your structure will eventually collapse. Often people try to use church attendance, good deeds, or financial giving as their foundation. These are good things, but they're not strong enough to build a wall of righteousness (a relationship with Christ).
2. *Be consistent.* Repeat after me: "I *will* build the wall of righteousness. I *will* stick it out. I *am* going to see this thing through." Brick upon brick. Step by step. Keep following Jesus. That's how spiritual growth happens.

Maybe you've had friends who started out excited about their relationship with Christ, but when the going got tough, they bailed. That's inconsistency, and a strong wall of righteousness will never be built with that ingredient.

BREW IT!
By building consistently on the foundation of Christ, you'll develop a strong, rock-solid relationship with him.

POUR IT!
Drink in the flavor from the following Scriptures: Nehemiah 6:2-3, 15-16; Proverbs 15:33.

SAVOR IT!
If you've never asked Jesus Christ to be your spiritual foundation, consider doing that right now.

BREW IT!
Check your foundation, be consistent, keep on keepin' on, refuse to be sidetracked, and realize that what you do for God is important to him.

POUR IT!
Drink in the flavor from the following Scriptures: Isaiah 59:15-17; Jeremiah 23:4; 29:11-12.

SAVOR IT!
Tell God you realize there's nothing more important than doing his will. Tell him that right now you know his will for you is to build a strong relationship with him. Commit everything you have into fulfilling this exciting task.

WALL STRATEGY

Not only does God call you to build a wall of righteousness (a relationship with him) around your own life, he also desires that you reach out and help others build a relationship with Christ in their lives.

Let's recap. The first two steps in building a strong wall of righteousness:

1. *Check your foundation.*
2. *Be consistent.*

And the next step?

3. *Keep on keepin' on.* Continue to do God's work in the midst of strife. The apostle Paul was beaten, shipwrecked, and imprisoned. But he remained consistent in completing the work God had called him to do. Action is always more important than talk! God calls us to do what's right, to keep on doing his work in spite of the conflicts around us.
4. *Refuse to be sidetracked.* There were several things vying for Nehemiah's attention. Many of them were extremely appealing. They were positive. Tempting. Alluring. But Nehemiah determined not to get sidetracked by them.

   We know we shouldn't get sidetracked with evil, but we often rationalize other things because they seem good. *Anything* that distracts us from doing God's work—even a good thing—is wrong. Remember, building a strong, rock-solid relationship with him isn't about good stuff; it's about the best stuff. It's not just something important that we want to focus on; it's zeroing in on what's *most* important.
5. *Know that your job is important.* Nehemiah learned the importance of each individual to God. "I am doing a great work," he said. What you do for God is important. It matters! You may think your role is small and goes unnoticed, but anything you do for Christ matters a great deal.

Does your church need help on cleanup day? Will your contribution to the offering really make a difference? Does your youth pastor need someone to send an e-mail to visitors each week? What you do matters. Your work is important. Never think that just because you're one person, your work won't help advance the Kingdom. God needs individuals just like you.

GIVING OF SELF

In Middle Eastern countries, there's an old story about the great Shah Abbas. He was a wealthy ruler who found it fun to disguise himself and hang out with the poorest of the poor. After putting on thin rags, he approached an impoverished area of the city and watched a servant tend the furnace.

The Shah struck up a conversation with the man, and the two spent the evening together. The poor servant even shared his meager lunch of bread and water with his new friend. The Shah continued to visit the poverty-stricken man and developed a deep friendship with him, even though the servant had no idea who the Shah really was. After some time, the Shah finally decided to reveal his identity to the servant.

After explaining who he was and proving his true identity, the Shah waited for the servant to ask him for something. He was ready to grant any request his friend had. But the servant sat silently and simply gazed on the Shah with love and admiration.

"Don't you understand?" the Shah asked. "I'm the great Shah Abbas, and I have the power to make you rich and noble. I can give you a city. I can appoint you as a great ruler. Don't you want to ask me for something?"

"Yes, I understand," the servant replied. "But you've already given me the most precious gift imaginable. You've left your glorious surroundings and have sat and fellowshipped with me all these months. You've cared about my worries. You've listened to my heart. You've shown me true love."

BREW IT!
Whom can you give the gift of your presence to this week? Whom can you simply spend time with and demonstrate Christ's love?

POUR IT!
Drink in the flavor from the following Scriptures: Matthew 7:1-2, 21; 19:29-30.

SAVOR IT!
Ask God to bring to mind a specific person you can reach out to this week.

You, too, have the opportunity to give the precious gift of your presence to others. By spending time with an elderly person, by going out of your way to befriend a new person on campus or at church, and by listening to the hurts of others, you are showing you care.

There's an elderly woman who lives on the corner of my street. She lives alone, and I often see her walking for exercise. I usually see her when I'm walking my 150-pound Saint Bernard, Bosco. Even though we're walking in different directions and across the street from one another, I make it a point to wave at her until I catch her attention.

When I walk by her house, she's often in the front yard. I stop and ask about her cats and make small talk with her. I can tell she cherishes each moment. I'm not really doing anything huge, but she loves that small bit of attention. I pray for her and ask Jesus to help her see himself through my actions.

HOW'S YOUR PRAYER LIFE?

The book *Twelve and One-Half Keys* tells the story of an innocent man who was unjustly sentenced to prison. He was a poor, yet honest, jeweler and a devout, godly man. After he had been imprisoned for several months, his wife visited with the guards and showed them a rug. "It's his prayer rug," she explained. "He's lost without it. Could he just have this one possession?"

The guards agreed that a small rug would not do anyone any harm and allowed the man to have it. Several weeks passed, and the jeweler presented an interesting proposition to the guards. "I'm bored sitting here all day with nothing to do," he said. "If you'll grant me a few scraps of metal and a couple of simple tools, I'll make jewelry for you. I just want to be able to keep up my trade. You can sell what I make for your own profit."

The overworked and underpaid guards quickly agreed, and each day they brought him a few scraps of metal and some tools. Each night they took the tools away from him and sold what he had made for their own profit.

Months later, when the guards approached his cell one morning, they discovered he was gone. The door was locked, and there was no sign of forced entry. It seemed he had just disappeared!

Later, the man who had actually committed the crime was found and sent to prison. Long afterward, one of the guards saw the innocent man's wife at the city market. He quickly explained that the real criminal was behind bars, but he wanted to know what had happened to her husband.

She told him that she had gone to the main architect of the prison. She obtained from him the blueprints of the cell doors and locks. Then she wove the design into a prayer rug. Each day as her husband knelt and bowed to pray, his head touched the rug.

Gradually, he began to see that there was a design inside a design inside another design inside yet another design, and he finally figured out that it was the design to the lock of his cell. From small bits of leftover metal, he created a key and simply unlocked his own door, walked out of the cell, then shut the door again!

Like interpreting the design on a rug, following Christ takes study, discipline, and consistency. And that's a plan that will move you toward a joyous relationship with him.

BREW IT!
How's your prayer life? Do you talk with the Lord consistently? If not, why? Don't use time as an excuse. You can talk to God in the shower, in your car, or during a part-time job. You can talk with the Lord anytime, anywhere. Do it.

POUR IT!
Drink in the flavor from the following Scriptures: Proverbs 15:8, 29; Matthew 21:22.

SAVOR IT!
Ask God to help you develop a daily prayer time with him. Start right now.

JESUS NEVER FAILS

Panic consumed Emma as she bit into the apple. *I wonder how many calories are in this piece of fruit?* she wondered. *I'll never look like the women in the magazines. I'm useless.*

She took another bite of the apple. Then another. And with each bite, Emma's panic multiplied.

The next day she punished herself by skipping breakfast and lunch. By evening, Emma was famished. She headed to the refrigerator and grabbed bologna and cheese. Then she opened the cabinets and pulled out chips and a couple of chocolate bars. Then she remembered the cookies.

In an hour, Emma hated herself so much she couldn't stand it. *I'm such a loser,* she thought as she sobbed herself to sleep. *Will this monster of an eating disorder ever end?*

Jesus never fails. Ever!

After Emma had struggled for two years with anorexia and bulimia, she finally sought help through Christian counseling. She learned that God saw her as beautiful. She began to memorize Bible verses that proved her worth in Christ. She gave the Lord total control.

Today, Emma eats three normal meals a day. She still struggles at times, but when she battles with insecurity, she knows where to turn. "God has never failed me," she says. "Jesus really is the answer!"

Alicia was a cutter. She'd been cutting herself for almost a year when her mom discovered the scars on her thighs. "I can't help it!" she screamed. "I hurt so badly inside that the pain on the outside seems to take my mind off of all my problems."

"Alicia, saying you can't help it is a lie straight from the pit of hell," her mom told her. "Satan is the master deceiver, and he wants you to hate yourself and destroy yourself. Honey, God has a beautiful plan for your life."

Jesus never fails. Ever!

Alicia and her mom sought help from their family physician. He referred Alicia to a Christian counselor who worked with other troubled teens. "I learned that Jesus sees me as his princess," she says. "My body is his holy temple, and I don't want to hurt him by destroying his temple. I've placed God in charge of my life and have given my hurt to him."

Does that mean Alicia will never hurt again? Of course not. But when she is hurting, she knows where she should turn.

JESUS NEVER FAILS

Mawee's mother died when Mawee was just six years old. Mawee lived in a Burmese village with her opium-addicted stepfather. When she was nine, a woman from Bangkok, Thailand, wandered into their village recruiting girls for prostitution. Mawee's stepfather—desperate to support his addiction—sold her for one hundred dollars to the Thai woman. To entice Mawee into leaving the village, they lied to her and said she was going to the big city of Bangkok to work in a restaurant and earn lots of money.

When Mawee arrived in Bangkok, she was kept in a locked room inside a brothel. Mawee was abused, frightened, and in shock when police rescued her. She was transferred to a children's shelter where she mopped floors for three years. She was safe, but it wasn't much of a life for a twelve-year-old.

One day a police officer approached her and said, "I've heard of a Christian ministry that takes in women off the street. They speak your language. Would you like to live with these women?"

Mawee quickly agreed and made a twelve-hour journey to the New Life Center in Chiang Mai, Thailand, where women introduced her to Christ and taught her personal life skills such as sewing, cooking, and weaving.

"I want to become an evangelist," she told me. "God has freed me and rescued me, and I want others to know of his love!"

Jesus never fails. Ever!

For a frightened, abused little girl who was thrown into a different culture and immersed in a language she didn't understand, Jesus was there. He was with Mawee in the dark, locked room inside the brothel. He guided her hands as she mopped floors for three years. He took her safely to another city and placed her in protective friendships with older women who loved her, nurtured her, and led her into his arms.

When bad things happen, we often scream, "Why, God?" We don't understand, and we often lash out in anger at the one who loves us more than life itself. God isn't causing bad things to happen to you, but because of sin in the world, bad things do happen. Someday, we'll live in a perfect eternal paradise with our heavenly Father where sin won't exist. There will be no more abuse, fear, confusion, illness, or anger. Until that time, continue to cling to the one who promises he will never fail you.

June 3

BREW IT!
When you encounter something so big and terrible that it doesn't seem as though you can even put one foot in front of the other, seek God. And instead of asking him why, simply cling to him and ask that his will be done.

POUR IT!
Drink in the flavor from the following Scriptures: 2 Corinthians 4:8-9; 6:10; 12:9.

SAVOR IT!
Pray for a godly perspective. Ask God to help you understand how you can bring glory to him through your trials.

BREW IT!
Let the Holy Spirit produce his fruit in your life!

POUR IT!
Drink in the flavor from the following Scripture: Galatians 5:19-25.

SAVOR IT!
Ask God to guide you through these two sections in Galatians. If he points out any sinful action or attitude in your life, seek his forgiveness and ask for the fruit.

JESUS *NEVER* FAILS

Samantha's dad didn't keep it a secret that he'd never wanted her. He told her often how he had tried to persuade his wife to abort her.

When Samantha was a teenager, an uncle sexually abused her. She developed an intense hatred toward men and felt as though she were a time bomb set to explode.

Jesus never fails. Ever!

Samantha desperately wanted to grow closer to Jesus and experience his healing. So she decided to participate in a Brio missions trip. While in Quito, Ecuador, she allowed God to do a miracle in her life. She forgave her dad and her uncle. She's now growing closer to Christ and blossoming into a beautiful woman of God.

"I realized how incredibly much Jesus loves me," she says. "He has freed me from my anger. I just want to serve him forever!"

Have you ever experienced so much anger you thought you'd explode? Jesus wants to help you through the anger, and then he wants to remove the anger from you and replace it with his joy. Will you let him do that?

Oftentimes we hold on to our anger. We don't want to let it go because it feels good to rant and rave and scream. But God has a higher calling on your life. He wants to produce the fruit of the Spirit in your life, including joy, peace, and patience. But if you're consumed with anger, that will prohibit you from experiencing the rich fruit God desires for you.

There's a great passage in Galatians 5. The first section lists sins of our sinful nature: impure thoughts, anger, jealousy, lustful pleasure, etc. And the next section lists the fruit of God's Holy Spirit: love, joy, peace, patience, kindness, goodness, faithfulness, gentleness, and self-control.

Go through these two lists carefully. If you're not experiencing one of the fruits, pop back up to the list before it and see if you're displaying one of the sinful actions on the list. If you are, that may be why you're not experiencing the fruit.

You can't have joy when you're angry. And you can't genuinely love someone if you're being guided by lustful thoughts. These two sections go hand in hand. Samantha realized she'd never fully experience God's fruit as long as she clung to anger. When she released the anger, she began experiencing the peace, joy, love, and other fruits God had intended for her all along.

JESUS NEVER *FAILS*

Mary was confused and hurt. Her brother Larry was sick, and she had contacted their best friend and physician as soon as he began showing signs of illness. But she was ignored by her best friend. Where was he? Why didn't he come? Larry's illness quickly escalated, and only a few days later, she buried her brother.

If only he had come when we sent for him, she thought, *Larry would still be alive.*

She and her sister began to slip into a tunnel of depression. They battled a whole range of emotions—shock, anger, grief, rage, bitterness. To continue living seemed pointless.

Jesus never fails. Ever!

Larry's real name was Lazarus. You may be familiar with his story recorded in John 11:1-44. He and his sisters, Mary and Martha, were extremely close friends with Jesus. Mary and Martha knew that Jesus was the Son of God, the Messiah, the Great Physician. They were certain if they sent word to their friend and Savior, he would respond quickly and heal their brother.

Yet when Jesus heard that Lazarus was sick, he stayed where he was for two more days. Two more days! You can understand why Mary and Martha were confused, angry, and depressed.

In the next few days we'll look at three lessons we can take away from this story.

Lesson #1: *Lack of immediate action is not due to lack of devotion.* Remember the violent storm on the Sea of Galilee? (You can check out the entire story in Mark 6:45-52.) Jesus left the disciples out in the boat all night! He didn't appear until the fourth watch—sometime between 3 a.m. and 6 a.m. When he arrived, he wasn't apologetic or rushed. He didn't sail to the disciples frantically while yelling over the crashing waves, "Sorry! I meant to get here sooner. Whoa, this is a mess! What a storm. Okay, here's what we need to do. . . ."

He came to them calmly. Walking on top of the water.

The wind and waves stopped, and the disciples learned that Jesus truly was the "I AM"—God himself, who has authority over nature.

Sometimes we need God's silence before we can see God's best. (Think about that for a second. Then read it again.)

Sometimes we need God's silence before we can see God's best.

BREW IT!
Just as Jesus came to the disciples in the midst of a horrific tempest, he'll come to you in the midst of your storms. Jesus never fails!

POUR IT!
Drink in the flavor from the following Scriptures (these sections are a little longer than usual, but dare to read them anyway, okay?): Mark 6:45-52; John 11:1-44.

SAVOR IT!
Ask God to strengthen your faith so you can learn to trust him even in the midst of your storms.

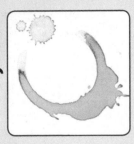

BREW IT!
You can give your friends a lifeline out of their dungeons. Do they see God's strength in your actions? Do they know you hold the lifeline in your relationship with him?

POUR IT!
Drink in the flavor from the following Scriptures: Psalm 40:1-3; Lamentations 3:21-26.

SAVOR IT!
Thank God that he's with you in whatever dungeon you're in.

GOD'S TIMING

Do you truly believe that Jesus never fails? If so, you'll learn to trust him even when you can't feel him. Let's grab a few more thoughts from Jesus' time with Mary, Martha, and Lazarus, as well as the storm the disciples battled.

Lesson #2: *God is never early, yet he's never late.* Jesus may have seemed late to the disciples when they were alone in the boat, but he actually came at the perfect time. Mary and Martha thought he was late, but we know his timing was perfect, because it allowed him to perform a great miracle (raising Lazarus from the dead) that convinced many people he was the Messiah. When you need a gentle reminder of this truth, memorize this: "This vision is for a future time. It describes the end, and it will be fulfilled. If it seems slow in coming, wait patiently, for it will surely take place. It will not be delayed" (Habakkuk 2:3, NLT).

How often do you grow impatient waiting for the Lord to act? God's timing is not our own, but his timing is perfect! Remember, he's promised he'll never fail you or forsake you. That's a powerful promise! When you are impatient and apprehensive with his timing, you're actually showing signs of doubt. When you truly believe that he'll never fail you, you can rest assured in the fact that he will act.

Remember the Old Testament story of Daniel in the lions' den? The Bible gives no hint of Daniel not trusting the Lord. For all we know, Dan could have even yawned and taken a doze. He could sleep because he trusted God.

The Bible doesn't show him as a man pacing the floor, wringing his hands, screaming at the top of his lungs, or trying to kick the lions. He experienced the presence of God even in a terrifying dungeon.

Thank goodness you're not actually in a lions' dungeon right now, but there are other kinds of dungeons, aren't there? Are you in a dungeon of despair? a dungeon of bitterness? a dungeon of lust? a dungeon of deceit? Whatever dungeon you're in, you're not alone. If you'll simply call on the name of the one who has promised to never fail you, you'll be blessed with the presence of God Almighty.

BE PART OF A MIRACLE

What have we learned so far from the fact that Jesus never fails us? Recap:

Lesson #1: *Lack of immediate action is not due to lack of devotion!*

Lesson #2: *God is never early, yet he's never late.*

There's one more lesson we can grab:

Lesson #3: *God is in the miracle business, but he wants to give us a chance to participate in the miracle.* Many times when God does a miracle, he does 100 percent, but he still gives us an opportunity to participate. Throughout the Old and New Testaments, we see God performing miracles. But let's take a closer look.

With Noah, it was as if God was saying, "I'll do the miracle, Noah. I'll save you and your family from a worldwide flood. But I want to give you a chance to participate in this miracle. You take responsibility for building the ark. I'll give you specific instructions, and I'll provide everything you need, but you build it."

With the children of Israel: "I'll give you a miracle. I'll free you from slavery and oppression under Pharaoh's rule. I'll lead you to the Promised Land. I'll even personally send food from heaven every day you're in the wilderness. But here's your opportunity to be involved in the miracle: You'll have the responsibility of collecting the manna each morning. You won't be able to save it; you'll actually need to gather it every single morning."

The blind man heard Jesus say, "I'll do the miracle. I'll give you sight! But here's how you can actively participate in the miracle: you have the responsibility of washing your eyes with mud in the river."

Jesus did the miracle of raising Lazarus, a dead man, to life. But he also invited Lazarus to participate in the miracle. Lazarus had to get up and walk out of the tomb. Then his grave clothes—the strips of cloth in which he was bound—had to be removed.

BREW IT!
God wants to do a miracle in your life too. But he doesn't want you to be a silent spectator. He wants to give you the opportunity to participate in the miracle.

POUR IT!
Drink in the flavor from the following Scriptures: Habakkuk 3:2, 17-18; Luke 5:18-20.

SAVOR IT!
Let God know you're willing to participate in a miracle. Ask him what he wants you to do, then trust him to work in his perfect timing, not your own.

BREW IT!

Is there an area in your life that seems too big for Jesus to handle? Not only can he handle it, he wants to handle it. Will you give that area to him right now?

POUR IT!

Drink in the flavor from the following Scriptures: Psalm 27:14; 34:1-3; 37:7.

SAVOR IT!

Ask God to teach you that he never, ever fails.

JESUS STILL FREES TODAY!

Flash back to the previous devotionals from June 2 to today. Remember Emma? Until she gave God complete control of her life—including her weight—she was oblivious to the fact that he created her and understands her body's chemistry and physiology. Now she knows the truth, because she's in love with the truth—God himself. Emma knows that Jesus never fails.

Alicia remained blinded by the deception that she was worthless until she began to believe the truth that God loves her passionately and wants to use her for his glory. Through the help of Christian friends and family, she prayed for wholeness. She's no longer a cutter, because she lives in Christ's victory. Alicia knows that Jesus never fails.

Mawee can reach out and minister to prostitutes by sharing the gospel and God's forgiveness with them. She understands the abuse they've experienced, and she's allowing God to use her past to bring him glory. "I want to build his Kingdom," she says. Mawee knows that Jesus never fails.

Samantha now lives a vibrant life in Jesus because she has allowed him to remove her anger toward men and replace it with Christ's joy. "Because of all he's doing in my life," she says, "I know he loves me and has a wonderful plan." Samantha knows that Jesus never fails.

Mary and Martha didn't see Jesus wearily drag himself to their home saying, "I'm sorry I'm late. It's just been so hectic. Blind people needed to see. Deaf people wanted to hear. I had to multiply bread so people could have lunch. It's been a whirlwind gospel tour! But hey, I'm here now. Where's Larry?"

Mary and Martha saw their Lord approach them confidently and heard him say that his purpose was greater than theirs. When all they were able to see was the immediate, he had the big picture in mind. If Mary could talk to us today, she might say, "It was beyond description. Jesus literally raised my dead brother to life! We'll never be the same. I know he truly never fails."

JESUS: THE BONDAGE BREAKER

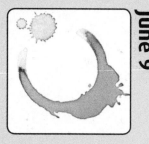

As Jesus approached the home of Mary and Martha, he didn't do so anxiously, wondering if Lazarus would be okay. Jesus knew his friend had died. Yet he approached the sisters with peace and confidence.

Yes, Mary and Martha were discouraged and full of questions. But can't you just imagine how their spirits must have soared with excitement as they watched the King of kings head to their brother's tomb? Wouldn't you love to have seen it happen? Let's imagine it in present tense:

Jesus takes each step in boldness. He doesn't even notice the grit of the sand between his toes and his sandals. He calls to Lazarus in a loud voice, "Come forth!"

The earth trembles. Dirt flies. The huge rock filling the tomb's entrance shakes uncontrollably.

The ground rumbles. The rock explodes! And Lazarus in the form of a mummy walks out of the grave. He approaches Jesus, Mary, and Martha. And rejoices that Jesus never fails!

Don't you love it? Jesus had the power to break the grave clothes in which Lazarus was bound. In those days, the strips of linen used to wrap a dead body were soaked in oils and ointments. They would have been wrapped tightly around his body, leaving him incredibly sticky and confined. But in raising Lazarus from the dead, Jesus freed him from the mess.

He can free you from your mess too! You see, Jesus is still in the business of removing bandages. He has the power right now to release you from whatever is keeping you from becoming all he desires.

What kind of bondage is it? The wrong chat rooms? Pornography? Gossip? Drugs? Wicca? Astrology? Cutting? An eating disorder? Steroids? Lying? Low self-esteem? Fear? Memories filled with abuse? He wants you to give him your filthy grave clothes, and he wants to dress you in his holiness. Will you let him?

Walk away from that habit, that relationship, that attitude. Give it up. Lay it down. Seek his help and forgiveness.

And as you do, remember that Jesus never fails! There will be times when you think, *I've prayed and prayed. Why hasn't he answered? Where is he?* Sometimes healing is a process. Remember, God's timing is not your own. He's on a totally different timetable.

BREW IT!
Can you hear Jesus calling to you? His message is the same as it was for Lazarus: "Come forth!" Leave everything else behind and come forth!

POUR IT!
Drink in the flavor from the following Scriptures: John 8:32; Galatians 5:1; 1 Peter 2:16.

SAVOR IT!
Ask God to reveal to you anything that has you in bondage. Be willing to place that area of your life in his control.

BREW IT!

How well do you know the voice of God? Are you making a genuine effort each day to get alone with him—to be still—to actually learn the sound of his voice?

POUR IT!

Drink in the flavor from the following Scriptures: 2 Samuel 22:29-31; Psalm 40:10; 46:10.

SAVOR IT!

Tell God you're willing to do whatever is necessary to be still on a consistent basis and learn the sound of his voice.

LEARNING TO BE STILL

We live in a fast-paced society, don't we? We want everything, and we want it now. We drive fast, eat fast, talk fast, walk fast. We're a generation of fast-paced people trying to go even faster. It's not enough to be on the Internet; we have to have high-speed Internet. Then we have to have wireless. Bigger. Better. Faster.

But as we study the life of Jesus, we notice he was never in a hurry. He was calm. He took his time with people. He looked them in the eyes. He listened to them. He prayed with them. He spent time with them.

The Bible tells us to be still. That's the exact opposite of how most of us live, isn't it? Though Jesus had an extremely full ministry and was flocked by huge crowds of people, he still took time to pace himself, to be still, to get alone with his heavenly Father.

If the Son of God made time to be still, we need it much more! *What's so important about being still?* you may be thinking. As we make a little time to be still on a daily basis, here's what happens:

- *We become more aware of God.* When we choose to focus on him during the still moments, it's easier to see him at work during the rushed times. We learn to watch for him and listen to him throughout our day.
- *We learn what his voice sounds like.* When we make time to shut out all the other noises of our lives for a few minutes each day and talk to God, we can hear him respond. Turn off the TV, the music, the noises of life. Shut your door. Get alone. Listen for God's voice.
- *We get in the habit of waiting for God.* Sometimes God acts quickly, and other times he asks us to wait for him. When we establish a daily quiet time with our Father, we learn the process of slowing down, of waiting. And it's usually during these times that God brings things to our mind, such as how we could have served him better today, someone who needs our prayers, and his affirmation and love for us.

Can't God speak to us when we're in a hurry? Of course he can. And he will. But when we first learn his voice in the silence, it becomes much easier to hear his voice through the noise.

SLOW AND SAVORY

By making time to be still each day, you're choosing to allow God to mold you to his image. That's a process. It takes time. It works kind of like a Crock-Pot.

You have a choice: you can either be a Crock-Pot Christian or a microwave Christian. If you'll allow God to make you a Crock-Pot Christian, you'll be much more effective in spreading his aroma. Think about it this way: The aroma of a roast inside a Crock-Pot permeates the entire house. As soon as you walk in the door, a smile spreads across your face and you're immediately aware that something very good is cooking. You can smell that roast from anywhere in the house.

That's the kind of relationship God wants to develop with you. When people are around you, he wants them to "smell the aroma" of Christianity. Wouldn't it be exciting if people smiled when you walked into the room and became acutely aware that something good was happening inside of you? They'd crowd you. They'd want what you have. You'd be so tender, people would be attracted to your "scent"—to God's presence within you.

It's hard to become a Crock-Pot Christian if you're living in a microwave. We need to cook slowly and be filled with his savory Spirit. Think about the disciples. They slowly "cooked" in the presence of God for three years. So after Christ returned to heaven, it's understandable they were ready to begin organizing the first churches.

They spread the gospel. They fulfilled God's mission. They had his savory Spirit. They had been tenderized. They were ready.

God also has a mission for you, but it will probably mean spending daily time in his presence becoming savory and tender before he reveals his full plan.

BREW IT!
When you decide to be a Crock-Pot Christian, God's Spirit through you will sweetly fill the atmosphere. You'll become tender. Be willing to go for the long haul. Don't be in such a rush in your relationship with Christ that you're not fully cooked.

POUR IT!
Drink in the flavor from the following Scriptures: 1 Chronicles 28:9-10; Isaiah 60:1; Jeremiah 15:19.

SAVOR IT!
Ask God to make you a Crock-Pot Christian.

BREW IT!
The choice is yours. And it will require action!

POUR IT!
Drink in the flavor from the following Scriptures: Psalm 139:23-24; Colossians 3:8, 17.

SAVOR IT!
Ask the Great Physician to help you examine your life for anything that's not pleasing to him.

EXAMINE YOURSELF

"I have a habit of saying bad things," Brendon told me. "I can't believe I even think about some of this stuff. And when I see people talking in front of me, I automatically assume they're whispering about me. I leave and start talking trash about them. I need help!"

Brendon's not alone. All of us struggle with thinking things that surprise us and with saying things we know we shouldn't. When you're struggling with thoughts you know aren't right, examine your media intake. Are you watching movies and TV shows that go against the lifestyle of Christ? If so, you're opening a door for those thoughts and ideas to dance around inside your mind.

What are you reading? Are you spending time on magazines and books that are filled with the world's view of sexuality? If so, you're opening the door to fill your mind with those thoughts.

What are you listening to? Does your music depict a lifestyle of lust and sexual intimacy outside of marriage? If so, you're willingly allowing that to enter your mind.

Fortunately, God has given us some advice in his Holy Word. The apostle Paul tells us in his letter to the Colossians to get rid of the stuff in our lives that gives us evil thoughts. This will take a conscious effort on your part. Getting rid of something requires specific action. You can't get rid of something while you're sitting around thinking about it.

Think of gossip, unclean language, and lustful thoughts as dirty socks. Everyone has dirty socks. To get clean ones, you actually have to remove the filthy socks from your feet. In other words, you must take action. You can wish the socks away. You can cry because they smell so bad. And you can pretend they're not dirty at all. But facts are facts: If you're wearing dirty socks, people will eventually find out.

It works the same way with our language and thoughts. You may think that whatever you play around with in your mind is private, but if you continue to live with lustful thinking, at some point those thoughts will show up in your lifestyle.

You can try to convince yourself that gossip won't really hurt anyone, but sooner or later—just like a pair of dirty socks—your language will begin stinking to those around you.

You can't always control what enters your mind (though you can influence it by what you choose to watch, read, and listen to), but you can control what you'll do with it. Once a lustful thought enters your mind, will you allow yourself to mentally play around with it? Or will you immediately take it to God?

THE THREE BOXES

Brendon's thought life took a positive turn when he took inventory of his media choices and made some changes. "My thought life is a lot better," he said. "But I'm still struggling with what I say behind people's backs. I know it's wrong to talk bad about others, but it's become such a habit, I don't know how to break it."

Can you relate? Gossip is an easy trap to fall into. People often gossip because they're insecure. They think spreading something negative about someone else will make them feel better about themselves. It seldom does. So they gossip more and more, but their self-esteem never rises.

Gossip is never the answer for a positive self-image. That answer is found in Christ. When you realize that you've actually been created in his image and you base your security and identity on a strong, intimate, growing relationship with him, your self-esteem rises to healthy heights.

If you, like Brendon, are struggling with what comes out of your mouth, try these tips:

Tip #1: *Develop some accountability.* Find someone you trust who will lovingly hold you accountable. Allow him or her to ask you the tough questions: "Did you trash-talk anyone today? If so, were you feeling insecure? Were you trying to make yourself look better by tearing someone else down?" Having someone hold you accountable—who will also pray with you—will help you break the bad habit of gossip.

Tip #2: *Think in terms of three boxes.* The box on top is labeled "True." The box in the middle has the title "Kind," and the box on the bottom has "Necessary" marked on it. Before you gossip, stop and mentally go through these three boxes.

First, ask yourself if what you're about to share is actually true. If it's not, or if you're not sure, forget it. If it is true, before you tell it, shift down to the second box. Is it kind? Once you've answered that question, go to the bottom box. Even if it's true, even if it's kind, is it necessary for you to share this information?

Tip #3: *Pray before you talk.* Many of us talk all the time. We talk without thinking. We talk without praying. We talk about anything and everything. We just talk . . . a lot! Guess what—we don't need to talk so much. Ask God if it's okay for you to say what you're about to say. You'll be surprised at how much gossip this will eliminate!

BREW IT!
The words you use are powerful. So take careful inventory of your speech. Does what you say build people up or tear them down?

POUR IT!
Drink in the flavor from the following Scriptures: Ephesians 4:29; James 3:1-2, 5-6; 4:11.

SAVOR IT!
Ask God to help you develop godly accountability with someone who can help you break bad habits and encourage you to develop good habits.

BREW IT!
It's really a matter of priorities, isn't it? How are you using the money God has entrusted to you? Is your focus more on people or things?

POUR IT!
Drink in the flavor from the following Scriptures: Matthew 6:19-21; 13:44; 19:21.

SAVOR IT!
Tell God you want him to be in charge of your money. Ask him to show you how to use your money to meet needs, help others, and build his Kingdom.

RICH BUT DEAD
It's tough enough to earn a decent living when you're alive . . . so wouldn't it be impossible when you're dead? Not for a select few. And Elvis Presley tops the list. Even though he's deceased, he still earns $40 million a year! And surprisingly, those earnings aren't from music sales. Elvis's manager sold the rights to pre-1973 recordings to RCA (now part of Sony) for $5 million. Elvis's huge annual earnings come from merchandising and admissions to his estate, Graceland.

Forbes lists the ten top-earning dead celebrities:

- Singer Elvis Presley ($40 million annually)
- "Peanuts" cartoonist Charles Schulz ($35 million annually)
- The Lord of the Rings author J. R. R. Tolkien ($23 million annually)
- Former Beatle John Lennon ($21 million annually)
- Children's author Theodor "Dr. Suess" Geisel ($18 million annually)
- Movie star Marilyn Monroe ($8 million annually)
- Former Beatle George Harrison ($7 million annually)
- Composer Irving Berlin ($7 million annually)
- Reggae singer and songwriter Bob Marley ($7 million annually)
- Songwriter Richard Rodgers ($6.5 million annually)

Though these dead celebs are raking in a fortune annually, what good does it do them? We enter this world with no material goods, and we leave this world with no material goods. We tend to forget that, don't we? It's easy to get caught up in making car payments, landing the perfect part-time job, buying new clothes, and purchasing songs off the Internet. We forget that all this is temporary.

That's why the Bible tells us to store our treasures in heaven instead of here on earth. What we store in heaven will last eternally, while material goods that we invest in on earth will someday erode, rust, or fade away.

Though we need money to live, God wants us to be wise stewards of our finances. First, he wants us to give him what's rightfully his (10 percent of all we earn), and second, he wants us to focus on people and needs instead of money and things. As we do this, it becomes more natural to store our treasures in heaven instead of on earth. In other words, when we invest our time and money in things that are important to God—like helping the poor and spreading the gospel—we'll someday see the results in heaven.

HE LEFT A LEGACY

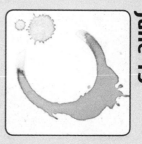

Though he's deceased, Charles Schulz, the cartoonist and creator of the "Peanuts" gang, still brings in $35 million each year. He left the world with a fun legacy—his cartoon characters. There aren't any new Peanuts cartoons—those now running in 2,400 newspapers are recycled from the 1970s—but there's always a new licensing gimmick. Recently, it was retro fashions sold at Wal-Mart stores.

Snoopy and the loveable Peanuts gang appear on one in every five Hallmark cards. The beloved beagle is also a pitchman for PepsiCo and MetLife. Though the Peanuts empire is sprawling, it's still very much a family business. Schulz's surviving family members have creative approval on every project.

Charles Schulz left his family with a thriving business centered around some much-loved cartoon characters who teach the world positive lessons about life, love, and loyalty.

That's a tremendous legacy! But as much as we love the Peanuts characters, they're not eternal. There will come a day when Charlie Brown and his four-footed friend, Snoopy, won't even matter. If we're going to leave a legacy that *matters*—one that makes a difference—it must be based on eternal truths.

What kind of legacy are you developing? *Hey! I'm still young. It's not time for me to be thinking about leaving a legacy yet!* you may be thinking. Though it may not be time for you to *leave* a legacy, it is time for you to be *developing* a legacy. How can you do that?

1. *Make sure your friends know what's important to you.* How will your friends learn what matters to you? You can tell them, but they'll really know what's important to you by how you use your time, what you purchase, and how you treat others.

So how are you using your time? Do you spend time at church? Are you involved in youth group and a Bible study? Do your friends know that you pour yourself into studying God's Word and growing closer to him?

What do they see you spending money on? Would they say you're more into things or people? And when it comes to people, do they hear you cracking jokes about someone, or do they see you treating others with respect and kindness?

Start developing your legacy right now by letting your friends see what's important to you. Talk openly about your relationship with Christ. Share your excitement about your church and what God is teaching you. Let them see you reach out to someone who needs a friend. Let them hear you affirm and encourage others.

BREW IT!
If your friends had to write a newspaper article about you today, what would they say? What kind of legacy do they see you developing?

POUR IT!
Drink in the flavor from the following Scriptures: Isaiah 1:17; 5:27-28; 8:12-13.

SAVOR IT!
Ask God what you need to change to begin developing the legacy he wants you to leave.

BREW IT!
What you have is God's gift to you. How you use it, however, is your gift to him. Use your gifts to glorify the Giver.

POUR IT!
Drink in the flavor from the following Scriptures: Romans 12:6-8; 1 Corinthians 12:27-31.

SAVOR IT!
Dedicate your gifts, abilities, talents, and skills to the Lord. Ask him to use you to bring glory to his name.

LEAVING A POSITIVE LEGACY

As you focus on developing your personal legacy, zero in on these two things:

1. *Make sure your friends know what's important to you.*
2. *Use your talents wisely and in a positive way.*

The famous composer Irving Berlin, though dead, still earns $7 million a year. Because he used his talents positively, his songs are still widely known and used in the world of musical theater.

He was born in Israel and sang for pennies in the streets of New York. His first major hit was "Alexander's Ragtime Band" in 1911. Over the next fifty years, Irving produced a repertoire that defined American music: musicals ("Annie Get Your Gun"), jazz standards ("Puttin' On the Ritz"), and novelty tunes ("White Christmas," "God Bless America").

Besides being blessed with huge publishing royalties, Berlin's heirs also own half of the historic Music Box Theater in New York. His musical genius continues through the legacy he left. What a positive way to be remembered—fun songs that bring happiness to people of all ages!

An even more powerful way to be remembered, however, would be to use one's talents for the glory of God. Though Berlin's music is wonderful and loved, it doesn't speak of Christ or an eternal hope. Berlin used his talents positively, but if he had known Christ, his talents could have influenced people's lives for eternity.

God has blessed you with tremendous gifts and special talents. How are you investing what he's given you? Are you using your skills to develop a lasting legacy? Are you using your gifts to bring glory to Christ?

Make sure those around you know what's behind your gifts. Determine to make your relationship with Christ known. Then when people applaud your gifts, they'll realize it's not you responsible for the success. Instead, it's because you've dedicated your life to using your gifts for God.

LEAVING A DAMAGING LEGACY

Think of those who have left not a positive legacy, but a negative one. Adolf Hitler left an incredibly negative legacy. When people hear his name, they automatically think of the Jews who were innocently slaughtered under his regime. What do you think of when you hear the names Dylan Klebold and Eric Harris? Your mind probably turns to the Columbine High School killings in Littleton, Colorado.

When you think of Rachel Scott or Cassie Bernall, however, you focus on the positive legacy they left. They died letting everyone within earshot know they believed in God. What a legacy!

Throughout history, people have lived and died. Some left legacies of worth and value; others left legacies of hate and negativity. It all boils down to a choice, doesn't it? You're in the midst of developing your own legacy right now. Be careful to make wise choices, because they'll help shape the legacy you're creating.

It's a simple fact: Good choices = good consequences. Bad choices = bad consequences.

Everything you do can have an impact on the legacy you're currently developing. Determine to be discerning regarding the movies you watch, the chat rooms you frequent, where you travel on the Internet, the friendships you develop, your dating life, how you spend your money, how you respond to the needs of others, and how you treat people.

BREW IT!
Take stock of everything that has an influence on your life—media, friends, your part-time job, money—and let God have charge of these influential areas so you can develop a godly, positive legacy.

POUR IT!
Drink in the flavor from the following Scripture: Acts 1:16-22.

SAVOR IT!
If you haven't surrendered everything in your life to the authority of Jesus Christ, right now would be a great time to do so!

God wants to help you make good choices. And if you've surrendered everything to his lordship, his Holy Spirit within you will help you make wise decisions. But everything matters! How people remember you will be determined by the legacy you leave. And the legacy you leave is determined by how you live and the choices you make.

When you think of the disciple Thomas, what comes to your mind? Most people immediately thinking of "Doubting Thomas." Thomas was an incredible disciple, and God used him in important ways to build the Kingdom. But because he let his doubts control his decisions at a critical time in his relationship with Christ, he's usually remembered as "Doubting Thomas."

What do you think of when you hear the name Judas? Like most Christians, you probably think of his betrayal of Christ. He left a negative legacy, didn't he? Although he had some wonderful skills and did some good things, because he allowed his own desires—not God's—to determine his actions, he's remembered for his damaging legacy.

WHOM ARE YOU TAKING TO SCHOOL?

Teen Kyle Dubrul was late to school one Tuesday . . . and he had a unique excuse. He had to wait for Detroit Lions quarterback Joey Harrington to pick him up in the stretch limo that delivered them to the front doors of Trillium Academy, Kyle's school in Taylor, Michigan.

Joey Harrington was Kyle's guest at school for the day. It was part of the "Bring an NFL Player to School" sweepstakes. The NFL donated $1.5 million to grants that funded after-school programs, and a lucky student in all thirty-two NFL markets won a chance to spend a day with a player from their team.

Can you imagine how lucky Kyle felt throughout the day? The Lions quarterback encouraged students to work hard, tinkered on the school piano for a few moments, and threw passes to students who attended his lecture. He made his time count.

Whom would you like to bring to campus for a day? A pro tennis player? A pro basketball player? A movie star? A popular singer? Imagine everyone watching you in envy as you stroll across campus with your guest. No doubt you'd be crowded with other students who wanted to get to know your friend. You'd be the talk of your school!

Guess what? You may not be able to talk basketball legend Michael Jordan into sitting through math with you or Tom Cruise into helping carry your books to chemistry. But you *do* have the ability to invite the world's most famous celebrity to your campus.

The world's most famous celebrity is Jesus Christ. All of time centers around him. We base our dates on the number of years before his birth or after his death. His letter—the Holy Bible—has sold more books than any other manuscript in history. And he wants to come to your campus with *you*!

If you truly brought Jesus to your school, wouldn't people notice? And wouldn't they want to be around you? Think about it: The most powerful being in all the universe . . . who created life itself . . . and gave his own body for the sins of every student in your school . . . why wouldn't people want to be with him?

They would. If you bring Jesus to school with you, people will see him through your life. They'll notice there's something positively different about you.

BREW IT!

People will see a deep-seated peace that saturates your life even when you fail a test, are made fun of, or are ignored by your crush. They'll notice your confidence and peace, and they'll want what you have. They'll want to meet your best Friend!

POUR IT!

Drink in the flavor from the following Scriptures: Psalm 16:3; 18:1, 30-33.

SAVOR IT!

Ask Jesus to come to school with you.

COOL, COOLER, COOLEST

For good or bad, families have a deep impact on their children. Specific qualities and characteristics are often passed down from generation to generation. Your priorities will determine whether you pass along traits that enhance or destroy others.

I don't think King Herod ever got that message. His kids, his grandkids, his great-grandkids, and even his nephews were all concerned about one thing—looking cool—and it all began with Grandpa Herod himself (Herod the Great).

Each generation was consumed with wanting more power, looking good in front of the crowds, and making their mark in history. Each followed the other in weaknesses, mistakes, and missed opportunities to do the right thing. Check out the havoc they created:

BREW IT!
How do you react to truth when it hurts? Are you defensive, or are you teachable and willing to learn and grow?

POUR IT!
Drink in the flavor from the following Scripture: Mark 6:14-18.

SAVOR IT!
Ask God if there's any sin he wants to bring to light in your life.

- Herod the Great murdered many of Bethlehem's children.
- Herod Antipas had a part in Jesus' trial and had John the Baptist executed.
- Herod Agrippa I murdered the apostle James.
- Herod Agrippa II was a sarcastic judge involved in the apostle Paul's trial.

Let's focus our attention on Herod Antipas. He had an opportunity that most of us would love to have. He got to meet Jesus face-to-face . . . but he failed to recognize who Jesus was. Let's back up a bit and soak in the details that led to that encounter.

It doesn't feel good to have someone notice your faults, does it? We all have them, but most of us either try to keep them hidden or strive to change them into strengths. Herod wanted to hide his sins, but he couldn't.

What about you? Are there some things in your life that aren't right with God? If so, it won't do you any good to try to hide them. God knows everything. Recognize your sins and seek his forgiveness.

Back to Herod. Everyone knew what was going on. You see, he divorced his wife so he could marry his brother's wife, Herodias. Not a smart move, but he had power, so he thought he could get away with it.

John the Baptist had been holding some desert revivals, and thousands had come to hear him. Good preaching is always filled with stories and examples, right? And guess what story John used to illustrate sin? Herod and Herodias.

You can imagine how ticked off Herodias was! Herod wasn't too happy about it either, but he liked John. Apparently this desert preacher was the only one who really told it like it was to Herod. Though he didn't always like what he heard, Herod liked that he heard the truth.

HEROD'S BIRTHDAY BASH

Herod Antipas had a major dilemma. He liked John the Baptist because he was bold enough to preach the truth. But he didn't like John the Baptist preaching the truth about *him*! Yes, what John said was true: Herod had divorced his wife so he could marry his brother's wife, Herodias. But he couldn't allow John to keep telling the people what a sinful leader they had.

Herodias was pressuring Herod to silence the desert evangelist. Yet he was afraid to have John killed, so Herod simply put him in prison. Because he didn't like conflict, this seemed like an easy solution. Herod was a man who wanted everyone to like him. He had to look cool in front of the crowd.

It's never cool when the desire to be cool overrides good judgment and God's will. That's a definite setup for failure. And sure enough, Herod had set himself up.

Putting John in prison took care of things for a while, but Herodias was still steamed. She finally got her chance to do something about it at Herod's birthday bash. This was a major event. Herod actually gave the party for himself. It was a stag party for his palace aides, army officers, and the leading citizens of Galilee. The wine flowed freely, there were lots of snacks (probably those little, bitty weenies stuffed in tiny biscuits served with mustard—stuff like that), and the crowd was big.

Herod asked Herodias's daughter to dance for all his male friends. And this was no country line dance she was doing. This dance was sin in action. Rhythmic wickedness. Vile filth in slow motion.

You can imagine how the drunken men reacted. They screamed for more. Herod was so proud of himself for looking cool in front of all his male friends, he arrogantly boasted, "That was . . . wow. I mean, that was really . . . Hey . . . You're hot! As an extra bonus, I'll give you anything you ask for."

He assumed she'd ask for a small piece of the kingdom or a few material possessions. Instead, she left the stage and found her mom. "What should I ask for?" she said. "They're all drunk. Help me think of something really big!"

Herodias had already been thinking. "Tell Herod you want him to kill John the Baptist!"

"Kill him?"

"Yeah. But let's make it interesting. Tell him you want John's head delivered to you on a platter!"

Things quickly escalate to extreme danger when someone's desire to be cool, look cool, and sound cool controls his life. How desperate are you to look cool? Do you find yourself doing and saying things you know aren't right just to impress others?

BREW IT!
God doesn't want cool. He wants obedience.

POUR IT!
Drink in the flavor from the following Scripture: Mark 6:19-25.

SAVOR IT!
Ask God to help you focus on obeying him rather than being popular with the crowd.

A SINFUL BIRTHDAY GIFT

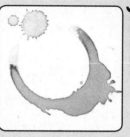

Herod's drunken friends were having the time of their lives watching Herodias's daughter's seductive dance. Their lustful appetites had been whetted, and they were wild with anticipation for more.

Herod boasted that the young woman could have anything she asked for. The crowd cheered. She climbed back on stage and grabbed the microphone. A hush fell over the drunken men as they watched her every move. She announced in full detail what her mom had planted in her mind. Herod's face fell. Kill John? Serve his head on a platter? Not only was that horrifying—it was evil!

Herod quickly scanned the room. Drunken men began to cheer again. They sounded like wild animals howling with glee. How could he disappoint his guests? He had to keep their approval. He had to look cool. He would have been embarrassed to back down now.

So, though he hated doing it, Herod demanded John the Baptist's head on a platter. He had caved in . . . but he looked cool in the eyes of his friends. Still, I imagine Herod didn't sleep much that night.

How did things go from bad to worse so quickly? When we allow ourselves to play around with sin— even for a little while—we're setting ourselves up for disaster. *What's a little sin?* you may think as you down a six-pack. *Everyone else is doing it. Gotta look cool.*

And when alcohol numbs your judgment and slows your thinking: *So what if we sleep together? Everyone else is having sex.*

Again, when we allow sin to have a foothold in our lives, bad can quickly escalate to depravity in a matter of minutes. Nothing—absolutely nothing—is worth compromising your relationship with Christ. Not being cool, having more friends, going out with the most popular person on campus, drinking . . . nothing!

Refuse even to play around with sin. Don't dance with it. Stay completely away, or you may find yourself at the equivalent of a birthday bash thrown by Herod!

BREW IT!
When Christ permeates your life, the desire to look good in front of others diminishes. Instead of wanting to appear cool, you'll find yourself growing more and more in love with your heavenly Father every day. Your main goal will be to please him.

POUR IT!
Drink in the flavor from the following Scriptures: Mark 6:26-29; 2 Corinthians 5:9-10; Galatians 1:10.

SAVOR IT!
Tell God you want to serve him with all your heart.

BREW IT!
Don't blow off your encounters with Christ like Herod did. Take advantage of meeting with the Savior each and every day. Learn from him. Listen to him. Draw near to him.

POUR IT!
Drink in the flavor from the following Scriptures: Deuteronomy 4:7; Psalm 73:28; James 4:8.

SAVOR IT!
Ask God to help your encounters with him become life-changing experiences.

STILL MAKING BAD DECISIONS

A few months after Herod's horrific birthday party, he met Jesus. Herod immediately associated Jesus with John because they were cousins. Again, Herod found himself in an awkward position. He didn't know what to do with Jesus. He didn't want to make the same mistakes he had made with John, yet he didn't want to take the action necessary to turn from his sins. That wouldn't look cool. His friends might not accept him anymore.

Not knowing what else to do, he tried to threaten Jesus just before his last journey to Jerusalem (see Luke 13:31). When he met with Jesus during one of his final trials, Jesus wouldn't even speak to him. Herod hadn't listened to John, and Christ didn't have anything to add to his cousin's words. Jesus knew Herod was interested not in hearing Jesus' message, but only in seeing miracles for entertainment. Herod's heart had been hardened. Because he had rejected God's message, he found it easy to reject God himself in the form of Jesus Christ. His response to Jesus' silence? Herod mocked him.

Herod met Jesus! If only he had recognized him for who he really is. But for years Herod had made choices to look cool in front of the crowd, and his heart had hardened so much that he couldn't recognize Jesus.

Herod could have turned his dysfunctional family history right side up. He could have influenced all of Galilee to follow God and spread the gospel. But being cool was more important.

We're all susceptible to letting our hearts harden toward the Savior. Don't let yourself get to that point! Keep a tender heart. Be receptive to the things of Jesus. The way to refrain from having a hardened heart is to seek God daily, read his Word, pray consistently, and listen for his voice. When he speaks, listen and obey. Don't ignore him.

Herod chose looking cool among his friends over spending eternity with Christ. As a result, as far as we know, he'll spend eternity completely separated from Christ. What a stupid choice! How in the world could he have allowed what others thought of him to determine where he'd spend eternity? Yet we can easily fall into the same trap if we don't allow Christ to be Lord over every area of our lives.

JUST WANT TO BE LOVED

It's natural to want to be loved. Even our pets desire our love. I have a big ol' 150-pound Saint Bernard who will allow a child to crawl all over him and even squeeze him too tightly, just because Bosco enjoys being loved. Everyone loves to be loved. In fact, God placed this desire within you. And guess what— you've had it since before birth.

If you're not receiving enough love, attention, and positive affirmation from your family, chances are you'll try to find it in other ways—such as standing on the cafeteria table and sticking french fries in the ear of an underclassman, being the class clown, putting someone down before he gets a chance to get to you, or hiding your old, smelly biology project in someone's locker.

Truth is, things and actions don't make you cool. Lifestyle and relationships do. A growing relationship with Christ results in a magnetic, hard-to-resist life-style. And *that's* cool!

Instead of trying to become more popular, pray about:

1. *Becoming a shining star.* Don't be obsessed with being popular, because God has a much higher calling on your life.

   Herod lived in a world darkened by sin. We live in that same darkened world. Your campus is filled with students who don't need one more cool friend. They need someone who (like John the Baptist) will shine brightly with God's truth. How can you do that? By refusing to go along with the crowd just to look cool. Ask God to keep your heart tender so you won't become hardened to his voice like Herod did.

2. *Being transformed in his image.* When you deter-mine to set a higher goal than popularity, you won't be able to look to your friends for an example of how to live. You'll look instead to Jesus Christ. Imitating him and yielding to his authority will totally transform your image.

3. *Living in love.* Rather than having you settle for fleeting popularity and acceptance from the crowd, God wants you to be saturated with something long lasting and genuine: his love!

BREW IT!
When Christ transforms your image, you become a brand-new person in him. And as you grow closer to him, being accepted by the crowd grows less and less impor-tant. The desire to be cool diminishes, and your desire to become all he desires you to be multiplies.

POUR IT!
Drink in the flavor from the following Scriptures: Romans 12:2-3; Philippians 2:14-16; 1 Timothy 4:16.

SAVOR IT!
Give God your desire to be cool, accepted, and popular. Ask him instead to help you focus on becoming who he wants you to be.

Students in Baton Rouge, Louisiana, get much more than just a cool breeze when they wear their trousers low. The state House of Representatives passed a bill that makes it a crime, enforceable with a five-hundred-dollar fine, to wear pants so low they expose your underwear.

What do you think? Are low, baggy pants out of hand? Should you be able to wear what you want without others making a big deal of it? Do you have a responsibility in the way you dress?

As a follower of Christ, you're called to reflect his image. That doesn't mean walking around in a suit and tie or heels and a new dress. But it *does* mean that you should dress in a way that will make Christ proud—not embarrassed.

Maybe you've heard one of your parents say, "Don't disgrace the family name." As a Christian, you carry the name of Christ. Doesn't it make sense then that you'd want to reflect his image in everything you do? The way you dress, the language you use, how you react to others, and your attitudes should all be reflective of your heavenly Father.

Guys, when you run around in the summer without a shirt, make sure there's a reason for it. If you're working outside and it's hot, it's understandable why you'd want to take off your shirt. But to run around without a shirt for no reason can cause girls to dwell on thoughts that lead to impure fantasizing.

BREW IT!

Go through your wardrobe with God. Be willing to toss anything that's suggestive or would embarrass him.

POUR IT!

Drink in the flavor from the following Scriptures: Proverbs 5:21; 10:8; 1 Corinthians 12:23-24.

SAVOR IT!

Ask God to help you make it a habit to seek his guidance when you're getting dressed each day.

Girls, when you go swimming, are you wearing a suit that's comfortable yet modest? Or are you wearing as little as possible? When you dress wearing too little—or when you wear clothing that's too short, too tight, or too low—you can cause guys to dwell on thoughts that lead to impure fantasizing.

Instead of tempting our guy and girl friends, our goal should be to help them become all that Christ wants for them. How much time and thought do you put into what you wear each day? How much prayer do you pour into what you wear? God cares about what you wear even more than you do!

Make time to consult him. Ask him about that shirt, those pants. Don't leave the house until he has approved your wardrobe. You'll get more than a cool breeze in Baton Rouge if you wear your pants too low—you'll face a fine. But if you're a Christian, you could also face the reality of embarrassing your Savior.

SURPRISE!

A man driving along a highway in Deerfield Beach, Florida, was stunned when he heard a loud crash. He looked down to discover the cab of his truck filled with broken glass and a turtle sitting next to him. "It seemed like it happened in slow motion," he said.

Even though most accidents occur as quickly as we can blink an eye, oftentimes they *seem* as though they're in slow motion. Maybe it's because we're in shock as things are coming to a crashing halt. Imagine how surprised you'd be, though, to see a turtle calmly sitting next to you after an accident!

Obviously the turtle can remain calm because he's not able to process what's happening around him. A turtle doesn't understand wreckage, death, climbing insurance rates, and so on. And because he doesn't understand what's going on around him, he can appear composed through a wreck.

The Bible tells us that someday the world will be extremely surprised. Someday—when Christ returns for his children and we're caught up in the air with him in the twinkling of an eye—the world will wonder what happened to the missing millions. Those familiar with the Bible will know that Christ has called his children home.

Do you get a little frightened when you think about the end times? It's natural to be apprehensive of the unknown, and though the Bible does give us several clues as to what will happen in the last days, none of us can imagine the scenario in detail. We don't understand all that will happen. Our minds aren't able to comprehend it.

BREW IT!
Determine to live inside God's peace by being ready at any moment to spend eternity with him.

POUR IT!
Drink in the flavor from the following Scripture: 1 Thessalonians 4:13-18.

SAVOR IT!
Tell God you don't want to be surprised about where you'll spend eternity. Ask him to show you anything in your life that's causing you to be fearful of the end times. Then ask God to remove your fear and replace it with his deep, settled peace.

But if Christ is truly Lord of your life, you can be calm amidst the surprises, just like the turtle in the wreckage. No, you don't know when Christ will return. You don't understand everything about the Tribulation and when the Rapture will occur. But you can experience the deep, settled peace of God and let it permeate your life so that a watching world sees that you're calm.

Of course, the only way you can live in his peace is if you're right with him. Take stock of your relationship with Christ right now. If the world ends tomorrow, do you know where you'll spend eternity?

If Christ returned tonight for his children, would you be taken with him? Or, like the truck driver, would you be caught totally off guard? Would you be shocked and surprised?

BREW IT!

Realize that non-Christians won't understand your desire for godliness. As your taste for the things of the world lessens, they may think you're weird. The only opinion that matters, though, is your heavenly Father's.

POUR IT!

Drink in the flavor from the following Scriptures: Proverbs 4:5-6, 11; 13:20.

SAVOR IT!

Tell God you want to grow as close to him as you can—even though doing so may make you seem weird to others.

THAT'S WEIRD

Almost everyone knows a football team has eleven players on the field at any given time, right? Not in Seligman, Arizona, not in Potter, Nebraska, and not in some towns in twelve other states in the nation. In small towns, football is played with eight team members on the field instead of eleven. The field is narrower and shorter than the one used by eleven-man teams, and because of that, eight-man teams usually run much higher scores.

The eight-man team was born during the Great Depression and takes a few other twists besides the number of players on the field. It subtracts the two tackles and a skill position player. Nebraska has the most eight-man teams of any state: 121. If you're used to watching or playing eleven-man football, you may think that eight-man football is weird. But the folks in Potter, Nebraska, don't think so. In fact, they're all for it!

The bleachers in their high school stadium only seat fifty, but two hours before the kickoff of a regular-season final, the field is bordered with empty vehicles. The residents of Potter (population 370) park early to save a spot, then walk home. At game time, everyone's back and in their cars or on the bleachers to cheer the Mullen Broncos.

Wow! Can you imagine what it would be like if people were so excited to go to church, they came two hours early just to get a good parking space or to find the best seat? Though it's probably not feasible for you to arrive at church that early, ask God to give you a brand-new excitement about being with his people.

For the folks who live in Potter, games are something they look forward to each Friday evening during football season. If you live in a large city, this may seem weird to you. What seems unusual to one person can seem entirely normal to another.

When you live a life of radical obedience to Jesus Christ, non-Christians may think you're weird. "What? You're not going to that party just because alcohol is being served? You're crazy!" some of your friends may say.

"What do you mean you're not going to the movie just because it's rated R? So what? Who cares?" another friend may say.

What seems weird to nonbelievers will hopefully become normal to you as you grow closer to Christ and strive to live a holy lifestyle.

WHO KNEW?

Here are some fun facts you may not be aware of:

- A beaver cuts down an average of two hundred trees a year.
- A pig's squeal ranges from 100 to 115 decibels.
- The average sled dog running in Alaska's annual Iditarod race burns ten thousand calories each day during the race.
- Cats sleep more than any other mammal. They average sixteen hours of sleep per day.
- The world's largest living bird is the male ostrich, and it can weigh up to 345 pounds.
- Every square inch of the human body has an average of 32 million bacteria on it.
- The average American will eat thirty-five thousand cookies in a lifetime.
- The human head weighs, on average, about eight pounds.
- Most mature oak trees shed about seven hundred thousand leaves in the fall.
- There are approximately 2,700 different species of mosquitoes.
- Most dogs can make about one hundred different facial expressions.
- Approximately 7 billion pounds of chocolate and candy are manufactured each year in the United States.
- Seawater is approximately 3.5 percent salt.
- There are approximately 75 million horses in the world.
- The human tongue contains about nine thousand taste buds.
- Our galaxy has approximately 250 billion stars.

Are there also some fun facts about the Bible you don't know? For instance, are you aware that there are sixty-six books in the Bible? Did you know the Old Testament contains thirty-nine books, and the New Testament has twenty-seven books? There are seventeen books of prophecy in the Old Testament, but there's only one in the New Testament (the book of Revelation). Approximately fifty Bibles are sold each minute across the world.

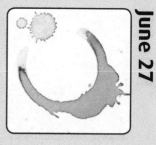

BREW IT!

There's a ton of incredibly exciting and challenging stuff in the Bible. Make it a point to read it, study it, and live your life by it. As you begin studying the Word of God, you'll automatically draw closer to your heavenly Father.

POUR IT!

Drink in the flavor from the following Scriptures: Psalm 119:105; John 1:1, 14.

SAVOR IT!

Ask God to give you a deep thirst for his Word.

BREW IT!
Take stock of your attitudes, words, and actions. Are they pleasing to Christ? Do they reflect him? Do you affirm others? Dare to be a disciple committed to damage control. Help a hurting friend feel better by reaching out to him.

POUR IT!
Drink in the flavor from the following Scriptures: Proverbs 12:25; Matthew 19:14; Ephesians 4:29, 32.

SAVOR IT!
Ask God to help you develop a sensitivity to the needs of others.

DAMAGE CONTROL

On a Sunday in October 2004, ninety-two vehicles crashed in seventeen separate accidents. What was the problem? A sudden, fast-moving hail- and rainstorm covered an eleven-mile stretch of highway near White Marsh, Maryland. No one died, but forty-nine people were injured. The highway had to be closed for a while due to the hail damage.

As much damage as hail can cause, your actions and attitudes can cause even more. What we say and how we act can make or break someone's day. The disciples knew this all too well. Jesus corrected them often for saying the wrong thing or having the wrong attitude. He knew his followers could damage the name of Christianity if they acted carelessly.

At one point the disciples scolded people for bringing their children to Christ. I can imagine the disciples thinking, *More kids! They're too noisy. They're too rambunctious. Take your kids home!* But Jesus let the disciples know that wasn't the right attitude, and he then instructed the disciples to let the children come to him.

In his New Testament letter, James wrote about how damaging the tongue can be. He reminded Christians that critical, negative talk can damage a person's spirit and reputation.

Andrew may have been known as the disciple who smiled and was nice to people. I can imagine he often tried to fix the damage others sustained from unkind words. Andrew was great at one-on-one relationships. He went out of his way to make the underdog feel special.

Remember the feeding of the five thousand? It was Andrew who brought Jesus the small boy with his lunch of fish and bread. Andrew had taken time to get to know a little boy in the midst of thousands.

Andrew was also the first disciple chosen by Jesus. Could it be that Christ chose him first because he knew Andrew had a tender, sensitive heart and would want to be involved in damage control when others were hurt?

Will you allow Jesus to use you on damage control? What would happen if you dared to affirm and encourage someone after he or she had been hurt by someone else's unkind words or attitudes? Will you dare to be an Andrew? A smiling, compassionate follower of Christ who reaches out to the underdog?

DO YOUR BEST

Many years ago a crew of students from Northwestern University, close to Chicago, was organized to serve as a rescue team when people needed help on Lake Michigan. One day they learned that a large vessel had wrecked just off the shore. The students hurried to the scene of the disaster and plunged into the frigid waters to rescue the people who were drowning.

After a while, the rescuers all returned to shore except for one young man. He finally arrived much later, carrying one man from the water. As soon as he released the man, he immediately returned to the water and brought another, and then another. He kept doing this until he had rescued ten people.

During this time, his fellow students on the rescue crew had built a fire and were warming themselves while trying to persuade this young hero to stop. By the time he had pulled the tenth person from the water, he was completely exhausted. He stopped for a while and rested. But it was only a matter of time until he plunged into the water again to rescue another man.

He was finally overcome with exhaustion. He went to bed feeling extremely ill. His friends knew he probably wouldn't make it through the night. While they stood around his bed and cried, they regretted that they hadn't done more. The young hero called one of his fellow crew members to his side and whispered, "Did I do my best?"

BREW IT!
How you live your life on earth will determine what Christ says to you at heaven's gates. Determine to do your very best for his sake.

POUR IT!
Drink in the flavor from the following Scriptures: Proverbs 12:27; Colossians 3:23-24; 2 Timothy 2:15.

SAVOR IT!
If there's an area in your life where you've been slacking off, seek God's forgiveness and ask him to help you do your best.

His friend instantly replied that he had. "Of course you did your best," he said. "You saved eleven men. But the doctors say you probably won't make it through the night."

The young hero was rapidly growing weaker, but he whispered again, "But tell me, did I do my very best?"

"Yes," his friend replied. "You did your very best."

A smile crossed the dying man's face as if to say, "Then I'm satisfied to die."

Someday, when we're in the presence of Christ, standing at heaven's gates, we'll want to be able to say, "I did my best. I did my very best!"

Think about yourself for a moment. Are you doing the best you can? Or are you half-heartedly coasting through life? If you're taking piano lessons, be disciplined about your practice time. If you're an athlete, follow your coach's instructions. If you're a budding writer, make time to keep a journal.

And if you're serious about being an all-out Christian, read your Bible consistently. Talk with God throughout each day. Do your best to become all he's calling you to be. Reach out to others. Think of their needs before your own.

BREW IT!
How have you praised God today? How have you worshipped him?

POUR IT!
Drink in the flavor from the following Scriptures: Jeremiah 29:11-13; Habakkuk 3:2; Malachi 3:2.

SAVOR IT!
Make a list of God's blessings in your life and praise him for each thing listed.

REFLECTING ON GOD

Spend some time today simply thinking about God and who he is.

God of glory
God of grace
God of hope
God of love and peace
God of retribution
God of the living
God of truth
God our Father
God our strength
God over all the kingdoms of the earth
God who gives encouragement
God who relents from sending calamity
Great and awesome God
Great and powerful God
He who blots out your transgressions
He who forms the hearts of all
He who raised Christ from the dead
He who reveals his thoughts to man
He who is able to do immeasurably more than all we ask or imagine
He who is able to keep you from falling
Holy Father
Holy One among you
I Am
I Am Who I Am
Judge of all the earth
King of glory
King of heaven
Living and true God
Lord
Lord God Almighty

WHICH ONES?

Try to guess which of the following holidays in the month of July are real and which ones are fake. Write an *R* by those you think are real, and write an *F* by those you believe are fake.

___ Be Kind to Cashiers Week
___ Eye Injury Prevention Month
___ National Baked Bean Month
___ AAA Baseball Awareness Month
___ Women's Motorcycle Month
___ Adopt a Kitten Month
___ National Try Some Tofu Week
___ International Foot Care Month
___ Take Charge of Change Week
___ National Salad Week
___ Celebrate Cinnamon Day
___ Cousins Day
___ Zoo Volunteers Day
___ Hot Enough for Ya? Day
___ Embrace Your Geekness Day
___ Hug Five People Day

BREW IT!
As a Christian, you should be having godly fun and living with joy. Are you?

POUR IT!
Drink in the flavor from the following Scriptures: Psalm 100; 115:12-13; 119:65.

SAVOR IT!
Ask God to help you get the most out of every day and to find joy in the little things.

Fake: Be Kind to Cashiers Week, AAA Baseball Awareness Month, Adopt a Kitten Month, National Try Some Tofu Week, International Foot Care Month, Celebrate Cinnamon Day, Zoo Volunteers Day, Hug Five People Day.

METICULOUSLY CARED FOR

Gene Sukie from Barberton, Ohio, has collected nearly ten thousand pounds of pennies during his life thus far—the greatest recorded feat of spare-change collecting. Gene is seventy-eight, and in 2004 he cashed in his record-setting collection of 1,407,550 pennies. It was worth $14,075.50 and took him more than thirty-four years to save.

Back in 1970, he cashed in his entire collection of forty thousand pennies to pay for his daughter's wedding. After the ceremony, he started collecting all over again. He collected an average of 112 pennies a day and inspected all the coins, separating them by year and mint location.

It would be an understatement to say that Gene was meticulous about his collection. He handled each coin carefully and could immediately show a guest exactly where coins minted in Denver were stored in his home. We could say that Gene really *knew* his coins.

Jesus talked a lot about sheep in the New Testament. He said that a good shepherd who truly cared about his sheep knew each one by name. In other words, a good shepherd was meticulous about the care he gave his flock. Jesus is called the Good Shepherd, and he knows each of his children by name. He not only knows the number of hairs on your head, he knows what frightens you, what makes you laugh, what frustrates you, and what you're passionate about.

Jesus cares for you much more intently than a record-setting coin collector cares for his precious pennies! Christ set a world record for demonstrating his love for you when he willingly sacrificed his own life for your salvation, and he meticulously cares for you each moment of each day, 24/7.

What are you meticulous about? Perhaps it's getting good grades or having the best clothes. Maybe it's keeping your hair perfect or staying in shape. But consider becoming meticulous about something that has eternal value or something that will have a major impact on others. For instance, if you treated those around you with meticulous concern, what kind of difference would it make in their lives? They'd probably see Christ in your actions.

What if you carefully shared your faith with those around you? You could make a difference for eternity! Instead of focusing on things that are temporary or don't have lasting value, consider becoming passionate about caring for the needs of others—just like a coin collector cares for his precious coins.

BREW IT!

Aren't you glad that God doesn't care for you halfheartedly? Imitate him in the way you care for those around you.

POUR IT!

Drink in the flavor from the following Scriptures: Ephesians 2:14-15; Philippians 4:17; James 3:17-18.

SAVOR IT!

Ask God to show you specific ways you can communicate to those around you how much he loves them.

THE FLAG OF THE UNITED STATES OF AMERICA

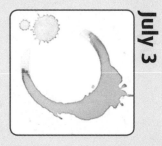

Did you know that the twenty-one-gun salute given at military funerals stands for the sum of the numbers in the year 1776? Perhaps you've noticed that when the honor guard captain removes the American flag from the coffin and prepares to hand it to the next-of-kin, he pays meticulous attention to folding the flag thirteen times. You may have assumed it was to symbolize the original thirteen colonies. But according to legend, it actually isn't connected to the thirteen colonies at all.

The first fold of our flag symbolizes life. The second fold symbolizes our belief in eternal life. The third fold is made in honor of the veterans who gave their lives to defend our country and to attain peace throughout the world. The fourth fold represents our weaker nature, for as American citizens trusting in God, we turn to him for his divine guidance during times of peace as well as in times of war.

The fifth fold is a tribute to our country. The sixth fold represents where our hearts lie. It's with our heart that we pledge allegiance to the flag of the United States of America and to the republic for which it stands, one nation under God, indivisible, with liberty and justice for all.

BREW IT!
Some traditions have important and deep meaning. Tomorrow, on Independence Day, remember these tributes when you see the American flag flown.

POUR IT!
Drink in the flavor from the following Scriptures: Isaiah 59:21; 61:1-3; 65:1.

SAVOR IT!
Ask God to help you show by your actions how proud you are of your country.

The seventh fold is a tribute to our armed forces, because it's through them that our country is protected. The eighth fold is in honor of Jesus, the one who entered into the valley of the shadow of death so we might see the light of day. The ninth fold is a tribute to womanhood and mothers. It's been their faith, love, loyalty, and devotion that has molded the character of the men and women who have made this country great.

The tenth fold is a tribute to fathers, for they, too, have given sons and daughters for the defense of our country. The eleventh fold represents the lower portion of the seal of King David and King Solomon and glorifies the God of Abraham, Isaac, and Jacob. The twelfth represents eternity and, in the Christian's eyes, glorifies God the Father, the Son, and the Holy Spirit.

At the thirteenth fold—when the flag is completely folded—the stars are uppermost, reminding us of our nation's motto, "In God We Trust." After the flag is completely folded and tucked in, it takes on the appearance of a cocked hat. This is to remind us of the soldiers who served under General George Washington, the sailors and marines who served under Captain John Paul Jones, and all their later comrades and shipmates in the armed forces of the United States, who preserve for us the rights, privileges, and freedoms we enjoy today.

BREW IT!

The United States of America was established on religious principles, and most of its founders had strong faith in God. Stand up for those values and be willing to speak out in boldness for God in America!

POUR IT!

Drink in the flavor from the following Scriptures: Isaiah 9:6; Matthew 22:17-22; Romans 13:7.

SAVOR IT!

Ask God to help you stand for what's right, even if you're criticized for doing so.

A COUNTRY THAT LOVES GOD = A STRONG COUNTRY

Have you ever been to Washington, DC? If you get a chance to visit our nation's capital, make sure you notice this: As you walk up the steps to the building that houses the U.S. Supreme Court, you can see near the top of the building a row of the world's lawgivers. The one in the middle—Moses—is holding two stone tablets, representing the Ten Commandments.

And as you enter the Supreme Court's courtroom, the two huge oak doors have stone tablets and ten Roman numerals—implying the Ten Commandments—engraved on the lower portion.

Make sure you visit the federal buildings and carefully notice the Bible verses etched in stone in various places throughout the buildings and on several monuments in Washington, DC. Our country's fourth president, James Madison, said, "We have staked the whole of all our political institutions upon the capacity of mankind for self-government, upon the capacity of each and all of us to govern ourselves, to control ourselves, to sustain ourselves according to the Ten Commandments of God."

Patrick Henry, one of the founding fathers of our country said, "It cannot be emphasized too strongly or too often that this great nation was founded, not by religionists, but by Christians; not on religions, but on the gospel of Jesus Christ."

Do you realize that every session of Congress begins with a prayer by an ordained minister? This was begun in 1789 and is still in practice today. Fifty-two of the fifty-five founders of the Constitution were members of established churches in the colonies. John Jay, our first Supreme Court Justice, said, "Americans should select and prefer Christians as their rulers."

It makes you wonder, doesn't it . . . how what we've done for more than two hundred years is now being interpreted by many as wrong and unconstitutional. Prayer in schools was an essential in the establishing of our educational facilities when our country was born. Traditional marriages between one man and one woman have always been deemed as sacred. Now states are trying to pass gay marriage rights, and many people want to keep prayer out of our schools. Several schools around the nation won't allow Christmas programs in assemblies if Jesus is mentioned.

It's hard to understand why there's such resistance to displaying the Ten Commandments in state courthouses, printing "In God We Trust" on our money, and keeping God in the Pledge of Allegiance.

MAN OF PRAYER

Starting on May 24, we took a quick peek at Nehemiah's life. You'll remember he was the one responsible for rebuilding the wall of righteousness that surrounded the entire city of Jerusalem. He and his crew completed this massive project in just fifty-two days. Throughout the Bible we see God working through ordinary people to do extraordinary things.

Nehemiah didn't have much power, but he had a lot of influence. You can too. The king Nehemiah worked for had a lot of respect for his employee. He trusted Nehemiah. Do people in positions of leadership and authority trust you? Does your lifestyle reflect integrity? Is your work ethic above reproach?

Let's think this through. What made Nehemiah so successful?

BREW IT!
Nehemiah was an ordinary man who accomplished extraordinary tasks because of God working through his life. God wants to work through your life too!

POUR IT!
Drink in the flavor from the following Scriptures: Psalm 9:10; Matthew 17:20; James 1:2-3.

SAVOR IT!
Ask God to help you develop the qualities of Nehemiah.

- *He was a man of prayer.* He knew the only way he could accomplish what seemed like an impossible task was through the power of God Almighty. So he spent time plugged into the Power Source himself through the avenue of prayer. What about you? Are you using prayer as a last resort? Or is it becoming a consistent part of your daily life?
- *He was an incredible organizer and motivator.* He was able to persuade men to volunteer their time and energy to rebuild Jerusalem's wall. They wouldn't receive any honor, pay, or awards for their work. Yet they were willing to spend time away from friends and family because Nehemiah had motivated them to become involved in something bigger than themselves. Do you try to motivate others in your Bible study, youth group, or church to rally together and do something great for God?
- *He was able to keep calm under pressure.* Nehemiah was tormented by neighboring governors Sanballat and Tobiah, yet he didn't become flustered or discouraged or threaten to quit. He continued even when the going got extremely tough. When others make fun of you for your faith, how do you react?
- *He was a spiritual leader who stood up for what was right.* When under intense pressure to quit, Nehemiah consistently did what was right. Regardless of how tough it was, he continued to stand for truth and morality by obeying God's instructions to rebuild the wall surrounding Jerusalem. Do you publicly take a stand for what's right?
- *He told it like it was.* When followers of God around him were sinning, he called them on it without worrying about what they'd think of him. What would it take for you to have this kind of boldness?

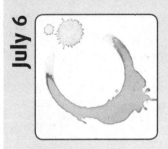

PRAYER MAKES A DIFFERENCE

What can we unpack and take with us from Nehemiah's life? We can actually learn quite a bit from this Old Testament hero. First of all, we're reminded that when God leads us to do something, he'll empower and equip us with everything we need to do it—and that includes the impossible!

Nehemiah didn't have any construction experience. Yet when God called him to be in charge of rebuilding the wall that surrounded the city of Jerusalem, Nehemiah obeyed. He could have easily argued, "Nah, I'm not the guy for this job, Lord. Now, my friend Jon has all kinds of experience in this field. He's been a roofer and helped his dad build custom-designed homes. He'd be great!"

Not only did Nehemiah not argue with God, he didn't even question God. Although his own abilities were extremely limited, he realized God could do the impossible through a willing life. Nehemiah was willing!

Still, this was an incredibly huge challenge. What did Nehemiah do first? He prayed. What an incredible lesson for us. The very first thing we need to do when facing any challenge is to talk to God. Nehemiah knew the power of prayer. He realized the opportunity he had to converse directly with the King of kings, and he took advantage of it.

Are there times when you feel as though you're facing the impossible? Does the task ahead seem insurmountable? Remember, the One who calls you is faithful to equip you with everything you need—not simply to get the job done, but to do the job extremely well. Nehemiah was motivated by prayer. Through talking with God, he received strength, encouragement, and power to do the task that he'd been called to accomplish.

What kind of difference can this make in your life? When you're doubting the task ahead of you, or even when you're dreading it, do you realize that prayer can actually enthuse you, motivate you, and equip you to accomplish the task with zeal? Take advantage of the wonderful gift of prayer God has given you. Think about it: Through prayer, he's made it possible for you to approach his throne. You can take your concerns directly to your heavenly Father and hear his response. That should make a huge difference in how you approach the tasks that lie ahead of you!

BREW IT!

Prayer is a powerful tool. Are you using it to its full strength?

POUR IT!

Drink in the flavor from the following Scriptures:
Mark 11:24; John 17:15; Acts 1:14.

SAVOR IT!

Ask God to help you rest in the assurance that he'll equip you with everything you need to accomplish all that he calls you to do.

PROMISES? TONS OF THEM!

What else can we learn from Nehemiah's life? He was a man of faith, and he was a prayer warrior. He also confessed his sins. Remember, Nehemiah was away from his home in Jerusalem when he heard the news about the wall being destroyed. So he could have said, "Hey, God, I understand it's important to have a wall around the city, but I didn't destroy it. I'm not even there right now. Could you get someone else for this task—someone who's right there and is familiar with what's happening in Jerusalem?"

Even though it wasn't directly Nehemiah's fault, he took responsibility for the actions of his people. He confessed that they had all sinned against God. He included himself in that prayer of confession. Have you ever stopped to realize that it was your sins that nailed Christ to the cross? Even though you didn't actually pick up the hammer and drive the nails through his flesh, your sins—as well as my sins—were responsible for Christ's death. Just as Nehemiah confessed for his people, we need to confess for the role each of us played in crucifying Christ.

After Nehemiah confessed, he acknowledged God's promises. Get this: God has given us 7,464 promises throughout Scripture. Don't you think it's time we started claiming some of them? Nehemiah knew God's promises, and he claimed them *before* he started rebuilding the wall.

BREW IT!
Recognize the difference God's promises can make in your life and let them be reflected through your actions.

POUR IT!
Drink in the flavor from the following Scriptures: Nehemiah 1:5-11; 2:4-5.

SAVOR IT!
Ask God to show you specifically what he's calling you to do, and pray the prayer included in today's devotional.

Think about the incredible difference this could make the next time the Lord assigns you what seems to be a huge task. Before throwing yourself into the assignment, first go to him in prayer. Draw strength and motivation from your prayer time with him. Confess anything in your life that could keep you from accomplishing the task he's set in front of you. Then thank him for his promises. Acknowledge those promises. Familiarize yourself with them by reading the Bible consistently. (If you're interested, check out your local Christian bookstore for books or Bibles that highlight God's promises.) Then claim what he has already promised you *before* you begin the assignment. And voice your prayer to him:

"Lord, this task seems huge! Show me anything in my life that I need to confess to you—anything that will hinder me from accomplishing what you've called me to do. I don't want anything to be between us. And thank you for your promise to make me strong in you, victorious in you, confident in you. Thanks that you have already promised to provide me with everything I need to accomplish this assignment. I claim those resources now, and in faith I'll move forward to do what you have called me to do."

FINDING YOUR PLACE ON THE WALL (PART 1)

The task given to Nehemiah was huge! For an ordinary young man to recruit volunteer construction workers and rebuild the wall surrounding the entire city of Jerusalem—amidst constant torment from two neighboring governors—may have seemed impossible, but Nehemiah was confident that God would give him victory.

Nehemiah knew how to involve those around him, and he also knew the value of teamwork. Let's take a peek at some principles of involvement Nehemiah used to accomplish his goal. As we walk through these principles, find your own spot on the wall of ministry. Let God speak to you about how you can make a difference right where you are.

1st Principle of Involvement: Have a team ministry. Nehemiah knew it would be impossible and even foolish for him to try to rebuild the wall all by himself. Very rarely does God call us into a "lone ranger" ministry. He wants us to work with others and to develop unity while doing it.

Nehemiah delegated. That doesn't mean he walked away from his responsibility; he merely shared the work with those around him. He was still very much involved, but he knew the wisdom in delegating. When you're facing a huge task, surround yourself with workers you can trust and delegate some of the task. That doesn't mean you're not responsible anymore, nor does it mean you can walk away. It means you're getting necessary help. As you delegate, concentrate on breaking down the job into manageable segments. When you do this, the task ahead doesn't seem so frightening.

2nd Principle of Involvement: Be a servant-leader. We read in Nehemiah 3:1 that Eliashib the high priest and his fellow priests went to work and rebuilt the Sheep Gate. The high priest could have easily said, "Let's find some homeless people to do this job. We have other things that are much more important. We're dignified. We're special. We shouldn't have to work on the wall."

But even the high priest and his fellow priests got their hands dirty. Let this be a reminder that the greatest leaders are the best servants. The most admired leadership comes through the act of servanthood. Always be willing to roll up your sleeves and get to work. As a leader, set the example for others by displaying your own work ethic.

BREW IT!
Be sure you're providing a great example of hard work for those around you before you start delegating.

POUR IT!
Drink in the flavor from the following Scriptures:
Nehemiah 3:1; Proverbs 10:9; Galatians 5:13.

SAVOR IT!
Ask God to help you develop into the servant-leader he desires.

FINDING YOUR PLACE ON THE WALL (PART 2)

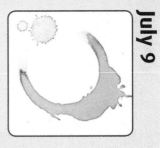

Nehemiah understood some important principles of involvement. Let's recap:

1st Principle of Involvement: Have a team ministry.
2nd Principle of Involvement: Be a servant-leader.
What else did Nehemiah recognize?

3rd Principle of Involvement: Don't let antagonists set the agenda. Neighboring governors Sanballat and Tobiah constantly threatened and mocked Nehemiah and his crew and tried to intimidate them into stopping their work. But Nehemiah refused to let the antagonists determine his course of direction.

When you're moving full-steam ahead doing the work of the Lord, there will always be people who taunt you, try to discourage you, and possibly even threaten you. Remember that they don't set your agenda for doing God's work; God sets your agenda! Refuse to succumb to your antagonists.

We halfway expect nonbelievers to give us a hard time, don't we? After all, the Bible tells us to expect persecution. So we really shouldn't be surprised when non-Christians try to discourage or defeat us. But what really hurts is when those within the body of Christ give us a hard time. And it happens! Again, don't let halfhearted Christians set the agenda for what God has called you to do.

We're told in Nehemiah 3:5 that some of the men "working" on the wall refused to do any labor. They simply wanted to play the part. Perhaps they thought it was cool to wear a tool belt and a hard hat and be a part of Nehemiah's construction crew. But when it actually came to real work, they didn't do much at all.

Do you have some friends who fall into this category? They may think it's cool to go to youth group and hang out with their friends. Maybe they wear a cool youth group T-shirt and get excited about going on a mission trip and participating in a variety of other fun church activities. But when it comes time to roll up their sleeves and really work at building the Kingdom, they balk.

They don't want to develop a testimony and learn how to share with those who don't know Christ. They have no desire to visit an assisted-living home for elderly people and be the hands and feet of Jesus. They're simply involved on a surface level because it feels good or because they think it looks good. Don't be discouraged by them! Keep your eyes focused on God and on doing all he has called you to do.

BREW IT!
When you stand before God, you want him to say, "Well done, good and faithful servant" (Matthew 25:21). So focus on him, not on what those around you aren't doing.

POUR IT!
Drink in the flavor from the following Scriptures: Nehemiah 3:5; Proverbs 11:3; 13:6.

SAVOR IT!
Ask God to keep you from becoming discouraged in doing what he has called you to do.

BREW IT!
Are you leading by example?
Are you willing to roll up your
sleeves and do a thankless
job? Remember, the best leaders are those who serve
zealously.

POUR IT!
Drink in the flavor from the
following Scriptures:
Nehemiah 3:14, 20;
Psalm 78:72.

SAVOR IT!
Ask God to give you zeal to
accomplish the work that he
has called you to do.

FINDING YOUR PLACE ON THE WALL (PART 3)

Nehemiah was clued in to several important principles that enabled him to accomplish the task God had
given him. And he also used these principles to help
others find their specific place on the wall. You, too,
can find your place on the wall of righteousness with
these principles. Let's recap:

1st Principle of Involvement: Have a team ministry.

2nd Principle of Involvement: Be a servant-leader.

3rd Principle of Involvement: Don't let antagonists
set the agenda.

4th Principle of Involvement: Serve regardless of
the job. The Bible tells us that the Dung Gate was
repaired by the ruler of one of the districts. His name
was Malkijah, and he could have easily argued, "I
have an important position of authority. Surely there's
a more prestigious job for me to do than fix the Dung
Gate!" But he, too, was willing to lead by serving.

Some gates were more important than others. But
for the wall to be built, someone had to repair the
Dung Gate—the place where people in the city came
to dump their garbage and human waste. It wasn't
very pleasant, but Malkijah was willing. Every project
needs people who say, "I'll do whatever it takes."
What a fantastic attitude! What an incredible example.

Are you willing to do whatever it takes? Or are
there some areas of service that seem beneath you?
God doesn't care about titles or positions; he's simply
looking for obedient and willing servants. There will be times when you'll need to do
the dirty work. You'll need to roll up your sleeves and do what no one else wants to do.
Be willing to get dirty. Have a good attitude about doing icky stuff for the glory of God.

5th Principle of Involvement: Serve with zeal. The Bible tells us that right next to
Malkijah was Baruch, who zealously repaired another section of the wall. There's a difference in doing a job because you have to or because it's expected of you, and doing a
job with joy and excitement because you want to! How do others see your involvement
in Kingdom business? Are you working with a halfhearted attitude and dragging your
feet? Or are you zealously throwing yourself into the task which God has given you?

What was Baruch doing? He was building a wall, clearing away rubble, picking up
trash, sweeping away debris. Yet he did these menial tasks with great zeal.

FINDING YOUR PLACE ON THE WALL (PART 4)

Nehemiah was able to accomplish this incredible task of rebuilding the wall surrounding the city of Jerusalem in just fifty-two days! Many would say that was a miracle. Think about it: In spite of opposition from neighboring governors, and in spite of difficult work, they completed the task. How? They did it because Nehemiah was operating by some extremely important principles that helped his crew find their own place of responsibility on the wall. God wants to help you find your place on his wall of righteousness as well. Let's recap and keep going.

1st Principle of Involvement: Have a team ministry.

2nd Principle of Involvement: Be a servant-leader.

3rd Principle of Involvement: Don't let antagonists set the agenda.

4th Principle of Involvement: Serve regardless of the job.

5th Principle of Involvement: Serve with zeal.

What was next?

6th Principle of Involvement: Watch each other's backs! Nehemiah's construction crew guarded each other. Through Nehemiah's quality leadership, his crew was transformed from merely a construction crew into a genuine community. They cared about each other. They picked up the slack for one another.

BREW IT!

Let God use other Christians in your life to fight the daily battles you'll encounter so you can continue to do the task he's given you.

POUR IT!

Drink in the flavor from the following Scriptures: Proverbs 29:10; Ecclesiastes 4:9-10; Titus 2:7.

SAVOR IT!

Ask God to help you surround yourself with godly people who will support your quest to do his will.

They developed friendships and unity. So when Sanballat and Tobiah began attacking the wall builders, Nehemiah reassigned some jobs. He had several stop what they were doing on the wall and protect the others, who continued to build.

The protectors may have been tempted to say, "Hey, wait a sec! This isn't what I signed up for! I'm a builder, not a warrior. I don't want to stand guard; I want to mix cement and lay brick." The Bible doesn't even give a hint of such an attitude. We're simply told that the men who were reassigned to stand guard did so. They protected their fellow crewmen so work on the wall could continue.

When others are giving you a tough time about doing what God has called you to do, you may be tempted to stop completely so you can fight the new battle that faces you. Instead, surround yourself with sold-out Christian friends who will support you and stand guard for you, so you can continue doing your task.

If you quit doing God's work every time a battle rages, you'll be stopping every other day to fight. Know that when you're truly doing what he has called you to do, battles *will* rage against you! The opposition will be relentless. Don't quit your most important task—that of doing God's will in your life—to stop and argue with those who oppose you.

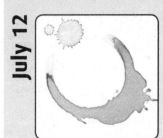

FINDING YOUR PLACE ON THE WALL (PART 5)

Let's recap the principles of Nehemiah's strategy:

1st Principle of Involvement: Have a team ministry.

2nd Principle of Involvement: Be a servant-leader.

3rd Principle of Involvement: Don't let antagonists set the agenda.

4th Principle of Involvement: Serve regardless of the job.

5th Principle of Involvement: Serve with zeal.

6th Principle of Involvement: Watch each other's backs!

And the final principle Nehemiah worked with was:

7th Principle of Involvement: Be motivated by God's plan. The only reason Nehemiah rebuilt the wall was because God had told him to. Think about your involvement in Christian service. Why are you doing what you're doing . . . really? Is it because you feel good or look good when you're busy? Or are you truly called by God to do what you're doing? Our utmost goal in everything we do should be to spread the gospel of Christ. Take stock of all the things you're involved in. Are these activities helping you reach your ultimate goal of spreading the gospel?

Hey, wait a sec! Are you saying I shouldn't be on the basketball team because it's not gospel oriented? No. But I hope your involvement on the team will be a witness to your fellow teammates. I hope you're allowing God to use you—including your actions on and off the court—to be a shining example of his love for your teammates, your opponents, and those who watch you play.

Our motivation should come from the bottom-line fact that we're here on earth to spread the gospel. That's why we do what we do. How do we get motivated? Through prayer—just as Nehemiah was motivated through prayer.

Nehemiah knew that rebuilding the wall around Jerusalem would serve two purposes: (1) It would be a physical wall of protection for those who lived in the city, and (2) it would symbolize a spiritual wall of righteousness. It would help keep out evil influences from surrounding cities, which would help the Jews grow stronger in their faith.

You're here on earth to build a wall. It's a wall of righteousness, and God first wants you to build it around your own life. Then he wants you to reach out and begin helping others build walls of righteousness around their lives.

Have you found your place on the wall? Don't be afraid to get involved in this incredible "building" project in the lives of those around you. Be willing to roll up your sleeves and do whatever needs to be done to spread the gospel of Christ.

REFINER OF SILVER

A group of girls was reading the book of Malachi in their Bible study. As they studied the third chapter, they came across verse three, which tells us that God will be like a refiner and purifier of silver. This puzzled them, and they wondered what it revealed about the character and nature of God. One of the girls offered to do some research on refining silver and said she'd report her findings to the group at their next meeting.

That week, she made an appointment with a silversmith. She wanted to watch him work. She didn't mention the reason for her interest beyond her curiosity about the process of refining silver. As she watched, the silversmith held a piece of silver over the fire and let it heat up. He explained that silver needs to be held in the middle of the fire where the flames are hottest so all the impurities can be burned away.

The girl thought about God holding us in such a hot spot. Then she thought again about the verse defining God as a refiner and purifier of silver. She asked the silversmith if he had to sit there in front of the fire the whole time the silver was being refined.

The man answered that he did. "Not only do I sit here holding the silver," he explained, "but I have to keep my eyes on the silver the entire time it's in the fire. If the silver is left even a moment too long in the flames, it will be destroyed."

The girl was silent for a moment, then turned to the silversmith. "How do you know when the silver is fully refined?"

He smiled as he answered, "That's easy. I know it's completely refined when I can see my image in it."

The girl was eager to report back to her Bible study the next week. "God will never give us more than we can handle," she reminded her friends. "He will stay with us the entire time we're experiencing the fire. He's faithful. And when he can see his image in our lives, we've been refined."

Being refined is a process, isn't it? God will spend our entire lifetimes refining us. He'll keep molding and reshaping and redefining us until his image is crystal clear in our lives. That takes time. Instead of being discouraged when you're feeling the heat, be grateful and recognize the fact that God is working his image into your lifestyle.

BREW IT!
Be glad that God cares about you enough to keep working with you so you'll become like him.

POUR IT!
Drink in the flavor from the following Scriptures: Malachi 3:2-3, 6, 10.

SAVOR IT!
Ask God to help you recognize the positive side of being refined when you're feeling the heat.

BREW IT!
Think about the difference between flippantly saying, "Sorry about that" and true repentance.

POUR IT!
Drink in the flavor from the following Scriptures: Isaiah 30:15; Jeremiah 15:19; Ezekiel 18:32.

SAVOR IT!
Spend some time thanking God for his grace and forgiveness.

YOU'RE FIRED!

If you've seen the reality television show *The Apprentice*, you're familiar with billionaire Donald Trump's famous line, "You're fired!" Contestants competing for a high-profile job in one of Trump's many companies engage in a variety of business and marketing activities, hoping to prove their competence. But as the show progresses, each week someone is fired from the competition.

Reality show contestants aren't the only ones who have heard "You're fired!" Some well-known celebrities went on to become successful in spite of losing a job.

- Larry King of CNN was fired as a columnist for the *Miami Herald* in the 1970s for writing about too many of his friends.
- Actor Robert Redford says he was fired once because he was caught sleeping in an oil tank instead of cleaning it.
- Lee Iacocca was fired from Ford but later became very successful as an executive with Chrysler.
- Walt Disney was fired from a department store because he "didn't have any good ideas."

Aren't you glad God doesn't fire you from being his child? The Bible is full of believers who made mistakes, but because we serve a God of second chances (and third, and fourth, and so on), they never heard "You're fired!" from their heavenly Father.

Does that mean we can do whatever we want to because God will always forgive us? No. If we truly love God, we'll strive to obey him in everything we do. And we'll *want* to obey him because we love him. Suppose you say, "I'm going to shoplift this pair of shoes today, and I'll ask God to forgive me tonight. Next week, I'll need to shoplift something for my best friend's birthday party, but I'll ask God to forgive me again." You're not truly repenting.

God will always forgive a genuinely repentant heart. But true repentance means turning around and not planning to repeat that same wrong action. After God forgives us, we need to set up some fences, hedges, or accountability to keep us from continuing in that same sin. And, of course, his Holy Spirit wants to empower us to get off that sinful road.

If we didn't serve a God who is willing to forgive genuine repentance, King David could have heard "You're fired!" after his sinful affair with Bathsheba. And Peter might have heard "You're fired!" after denying he even knew Christ . . . three times!

What could you have been fired for? Aren't you grateful you serve a God who wants to forgive, forget, and restore?

DANGER ZONE

Do you remember show-and-tell? Many elementary school students get to bring something to school to show the class and tell about it. It's a great exercise in getting students to become comfortable addressing a group, and it's a fun way to teach kids how to make oral presentations.

You may remember getting excited about sharing stuff that was cool to you with your classmates. You probably brought in some pretty harmless objects, but a first grader in New Jersey recently brought a grenade for show-and-tell! His teacher took it to the principal and they evacuated the building. It turned out to be harmless and not live, but they followed safety procedures anyway.

Has your school become more dangerous in recent years? Do you get a little nervous when you think about the Columbine High School tragedy in Littleton, Colorado, or a variety of other school shootings? It's normal to be frightened of some things. Though God doesn't want us to live in fear, there *is* such a thing as healthy fear. If you're afraid of poisonous snakes, you simply have a healthy fear of something that could potentially kill you. But if you're afraid to ride in a bus or car to school each day because of the relatively low possibility of having an accident, that's an unhealthy fear.

Do you have some unhealthy fears? God desires to give you victory over those fears. He wants you to live in confidence. He wants you to experience his peace on a daily basis. The Bible tells us that the peace of God passes all understanding. In other words, when his peace floods your soul, there aren't words to describe it!

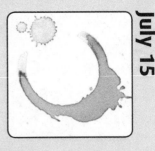

BREW IT!
Think about your fears and label them as healthy or unhealthy. Are there some unnecessary fears in your life you can get rid of?

POUR IT!
Drink in the flavor from the following Scriptures: Psalm 3:6; 27:1; 46:2.

SAVOR IT!
Ask God to remove your unhealthy fears and replace them with his solid peace.

The apostle Peter denied that he knew Christ three times just hours before the Lord's crucifixion. Why did he do that? He had walked with Jesus for three years, heard his preaching, witnessed his miraculous healings, watched him raise the dead to life, and grown to love his Master. He denied knowing Christ because he was afraid.

Fear can cripple even the strongest people. Some of the twelve disciples were professional fishermen and knew the Sea of Galilee like the backs of their hands. Yet when they were out in the middle of the sea and a violent storm came up, they were frightened beyond words. Jesus calmed the disciples and the storm by commanding the winds to stop. He cares about our fears—the big ones and the small ones, the healthy fears and the unhealthy fears. Jesus wants to saturate you with his deep, settled peace.

BREW IT!
Instead of questioning God and his ways, simply accept them and trust his sovereignty.

POUR IT!
Drink in the flavor from the following Scriptures: Jeremiah 39:18; John 14:1; Hebrews 2:13.

SAVOR IT!
Ask God to deepen your faith in him.

WAS IT GOD?

A woman in Indianapolis said that God led her to a parked van whose driver was responsible for her son's death in a hit-and-run accident. She wrote down the license plate number and discovered four days later that she was right. The sheriff's department confirmed her suspicions. It *was* the same van that hit and killed her son.

Did God really lead her to the van? Was it just a coincidence? We may have to wait until we get to heaven to find out, but we *do* know from reading the Bible—God's Holy Word—that he often works in mysterious ways.

Do you remember the Old Testament story about Balaam (see Numbers 22)? He wouldn't listen to God, but God was determined to get through to him, so the Lord caused his donkey to speak! Can you imagine? What if your dog or cat began speaking to you and told you what God wanted you to hear? Would you believe your pet? You probably would, because you'd realize you were witnessing a supernatural event. When Balaam's donkey spoke to him, he listened. God can work in mysterious ways!

Remember the Old Testament prophet Jonah? (For a quick preview, turn to September 22–26.) God worked in mysterious ways in his life too. God allowed Jonah to be swallowed by a large fish and enabled the prophet to live inside the animal for three days and nights! When the fish finally vomited Jonah onto shore, Jonah realized God was speaking to him.

God actually lengthened a twenty-four-hour day so his army could continue fighting and receive victory over the enemy in an important battle. He took Elijah up to heaven in a whirlwind.

God spoke to Moses through a burning bush. He told Noah to build a boat that would save him and his family from the rain. (The people in Noah's day had never even heard of rain. In fact, Genesis 2:5-6 tells us that water came up from the ground to irrigate the earth. Rain was a brand-new concept for them!) God works in mysterious ways.

Never underestimate the creator of the universe. He can do *what* he wants, *when* he wants, and *how* he wants. The issue is simply to trust him implicitly.

BACK TO YOUR FIRST LOVE

The apostle John recorded seven letters that Jesus "dictated" to him to send to the seven churches in Asia Minor—now known as Turkey. On April 28–30, we talked about the first church John sent a letter to— the church in Ephesus. Jesus affirmed that church for several things, but he condemned them for one thing. "I hold this against you: You have forsaken your first love. Remember the height from which you have fallen! Repent and do the things you did at first" (Revelation 2:4-5).

Jesus didn't say these Christians had *lost* their first love; they'd simply *left* it, or forsaken it. Their first love, of course, was Jesus Christ. It was as if Jesus was saying, "Do you remember when you first became a Christian? You were excited and on fire for the Lord. Remember when you used to be enthusiastic about going to church and youth group? You looked forward to reading the Bible and learning what God wanted to teach you. What happened? You haven't lost your love for me, but you've certainly walked away from it."

Can you remember a time when you were closer to God than you are now? Jesus gives you three *R*s that will help you recover that closeness.

Remember. The first thing he told the Ephesians to do was to remember, and he says the same thing to you. Remember how it used to be. Remember that vibrancy you used to have in your relationship with Christ. Memory is a good thing. You *can* get back to that solid spiritual place you used to be.

Repent. Next, Christ instructed the Ephesians to repent. Remember what your relationship with Christ used to be like and repent that you've taken some backward steps or some side steps. Repent that you've veered off the "straight and narrow" with him.

Return. Finally, Jesus told the Christians in Ephesus to return to the in-depth, solid relationship they used to have with him. Will you do that?

Think for a moment. What were you doing when you were so on fire for God? *Umm, let's see. Well, I got up early to have a quiet time with him.* Great! Do it again. What else were you doing? *Uh, I used to sing praise choruses to him in my car instead of listening to the radio.* Really? Sing again!

BREW IT!
Whatever you were doing before, do it again! Remember, repent, and return to that solid, growing, exciting relationship with the Lord you once had.

POUR IT!
Drink in the flavor from the following Scriptures: Psalm 62:8; 91:2; 115:10-11.

SAVOR IT!
Ask God to help you become all he wants you to be spiritually.

THE CUTTING EDGE

Elisha, an Old Testament prophet, was president of a small, crowded seminary. One day his students approached him and complained that their dormitory was too small. "Can we have permission to build a new one down by the Jordan River?" they asked. "There are plenty of logs down there."

Elisha granted them permission, and the students enthusiastically got to work cutting logs and clearing land. One student chopped so vigorously that his ax head flew off the handle. He could have looked around to see if anyone had noticed. Then he easily could have thought, *Hey, I still have the ax handle in my hand. I can just keep swinging at this tree, making all kinds of noise, and maybe no one will notice I'm not really doing any work. Maybe no one will realize that ministry isn't actually taking place.*

But this student didn't want to see how much he could get away with; he wanted to make a difference. He wanted to do what was right. So he did exactly what Jesus wants us to do—he asked for help. He ran to Elisha and said, "Master! I've lost my cutting edge. It's gone!"

Elisha asked him where he had seen it last. "Down by the Jordan River," the student answered.

"Let's go," Elisha said. And they went to the Jordan. Elisha tore a limb off of a tree and stuck it in the river. Miraculously, the ax head came right to the surface of the water. "Now reach in and grab it," Elisha instructed. The student did.

Okay, we had a little fun with that story. But what about you? Is the cutting edge missing from your life? Is the power gone from your relationship with the Lord? As Jesus instructed the Ephesians, "Remember, repent, and return." The seminary student remembered where he had lost the cutting edge. He repented—he confessed to Elisha that he'd lost his cutting edge. And after retrieving the ax head, he returned to his effective, enthusiastic service.

Jesus wants to empower you and enable you to have a cutting-edge relationship with him. He wants you to live enthusiastically for him. There should be zing and excitement in the fact that you walk hand in hand with the King of kings every day.

TO THE CHURCH IN SMYRNA

While the apostle John was exiled on the rocky, volcanic island of Patmos, Jesus revealed himself to John. From this *revelation,* John wrote the last book of the Bible: Revelation. Jesus told the apostle to send a letter to the seven churches in Asia Minor. John's first letter was to the church in Ephesus, and his second letter was to the church in Smyrna.

Jesus' message to the church in Smyrna was the briefest of all his messages to the seven churches, and he had only words of praise and affirmation for them. It's interesting that out of these seven churches, only two still exist today. Smyrna's actual church building has been relocated, but there are still Christians vibrantly serving the Lord in Izmir (today's name for the city of Smyrna). They're undercover. They don't openly express their faith in public, because Christians are persecuted in modern Turkey. But the church of Smyrna still exists.

In John's day the Christians in the church of Smyrna were being persecuted for their faith. Jesus encouraged them through John's letter. He reminded them that he understood their persecution and suffering, and that he was experiencing it with them. These Christians needed to hear that. They also needed to hear that Christ was in charge. Though he didn't cause their persecution, he let them know he was allowing it for a greater purpose. He encouraged them to stay faithful to the very end.

BREW IT!
When you're in the midst of trials and being "crushed," do you complain or do you allow Christ's fragrance to be released through your reaction to trouble?

POUR IT!
Drink in the flavor from the following Scriptures: Romans 5:3-4; 2 Thessalonians 1:4; Revelation 2:8-9.

SAVOR IT!
Tell God you'll be faithful to him no matter what the cost!

Most Christians in North America today don't have a clue about spiritual persecution. We get bent out of shape when someone doesn't say hi to us or when someone spreads a rumor or makes fun of us. But we have no idea what it would feel like to be physically beaten for our faith. We can't imagine being tortured or burned simply because we love Jesus.

According to *Foxe's Book of Martyrs,* 5 million believers died for Christ during the first three hundred years after his death and resurrection. These Christians were not only being persecuted; they were being killed. They desperately needed the encouragement Jesus gave them through John's letter to their church.

Smyrna means "myrrh"—a fragrance that is only released when crushed. It was as if the Lord was saying to the Christians in Smyrna, "I understand your suffering. Realize, however, that as you're being crushed, my fragrance is released through you. Let my fragrance be known to all around you. Stay true to me no matter what the cost."

BREW IT!
Ask the Lord to give you a spiritual examination to see if there's anything in your life that doesn't add up spiritually.

POUR IT!
Drink in the flavor from the following Scriptures:
Psalm 26:4; Matthew 6:2-6; Mark 7:6.

SAVOR IT!
Seek God's forgiveness for any area in your life in which you tend to be hypocritical.

THE LORD'S AFFIRMATION

Christ commended the Christians at Smyrna for their perseverance through seven things:

1. *Tribulation.* This wasn't the Great Tribulation; that hasn't occurred yet. This tribulation was trouble—big trouble. The Christians in Smyrna were suffering for the Lord. They were greatly persecuted for professing their faith in him.

In AD 155, Polycarp was the pastor of the church at Smyrna. He was the last man to be personally discipled by the apostle John. When Polycarp was eighty-six years old, he was commanded by the Roman government to burn incense at the altar of Caesar. Doing this would signify that he was renouncing his faith in Christ and devoting himself fully to Caesar. Polycarp refused and was sentenced to be burned at the stake. When the fire failed to come near him, an anxious guard thrust a spear into Polycarp's shoulder, and it began to bleed. It's said that his blood extinguished the flame.

There were times that the only substance powerful enough to put out the fire of persecution was the blood of the saints.

The Christians in Smyrna were willing to bleed, suffer, and even die for their Lord Jesus. Christ knew and understood their tribulation and encouraged them through this letter.

2. *Poverty.* The early church was made up largely of poorer classes of people. When the wealthy did profess faith in Christ, the government often seized their possessions. Even though the Christians in Smyrna didn't have many material possessions, Christ told them they were rich. They were spiritually wealthy, because he was bestowing many spiritual blessings on them.

3. *Blasphemy.* Some Jews in Smyrna were extremely hostile toward Christianity. They still called themselves Jews—because they were Jews physically or outwardly—but since they had rejected Christ, they were no longer considered part of God's chosen people. Jesus affirmed the Christians for recognizing this blasphemy and for using discernment and wisdom to bring it out in the open.

God is frustrated with hypocrisy. We break his heart when we claim one thing but do another. What about you? Does your walk match your talk? Or do you live one way on Sunday but act differently throughout the week? If so, you're not living a genuine Christian life.

THE LORD'S ENCOURAGEMENT

Christ encouraged and affirmed the believers in Smyrna for how they handled seven things:

1. *Tribulation.*
2. *Poverty.*
3. *Blasphemy.*
4. *Fear.* Remember, these particular Christians were suffering great persecution for the Lord. Right in the middle of their torment, Christ encourages them with these wonderful words: "Fear not." History tells us that multitudes of Christians sang praises to God up to the very moment they were killed. They not only heard the Lord's encouragement, they took it to heart. They lived it out.
5. *Satan.* Christ told the Christians in Smyrna that Satan would throw some of them into prison. Christ didn't dance around the fact that Satan was the cause of the persecution they were experiencing. He placed the blame where blame was due: on Satan himself.

Today we often blame other people or circumstances instead of Satan directly. But the Lord was very clear in labeling Satan as responsible for the suffering. Many today would blame our international terrorism on Osama bin Laden or Saddam Hussein. But they're merely tools through which Satan has chosen to work. The direct blame goes deeper than men; it goes directly to Satan, who is intent on killing and causing havoc in our world. He's the root of all evil. He is sin personified.

Jesus encourages the believers to keep on keepin' on. He tells them to stay true, to be faithful even in the midst of battles with Satan himself.

6. *Tribulation of ten days.* At the beginning of the letter, the Smyrna Christians were affirmed for the way they were handling their tribulation. Now, in Revelation 2:10, they're being affirmed for a specific wave of persecution that had already begun and that would continue under various Roman emperors for the next two hundred years. They launched massive attacks against the believers, and some estimate that between 5 and 7 million Christians were killed during their rule.

The apostle Paul was beheaded under Nero's rule. Domitian exiled John to the Isle of Patmos, where John wrote the book of Revelation. Trajan sent a well-known Christian named Ignatius to Rome's amphitheater to be killed by wild beasts. Polycarp, the pastor of Smyrna, was martyred under the rule of Marcus Aurelius. Many others followed.

BREW IT!
How would you handle true persecution? How do you handle the daily trials you currently experience?

POUR IT!
Drink in the flavor from the following Scriptures: Matthew 5:10-12; John 15:20.

SAVOR IT!
Ask God to help you identify the source of evil (Satan) instead of simply blaming things on circumstance. Know what you're up against.

BREW IT!
Be ready at any moment to share what God has taught you, spoken to you, or shared with you on any given day.

POUR IT!
Drink in the flavor from the following Scriptures: Deuteronomy 30:10; Psalm 119:86; Revelation 2:10-11.

SAVOR IT!
Deepen your commitment to God to stay faithful to him no matter what the cost.

BE FAITHFUL!

As we've been discussing, the Lord gave the apostle John seven letters to send to the seven churches throughout Asia Minor. He sent the first letter to the church in Ephesus. The Lord commended them and also condemned them.

John sent the second letter to the church in Smyrna. The Lord had only encouragement and praise for this particular group of Christians. He affirmed them for the way they handled seven things:

1. *Tribulation.*
2. *Poverty.*
3. *Blasphemy.*
4. *Fear.*
5. *Satan.*
6. *Tribulation of ten days.*
7. *Death.* In Revelation 2:10, Christ encourages the Christians to be faithful to him even unto death. You'll notice when you read this Scripture that Jesus didn't promise to lighten their persecution. He didn't say he'd make the pain go away. He encouraged them to be faithful to him. Because Christ was faithful to God even unto death, we must follow Christ's example and also remain faithful—even if we have to die for our faith. The Christians in Smyrna truly were faithful. They were martyrs for him.

This letter to the church in Smyrna ends with Christ telling all who have ears to hear to listen to what the Holy Spirit is saying to the churches. Who is the church? It's you and me. The church isn't a specific building on a certain street—though we tend to label it as such. The real church is the body of Christ—those who have placed their trust in God and are following him.

So to all Christians (that's us!), Jesus tells us to tune in to what the Spirit is saying. Many people hear, but they don't listen. You may vaguely hear your mom telling you to empty the trash as you're watching TV, but it's possible to ignore her and not really listen to what she's saying.

What is God saying to you? Instead of responding with, "Well, he doesn't speak to me a lot," focus instead on learning the sound of his voice. God *does* speak to you. In fact, he speaks to you often. But if you're not hearing him, it could be because you haven't learned to listen to his voice. Or perhaps you don't recognize his voice when he speaks. (For more information on learning the voice of God, flip to devotionals found on May 6–13.) God is speaking. Are you listening?

THE CROWN OF LIFE

As the apostle John wraps up his letter to the church in Smyrna, Christ instructs him to inform the believers that if they're faithful, they'll receive a crown of life when they enter heaven.

You may know of people in today's society who have been martyred for their faith in Christ. They, too, will receive the crown of life for all eternity. But what about you? Chances are you're not currently undergoing massive persecution for your relationship with Christ (or you probably wouldn't be allowed to read this book). But who's to say? Perhaps in ten or twenty or thirty years you and I may both undergo intense persecution for our faith.

Stay faithful! Draw encouragement from this letter to the Christians in Smyrna. Not only did it affirm them in the midst of their suffering, but what Christ says is still extremely relevant today. Yes, the letter was directed to a specific church in Smyrna, but on a larger scale, we are the church. So take the words of Jesus in this letter personally.

The final words of encouragement given to the Smyrna Christians are: "He that overcometh shall not be hurt of the second death" (Revelation 2:11, KJV).

What's the second death? It's a death that no Christian will have to experience. Everyone will experience the first death—it concerns the body. We'll all die a physical death. But the second death concerns a human's soul and spirit. This second death is eternal separation from God. No one who's a Christian will ever be eternally separated from God. Draw encouragement from that fact!

The person who overcomes won't have to be separated from God. If you are ever persecuted for your faith, how will you overcome?

BREW IT!
Do you have many Bible verses memorized? Strive to memorize some that you can recall and draw comfort from in times of persecution.

POUR IT!
Drink in the flavor from the following Scriptures: Matthew 28:18-20; Romans 8:35-39.

SAVOR IT!
Be honest with God. Admit your fear of persecution to him. But also tell him that you trust him completely.

- *Remember what God has said.* He has promised never to leave you or forsake you. He has also promised you the crown of life for your faithfulness. Remember and reflect on his truth.
- *Trust God's faithfulness.* You serve a God you can certainly trust. Through the ages, he has never lied. He can't lie; he doesn't have it in his character to lie. What he says, he will do. He won't change. He's solid. Dependable. Trustworthy. Think of all the Bible heroes he was faithful to, and trust his continued faithfulness in your own life.
- *Pray for strength.* No doubt you'll be frightened and confused. You may even feel as though God has forsaken you. He hasn't. Pray constantly for him to strengthen and bless you with his very presence.

BREW IT!
Are you harboring an unforgiving spirit against someone who has hurt you? That can hinder your spiritual growth.

POUR IT!
Drink in the flavor from the following Scriptures: Matthew 6:14-15; Luke 6:37; 23:34.

SAVOR IT!
Ask God to bring anyone to your mind whom you need to forgive. Seek his help in forgiving.

FORGIVEN!

Fifty-seven-year-old Jean-Claude Godrie, an architect from Douai, France, attempted to commit suicide a couple of years ago because he was overwhelmed by his mounting financial debts. He decided to kill his wife first, so she wouldn't have to face the financial burden without him. Then his plan was to kill himself.

After he shot his wife while she was asleep, his son stopped him from killing himself. His wife, Chantal, survived the shooting, but she lost her sight because of it. Jean-Claude was given a five-year suspended sentence after his wife publicly forgave him and begged the court to acquit him.

Would you have been able to forgive? With God's help, you can always forgive. It may seem humanly impossible to forgive someone who has deeply hurt you, but God can empower you to forgive anyone who has ever wronged you.

Because God freely forgives you, he commands that you freely forgive others. But when you pray, be honest. Pray exactly where you are—not where you want to be. For example, say Hannah spread lies about you and almost ruined your reputation. Pray exactly where you are: "Jesus, I'm angry with Hannah! I hate it that she lied about me. I don't feel like forgiving her. But I know I need to. So I'm asking you to help me want to forgive her. Because you have forgiven me, I know I also need to forgive Hannah."

Keep praying that honest prayer over and over. You'll reach the point where you'll honestly be able to pray, "Lord, I'm really struggling with this. I don't know how I'm going to forgive Hannah, but I want to forgive her. Help me to forgive, Father."

Pray that prayer over and over. Also pray for Hannah's well-being and that she would be led into a close relationship with Christ. After a while, you'll be able to pray, "Dear Jesus, I want to forgive Hannah. I'm deeply hurt by what she did, but in obedience to you, I choose to forgive her. I've decided to let go, Father. I give you the hurt I've experienced because of her, and I ask you to mend my wounded heart. I decide to forgive. I choose to forgive Hannah. Lord, help my feelings eventually match my words."

You may not feel like you've forgiven Hannah when you pray this prayer, but forgiveness is a decision. And as you continue to pray exactly where you are and where you want to be, God will eventually help your feelings catch up with your words.

If Chantal Godrie can forgive her husband for shooting and blinding her, and if God can forgive you for nailing his Son to the cross, you can forgive those who hurt you—with the Lord's help.

TURNING FAILURE INTO VICTORY

"Abby, Cassandra, and Natasha all made the volley-ball team," Sami angrily scribbled in her journal. "Everyone made it but me. I can't do anything right!"

Ever feel like Sami? Perhaps you've tried several different things and haven't succeeded at any. How can you keep your sights high and not get discouraged?

First of all, remember that you're not alone! Even though you feel like you're the only one in the world who has failed, you're actually in good company.

- Napoleon graduated forty-two out of forty-three in his class, yet he went on to conquer Europe!
- Despite all his home runs, Babe Ruth struck out 1,330 times.
- George Washington lost two-thirds of all battles he fought, but later he won the Revolutionary War and became the first president of the United States!

Allow yourself the freedom to fail so you won't become frightened of trying. Let's use the word *try* as an acronym that will help motivate you to get back in the saddle.

BREW IT!
With God's help, determine to turn your failures into victory.

POUR IT!
Drink in the flavor from the following Scriptures: Psalm 55:1-2, 4-5; Ephesians 3:20-21.

SAVOR IT!
Give your dreams to God and ask him to replace them with his own.

- **T**ry again. Maybe you'll make the team next year. Who knows? You could get a three-inch growth spurt! You may be better developed physically in another year. Your stamina and determination may be stronger.
- **R**efuse to make excuses. There may be a good reason you didn't make the volleyball team. Maybe you should get help with your serve, your spikes, or your eye-hand coordination. If you've skipped practices, you probably haven't developed the necessary skills. Don't blame your failure on unfair treatment or a bad day. If there's an area in which you're making excuses, recognize it and do something about it.
- **Y**ield to the heavenly Father. Could it be that God has other plans for you? Instead of volleyball, maybe he wants to help you develop the musical abilities he's planted within you. Or instead of the school newspaper, perhaps he desires to cultivate your cooking interests or your love for the outdoors. Spend time praying with your Christian friends and your parents, and seek God's will together. Try everything that interests you. If you enjoy taking pictures and arranging them in a photo album, consider joining the yearbook staff. What about computers? Do you thrive on modern technology? Develop that interest.

As you seek out a variety of interests and consistently ask for God's guidance, trust him. Yield your interests, plans, frustrations, and dreams into the hands of the Creator. According to Ephesians 3:20-21, he dreams much bigger for you than you ever will! How about memorizing those verses?

BREW IT!
Could it be that you're making more withdrawals from your friendship accounts than deposits?

POUR IT!
Drink in the flavor from the following Scriptures: Proverbs 17:17; 18:24; Philippians 2:4.

SAVOR IT!
Ask God to help you develop quality Christian friendships.

THE FRIENDSHIP ACCOUNT

You're trying to earn enough money to buy a car before school starts, so three evenings a week you babysit for Terra, a ten-year-old from your church. This evening you just overheard Terra slam the phone in its cradle and murmur, "Crystal's no fun anymore!"

"What are you talking about?" you inquire. "You two are always up to something."

"I know. I don't get it. I asked her to come over and watch *The Princess Bride* with me, and she said she had other stuff to do."

"Didn't you two just watch that a couple of nights ago?"

"Yeah, but it's my favorite! She could watch it again with me!"

You think for a second, then continue. "And what did you two do last weekend?"

"I wanted her to help me with a puzzle I was trying to put together, so I asked her to come over."

"Terra, it could be you're wearing Crystal out. It sounds like you're making several withdrawals from this friendship without putting in many deposits. You're *getting* a lot from Crystal, but you're not investing much in her."

Understanding the intricacies of friendship will help you establish solid relationships throughout your life. So let's take a peek at some strategies that will not only help you help others (such as kids you may babysit), but will also help you become a winning friend!

- *Invest interest.* Show genuine interest in your friends (memorize Philippians 2:4). Probably the easiest way to develop your interest in others is to ask meaningful questions. This will bring out what's important to your friends. A friendship without intention to grow and deepen becomes routine and eventually fades.
- *Listen to your friends.* It's tempting to look at a friend but actually be thinking about last night's movie or what you want to say as soon as you can jump into the conversation. Listen carefully! And remember that good listening requires eye contact. If you catch yourself playing with your hair or looking at your shoes, determine, instead, to look into the eyes of your friend who's speaking.
- *Make an investment of faith.* Bring Jesus into each one of your friendships. Bring friends to church and youth group. Pray for your friends and share favorite Scriptures with them.

SO LITTLE TIME . . .
SO MANY FRIENDS

It's likely that the friends you make during your teen years won't be your friends for a lifetime. Though you may feel as though your high school pals will be around forever, you'll probably only maintain a few of those friendships. Most of the friendships you'll take through life are the ones you make during college and the years after.

But it's important to learn how to develop great friendships now, so that when you do make the friendships that will last for years, you'll understand how to nurture these relationships.

First, understand the different types of relationships we form: acquaintances (people we know well enough to say hi to), friends (established from time spent talking together), and valued others (requires vulnerability, nurturing, and common depth).

It's good to have as many acquaintances as possible—to be friendly with everyone. These are the people you may wave to, smile at, ask how they're doing. You know them on a very casual basis. Everything is surface. You don't share deep secrets with them because you're not that close to these people.

Strive to spend time with friends who are positive and share your value system. These are the people with whom you go see a movie, grab a cup of java, or enjoy a concert. You have shared interests with these people. You've invested time in them. You may call each other on the phone, e-mail, and chat several times throughout the week.

Choose your valued others wisely. These are the relationships you'll want to be selective about, because it's with these valued others that you'll share your heart, your character, and your secrets. And probably your life. Make it your prayer that your future spouse will be your soul mate—one who has grown from a "valued other" friendship.

BREW IT!
Do you have some great "valued other" friendships? If not, strive to develop some with God's guidance.

POUR IT!
Drink in the flavor from the following Scriptures: Job 2:11; 42:10; John 15:13.

SAVOR IT!
Ask God to give you wisdom in developing genuine friendships.

Over the next few weeks—while you still have some summertime remaining—read about some "valued other" friendships from the Bible that will inspire you. Check out Ruth and Naomi. Then check out Ruth and Boaz. Read about David and Jonathan's friendship. Jonathan willingly gave up his right to the throne because of his friendship with David. And read about Daniel and his closest friends: Shadrach, Meshach, and Abednego.

COUNTING THE COST

Do you know—really know—that Christianity is much more than a fun youth group? Jesus told his disciples it would cost them to follow him. It's easy to get so caught up in the fun of belonging to a great youth group, being plugged into a growing church, and establishing tight friendships within the youth group that we fail to see the bigger picture of following Christ.

If church involvement and Christian friends are what you're equating with following God, you need to discern the difference between casual Christianity and living in radical obedience to the lordship of Jesus Christ.

Let's refresh our memories on what Jesus had to say about the cost of Christianity: "Suppose one of you wants to build a tower. Will he not first sit down and estimate the cost to see if he has enough money to complete it? . . . In the same way, any of you who does not give up everything he has cannot be my disciple" (Luke 14:28, 33).

Wow. Jesus places a high premium on following him. Do you realize what it actually costs to be totally devoted to your heavenly Father? Do you understand absolute surrender? Do you have an accurate view of the big picture of Christianity? Are you spiritually naive, or are you sold-out and excited about an intimate, growing relationship with your heavenly Father?

BREW IT!
You'll fall more and more in love with your heavenly Father the deeper your relationship with God becomes.

POUR IT!
Drink in the flavor from the following Scriptures: Psalm 77:13; 78:1-4; 81:9.

SAVOR IT!
Ask God to teach you the difference between casual Christianity and radical obedience to his lordship.

Here's a quick recap of some foundational truths to think about:

- *It's not enough just to believe.* Hey, even Satan believes in God. Simply acknowledging that God exists doesn't make anyone a follower of God. The word *believe* in Greek means to totally adhere to. That's different from intellectual knowledge, isn't it?
- *We must confess our sins with a repentant heart.* Believing you can do anything you want because God will always forgive you doesn't reflect someone living in radical obedience to his lordship.
- *Grow in Christ.* This is best done through consistent Bible reading, an active prayer life, being involved in church, and sharing our faith.
- *Count the cost.* What do you think this means? Does God want to make your life miserable? No. According to Jeremiah 29:11, he wants to fill your life with purpose and meaning. So anything he prompts you to give up is really for your own benefit.

Are there some friendships you need to reevaluate? some habits you need to give up? Consider praying with your parents, your youth pastor, or your Sunday school teacher regarding the cost for you to follow Christ.

LETTERS

Check out a few of these letters from children to their pastors.

Dear Pastor:
I heard that God loves everyone in all the world. But he hasn't met my sister! —Nolan

Dear Pastor:
Please try to work it into your sermon this week that Geoffrey Smith has been a good boy all month. I am Geoffrey Smith. —Geoffrey

Dear Pastor:
Are there devils that live on earth? I think there's one in my class at school. —Carlita

Dear Pastor:
I liked your sermon last Sunday. Especially when you finished. —Matthew

Dear Pastor:
How does God know the good people from the bad people? Does he read the newspaper, or do you tell him? —Louis

Have you thought recently about the responsibilities your pastor has? He prayerfully prepares sermons each week that will motivate people in your church to grow spiritually and seek forgiveness. He conducts funerals and weddings. He attends special community events, visits sick people in the hospital, prays for people before surgery, calls on visitors, prepares the order of the worship service, counsels people who need spiritual advice, manages a staff, and strives to be the hands and feet of Jesus to his congregation.

When was the last time you told your pastor how much you appreciate all he does? Though October is the official Pastor Appreciation Month, surprise him by doing something special for him this week—right in the middle of summer!

Take time to send him an e-mail, make him a card, write him a note, make a phone call, or get him a gift certificate to one of his favorite restaurants. Let him know how much you appreciate his ministry.

BREW IT!
Make a list of other people you can show appreciation to.

POUR IT!
Drink in the flavor from the following Scriptures: 1 Corinthians 1:4-6; Philippians 1:3-5; 1 Thessalonians 1:2-3.

SAVOR IT!
Pray for your pastor and your entire church staff.

BREW IT!
Take some time today to reprioritize what's truly important in your life.

POUR IT!
Drink in the flavor from the following Scriptures: Proverbs 24:5; Isaiah 1:17; 61:1-2.

SAVOR IT!
Ask God to help you keep him as the center of your life so that everything you do will revolve around him.

ARE YOU AWARE?
Did you know that . . .

- 1.3 billion people in the world live on less than one dollar a day?
- 3 billion people live on less than two dollars a day?
- 1.3 billion have no access to clean water?
- 3 billion have no access to sanitation?
- 2 billion have no access to electricity?
- approximately $11 billion is spent each year in Europe on ice cream?
- a few hundred millionaires now hold as much wealth as the world's poorest 2.5 billion people?
- approximately $6 billion is spent on cosmetics each year in the United States?
- approximately a billion people entered the twenty-first century unable to read a book or sign their names?
- the annual cost of pet food in America and Europe is approximately $12 billion?

Where are our priorities? Clearly, we're a little messed up when it comes to spending our money and helping the poor. But what if a research company tracked *you* for a specific period of time—say one week. What kind of statistics would we read?

- Spent twenty-five dollars a week on coffee or soft drinks.
- Sat in front of the TV for twenty hours.
- Read the Bible for fifteen minutes.
- Spent two hours at church.
- Went out of his way for someone else one time.
- Prayed for six minutes.

Would your list would read a lot better . . . or a lot worse? Are your priorities what they should be?

"I'M SORRY"

It's not that hard to say. And learning to admit when you're wrong is a skill that will serve you the rest of your life. You probably know people who just can't admit when they're wrong. They rationalize, get defensive, and are even tempted to lie rather than acknowledge something was their fault. That's really sad. But it's especially sad—and frightening—when we find this among Christians.

When certain people always have to be right, I can't help but wonder about their lives as children. *Didn't their parents teach them how to apologize?* I find myself thinking.

If you can learn to admit your faults and seek forgiveness with your family members, it will carry into your relationships outside of the home. I wonder how many marriages could be stronger if the husband and wife had learned to say "I'm sorry" when they were children.

When I was growing up, my brother and I learned early to accept responsibility for our actions and apologize when we were wrong. How did we learn that? Our parents made us ask forgiveness of each other over hurt feelings, broken toys, and stolen dessert. There were times when "I'm sorry" wasn't enough—we were instructed to ask, "Will you forgive me?" Then we had to hug each other.

BREW IT!
Dare to swallow your pride and seek forgiveness from someone you've hurt.

POUR IT!
Drink in the flavor from the following Scriptures: Matthew 5:23-24; 2 Corinthians 2:7; Ephesians 4:32; Colossians 3:13.

SAVOR IT!
Ask God to help you admit it quickly when you're wrong.

Actually, now that I'm an adult, I'm extremely grateful to have learned that lesson early. Because I'm always in a hurry, too loud, and usually impatient, I quite often find myself saying, "I'm sorry" or "Will you forgive me?" to a coworker. I'm not proud of my faults, but I am glad that I can admit it when I'm wrong and seek forgiveness.

What's the big deal about apologizing? If you don't accept responsibility now when you're wrong, it'll become more difficult to accept it later in life. It will also affect your relationship with Christ.

The most valuable quality in an employee, friend, or spouse is a teachable spirit. When I was a high school drama teacher, I would have much rather cast a student with less talent and a teachable attitude than the most gifted student who would never apologize or admit his ways weren't always the best.

Let's develop an action plan. When you're wrong and you've blown it:

- *Pray.* First seek God's forgiveness.
- *Remember.* Remind yourself that failure to seek forgiveness from those you've hurt can harden your heart and eventually make you feel distanced from God.
- *Know the ground rules.* When you're wrong, admit it. Apologize when it's your fault. Seek forgiveness from those you have hurt. These aren't suggestions; this is the Christian's lifestyle. We operate with integrity. We strive to reflect Christ.

CAN YOU GUESS?

Guess which of the following holidays in the month of August are real and which ones are fake. Write an *R* by those you think are real, and write an *F* by those you believe are fake.

___ Vinegar Day
___ I Love Fruit Pies Day
___ Cataract Awareness Month
___ Air-Conditioning Appreciation Day
___ Reduce the Clutter Week
___ International Quit Smoking Month
___ Visit the Zoo Week
___ Mow Your Neighbor's Lawn Day
___ Serve a Pancake Day
___ National Fresh Breath Day
___ National Pet Flea and Tick Week
___ Work like a Dog Day
___ Doctor Appreciation Week
___ National Mustard Day
___ Bad Poetry Day
___ Thank Your Coach Week

Who would have guessed these special days actually exist in the month of August? It's amazing what you can find with some creative research. But remember—not all these holidays were real. Don't believe everything you hear.

BREW IT!
Learn to discern. Discover for yourself what's true and what's fiction.

POUR IT!
Drink in the flavor from the following Scriptures: Proverbs 17:24, 28; 19:25.

SAVOR IT!
Ask God to help you learn to separate truth from fiction.

Real: Vinegar Day, Cataract Awareness Month, Air-Conditioning Appreciation Day, Reduce the Clutter Week, National Fresh Breath Day, Work like a Dog Day, National Mustard Day, Bad Poetry Day.

THE THIRD LETTER

When the apostle John was exiled to the rocky, volcanic island of Patmos, he received a revelation of Jesus Christ in all his glory. He wrote the book of Revelation based on that vision. The Lord gave him seven specific letters to send to the churches in Asia Minor—modern-day Turkey. We looked at the first two letters on April 28–30 and July 17–23. Now we're ready to dive into the third letter. It was written to the church in Pergamum.

We should be able to identify with this church, because it struggled for its identity in a pagan, hostile environment. Does that sound like our culture today? Pergamum was full of false religions, and some of these philosophies and beliefs had crept into the church.

The Lord commends and condemns this church. He commends them for three specific things:

1. *Striving to stay strong in spite of their circumstances.* God knew what these Christians faced. He understood they were living in a very difficult place. Pergamum was the center of emperor worship in Asia; as early as 29 BC the town had erected the first temple where citizens could worship Augustus Caesar. The city was also considered the birthplace of Zeus. The Lord used the term "Satan's seat" in Revelation 2:13 (KJV) to describe their environment. "Satan's seat" may have referred to the 150-foot-high structure in the middle of the city dedicated to Zeus.

Many people assume Satan is in hell right now. But Satan won't be in hell until the events recorded in Revelation 20 finally occur. Right now, Satan is loose and is prince of this world, roaming up and down the earth as a roaring lion, hunting for someone to devour. But he does have headquarters, and Jesus said they were in Pergamum at that particular time. Satan has the power to move his headquarters to different places, and he has probably done so throughout the years.

Beyond the focus on emperor worship, the city also contained several significant pagan temples. Let's just focus on one for a moment: the temple of the god Asklepios. Just down the street from this temple was the greatest hospital of the ancient world. It was considered the Mayo Clinic of that day. There they used every means of healing imaginable—medicine, psychology, and everything else. No doubt there were some sincere physicians who practiced in that hospital, but it was also filled with satanic healing.

Not only did God take note of the circumstances in which the Pergamum Christians lived, but he understands your situation as well. He desires to empower you to live a holy life inside a secular society.

THE GOOD AND THE BAD

Christ affirmed the church in Pergamum for three specific things:

1. *Striving to stay strong in spite of their circumstances.*

2. *Remaining faithful to the name of Christ.* The Lord commended the Christians for their defense of the deity of Christ.

3. *Not denying their faith.* The Christians remained true to the Word of God—the message of the gospel believed by those who genuinely know the Lord.

Though Christ commended the Christians for the above three things, he also condemned two teachings in the Pergamum church:

The doctrine of Balaam. The "doctrine of Balaam" is different from the error of Balaam (Jude 11) and the way of Balaam (2 Peter 2:15), which was selling out—being willing to do something wrong to gain a financial reward. In this particular church, the problem was the "doctrine" of Balaam.

Balaam taught King Balak the way to corrupt Israel—by encouraging intermarriage with the Moabite women, which led to the Israelites worshiping idols and being involved in sexual immorality. *Per* in Greek means "opposition." We get the word pervert from this. *Gamos* means "marriage." We get words like monogamy and bigamy from this. *Pergamos* means "objectionable marriage with the world." Apparently some corrupt teachers in the church were deceiving believers into compromising their faith with worldliness.

The doctrine of the Nicolaitans. In John's letter to the first of these seven churches addressed in Revelation—the church in Ephesus—we see that Christ affirmed them for not tolerating the Nicolaitans. But in Pergamum, he condemns the church for tolerating them. The Nicolaitans were people who had crept into the church believing they were infallible. Christ tells us that he hates this. We serve a God of love and a God of hate. He loves his children, but he hates sin.

The Nicolaitans also taught that it was okay to indulge in sin so they could understand it and adequately teach against it. They were involved in much sensuous sin and claimed it didn't matter because sin could only touch or damage the outer self, not the spirit.

Christ told the church in Pergamum to repent, turn around, and change their hearts and lives. If they didn't, he said he would fight against them with the sword of his mouth. What's that? It's his Holy Word.

How can we know who's who and what's what in our world today? By stacking it all against God's Word. We're mistaken if we think the church has the authority to decide what's right and wrong. Who is the church? We are—the Christians. And we're called to be a light in a dark world. For us to shine adequately, we need to be careful to identify with the Master, Jesus Christ, and to recognize his Holy Word as our authority.

BREW IT!
Be careful! Watch out for false doctrine. Look to the Bible for absolute truth.

POUR IT!
Drink in the flavor from the following Scriptures: John 1:9; 4:23; Revelation 2:14-15.

SAVOR IT!
Ask God to help you remain strong spiritually in a society that offers so many false religions.

BREW IT!

Instead of getting discouraged when you recognize false teachings around you, thank God for helping you recognize what's true and what's not.

POUR IT!

Drink in the flavor from the following Scriptures: Matthew 5:14-16; John 6:32-35; Revelation 2:16-17.

SAVOR IT!

Tell God that you want to be an overcomer—no matter what you're up against. Thank him for the special white stone he wants to present to you in heaven.

WHAT ARE YOU EATING?

The Lord wraps up his letter to the church in Pergamum by repeating something he has said in the other letters: "He who has an ear, let him hear what the Spirit says to the churches" (Revelation 2:17, NKJV).

Who is the church? Again, it's us. Those who have placed their trust in Jesus Christ and are living for him are considered the body of Christ. How does it make you feel to be considered Christ's church? Are you living up to the definition?

The Spirit mentioned here is, of course, the Holy Spirit. He's speaking to us. Have you heard what God's Spirit has said to you this week? If you haven't, it's not because he's giving you the cold shoulder. He's speaking, but you may not be listening.

The Holy Spirit tells us to listen to what he's saying. What Christ says must be important, or he wouldn't keep telling us to use our ears to listen to him. If the Lord talks, we need to take note and catch every single word!

Then Jesus mentions "hidden manna." This is a reference to himself. Manna was the breadlike substance that God provided for the children of Israel as they journeyed out of Egypt and into Canaan, the Promised Land.

We're told in the Gospel of John that Jesus is the Bread of Life. As Christians, that's what we need to be eating. We need to feed on Jesus himself. Christ and his Holy Word are essential for spiritual growth. Christ labels himself as "hidden" manna because he's hidden to much of the world today. People misrepresent him and abuse his name all the time.

Christ closes this letter by promising the Christians that if they overcome, he will give them a white stone when they spend eternity in heaven with him. This white stone could be a piece of exquisite jewelry or it could symbolize his "vote" for each Christian. Christ stands before God and vouches for those who have placed their trust in him.

Christ wants you to overcome. He understands the environment in which you live. He knows what you're up against, and he realizes that Satan is fighting for your soul. But Jesus is also fighting. He's not giving up. He wants you in heaven with him forever. He can't wait to present you with that special white stone with your name engraved on it.

THE HOLY SPIRIT

Spend some time today simply reflecting on the Holy Spirit and all that he is.

The Holy Spirit is . . .

Another counselor
Breath of the Almighty
Holy One
Holy Spirit of God
The seal
Spirit of Christ
Spirit of power
Spirit of faith
Spirit of fire
Spirit of glory
Spirit of grace and supplication
Spirit of holiness
Spirit of judgment
Spirit of justice
Spirit of knowledge and of the fear of the Lord
Spirit of life
Spirit of truth
Spirit of wisdom and of understanding
Voice of the Almighty
Voice of the Lord

BREW IT!
Have you yielded control of your life to the authority of the Holy Spirit?

POUR IT!
Drink in the flavor from the following Scriptures: Psalm 51:11; Isaiah 63:10; Matthew 1:18.

SAVOR IT!
Ask God to release the power of his Spirit within you.

BREW IT!

To avoid an ice cream head-ache (brain freeze), keep the ice cream away from the roof of your mouth.

POUR IT!

Drink in the flavor from the following Scriptures: Matthew 16:18; Acts 20:28; Colossians 1:24.

SAVOR IT!

Ask God to help you find the church where he wants you to get involved. He'll lead you to the right place.

I SCREAM, YOU SCREAM, WE ALL SCREAM FOR ICE CREAM

People who *don't* enjoy a big ol' scoop of ice cream are very rare. It's tough to find someone who actually dislikes the soft, cold stuff most of us love to eat—especially during the hot months.

Did you know that it takes approximately fifty licks to finish a single-scoop cone? The United States leads the world in ice cream production. We churn out about 1.6 billion gallons a year, and the average American eats more than twenty-three quarts of it a year. Texas boasts the most Dairy Queens in the nation—approximately six hundred! About 65 percent of all ice cream eaten in American is consumed at ice cream shops. But 93 percent of Americans have ice cream in their freezer.

You probably have your favorite flavors. Maybe you even have the thirty-one varieties at Baskin-Robbins memorized. But other countries boast flavors you might find a little unusual.

In the United States, the "brown flavors" are extremely popular: caramel, chocolate, and coffee. But you'll find squid, ox tongue, eel, cactus, and chicken wing ice cream in Japan.

Just as there's a variety of ice cream flavors, you've also noticed the huge variety of churches in our nation. We try different ice cream flavors to discover the ones we like the best, but we can't visit every kind of church to find our place of worship. That would almost take a lifetime! So how can you know which church to plug into?

Flavor Secret #1: *Talk to your parents.* If you're still living at home, and if your parents are involved in a church, they probably desire that you go together as a family. If your church doesn't meet the next two requirements, however, respectfully ask your parents to consider finding a new church home for your family.

Flavor Secret #2: *Is the Word of God preached diligently and consistently?* I've been to some huge churches with the latest and best technology, the most fun youth stuff, and tons of excitement within the congregation, but I'm wondering how long they'll actually last . . . because the Bible isn't actually preached. The sermons are simply feel-good, positive teachings.

Flavor Secret #3: *Are there opportunities for you to get involved?* It's not enough to simply be ministered *to*; we each need to be involved in a ministry of some sort. Can you greet people as they enter the church? fold bulletins? teach a Sunday school class? help out in the nursery? What ministries are available for you?

Don't settle for church hopping—going to whichever church has the best burger bash or serves free Starbucks. Seek God's divine direction for where he wants you.

JESUS, WE HAVE A PROBLEM!

The story is found in the sixth chapter of Mark. Jesus was teaching thousands, the hour was late, and the people needed to eat. So the disciples asked the Lord to send the crowd home while it was still light, so they could get food.

But Jesus expected the disciples to do something about the food problem. After all, they were in the company of the one who created life itself. Obviously, the disciples didn't have enough resources, and they couldn't believe it when Jesus commanded them to feed the crowd.

News flash! Jesus always calls us to something bigger than ourselves. The disciples were able to serve food to the crowd, but they needed Christ's help to do it. Do you realize that there are hungry people all around you? They're spiritually hungry and desperately searching for answers. What will you do about it? You *can* do something—with Christ's help!

When we're willing to give all our resources to Jesus, he multiplies them. When we hoard them, we're missing out on opportunities to see Christ working in our lives in the big way he desires. When Jesus asked the disciples how much food they had, they said there were only five loaves of bread and two fish. But when they gave the Lord everything—though it wasn't much—he multiplied it over and over again.

BREW IT!
As much as we need God's help to do effective ministry, he wants to provide it even more.

POUR IT!
Drink in the flavor from the following Scripture: Mark 6:30-44.

SAVOR IT!
Admit to God that you need and want his help.

That's what God wants to do with what *you* have! Instead of clinging to your talents, your money, or your gifts, give them completely to Christ and watch him multiply what little you have into much for the glory of his Kingdom. When we want to see Jesus move as he did in this story, we must:

- *Identify the problem.* You'll notice that Jesus didn't approach the disciples and say, "Oh, no! Now what are we going to do?" He waited for the disciples to recognize the problem, take initiative, and come to him.
- *Take the problem to Jesus.* Once we come to the Lord, we need to pray specifically. "Here's the problem, Lord. Here's what I need."

Instead of automatically coming to Christ, we often find other avenues to explore. We:

- *Procrastinate.* "Maybe Jesus will quit talking soon, and the crowd can go home and eat. Let's just hang out and see."
- *Pass the buck.* "Let's send the people away to someone else. If they leave now, maybe they can still find some vendors selling food along the road." Or, "Jesus, you just deal with it."
- *Worry about it.* "How much will it cost? Where will we get the money?"

The cost of ministry is high. It requires all our resources and then some! In fact, we can't accomplish true ministry on our own. We have to have God's help.

BREW IT!
Are you asking the right question? And are you giving God what you have?

POUR IT!
Drink in the flavor from the following Scriptures:
Psalm 37:21; Ecclesiastes 5:10; Matthew 6:24.

SAVOR IT!
Ask God what he wants you to do, and pray for the willingness to do it, no matter how big or small the challenge.

THE RIGHT QUESTION

When it comes to Christ working through you, the only question you need to ask is, "Father, what do you want me to do?" You don't need to ask: "How much will it cost?" "How is that possible?" or "What will people think?"

Simply ask God what he wants you to do; then obey.

Let's recap. When you want to see God work through your life:

- *Identify the problem.*
- *Take the problem to Jesus.*
- *Do what you can.*

The little boy in the story we discussed yesterday gave his fish and bread to Jesus. The boy wasn't worried about how the miracle would get done. He simply released what he had to the Lord. He did what he could.

God wants you to do what you can. He'll take what you have, multiply it, solidify it, and use it to work through you in an exciting way. The boy gave what he had. He didn't hold anything back. He didn't hesitate. "Here it is, Jesus. Take it. I trust you."

Don't get caught up in the fact that your gift is small. Jesus is the one doing the miracle, so it's totally okay that your gift is small. You might think, *If I had a million dollars, I'd give it to the Lord.* Well, you don't. Instead, give what you have.

Chances are . . . if you're not giving to God right now, you probably wouldn't give to him if you had a million dollars. You *think* you would, but you'd simply increase your cost of living. You'd buy a bigger house with larger payments. You'd get some expensive cars. You'd probably travel and maybe give cool gifts to your friends. You'd upgrade your wardrobe. And you'd still hesitate to give to God, because your expenses would be so much greater.

Let's pretend you're making $500 a month and have $300 worth of expenses. Hopefully, you're giving God at least 10 percent, which would be $50. But if you're thinking, *Nope. Can't afford to give him $50. I'd only have $150 left for me,* then you're not going to give to God when you're bringing home $10,000 a month. You'll be thinking, *I should be giving God at least $1,000 a month, but I have so many expenses I can't afford it!*

You see, our finances are relative. The issue isn't how much we have in resources. The issue is, will you give God what little you do have and allow him to work through you?

LEVELS OF GIVING

God wants to work through you and your resources as he did with the little boy who offered his fish and bread. But for him to do that, you need to be willing to offer him all you have. There are three levels of giving, which are reflected in our attitude.

1. *What can I afford?* This person isn't thinking about what God can do; he's focused on himself. He's thinking, *How much can I afford to let go of?* We need to focus consistently on what God wants, not on what we can afford. What if the little boy had asked himself what he could afford that day when Jesus wanted to feed the multitudes? Chances are the boy had no money at all. But he gave all he had. He gave his resources.

2. *What can I sacrifice?* This level of giving sounds heroic. Anyone willing to make a sacrifice is thinking in the right direction, right? Not always. The focus is still on the giver instead of God. *I can sacrifice going out to eat once a week. I can sacrifice the large pizza and go with the medium.* Unless it's total sacrifice, the focus is still a bit off. This level of giving is headed in the right direction, but it's not quite there yet. What if the little boy had thought, *I guess I can sacrifice one fish and one slice of bread.* He wouldn't have been trusting the Lord completely.

3. *What can I trust God to do through me?* This is the ultimate level of giving. God loves this attitude. The focus is on him—the one with a million and one resources. The person at this level of giving isn't concerned with how much money he has. He realizes that money isn't the issue—the issue is what God wants to do! The little boy didn't worry about all he *didn't* have. He simply trusted Jesus to take what he had and perform a miracle.

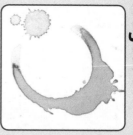

BREW IT!
Will you dare to trust the Lord to do all that he wants to do through you?

POUR IT!
Drink in the flavor from the following Scriptures: Psalm 36:5; 89:1; Isaiah 49:7.

SAVOR IT!
Ask God to help you trust him in the area of giving. Give him the freedom to do whatever he desires through you and your resources—no matter how big or small they are.

BREW IT!
Don't settle for merely looking the part when you can be the real thing.

POUR IT!
Drink in the flavor from the following Scriptures:
Luke 15:7; Romans 3:23; Hebrews 10:26.

SAVOR IT!
If you've never established a relationship with Jesus Christ, consider praying the prayer of salvation (see the devotional on February 21).

WHAT DO YOU GET WHEN . . .

What do you get when you cross a rug with some wood flooring? You get a teak rug! Does that seem odd? Actually, wood rugs are being sold by several popular U.S. retailers at prices ranging from fifty to six hundred dollars!

They're traditional in many Eastern countries, yet they also have a sophisticated contemporary style. They're clean and simple, and they're warm looking and rich because of the color of the wood.

Teak rugs are handmade, created from small rectangles of wood joined with hidden nylon cord. The idea is to combine the best features of hardwood flooring and a traditional textile rug. A teak rug allows you to get that special look without having to redo your entire floor. Wood rugs are also easy to clean. They're lighter than tile, and dust mites can't hide in them like they can in other floor coverings such as carpet.

That sounds kind of appealing, doesn't it? No need to vacuum or wax the floor! But still . . . as nice as a wood rug is and as much as it gives that special look to a floor . . . the bottom line is: It's still simply a wood rug.

It might *look* like a wooden floor. It may *feel* like a foot-friendly floor covering. But it's still not carpet or tile or wood. It's merely a rug with wooden pieces woven into it. It's not the real thing. It's a great substitute, but it's not the real thing.

Unfortunately, there are some people who fall into a similar category. They desperately try to play the part of a Christian by going to church, getting involved in youth group, or singing in the choir. And they fill their lives doing good things for others. From all outward appearances, they look, feel, sound, and act like Christians. But if they've never established a personal, growing relationship with Jesus, they've merely woven a few pieces of Christianity into the fabric of their lives. Bottom line: They're not the real thing!

AN UNLIKELY HERO

The eleventh chapter of Judges contains an interesting story. It centers around a man named Jephthah. The first verse in this chapter describes him: "Jephthah the Gileadite was a mighty warrior. His father was Gilead; his mother was a prostitute" (Judges 11:1).

This description mixes the good with the bad, doesn't it? Don't you wonder why the writer even mentioned the fact that his mom was a prostitute? Why not just stick with the good stuff—this guy was a mighty warrior! As you study the Bible, however, you'll notice that genealogy is important throughout Scripture. It's important to know where we came from. We need to understand our history. All through the Bible, God has done extraordinary things through ordinary people, regardless of their backgrounds. He doesn't define us by our past, and our past doesn't determine what he'll do in our future.

God had big plans for Jephthah. But what an unlikely hero! Jephthah was the result of his dad's relations with a prostitute. And in his time and culture, being born illegitimately was a terrible social stigma. Growing up, he was always the punch line for jokes. He was teased and taunted by those around him.

I hope Jephthah's story encourages you. You don't have to have a perfect home life for God to use you. You don't need money, prestige, or popularity. You simply have to be willing and available. Jephthah was both of those things, and God used him in mighty ways. In fact, in Hebrews 11 (the faith chapter), Jephthah's name is recorded for all eternity as one of the giants of faith—one of the heroes of God's people.

Perhaps, like Jephthah, you've been teased and taunted. Maybe you feel like an outcast for something that's not even your fault, something you can't do anything about. Draw encouragement from the fact that God dreams big dreams for you! Regardless of your past or your circumstances, God can use you. He doesn't call the qualified. He qualifies those he calls.

BREW IT!
Are you tired of being teased? Are you worried that God won't use you because of your past? Rest assured, he wants to use you to bring glory to him.

POUR IT!
Drink in the flavor from the following Scripture: Hebrews 11:1-16.

SAVOR IT!
Thank God for his willingness to do extraordinary things through the lives of ordinary people. Ask him to use you in a special way.

FROM THE PIT

Yes, Jephthah came from an interesting background. But when you think about it, haven't all of us come from the pit? Each one of us was born with sin and has been pulled out of the pit through God's grace.

Take Abraham, for example. He was ordained by God to be the father of Israel, but he still wavered in his faith. He even lied twice about his wife to save his own skin. And Jonah was called by God to usher in the world's greatest revival. But when the people of Nineveh began to acknowledge God and repent of their sin, Jonah complained to the Lord and wished they'd been blasted instead of blessed.

Moses murdered a man, buried him in the sand, and ran for his life. Peter spent three years with Jesus. He watched the miracles, heard the teachings, shared meals with the Master, and conversed with him constantly. Yet Peter denied he ever knew Christ.

And what about Paul? He was so cruel and callous, so barbaric and brutal that when he finally *did* get saved, the early church hesitated to believe it. And then there's John Mark (author of the Gospel of Mark). He received a call to the mission field but got homesick and ran back to Jerusalem.

Throughout the Old and New Testaments, we can find individuals who were in the pit of sin, but who were brought out by God Almighty and used to build his Kingdom. So don't be tempted to think, *I've blown it too many times. God can't use me.* God can use anyone who's willing, available, and committed to him.

Let's keep following Jephthah's life. In Judges 11:1-2, we get a little more information. "His father (whose name was Gilead) had several other sons by his legitimate wife, and when these half brothers grew up, they chased Jephthah out of the country. 'You son of a whore!' they said. 'You'll not get any of our father's estate' " (TLB).

Growing up unloved and unwanted, Jephthah compensated by becoming the roughest kid on the block. How do we know? Read what happened next:

"So Jephthah fled from his father's home and lived in the land of Tob." Tob was an area known for its murderers, thieves, and gangs. Read what else happened: "Soon he had quite of band of malcontents as his followers, living off the land as bandits" (Judges 11:3, TLB).

He didn't have the ideal home life, so he left and became a tough guy. Do you know people like this? They're hurting so deeply inside that they put up a hard exterior to hide the pain.

HE KNEW HIS STUFF

Jephthah got his own gang. You can imagine it, can't you? The Tob Mob, dressed in black leather jackets and riding loud, unmuffled camels from party to party. Yep, he was definitely Mr. Tough Guy.

But about that time, the Ammonites declared war against Israel. And wouldn't you know it? The leaders of Gilead needed a tough guy to lead their army into battle. So whom do you think they sent for? You guessed it! They wanted Jephthah back. But the tough guy wasn't so quick to consent.

"How come you want me now when you're in trouble? All my life you haven't wanted me. In fact, you drove me out of your sight!"

"Yeah, we know," they admitted. "But we need someone really tough to lead our army, and . . . well, you're the toughest guy we know!"

So the tough guy from Tob was made head of the entire Israelite army. Growing up, Jephthah would have never dreamed he'd have such a position of importance. But again, God doesn't base our future on our past. He can work through anything to accomplish his will. And God was determined to use Jephthah.

You might think that because Jephthah was such a tough guy, he'd just wipe out those who were giving the Israelites trouble. But he didn't. Before engaging in battle, Jephthah tried to bring about peace through diplomatic channels.

BREW IT!
Instead of jumping into a fight, first try to bring about a solution through peaceful measures.

POUR IT!
Drink in the flavor from the following Scripture: Judges 11:4-15.

SAVOR IT!
Ask the Lord to help you establish a strong spiritual heritage that you can some-day pass on to others.

He sent messengers to the king of Ammon and demanded to know why they were attacking Israel. The king answered Jephthah with something like this: "Yeah, well, it's really our land. Back when you Israelites came here from Egypt, you guys stole it from us. So give it back. And give it to us peacefully."

You'll be amazed at what our tough guy did next. We read in Judges 11:14-19 that Jephthah dug way back into history and recounted what had really happened. He knew his past. He knew the spiritual record and heritage of his forefathers. In fact, Jephthah looked back three hundred years into history and related the facts to the Ammonite king. "That's not what happened at all," he explained. "When my people, the Israelites, left Egypt for the Promised Land, they asked Sihon—who was then king of the area—if they could pass through the land to go into Canaan. They sought permission."

It's impressive that this gang leader knew his "church history." The spiritual heritage of his forefathers was important to him. What about you? Would you be able to go back through the years and recall your spiritual heritage or your church history?

BREW IT!
When God makes a promise, you can depend on him to keep it.

POUR IT!
Drink in the flavor from the following Scripture: Judges 11:16-22.

SAVOR IT!
Ask God to help you speak out for him in confidence.

CONFIDENCE!

Before the king of Ammon could even answer, Jephthah kept recounting history. "My people asked permission of King Sihon to cross through your land so we could get to the Promised Land, but Sihon didn't trust Israel. Instead of allowing us to pass through peacefully, he mobilized an army at Jahaz and attacked the Israelites."

Do you think the king got to speak then? No way! Jephthah just kept going. "Your people attacked us unjustly! What's up with that? We hadn't done anything to you!"

King Ammon opened his mouth to say something, but Jephthah was on a roll. "When God gives a promise, he always fulfills it," he continued. "And he promised us the Promised Land. So when your people attacked my people, they were trying to interfere with God's plan of getting us to Canaan—the Promised Land. God was with Israel. He enabled us to defeat Sihon's army. At that point," Jephthah said with great emphasis, "the land became Israel's!"

Wow. You have to admire this guy for knowing his stuff! He had the answers. He knew God was with his people. "So it was actually God who took your land and gave it to us," Jephthah said. "Why in the world should we take what the Lord has given us and turn it over to you?"

This guy was confident! He was sure of God's leading. He could have gone to college on a debate scholarship! And he probably could have stopped right there. After all, he'd made his point. He accurately recalled history, and you can't argue with historical facts. But he didn't stop there.

Jephthah kept going, and I like the fact that he kind of pushed it a step further. "So who do you think you are?" he said to the Ammonite king. "The kings who served after Sihon and before you didn't try to take the land back. They knew better. So do you think you're better than all your predecessors? Huh? You think you're greater than King Balak? And why are you being so petty to go back three hundred years in history to make an issue of this now?"

Then Jephthah announced that his people hadn't sinned against the Ammonites, and he knew God Almighty would prove he was right.

OBEDIENCE IS THE KEY

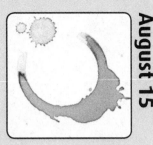

Though Jephthah confidently and accurately presented the facts to the king of Ammon, the king ignored him. But even though Jephthah was ignored by royalty, the King of kings had already spoken. God had said to Jephthah—an illegitimate son, a hoodlum, a gang member—"You're my man! You're the one I want for this job. You'll lead my army."

God can use anything and anybody to accomplish his will. You may know some people who aren't into Christianity, and you're hesitant even to invite them to church because they're stoned all the time or just seem hopeless. Who knows that God won't use one of those people to be the world's next great evangelist or missionary? Never underestimate the Lord. If he places someone on your heart, reach out to her. Invite her to church. Pray for her.

Jephthah responded to God's call to become the leader of the Israelite army. But he didn't immediately jump into a fight. He sought peace and was obedient to the Lord's leading.

It all comes down to obedience, doesn't it? The issue isn't what kind of family you're from, what kind of past you have, or what kind of grades you get. The real issue is, will you be obedient to God's call on your life?

I recently asked a group of high schoolers what would happen if they abandoned their lives to God in ultimate, total obedience. Here are some of the responses I received:

BREW IT!
Are you living in total obedience to him?

POUR IT!
Drink in the flavor from the following Scriptures: Judges 11:23-29; 2 John 6.

SAVOR IT!
Ask God to show you anything in your life that's keeping you from being totally obedient to him.

- I'd quit going to R-rated movies.
- I'd change my dating habits.
- I'd ask my parents to forgive me for the way I've treated them.
- I'd choose a different group of friends.
- I'd be honest with my parents about the things I've done behind their backs.
- I'd join the worship team at church.
- I'd carry my Bible to school.
- I'd become a missionary.
- I'd get serious about school.
- I'd start sharing my faith with others.

And I love what one girl said. She was from a town of thirty-five thousand, and she felt God was calling her to try to get everyone in her city to attend a church at least one time during the next year.

Question: What can God do through an obedient life?

Answer: Anything. Absolutely anything!

BREW IT!
God doesn't want his children trying to strike deals with him. He wants your trust.

POUR IT!
Drink in the flavor from the following Scriptures: Judges 11:30-35; Mark 6:26-29.

SAVOR IT!
Ask the Lord to help you think through a promise completely before you make it.

A PROMISE THAT SHOULD NEVER HAVE BEEN MADE

There's a good side and a bad side to Jephthah's story. The good side is that he prayed, followed God's leading, and spoke out in confidence about what was right. He was determined to defend the Lord's honor. The bad side is that after he agreed to lead Israel's army, he still didn't really trust God. He tried to cut a deal with God and in the process made a hasty promise. You can believe that almost anything done in haste will bring regrets. Yes, there are a few exceptions. But generally speaking, it's true.

Jephthah promised that if God would grant him victory in battle, he'd give the Lord whatever he first saw coming out of his home when he returned. Why would he make such a promise? Maybe he wanted to look good in front of those who had taunted and teased him growing up. Perhaps he was desperate to make a good impression to all who were watching him.

It reminds me of another story recorded in the Gospel of Mark. King Herod was so pleased with the sinful dance he saw performed that he hastily promised to give the dancer anything she asked for. She asked for John the Baptist's head on a platter. Herod felt he had to keep his word, so he ordered the cousin of Jesus murdered. (Read the devotionals on June 19–22 for more information about this story.)

Back to Jephthah. He may have assumed the first thing he'd see upon returning home would be an animal running out of the house. And because animal sacrifice was required for forgiveness of sins before Jesus willingly became our sacrifice, his vow would have seemed logical.

But the tragic truth is that when Jephthah approached home, his daughter—his only child—ran out to greet him. She was celebrating his victory in battle and his homecoming. She ran to him, playing a tambourine and dancing in joy.

You can imagine how his heart must have broken. I'm certain he was completely shocked to see his only child run out the door and across the field to meet him.

TRUE TO HIS WORD

When Jephthah saw his daughter, he was so over-whelmed with grief regarding his promise, the Bible tells us he tore his clothes in anguish. I can imagine him falling to the ground and screaming through his tears. The pain must have been unbearable.

He told his daughter about his vow to the Lord, and her response was nothing short of amazing. Instead of saying, "Yeah, but you didn't know what you were saying," she said, "Dad, you're a man of integrity. God has his hand on your life. Don't back down now. You have to keep your word to the Lord."

Do you realize that people watching you want you to be a guy or girl of integrity? They want to know you're a friend who's dependable. Trustworthy. Some-one who keeps his or her word. They want to see your character, and they need to see that it's possible to make it as a godly person in an ungodly culture.

In the back of Jephthah's mind he may have been thinking, *Maybe no one will remember me making that vow. Hey, I was under lots of stress.* It would have been easy and convenient to rationalize this vow, but watch what happens next. His daughter says, "But first let me do this one thing: Let me go up and roam in the hills and weep with my friends for two months, because I will die a virgin" (Judges 11:37, NLT).

Did Jephthah really kill his daughter? There are a few different theories. Many Bible scholars think he wouldn't contradict God's desires, and God wouldn't have approved of the "deal" in the first place. Some scholars say it's not clear whether he killed her or sat-isfied his vow by consecrating her to a life of single-ness and perpetual virginity.

Whether he killed her or sent her away to live a life alone, it was a tremendous sacrifice. He made a rash promise outside of the will of God. We can learn a couple of things from Jephthah's story:

- *Think and pray before you make a commitment.* Making rash vows in haste isn't smart. Seek God's will first.
- *Be a man or woman of your word.* God wants us to be dependable disciples who keep our word, but he doesn't want us to make stupid promises.

August 17

BREW IT!
Are you a dependable person? Can others count on you?

POUR IT!
Drink in the flavor from the following Scriptures: Judges 11:36-40; Psalm 25:5; Isaiah 58:11.

SAVOR IT!
Ask the Lord to help you become a trustworthy disciple.

BREW IT!
Go ahead: Give like you've never given before. But seek God's direction first.

POUR IT!
Drink in the flavor from the following Scriptures:
1 Samuel 1:9-11; 2:3; Mark 12:41-44.

SAVOR IT!
Ask God to help you make a sacrificial commitment that will bring glory and honor to his name.

SMART COMMITMENTS

It's not that God doesn't want us to make commitments, but he wants us to make smart ones. That's why it's so important to pray before you make a promise or commitment. If someone asks you to help with something and you're not sure you can follow through, don't even make the commitment.

God wants us to make commitments, and he'll empower us to keep the commitments we make. But he wants us to seek his guidance first. Perhaps your church launched a fund-raising campaign for a new building or for missions. Maybe you prayed and felt God leading you to pledge two hundred dollars to be paid off during the next year. Are you keeping your word? Are you a man or woman your church can depend on?

The Bible is full of people who made smart commitments and kept them with God's help:

- *Hannah.* She desperately wanted to have children but hadn't been able to. Each year she'd go to the temple and weep and pray for the Lord to bless her with a child. After years of praying, she felt led to make a promise to her heavenly Father. "You know I don't have any children, but if you'll give me a son, I'll give him back to you for your glory." God responded by giving her Samuel, who became a great prophet.
- *Shammah.* When the enemy Philistines attacked and all of God's army fled in fear, Shammah said, "I'm not leaving! I'll remain committed to God's battle." God responded. The Spirit of the Lord came upon Shammah, and he single-handedly defeated the entire Philistine army.
- *The widow.* She gave her last two cents to the Temple treasury, not knowing that the King of kings was sitting across the street watching her, smiling and observing her sacrificial commitment.
- *Mary.* She broke her alabaster jar and poured the expensive perfume over Jesus. Her commitment to him was so important, he told his disciples that wherever the gospel was preached, her story would be told.

God wants you to make commitments. And he responds to sacrificial commitments. He simply wants you to make them with his wisdom and not in your own rash thinking. Are there people you can help this week? Think of people you can give to who can't repay you. Ask God to direct you to such people. Then trust him to empower you to keep your commitments.

THE FOURTH LETTER

When the apostle John was exiled to the rocky, volcanic island of Patmos, he received a revelation of Jesus
Christ in all his glory. He wrote the book of Revelation
based on that vision. The Lord gave him seven specific letters to send to the churches in Asia Minor—
modern-day Turkey. We looked at the first few letters
on April 28–30, July 17–23, and August 2–4. Now
we're ready to dive into the fourth letter, written to
the church in Thyatira. This church is representative of
the body of Christ in the Dark Ages.

This city was the center of the dyeing industry. It
also boasted the headquarters of ancient trades such
as pottery, robe making, tanning, and weaving. Lydia,
who was Paul's first convert in the city of Philippi and a
woman who sold purple material, came from Thyatira.

Christ has words of affirmation, or commendation,
for this church as well as words of condemnation. He
tells the Christians that he has noticed their good
works and affirms them for that. Though we're not
saved by our works, it's important for us to be
involved in serving others. The apostle James tells us
that faith without works is meaningless.

Are you a Christian who's merely coasting in a
relationship with the heavenly Father? Or are you
involved and working in building his Kingdom? Again,
works can't save us from our sins, but they *are* an
important way to show our love for God once we
come to know him.

BREW IT!
Be willing to allow God to
change you and remake you
in his image.

POUR IT!
Drink in the flavor from
the following Scriptures:
Acts 16:14; James 2:18;
Revelation 2:18-21.

SAVOR IT!
Ask the Lord to show you
anything that may have crept
into your relationship with
him that shouldn't be there.

The Lord also affirms the believers in Thyatira for their love. He commends them for
faith, ministry (or service), patience (they continued to endure during their days of spiritual darkness), and their "last" works—meaning that their good works continued to
increase instead of decrease (see Revelation 2:19, NKJV). All of these virtues are produced within Christians by the Holy Spirit.

Although Jesus affirms the church for six specific areas, he also condemns them.

You may be familiar with Jezebel from the Old Testament. She's one of the most
wicked women on record (see 1 Kings 19:1-2 to get an idea of her character). There was a
woman in the church of Thyatira with a reputation as a prophetess and teacher who was
the counterpart of Jezebel. Remember, this church is in the midst of the Dark Ages, and
pagan practices and idolatry were getting mixed up with Christian works and worship.

Christ says in Revelation 2:21 that he had given time for repentance, meaning he had
patiently dealt with this false system of paganism for more than one thousand years,
and yet there had been no real change. There still hasn't been a total change today.
Paganism, Wicca, New Age—it's all subtly mixed in with people who call themselves
Christians and believe there are many paths to God.

Are you heeding the warnings of the Lord? Or do you find yourself trying to get ahead by mixing a little evil, deception, and manipulation into your works?

POUR IT!
Drink in the flavor from the following Scriptures:
1 Kings 21:11-16; 1 Corinthians 6:2; Revelation 2:22-27.

SAVOR IT!
Ask God to help you remain forever true and committed to his teachings and to his Word.

WARNINGS!

Christ says that Jezebel and her children will experience great tribulation unless they repent of their actions. He is referring to everyone who mixes paganism with Christianity, as well as all those who don't have a personal relationship with the Lord. This tribulation may refer to the poverty and affliction much of the world is currently suffering, or it may mean the Great Tribulation during the end times.

Jesus says in Revelation 2:23 that he will search the minds and hearts of each person. The King James Version translates this "reins and hearts"; "reins" literally means *kidneys.* It refers to the entire psychological makeup of humans—our feelings, thoughts, and purposes. When the Lord searches us, he searches our entire being.

Christ refers to "the depths of Satan" in Revelation 2:24 (KJV). He's talking about the false, cultic religions that originate with Satan. When we tap into false religions, we're actually bowing down to Satan, the father of lies and falsehood. In this letter to the Christians in Thyatira, Christ warns them—and us—not to fall for those false teachings and deceitful teachers, who will face his judgment.

The Lord also encourages the Christians to "hold fast." In other words, keep believing the truth of God. Keep reading and studying the Holy Bible. Don't be susceptible to false religions. Hold fast to your commitment to God. And the reward?

He goes on to say that the Christians who overcome and continue to obey him will eventually have power over nations. This corresponds with what Paul told the believers in Corinth—that someday the saints will rule the world with Christ. These are the Christians who refuse to fall prey to Jezebel's seductive teachings. The original Jezebel, wife of King Ahab, wanted to rule. In fact, she married Ahab so they could increase their power by merging countries and joining religions. They were power-hungry, egotistic rulers who stole land quickly. (Read the entire chapter of 1 Kings 21 for a peek at how they took control of Naboth's vineyard.)

Jesus is saying to us today, "If you're not part of the Jezebel scene—the scene of false beliefs—and if you'll worship me and me alone, you'll get to reign with me. You can't win by trying to reign and conquer as Jezebel did."

WALKING IN THE LIGHT

The Old Testament presents an image of Christ as the "sun of righteousness." Here in Revelation, he's seen as the "morning star." He is a bright, all-consuming light. The Bible instructs us to "walk in the light." In other words, we are to walk hand in hand, side by side with our Savior. As he illuminates the path before us with his all-powerful light, we are to walk in the light that he provides.

His light also refers to understanding. As he brings things to light, we're to heed what he reveals to us and live according to what he teaches. There were some people in the church of Thyatira who weren't truly living in the light. God had revealed truth to them, but they continued to ignore it and live in darkness.

The Holy Spirit is faithful to help us learn all that God wants to teach us. It's his responsibility to reveal—or to bring to light—that which God wants us to know. Are you walking in the light as he reveals it to you? Or are there still some areas in your life where you're in the dark?

It's easy to allow idols into our lives—to focus all our energies, attention, and devotion on a person, a program, or an activity (sports, drama, music)—instead of focusing 100 percent on God.

Christ ends his letter to the church in Thyatira by telling those who have ears to listen to what the Spirit says to the churches. Are your ears tuned in to the voice of the Holy Spirit? Can you hear him whisper? Can you feel his nudge?

As Christians, we need to use our ears to hear what God wants to say to us instead of filling them with the voices of the world. Though it's important to be aware of what's happening around you, don't let the world's influence fill your ears to the point that God's voice can't come through loud and clear.

BREW IT!
Is it time to clean out your ears? God has so many things he wants to teach you, but he needs disciples with open ears and children who are willing to walk in his light.

POUR IT!
Drink in the flavor from the following Scriptures: Malachi 4:2; Revelation 2:28-29; 22:16.

SAVOR IT!
Ask God to shed new light on your path so you can follow his guidance.

BREW IT!
You can reach out to those who don't know the Lord. God wants you to do that! But be wise and seek his direction first.

POUR IT!
Drink in the flavor from the following Scriptures: Habakkuk 2:4; 2 Corinthians 5:7; 2 Timothy 1:7-8.

SAVOR IT!
Ask God to show you how to live in the world without compromising and becoming part of the world.

IN . . . BUT NOT OF

Do you like to snoop? Scoot a little closer and I'll let you take a peek at a letter I received, okay?

Dear Susie,

My parents don't want me hanging around with the wrong crowd, but doesn't Jesus want us to be friends with people who don't know him? How can I reach out to the "bad" kids if I don't hang out with them?

Great letter. Common question. You may be wondering the same thing. If so, I appreciate your concern for those who don't know Christ. I think you and your parents are both right. Yes, Jesus wants us to reach out to those who don't know him. But there's a big difference between *reaching out* and *forming intimate relationships.*

You can purchase soft drinks in a bar, but why go into the bar just to get a Coke? That's placing yourself in an unnecessary environment of temptation. Should you attend the big party Friday night just so you can make a stand?

Yes, Jesus hung out with sinners . . . but they weren't sinners for very long. They couldn't help but notice he was different, and they wanted what he had to offer. Most parents are concerned that if you become really tight with the wrong crowd, it could influence your actions and decisions. Know what? They're right! You can't help but be affected by those you hang out with. Either they influence you or you influence them.

So how can you be in the world but not of the world?

Make contact. If you're going to impact others for Christ, you'll have to make contact. A silent witness can be powerful, but at some point you're going to have to say or do something. God doesn't want you to be a wallflower and simply withdraw from non-Christians. In fact, 2 Timothy 1:7-8 tells us that he wants just the opposite.

How can you reach out and make contact? Be friendly. Keep a smile on your face. Laugh a lot. Non-Christians don't have the joy you have from a close relationship with the Lord. Believe it or not, they'll be attracted to your lifestyle.

Your campus has tons of built-in ways of making contact: clubs, lunchtime, classes, sports, and various other activities. Take advantage of these opportunities (without becoming overloaded, of course), and use them to make contact with people who don't know Christ.

YOU CAN MAKE A DIFFERENCE

How can you be in the world but not of the world?

Make contact.

Find common ground. Many times in the Gospel of Luke, we see that Jesus interacted with people based on what they were interested in. If the non-Christian guys in your second-period class are really into championship wrestling, you probably won't get very far trying to talk with them about painting. There's no common ground. Build a bridge and deal with *their* interests.

Always? No. There will be exceptions. For example, if the students at your cafeteria table are interested in slamming the new girl and are making sexual comments about her, it obviously wouldn't be a good idea for you to jump in and join them just to find common ground. Use your head. You want to be Jesus to them.

How can you find common ground? Ask questions and listen. You'll be surprised how much you'll learn if you really try. People love to talk about what concerns them. Many Christians make the mistake of talking too much. You'll find out a ton of information by simply giving others a chance to express themselves.

Sound elementary? We often overlook the most obvious.

Don't put others down. Your non-Christian classmates don't need you to be a preacher. Chances are, they've had their fill of TV preachers and other adults who try to "preach" their convictions at them. What they need is to see a positive difference in your life!

BREW IT!
See how you're reaching out without becoming intimate? You're in the world but not of it.

POUR IT!
Drink in the flavor from the following Scriptures: Luke 5:7-8; Romans 12:1-2; Titus 2:1.

SAVOR IT!
Ask God to help you become sensitive to the needs of the non-Christians around you.

Imagine Joey comes to first period with bloodshot eyes from his wild weekend. Mr. Buchanan gives a written assignment to the class that's due at the end of the hour. Joey has barely managed to get *himself* to class. He couldn't even think about supplies such as a pen or a notebook. How will you respond?

a. "Hey, Joey! Got blasted again, huh? Man, you look terrible! When you gonna learn? Now, lookit . . . you don't even have a pen or paper."

b. "Here, Joey. Need some paper? I have an extra pen too. I know, I know. Another wild weekend. I had a wild time, too—only it was pizza and paintball and a crazy youth group. One of these days I'm gonna talk you into trying it *my* way, okay?"

Hope you chose the second response. If so, you're letting Joey know you care about him without putting him down. You've also given him something to think about without being pushy. Now you can pray that the Lord will continue to give you opportunities to reflect his love to Joey.

BREW IT!

Yes, God wants you to reach those who don't know him. But he doesn't want you to identify so closely with them that you're affected by their lifestyle.

POUR IT!

Drink in the flavor from the following Scriptures: Isaiah 2:5; 9:2; Luke 5:18-26.

SAVOR IT!

Ask the Lord to use his Holy Spirit to teach you the difference between being in the world and being of the world.

WHAT'S *REALLY* HAPPENING?

How can you be in the world but not of the world?

Make contact.

Find common ground.

Don't put others down.

Focus on the real issue. Remember the story of the lame man whose friends broke through the roof of the house where Jesus was teaching and brought their pal to him? Jesus didn't let them down. He physically healed the guy, but he also knew there were other issues in his life that were even more important than his disabled legs.

Jesus took a deeper look. He saw *inside* the man. Jesus knew that the man's misery came from being separated from his heavenly Father. So Christ healed him spiritually as well as physically. In other words, the Lord dealt with the outside stuff, but he focused a little deeper on the *real* issues that were troubling the paralytic.

When your friends brag about their sexual escapades, the party scene, or how much they get away with . . . that's the *outside* stuff. The real issue is the *inside* stuff . . . the "why" of what they're doing.

They're going too far with their girlfriend or boyfriend because they're looking for love. If they knew God's love, they'd have what they're searching for.

They're partying hearty because they have no purpose in life. Anything that feels good for the moment is attractive because they have nothing to make them feel good enough to last for eternity.

You know better. So try to deal with what's happening on the inside.

Karla confides that she and her boyfriend, Mitch, went too far, but she did it because she's afraid of losing him. How will you respond?

a. "Karla, that was really stupid! Weren't you even thinking about STDs, pregnancy, or AIDS? You're seventeen. Think Mitch is gonna stick with you forever? No way."

b. "How do you feel about going too far? Guilty? Scared? Pressured? Proud? Karla, *no one* should pressure you into doing something you're not comfortable with. You say you're scared of losing him. Why? Because you feel more secure when he's around? Because you're scared of being alone? Those are inside reasons that would make a lot of people respond outwardly to things they really don't want to do. Can we talk more about this later?"

I hope you selected the second response. By saying what you did, you've caused Karla to do some heavy thinking. Pray that Christ will help her keep an open mind toward the gospel. She'd be an excellent candidate to come to youth group when you have a special series on sex and dating.

DO YOU HAVE A HEART? (PART 1)

God smiles when we reach out to others. But to reach out, we really have to care. Do you have a genuine burden for those around you who don't know him? Check your caring quotient with this heart-for-others quiz:

1. Kyle comes to school every Monday morning still halfway bombed from the night before. You

    a. ignore him. Maybe someday he'll learn his lesson.
    b. speak to him. "Hi, Kyle. I think we're having a test in Mrs. Kraft's class today."
    c. invite him to church. "Hey, Kyle, wanna come to 'The Cave' this Wednesday with me? It's our weekly youth meeting, and you might think it sounds like a drag, but it's really a lot of fun. Try it just once, and I'll never hassle you again. But if you turn me down, I'm gonna hound you, man, because I want you to give it a shot."
    d. quietly tell the vice principal Kyle's bombed again.

2. There's a new student in your English class. You

    a. introduce yourself and ask if she wants to have lunch with you and your friends.
    b. tell a few students from your church to make her feel welcome.
    c. are too caught up with your own friends to even notice her.
    d. feel for her because you know what it's like to be new, but you don't have the courage to do anything about it.

3. Someone you know (not super well, but well enough to say hi to because you have a class together) has just been dumped by her boyfriend. You

    a. silently breathe a prayer for her.
    b. send a note telling her that you care.
    c. make a point to speak with her: "Listen, I'm really sorry about what you're going through. If you need a cappuccino, it's my treat, okay?"
    d. note that it's none of your business and steer clear.

BREW IT!
God can use you to make a huge difference in the lives of others if you're sensitive to their needs.

POUR IT!
Drink in the flavor from the following Scriptures: Matthew 5:16; Luke 8:16; John 1:4-7.

SAVOR IT!
Tell God you truly want to be his voice to those around you.

No, we're not finished with this quiz yet, but we'll take a break and finish it over the next few days. But right now think of the people on your campus who don't have a personal relationship with Christ. Jot their names down on a sheet of paper or in your computer and label it your prayer journal. Pray daily for these students. Ask God to help you know how to show them you care.

BREW IT!
God wants to give you a heart for others.

POUR IT!
Drink in the flavor from the following Scriptures:
Proverbs 22:9; John 13:14; Acts 4:32.

SAVOR IT!
Thank Jesus for being the perfect example of reaching out to others.

DO YOU HAVE A HEART? (PART 2)

Ready to continue our quiz? Let's go!

4. Your youth group just had an incredible back-to-school bash complete with laser tag, a Velcro wall, and all kinds of cool stuff. It's almost 11:30 p.m., and you have to be home by midnight. The gym's a mess. Everyone except your youth pastor and a couple of adults are still just hanging around. You
   a. leave immediately so you won't be late.
   b. tell a few of the younger students they need to stay and help clean up the place.
   c. say thanks to the adults for the great party and head home.
   d. call your folks and explain that the gym looks like a hurricane hit. Then ask permission to stay a little later to help clean up.

5. The star forward for your school's basketball team has just been hospitalized for knee surgery. He'll be out the rest of the season. You
   a. stop by the hospital and let him know you care.
   b. ignore the entire situation. After all, you're in the band. He doesn't really care about you, so why should *you* care about him?
   c. send him a funny card because hospitals give you the willies.
   d. ask your youth minister to visit him.

6. Sara has been hanging around some different students on campus. Everyone knows they have bad reputations. She's missed a few of your youth group's Bible studies, and you can't even remember the last time she was in Sunday school. You
   a. think she's probably getting what she deserves hanging around jerks like them.
   b. call your youth pastor and share your concern with him.
   c. call Sara and tell that her if she knows what's good for her, she'll get back in church.
   d. make a point to catch her between classes and let her know she's missed. You also offer to give her a ride for this week's meeting.

7. There's a student at your school who's obviously from a very poor family. He always wears the same pair of jeans and has only a couple of T-shirts. His tennis shoes aren't the cool kind, and they even have a hole in the bottom. You
   a. ask your parents if you can go through the family's clothes and pull out stuff that might fit him. Then you take it to the school counselor and ask him to make sure it gets to the student in a nonembarrassing manner.
   b. think, *If his dad would get a decent job maybe he wouldn't look like such a geek!*
   c. leave an anonymous note on his locker with the address of Goodwill on it.
   d. have your youth group collect some money or clothing for the family.

DO YOU HAVE A HEART? (PART 3)
Ready to wrap up this quiz? You're almost finished!

8. Your youth leader has just announced the spring break trip. This year you're going on a short-term, inner-city mission trip out of state. You
   a. help come up with fund-raising ideas.
   b. feel extremely disappointed. After all, you'd been saving for a ski trip during spring break.
   c. decide not to go since none of your friends are going.
   d. realize that even though this may not be as fun as skiing, it will probably be a life-changing experience, so you display a positive attitude.

9. Your Sunday school teacher is really boring. You
   a. quit going to Sunday school.
   b. hang around for a while after class and ask if you can help implement some new ideas for part of the class time, like playing a Christian music video for the first five minutes of class; taking five minutes at the end of class to ask students what's going on in their lives; sharing prayer requests and answers, etc.
   c. complain to your youth minister that if he doesn't do something soon, the entire class will fall apart.
   d. switch churches.

BREW IT!
Strive to see those around you through God's eyes.

POUR IT!
Drink in the flavor from the following Scriptures: Psalm 95:7; Proverbs 29:7; Zechariah 7:9-10.

SAVOR IT!
Ask God to help you honestly evaluate your caring quotient.

10. Your youth group is small, and when your leader is out of town, things seem to fall apart until he returns. When he leaves on vacation this summer you decide you'll
   a. volunteer to lead a two-week Bible study to keep things running consistently.
   b. open your home for fun, games, refreshments, and videos a few times while he's gone so students will stay tuned in to church activities.
   c. look forward to a nice break from having to go to church all the time.
   d. sit around and complain with your friends that there's nothing to do.

Scoring: Add your points according to the chart below.

1. A = 0, B = 1, C = 2, D = 0
2. A = 2, B = 1, C = 0, D = 0
3. A = 1, B = 2, C = 3, D = 0
4. A = 0, B = 0, C = 1, D = 2
5. A = 3, B = 0, C = 2, D = 1

6. A = 0, B = 1, C = 0, D = 2
7. A = 3, B = 0, C = 0, D = 2
8. A = 2, B = 0, C = 0, D = 1
9. A = 0, B = 2, C = 0, D = 0
10. A = 2, B = 2, C = 0, D = 0

BREW IT!
Be willing to do whatever it takes to be the hands and feet of Jesus to those around you.

POUR IT!
Drink in the flavor from the following Scriptures: Psalm 145:7; 1 John 5:4-5.

SAVOR IT!
Thank God for helping you see yourself in an honest light. Ask him to mold you into his image.

DO YOU HAVE A HEART? (PART 4)

Have you added up your score? It's time to evaluate your caring quotient.

19–23 You definitely have a heart for others! You truly care about those around you and have developed some terrific skills for reaching out. Congrats! You're striving to be Jesus to your world.

10–18 You have a heart that wants to care for others. You care about people, but sometimes you're afraid to reach out. You feel a little insecure about letting others know you care. But guess what? You're headed in the right direction. Increase your time spent with the Lord, and ask him to increase your confidence.

5–9 Your heart is beating, but not for others. Whoa! Quit thinking about yourself so much, and start focusing on the needs of those around you. Ask your youth pastor (or a trusted friend) to help you become more concerned about the world around you. Strive to come up with some specific ideas that will help turn your heart around.

0–4 Do you even have a heart? Wowsers! I sure am glad you took the quiz, but will you seriously think about your answers? From your responses, you've indicated that you don't care much at all for others. Is that really true, or did you just want to come in last to be funny? Ask your parents, youth minister, or friends for suggestions on becoming more caring. Then seek God's forgiveness for being so coldhearted. God wants to warm your heart. Let him!

WANT MORE FAITH?

You may know someone who has deep faith. Do you ever get discouraged because you don't seem to have as much faith as he does? It seems as though some people are just really trusting. For others, faith is more difficult. Remember the disciple Thomas? (His nickname is "Doubting Thomas.") He wanted to see the nail scars in Christ's hands before he would believe. Faith was hard for him.

But guess what? You don't need a lot of faith. Jesus tells us all we need is a small amount. In fact, he compares what we need to a mustard seed. Have you ever seen a mustard seed? It's about the size of a pinpoint. We're talking microscopic!

The fact that you're a Christian and have trusted God to forgive your sins proves you have faith. And yes, there are some things you can do to increase the little bit of faith you have:

1. *Read your Bible consistently*. Think of God's Word as your soul food. It nourishes, instructs, encourages, and strengthens us. You need its contents to help deepen your faith.
2. *Pray daily*. Set a small goal for yourself. Start with something you know you can accomplish. For instance, say, "I'm going to read the Bible and pray for one minute every day." Anyone can spend one minute with God! You'll easily meet your goal, and after a few weeks you'll probably want to increase it to two minutes, then three or five or thirty. Be realistic and set a goal you know you can easily reach. Then discipline yourself to extend that goal.
3. *Surround yourself with other Christians*. By hanging out with like-minded believers, you gain a sense of what God is doing in others' lives. This helps deepen your faith. Also, as you share prayer requests with each other, you'll learn how faithful God is.
4. *Memorize the Word*. Look up some verses on faith and jot them down on some index cards. Hang them in obvious places where you'll see them often. Take time to memorize those verses and say them out loud in the car, in the shower, or when you're exercising. You'll be amazed at how God's Word will deepen your faith.
5. *Get involved in your church*. Use your gifts to serve your congregation.

If you're already doing all these things, watch your friend's life. What is he doing that you're not? Ask him. Close friends should be able to share their spiritual highs and lows. Ask him to pray with you about your concerns regarding faith.

BREW IT!
Determine to participate in each of these five areas for at least a month, and then assess how your faith has grown.

POUR IT!
Drink in the flavor from the following Scriptures: Matthew 8:10; 9:2, 29.

SAVOR IT!
Thank God for giving you the faith you have, and ask him to deepen it.

BREW IT!
Make your own list of favorite names for Jesus.

POUR IT!
Drink in the flavor from the following Scriptures: Isaiah 40:5, 7-8, 21-23.

SAVOR IT!
Ask God to reveal himself to you today in a variety of ways.

WHO HE IS

Spend some time today simply reflecting on the character of the Lord and some of the different facets of his holy character.

Jesus is . . .

A banner for the peoples
Alpha and Omega
Ancient of Days
Anointed One
Apostle and High Priest
Author and perfecter of our faith
Author of life
Author of our salvation
Blessed and only Ruler
Branch of the Lord
Bread of Life
Bridegroom
Chief Cornerstone
Chief Shepherd
Consolation of Israel
Covenant for the people
Crown of splendor
Eternal life
Faithful and true
First to rise from the dead
Firstborn over all creation
Fragrant offering and sacrifice to God
Friend of tax collectors and sinners
God's Son
Great High Priest
Great Light
He who died and came to life again
He who loves us and has freed us from our sins
Head over every power and authority
Heir of all things
Holy and righteous One
Hope of Israel
Horn of salvation
Image of the invisible God

IT'S A MATCH!

Imagine having a disease that could kill you.

Imagine finding out that a life-sustaining substance could save you . . . but the substance is extremely rare and your chances of getting it are slim at best.

If you can imagine that scenario, you might have a small clue to what twenty-nine-year-old Pia Awal was feeling. She was diagnosed with leukemia and desperately needed a bone-marrow transplant. But because she and her family immigrated from India to the United States, she knew her odds of receiving the right match weren't too hopeful. She needed a South Asian match, and that particular group is among the most underrepresented in the nation's bone-marrow registry.

Her friends and family members, however, refused to throw in the towel. They built a Web site and helped get 12,442 people tested in fourteen weeks. Finally, a donor in Britain was a match. Pia received the lifesaving transplant in Seattle and will be forever grateful for getting a second chance at life.

Whether or not you've battled leukemia, you've actually faced a situation similar to Pia's. Each one of us was born with the disease of sin. Left untreated, it will eventually kill you. And, as in Pia's situation, there aren't many people who are matched donors to fight your disease. In fact, there's only one.

Jesus Christ is the only one who has the cure for your sin. You'll never have enough money to buy salvation; you'll never be able to do enough good things to earn it. The only way to receive forgiveness for sins is by confessing to Christ that you are a sinner and asking him to forgive you.

But unlike Pia, you don't have to wait and search and build a Web site to catch Christ's attention. As the Great Physician, he's already aware of your diseased condition, and he's ready and willing to step in. But he won't do it uninvited. He's waiting on you to seek his forgiveness—his one and only cure.

Because of our culture, we've become accustomed to sin. We've become used to hearing it, seeing it, and—unfortunately—even participating in it. We tend to overlook that it's a deadly disease that will eventually kill us. If you've never sought forgiveness for your sin, you can do that right now by praying the prayer of salvation in the devotional on February 21.

BREW IT!
Don't delay in making things right with God.

POUR IT!
Drink in the flavor from the following Scriptures: Psalm 51:5; Romans 7:5; 8:3-4.

SAVOR IT!
Tell God how grateful you are that he was willing to pay for your sins through the death of Christ, his only Son.

GO FIGURE!

Some of these September holidays are real, and others are fake. See if you can guess which is which by writing an *R* or an *F* in the blank.

___ Children's Good Manners Month
___ Increase Your Octane Month
___ Write a Senator Month
___ Scrub Your Gutters Week
___ Library Card Sign-Up Month
___ National Biscuit Month
___ National Plant a Cactus Month
___ National Potato Month
___ Try a Parrot for a Pet Week
___ National Wear Purple Day
___ Everything Dutch Day
___ Substitute Teacher Appreciation Week
___ National Farm Animals Awareness Week
___ Roast Beef Day
___ Talk like a Pirate Day
___ Elephant Appreciation Day
___ Ancestor Appreciation Day
___ Hairstylist Appreciation Day
___ Tap Dancing Day
___ National Waffle Week

BREW IT!
It's not always easy to discern the real from the fake, is it? Strive to become spiritually discerning, so you'll be knowledgeable about what's real and what's not in the arena of religion.

POUR IT!
Drink in the flavor from the following Scriptures: Proverbs 14:6; 15:14; Philippians 1:9-10.

SAVOR IT!
Tell God you want to be a discerning disciple.

Fake: Increase Your Octane Month, Write a Senator Month, Scrub Your Gutters Week, National Plant a Cactus Month, Try a Parrot for a Pet Week, National Wear Purple Week, Everything Dutch Day, Roast Beef Day, Hairstylist Appreciation Day, Tap Dancing Day.

BREW IT!
Think about it: Are you bowing down to certain things in your life when God is actually calling you to stand against them?

POUR IT!
Drink in the flavor from the following Scripture: Daniel 3:1-12.

SAVOR IT!
Ask God to give you the courage you need to refuse to bow to worldly things.

REFUSE TO BOW

Instead of calling him Mr. President, they called him King. His real name was King Nebuchadnezzar, but most people called him "King Nebbie Baby." KNB was really stuck on himself. His ego was so huge, he commissioned the Sizzling Sculpture Guys to create a solid gold, ninety-foot statue of himself.

On the day of its completion, KNB decided to mark the unveiling with a great celebration. He announced the world's first, largest, and loudest rock concert. Then he passed a law that forced every citizen to attend his bash. It was massive! They had amps lined up the distance of a football field. And anyone who was anywhere on the music charts was there to play.

KNB grabbed the microphone and announced the party rules. "When the music starts to blast, I want everyone to do the new national dance I've created. I'm calling it 'The Bow.' As we unveil the ninety-foot golden replica of me, the music will crank, and you'll bow. Got it?"

Thousands nodded their empty heads in agreement. The music blasted. The golden giant glistened in the sun as it was carefully unveiled. KNB eyed his citizens swaying and bowing to the new national dance. They all bowed—literally thousands. All of them.

Okay, maybe you've heard this story before. The actual version is found in Daniel 3. And if you're familiar with the story, you know that three young men didn't bow. We'll use their nicknames: Shad, Mad, and Bad. There they stood, refusing to bow.

KNB was furious! He grabbed the microphone again and spit out the rules. "We're cranking up the tunes. When you hear the music, bend those knees. If you don't do 'The Bow' in allegiance to me, you'll be tossed into this fiery furnace."

They cranked. You know how it sounds when you can *feel* the music? The point where it's so loud you can actually feel the ground beneath you vibrate? This music was so loud, it was way past that. It was electric. Not only could you *hear* it, you could *taste* it as the notes slid down your throat. You could *smell* the rhythm as it throbbed against your body. You could see the beat wrapping itself around your life. And you could *feel* the chords as they danced through your soul. Oooh. It was wild, like you became one with the music.

Thousands bowed. But Shad, Mad, and Bad continued to stand. And they stood tall. In fact, they stood head and shoulders above the rest. That's what happens when you take a stand for God; you stand head and shoulders above everyone. But if you don't stand for God, you'll fall for anything the world tosses your way.

TEMPER TANTRUM

KNB was livid that Shad, Mad, and Bad still refused to bow! He brought them right down front where everyone could see. Sometimes that happens when you take a stand for God. But taking a stand for Christ guarantees that God will definitely use you to bring glory to his name.

Right there, in front of thousands, KNB ordered those three young men to be bound tightly with ropes and thrown into the furnace of fire. He ordered the fire be cranked up seven times hotter than usual. And those three men of God were tossed into the furnace. The flames were so intense, they killed the soldiers who had thrown the men into the fire.

Before we get to the end of the story, we need to pause for a moment and take a look at Shad, Mad, and Bad's attitude right before they were tossed into the furnace, because there are some terrific lessons we can learn from them.

1. *They continued to act respectfully toward authority.* Maybe you'd be tempted to scream, "You're a jerk, KNB! Our God could simply sneeze on you and blow you to pieces. Nyah, nyah, nyah."

But these three Hebrew teens recognized that even though KNB was wrong, he was still in authority over them. They refused to bow because they worshipped a higher authority, but they still acted like gentlemen toward this monster. When they spoke with KNB, the New International Version records them referring to him as "O king." *The Living Bible* translates it "sir." The three men maintained respect for the king's authority without agreeing with his command.

Your campus administration may not be a godly group. Your boss may not be a Christian. God still wants you to maintain a Christlike attitude when interacting with them. You can respect their position without agreeing with their lifestyle.

How do you tend to react to someone in opposition to the gospel? Your natural inclination may be to rise against that person in anger, yelling and screaming that he doesn't know what he's talking about. But people aren't won to the Lord through angry arguments. They're won to the Lord because of our testimony, because of God's love shining through us, and because they are treated with kindness.

There are certainly moments for righteous anger, but the Holy Spirit will reveal to you when those moments are, and how to handle them. Righteous anger usually isn't called for when God is trying to work through you to win someone to him.

September 3

BREW IT!
Though KNB threw a temper tantrum, the three young men refused to play that game. They remained obedient to God, and they still showed respect to the king. Is it more common for you to throw a temper tantrum than to show respect?

POUR IT!
Drink in the flavor from the following Scripture: Daniel 3:13-23.

SAVOR IT!
Ask God to help you control your temper and give those in authority the respect that's called for.

BREW IT!
Does your faith remain constant during smooth times and tough times?

POUR IT!
Drink in the flavor from the following Scriptures:
Psalm 9:10; Habakkuk 2:4; Matthew 17:20.

SAVOR IT!
Ask God to strengthen your faith as you meet with him on a daily basis.

FAITH IN THE FIRE

When they may have been tempted to lash out in rage or start a fight, three Hebrew guys refused to let their tempers fly. Shad, Mad, and Bad didn't obey wicked KNB, but they respected his position of authority. Their decision cost them! They were thrown into the fiery furnace. What can we learn from them?

2. *They continued to trust in God.* Even in the midst of intense fire, their faith didn't waver. They knew beyond all doubt that the God they served—Jehovah, God Almighty—had the power to save them from being burned alive. They also knew, however, that for reasons they wouldn't understand, God might choose not to save them. But though they didn't know the outcome, their faith remained solid. They never doubted the power of God. They had settled in their minds that if God chose not to save them, they had still made the right choice. They would still worship him; their relationship with him wouldn't be affected in the least. He was still on the throne.

Wow! Are you serving God with that kind of commitment? Are you living with that kind of faith?

Check out their incredible response to the king as he announced they would be burned alive:

"O Nebuchadnezzar, we do not need to defend ourselves before you. If we are thrown into the blazing furnace, the God whom we serve is able to save us. He will rescue us from your power, Your Majesty. But even if he doesn't, we want to make it clear to you, Your Majesty, that we will never serve your gods or worship the gold statue you have set up" (Daniel 3:16-18, NLT).

Their faith remained solid even though they couldn't see the immediate outcome. They knew God could save them, but they didn't know if he would choose to. They simply trusted his wisdom, his judgment, and his plan.

That's the kind of faith God wants you to have. He wants to enable you to live your life every single day with a no-compromise, no-doubt trust in his plan for your life. Even though you can't see what he has in store for you next week, next month, or next year, will you trust him with unswerving faith?

How can I develop that kind of faith? you may be wondering. It all boils down to an intense, intimate, growing relationship with him. You see, the better you know your heavenly Father, the more you trust him. And the way you get to know him better is by spending time with him, talking to him, listening for his voice, and reading his Word.

If that sounds familiar, it's because it is! This is the basic truth of spiritual growth: Get to know God better by spending time in prayer and reading the Bible on a daily basis.

SURPRISE!

Shadrach, Meshach, and Abednego were three young men who had a strong relationship with their heavenly Father. They chose obedience to him even though it meant risking their lives. Because of their faith, we learn some powerful lessons:

1. *They continued to act respectfully toward authority.*
2. *They continued to trust in God.*
3. *They chose obedience over comfort.* And because of this, God was able to influence a nation for his glory. When King Nebuchadnezzar ordered the three guys thrown into the furnace, and even the soldiers who carried out the order were killed by the flames, he expected these enemies of his to die immediately.

But as he observed from a distance, KNB squinted his eyes and was astonished at what he saw in the furnace. Imagine his surprise when he saw four men instead of three—and the fourth looked like an angel or God himself! And imagine his amazement when he saw them walking around in the furnace, unharmed, without the ropes with which they'd been bound.

Was the king more surprised that Shad, Mad, and Bad's God rescued them? Or that their God had chosen to walk through the fire *with* them? No doubt he was impressed with both facts! He got as close to the furnace as he could without being injured, and he commanded the three young men to come out.

King Nebuchadnezzar was so moved at this miracle that he gave Shad, Bad, and Mad promotions and told his entire nation about their God of everlasting power.

It's amazing, isn't it? In the most unthinkable and unexpected places, God shows up. You can depend on him wherever you are.

BREW IT!
You have a choice: When in the furnace, you can complain and question, or you can thank God for being with you!

POUR IT!
Drink in the flavor from the following Scripture: Daniel 3:24-30.

SAVOR IT!
Thank God for specific times he's stood in the fire with you. And thank him ahead of time for his promise to keep standing with you in future trials.

What kind of furnace are you experiencing? God stands in the fire with you. He feels the heat you're experiencing, and he wants to give you the strength to keep standing. You don't serve a God who says, "Take a stand! I'll check back with you next year during spring break to see how you're doing." The God you serve says, "Take a stand! And I'll be right here with you, holding you up, empowering you, and letting you lean on me."

When others notice that you're standing in the fire—going through a tough time—do they see you standing alone, or are they pleasantly surprised to discover that God stands with you, even through your trials?

BREW IT!
Are you taking advantage of the opportunities that come your way? Are you standing tall? Are you speaking out? Never forget that you don't stand alone! God is with you.

POUR IT!
Drink in the flavor from the following Scriptures:
Psalm 119:2-3; Jeremiah 1:6-8; Hebrews 12:12-13.

SAVOR IT!
Ask God to give you an opportunity this week to stand for him.

FEELING THE HEAT?

You may feel as though you're in a fiery furnace right now. Maybe some students on your campus are making fun of you because of your faith. Perhaps you're being pressured to drink, cheat, or become sexually involved. As a Christian, you can find comfort in knowing that God is already committed to being with you. You don't have to beg him to show up. He's already there.

Read this out loud: *If I don't take a stand for Christ, I'll fall for anything. But when I stand for him, I stand head and shoulders above everyone else.* Read it again; it bears repeating. Let it soak into your mind and your heart. Act on this principle. Live out its truth.

It's kind of funny. At the beginning of this story, three young men stood at the back of the crowd. But because they continued to stand in the midst of pressure, God moved them right down front. The statue of King Nebuchadnezzar? No one seemed to notice anymore. Even ninety feet of solid gold pales when three godly people stand in front of it.

Taking a stand isn't always easy, is it? Sometimes it hurts to go against the crowd. Yet when we're confronted with something we know is morally wrong, unethical, or distracting to our walk with Christ, we know he wants us to stand tall. And the same God who calls you to stand holds you up!

Here are some steps that will help you to stand:

Pray for courage. You may be the only one in biology class who's equipped to speak out against evolution. You may be the only one in health class who doesn't support abortion. Seek the Lord's boldness to speak out.

Pray for strength. When you take a stand, you'll undoubtedly face opposition and you may feel attacked. Seek God's power to continue standing—even on shaky legs.

Pray for opportunities. Ask God to make you aware of situations in which you can stand tall for him. Tell him you want to recognize opportunities to share your beliefs, convictions, and faith.

WILL MAGGIE PACK HER TRUNK?

Maggie, a twenty-two-year-old African elephant, lives in the zoo in Anchorage, Alaska. Zoologists are concerned about her—not because of the cold weather, but because Maggie is the only elephant in Alaska.

But Maggie's not going to be packing her trunk anytime soon. Zoo officials have decided to keep her in the Alaska Zoo in Anchorage and simply try to make her more comfortable. Maggie's barn will get better ventilation and a softer floor. A second handler has been hired to tend to the elephant's needs. An elephant treadmill has also been added to Maggie's home so she can be more active.

Maggie arrived at the zoo as a baby in 1983 and joined Annabelle, an older Asian elephant. When Annabelle died in 1997, Maggie's loneliness and socialization became a problem. The American Zoo and Aquarium Association recommends that female elephants be kept in groups of three or more. One of the animal experts says, "Elephants have an innate need for other elephant companions."

Just as elephants have a deep need to connect with other elephants, you were created with an innate need to connect with your heavenly Father.

BREW IT!
Spend a few minutes in worship. You don't have to be in church; you can worship God right now wherever you are.

POUR IT!
Drink in the flavor from the following Scriptures: Psalm 95:6; 97:7; 100:2.

SAVOR IT!
Seek God's forgiveness for worshipping anything other than him.

Since the beginning of time, humans have expressed their need to worship a higher being. Whether it was cavemen making stone gods, Greeks creating extensive myths about their gods, or people worshipping the sun and stars, there's something deep within us that drives us to recognize a higher being.

We realize we are not alone. Deep inside we know there is something—someone—greater than ourselves. We feel it so deeply that if we don't know Jesus Christ, we somehow create something else to worship.

The interesting thing, though, is that because God created us, only God can satisfy us. The void we feel is a God-shaped void. We can try to fit other things in the hole—relationships, jobs, cars, new clothes, alcohol, chat rooms—but the only one who completely fills the void is God himself.

Our lives are like a puzzle, and he is the missing piece. No matter how hard we try to squeeze something else into that vacancy, only God will truly fit. Until we realize that God and God alone is the answer, we'll feel a need to worship a number of other things.

The Alaska Zoo is going out of its way to meet Maggie's needs with a treadmill and plenty of other extras. Yet what she really desires is simply another elephant.

Are you trying to meet your needs with things besides God? Are you putting too much emphasis on things of the world? He alone is worthy of our worship.

YOU CAN RUN, BUT YOU CAN'T HIDE

The Bible tells us that our sins will find us out. In other words, we can't hide anything from God. People often run from the authorities and go to great measures to hide a crime from the police. But even if we can fool the authorities, we'll never be able to fool God.

Recently a man named David Jones was convicted of voluntary manslaughter for a crime committed in 1975. For almost thirty years he was able to hide his crime, but the truth eventually caught up with him.

David lived in the same neighborhood as fourteen-year-old Robin Gilbert when her dead body was found on a golf course. A medical examiner ruled that she died of heart disease. David no doubt thought he was home free. But twenty-one years later, police received a tip that led them to a diary kept by David's mom. The details inside the book revealed that Robin hadn't died of heart disease; David had killed her.

Her grave was opened, and her body was exhumed. In 1997 a different medical examiner conducted an autopsy and discovered that Robin had been strangled. David was convicted by a jury and is currently in prison.

People often go to extreme lengths to hide their sins, don't they? Lying, running, changing names, relocating, and living in denial are all ways people try to cover up something wrong. And though we may be able to get by for the time being, God always knows, and he says our sins will eventually catch up with us.

Doesn't it make sense, then, to confess our sins? What good does it do to run and hide? Adam and Eve tried to hide from God in the Garden of Eden. They soon realized, though, that God knew exactly where they were, what they had done, and why they were hiding.

When God found them, they could have responded, "We're so sorry, Father. We've disobeyed you. We broke your command. We were wrong. Will you forgive us?" Instead, they immediately made excuses. Adam blamed the whole thing on Eve, who in turn blamed Satan.

In our culture, it's not popular to take responsibility for our actions—especially when we're wrong. After all, if no one sees us do something wrong, it doesn't really matter, does it? Yes, it does. It always matters to God.

RESPONSE ABILITY

I had been invited to Dan and Becky's for dinner. As I pulled into their neighborhood, I parked my car by the curb. After an enjoyable evening, I walked to my car in the dark and didn't notice that another car had pulled in just a few inches behind me.

As I backed up, my heart sank with the sound of metal crashing against metal. I had hit the car and damaged the front end. It was dark. I was alone. . . .

Though you may think it would have been easy for me to stay in my car and simply drive away, it really wouldn't have. Because Jesus is Lord of my life, I wouldn't have been able to sleep that night if I had tried to hide what happened.

God and I both knew what needed to be done. I had to take responsibility for my actions. Even though it was a mistake, the damage had been done. I wrote a note explaining that I had hit the car and left my name and phone number at the bottom. Then I placed the note underneath the car's wiper blade.

The owner of the car called me the next day, and I ended up footing the bill for an unexpected, unplanned expense I couldn't really afford. But I did it, because it was the right thing to do.

It doesn't always feel good to do what's right—especially when doing so hits your wallet. And it's not always fun to take responsibility for our actions. But as Christians, we do so because we're committed to integrity and dedicated to imitating Christ.

Responsibility actually boils down to "response ability." How's yours? Are you willing to admit it's your fault even when it costs you? Think of it this way: It will cost you more in the long run if you don't accept responsibility for your actions right now.

The book of Acts tells about a man named Ananias and his wife, Sapphira, who lied to Peter about their money then tried to hide the fact that they were lying. They didn't get very far. They died before they even left the church. Sin is deadly. It will kill us spiritually if we don't give God control.

BREW IT!
What are the disadvantages of trying to hide something you know isn't right?

POUR IT!
Drink in the flavor from the following Scriptures: Psalm 32:5; 38:18; Hebrews 4:12-13.

SAVOR IT!
Ask God to help you develop a strong sense of "response ability."

BREW IT!

If you've never actually been rescued by Christ, you can pray a prayer of salvation right now and accept him as your personal Savior. Turn to the devotional on February 21 if you need help praying.

POUR IT!

Drink in the flavor from the following Scriptures:
1 Chronicles 16:23;
Psalm 51:12; Isaiah 12:2-3.

SAVOR IT!

Spend some time thanking God for the miracle of your rescue.

RESCUED!

More than one hundred people gathered at a vacant lot to watch rescuers bring twenty-two-month-old Da'jour McMillan to the surface of an abandoned well. Da'jour had been playing with his older brother and sister near his grandparents' house when he fell down the fourteen-foot well that was overgrown with grass.

After police arrived at the scene, they called for a rescue team with special training. Authorities were concerned that Da'jour might not be able to breathe in the narrow hole, and they knew that only a little bit of dirt could suffocate him.

A drill from a local power company was used to dig a shaft next to the one where Da'jour was trapped. Workers from the rescue team then tunneled over to the well. Though it took all night, Da'jour was finally rescued around 5:45 a.m.

Firefighters said this incident reminded them of another similar accident—the 1987 rescue of eighteen-month-old Jessica McClure. She fell into an abandoned well and was trapped twenty-two feet down inside a hole only eight inches wide. It took emergency workers two and a half days to rescue her.

People striving to rescue Da'jour didn't mind that it took all night. And workers rescuing Jessica were determined to keep going until the two-and-a-half-day operation was completed. In both cases, these people were dedicated to their jobs. They had a goal to reach, and they continued to focus straight ahead until it was complete.

Isn't it comforting to know that Jesus Christ is far more dedicated than a professional rescue worker? He's willing to do whatever it takes to rescue you from eternal separation from him. Those who haven't repented of their sins and placed their faith in Christ are headed for hell. Does that sound blunt? It is. No sense dancing around it or trying to sidestep the issue.

It's frightening to imagine a friend spending eternity in hell, isn't it? But the exciting news is that God doesn't want *anyone* to go to hell. That's why he gave his own Son, Jesus Christ, to pay the price for everyone's sins. All we have to do is repent, accept his forgiveness, and follow him.

What a rescue! Though it was undoubtedly difficult and tense for workers to spend hours pulling Da'jour and Jessica out of wells, it was beyond what we can comprehend for Christ to willingly be tortured and die on the cross to rescue us. It was the rescue of all rescues!

And it didn't end at the Cross. After Jesus had been dead for three days, God raised him from the dead, and he is preparing an eternal home for you *right now* in heaven. That's love!

STAR POWER

Americans spent $72 billion on furniture in 2003—and that's down from previous years. Many furniture makers are worried about declining sales, so some of the top U.S. furniture manufacturers have recruited celebrities to lend their name to their products, hoping the "star power" will help sell everything from tables to recliners to sofas to bedroom suites. John Elway, former Denver Broncos quarterback, has connected his name with the Bassett furniture line. Designers Oscar de la Renta and Ralph Lauren have associated their names with Century Furniture and Henredon.

Golf pro Arnold Palmer's name is now with Lexington Home Brands, and Martha Stewart has a signature line with Bernhardt Furniture. These licensing deals are used to create instant credibility. Even though many of these furniture makers are already well-known, they believe the power of a celebrity's name will set them apart.

What if Christianity relied on celebrities to sell forgiveness? Can you imagine Jesus standing in heaven wringing his hands thinking, *Wow! I'd better recruit a few more movie stars, singers, and athletes to push forgiveness so I'll get more business.*

It sounds like a pretty good idea. After all, most people will listen to what someone famous has to say, and if a popular movie star talks openly about his faith in Christ, fans take notice. Why hasn't God thought of that?

Why doesn't he create a worldwide marketing plan? Or speak audibly through a hurricane and scare people into coming to him? Or what about designing a brand-new clothing line that everyone would want—and it would advertise how to receive forgiveness for sins? Imagine, if millions of people wore those clothes, everyone would know how to come to Christ.

Wait a minute. Salvation already has a celebrity: Jesus Christ. And God already has designed a marketing plan to reach the world. It's you and me. That's right. No big air show. No new clothing line. No gimmicks. Just you and me and a whole lot of love.

It's hard to resist genuine love. If you truly love the people in your own little world, they'll notice. They'll be drawn to you, and they'll want what you have. If every Christian in the world loved others and was open to opportunities to witness, the world could probably be won in no time at all. But we each have to do our part. God is counting on us. We're his marketing plan.

BREW IT!
Have you ever prayed with someone to accept Christ as their Savior? If not, why? God can replace your fear with boldness. If you have led someone to the Lord, keep looking for more opportunities!

POUR IT!
Drink in the flavor from the following Scriptures: Psalm 37:39; 40:10; Lamentations 3:26.

SAVOR IT!
Ask God to bring to your mind someone who needs him. Ask him to help you lead that person to a saving relationship with him.

BREW IT!

Are you taking advantage of meeting with the "Doctor in the house"? There's no need that's too big for his care, and nothing you face is too small to be considered important to him.

POUR IT!

Drink in the flavor from the following Scriptures: Deuteronomy 4:7; Psalm 145:18; Romans 8:35.

SAVOR IT!

Thank God that you can't ever travel far enough to get away from his love and care.

A DOCTOR IN THE HOUSE

Imagine you're flying from Boston to Dallas with a layover in Chicago. While in Chicago, you decide to pass the two-hour wait by heading toward the food court to grab some cookies. On the way, though, you trip getting onto the moving walkway, fall down, and sprain your ankle. Do you hobble around during the rest of your layover and wait until you reach Dallas to seek medical help?

If you're traveling in a select number of airports, you'll be in luck if you have an accident! Some airports now offer medical assistance for anything from indigestion to heart attacks to cuts and scrapes. At least eleven major U.S. airports have medical offices accessible to travelers, and they range from one-person emergency care facilities to multiservice operations with sixty staffers.

Many provide nonemergency services such as giving shots and drawing blood, and most have a doctor on duty and equipment such as X-ray machines. Three airport medical clinics never close: New York, Los Angeles, and Honolulu. The medical facility at the Los Angeles International Airport is the largest of its kind; it has an eight-bed emergency area and handles about forty-eight thousand patients each year.

The medical facility at New York's John F. Kennedy International is the second largest and has about twenty-five examining rooms. It even has a sonogram that can detect blood clots developed during a long flight.

Though it's comforting to know you can find medical help in at least eleven airports throughout the nation, there are still many places you won't be able to receive medical assistance during a layover. Fortunately, there *is* a Physician who's available anytime, anywhere, for anything. God is the Great Physician, and for Christians there's no place you can travel outside his care.

You can fly to a third world country and be surrounded by people who don't speak your language, and the Great Physician will be there to meet your needs. You can dive to the depths of the ocean on a high-tech navy submarine, and the Great Physician will be there. You can climb Mount Everest, blast off into space, or go spelunking in any cave in the world, and the Great Physician will be right beside you.

MY FRIEND, THE ATHEIST

"I've been trying to share Christ with a friend on my campus," Megan told me. "But every time I bring God into the conversation, he interrupts me and says, 'Don't wanna hear it. I'm an atheist.' What can I do?"

Have you crossed paths with someone who claims to be an atheist? If so, I hope you're trying to share your faith with him as Megan is doing. You've probably already realized that it won't do you any good to argue. Heaven won't be filled with people who lost the argument; it will be filled with those who have been loved into the Kingdom of God.

Yes, it's important to state your beliefs and to articulate why you believe what you do. But be careful not to get involved in a battle zone of arguing simply for its own sake.

Be up front with your friend. "Really? You're an atheist? That's interesting. Do you have proof that God doesn't exist?"

It shouldn't be surprising when your friend can't produce proof. So help him clarify his terms. "If you don't have proof that God doesn't exist, perhaps you're not really an atheist. Maybe you're an agnostic—someone who simply chooses to believe there's no God."

He'll probably agree to that term and definition. Then gently ask what led him to that conclusion. He may say what many unbelievers say, "I prayed that God would do something specific, and God didn't answer."

BREW IT!
Your lifestyle can shout volumes over your words. Make sure your actions are Christlike.

POUR IT!
Drink in the flavor from the following Scriptures: Isaiah 43:10; Acts 1:8; Philippians 1:27.

SAVOR IT!
Ask God for boldness in sharing your faith with others.

You can lovingly show him that the Bible clearly says that God has committed himself to hearing only one prayer from a sinner, and that's the prayer of repentance. Help your friend understand that before he can expect two-way communication from God, he first needs to give God his life and place his faith in him.

There's an old story about an atheist who spoke to a large audience about his disbelief in God. After his lecture, he invited anyone who had a question to approach the platform. There was a man in the audience who had been an alcoholic for years, but recently he had given his life to Christ and had now been delivered from drinking.

This man approached the platform and presented an orange to the lecturer. "Is this a sweet orange?" he asked.

The lecturer was indignant. "What a stupid question!" he snarled. "How can I know whether it's sweet or sour if I haven't tasted it?"

"Good point," the Christian replied. "And how can you know anything about Christ if you haven't tried him?"

BREW IT!
Remember, as you share your faith, your goal isn't to argue. It's to confront others with the truth in love.

POUR IT!
Drink in the flavor from the following Scriptures: Psalm 67:1-3; Proverbs 12:17; Acts 13:32-33.

SAVOR IT!
If you're not sure what God is teaching you, ask him to make it plain.

SHARING YOUR FAITH

Megan lovingly confronted her atheist friend, who admitted to not having any proof that God doesn't exist. Then she gently asked if she could share what God was doing in her life. Megan was surprised when her friend agreed to listen.

Megan was smart in asking if she could share. When someone gives you permission to share your faith, it's hard for him to walk away. After all, he's already agreed to listen!

Megan also knew her testimony would go a little further with her agnostic friend if she didn't come off as "telling" him or pointing a finger in his face. Instead, she simply shared. "Telling" feels very different from "sharing." Strive to share.

One of the most powerful testimonies you can give is simply to share what God is doing in your life. No one can refute that. No one can say, "No, he didn't do that. That's not true." Only you can testify to what God is teaching you.

Your friend may say, "That's hard to believe," or "I don't understand," but he can't dismiss what you say God is doing right now in your life—especially if your actions support what you're saying.

So what is God doing in your life? If your time with him is sporadic and rushed, it'll be hard to answer this question. But if you're establishing the good habit of spending time with God daily, reading the Bible, talking with him, and listening to him, you'll be ready to respond.

You can always share what God is teaching you through this devotional book and the Scriptures you're reading. After you begin sharing what God is currently doing in your life, your friend may be curious to know more. I suggest you grab the student edition of a book called *The Case for Christ* by Lee Strobel. It's easy to understand, it's a quick read, and it will provide a ton of things for you and your friend to discuss.

Strobel was an award-winning journalist who didn't believe in God. He determined to prove that God didn't exist and set out on a journey for evidence. During his research, he realized there's actually more proof that God does exist and that Jesus really is who he claims to be, than there is that God doesn't exist.

Strobel committed his life to Christ and is now enthusiastically serving him. Some of his research is included in *The Case for Christ*, and it would be a great book for you and your friend to read together. Ask him to read one chapter; then get together and discuss it.

SEEING THE LIGHT

As you grow closer to the Lord, you'll realize it's important for you to spend daily time with him—not only for your own spiritual growth, but also so you'll have something to share with your unsaved friends. The apostle Paul told his young friend Timothy to always be prepared to share his faith. We, too, need to be ready to share Christ with the dying world around us.

As you walk through the halls on your campus, as you shop in the malls of your city, and as you drive through your local streets, imagine that everyone you see has the word *dead* written across their foreheads. Unless you know for sure that someone has a relationship with Christ, you can assume he doesn't. And those who haven't placed their trust in him are spiritually dead.

When you see people as though they're spiritually dead, you realize the urgency in sharing the Good News with them. That's why the great commission is so important. The great commission is Christ's command for us to spread the gospel. People who don't know Christ will spend eternity separated from him. They're living in spiritual darkness. So it's imperative that we be willing to share Jesus, the Light of the World.

Dustin was born blind, but when he reached the age of five, he had an operation that doctors believed would restore his sight. After the surgery, they exposed him to only a little light at a time. A couple of weeks passed, and finally Dustin's mom took him outside and uncovered his eyes. For the first time in his life, the little boy was able to see the mountains, the sky, and the trees. "Mom!" he screamed. "It's beautiful! Why didn't you tell me it was so beautiful?"

Tears streamed down his mom's face. "I tried to, Dustin. But you just couldn't understand me."

Nonbelievers are blind to the glory and light of the gospel. The only way they'll ever understand is if the light shines in through the enabling of the Holy Spirit. Every time you share your faith with someone, you're allowing the Holy Spirit to shine some light into that person's life.

BREW IT!
Whom can you share the light of Jesus with this week?

POUR IT!
Drink in the flavor from the following Scriptures: Matthew 28:18-20; John 1:1-5; 2 Timothy 4:2.

SAVOR IT!
Ask God to shine brightly through your life.

BREW IT!

It's normal to get a little nervous about taking a stand for the Lord. But you can ask him for strength, and he'll provide it for you. You can also rest in the fact that he has promised to never leave you.

POUR IT!

Drink in the flavor from the following Scriptures: Psalm 27:1; Romans 1:16; 2 Timothy 1:6-8.

SAVOR IT!

Be honest with God. If you're nervous about witnessing, tell him. Then ask him for his strength.

SEE YOU AT THE POLE!

It's an annual event that happens on school campuses and universities around the world the third Wednesday of every September. "See You at the Pole" involves students who are willing to take a stand for Christ by praying for themselves, their student body, and their school while standing at their school's flagpole. (See www.syatp.org for more information.) For some, this is an easy thing to do. Perhaps they're involved in Fellowship of Christian Athletes, Young Life, Campus Crusade, or Youth for Christ, and they're able to stand with several other Christians.

For others who may be the only Christian on their campus, praying at the flagpole can be difficult. What about you? Whether you stand alone or with other Christians, it's important that you make a statement for Christ. He was willing to go to the Cross for you; will you be willing to stand beside your flagpole for him?

Why is this so important?

#1: *God not only wants you to enjoy your relationship with him, he wants you to tell others about it.* By taking a stand at your flagpole, you're letting everyone who walks through your school's doors know that you're a Christian.

#2: *God wants you to be able to articulate your faith.* Letting others know you're a Christian is great, but God's desire is that you also explain *why* you believe what you do. By taking a stand at your flagpole, you're inviting others to ask you about it. And when they do, you'll want to share why you've chosen to place your faith in Christ.

#3: *God wants you to be bold and confident with your faith.* Taking a stand at your flagpole may bring about some ridicule. If so, that's okay. Know that God will use this to strengthen your faith and make you stronger in him. The more often you take a stand for Christ, the bolder you'll become in witnessing to those around you.

If you do get mocked for your faith, realize you're not alone. In fact, you're in good company! The Bible is full of believers who were mocked, tortured, and even killed for their faith in God. Don't let a nonbeliever intimidate you into being shy about your relationship with Christ. God within you is much stronger than anyone in the entire world!

CHANGED LIVES!

Students' lives have been changed by "See You at the Pole" events. One of the student athletes from a high school in Wauseon, Ohio, shared with his peers that a year ago he was involved in drugs and alcohol but now was serving Christ. One of the girls spoke up and reminded the group that last year as they stood at the pole they had specifically prayed for this student!

Bryan, a sophomore from Memphis, shared with his youth pastor that he'd probably be the only one to stand at his school's flagpole. The youth pastor prayed for Bryan and told him he'd drop by the school the next morning to support him. As he walked through the parking lot filled with students, he was impressed to see Bryan sitting at the base of the flagpole with his Bible, praying for God to use his solo witness and silently pleading for revival at his school.

Kristen had been witnessing to her friend Julie for two years. She talked Julie into going to the pole with her last September, and they both ended up in different small groups for prayer. Kristen asked God to help Julie respond to the gospel presentation. As they walked to class after the meeting broke up, Julie told Kristen she needed to receive Christ. Less than thirty minutes after Kristen prayed, God answered. Julie accepted Christ as her Savior that very morning!

At a school in Woodland Hills, California, students at the flagpole endured mocking laughter and taunts from their peers. One of the boys was challenged to get into the circle. He grabbed their hands, laughing, and continued to taunt the group until he heard their prayers. He bowed his head and became silent as they continued. As the meeting ended, twenty-five students began talking with three of the "mockers" about what had happened, providing an opportunity to "give the reason for the hope that you have" (1 Peter 3:15).

BREW IT!
You can be part of a success story by taking a stand for the Lord at your flagpole this month. Whether it's with a large group or all alone, determine to stand tall for God.

POUR IT!
Drink in the flavor from the following Scriptures: Joshua 1:7-9; 2:11; Isaiah 41:10.

SAVOR IT!
Ask God to give you courage to share your faith with others and to participate in the worldwide "See You at the Pole" this month.

At a school in Fargo, North Dakota, a small group of students prayed as more than fifty others tried to distract them. Some of the nonparticipating students even threw garbage at the Christians. Others maliciously shoved passersby into the group. One of the Christians reported, "It was very hard to stand out there and pray with all this going on, but I'm glad I made a stand for Christ by participating in 'See You at the Pole.' "

BREW IT!
We often forget that when we enter into a relationship with Jesus Christ, it's big. In fact, it's so big and so sacred, it transcends our comprehension. Are you merely feeling secure in your own group of friends? Or are you thinking and praying globally?

POUR IT!
Drink in the flavor from the following Scriptures: Psalm 34:1-3; 69:32-33; 77:13-14.

SAVOR IT!
Thank the Lord for being bigger than you can imagine. Ask him to enlarge your worldview so you can pray and care for others around the world.

IT'S BIGGER THAN YOU

One year I received a letter from a girl who was homeschooled. She expressed her desire to be part of the recent "See You at the Pole" event but felt left out because she didn't attend a traditional school. She said she prayed about it for days and knew God wanted her to be involved somehow; she just didn't know how to respond.

"On the morning of the event," Sheila wrote, "I rummaged through our garage and found a little flag on a stick. I went outside to our front yard and just stood there, holding the stick with the flag on it, and prayed for myself, my neighbors, and the nearby schools."

That's exciting! Sheila realized the importance of being a part of something bigger than her own ideas. It's easy to get so caught up in our own little world that we forget Christianity is global and eternal. It's not just about you and your youth group. It's more than your Bible study. It reaches much further than your Christian friends at church and in your school.

Christianity is worldwide, and God wants to enlarge your worldview. He wants you to pray at your flagpole for yourself and your school. But he also wants you to pray for other Christians around the world. Instead of simply asking God for this and that, consider praying about Christians your age who are being persecuted for their faith.

I received another letter from a homeschooled teen. He, too, wanted to be part of the SYATP event, but he didn't know how. Kevin spent a few days praying about it, and the morning of the event, he walked several blocks to the public school in his district and stood at the pole and prayed.

I admire his courage. I also admire that he was serious enough about his faith to think bigger than his own life. Both Sheila and Kevin joined something much bigger than themselves when they dared to become part of an event that has a global outreach.

COURAGE AMMUNITION

When you're feeling frightened or mocked because of your faith, meditate on these verses. Pray these Scriptures. Write them on index cards and carry them with you, or place them on the visor of your car. Memorize them. Make them part of your lifestyle.

- "Act with courage, and may the LORD be with those who do well" (2 Chronicles 19:11).
- "Jesus quickly spoke to them, 'Have courage! It is I. Do not be afraid' " (Matthew 14:27, NCV).
- "When they saw the courage of Peter and John and realized that they were unschooled, ordinary men, they were astonished and they took note that these men had been with Jesus" (Acts 4:13).
- "After they prayed, the place where they were meeting was shaken. And they were all filled with the Holy Spirit and spoke the word of God boldly" (Acts 4:31).
- "I will not abandon you or leave you as orphans in the storm—I will come to you" (John 14:18, TLB).
- "On the day I called to you, you answered me. You made me strong and brave" (Psalm 138:3, NCV).
- "The righteous are as bold as a lion" (Proverbs 28:1).
- "Though an army besiege me, my heart will not fear; though war break out against me, even then will I be confident" (Psalm 27:3).
- "Wait for the LORD's help. Be strong and brave, and wait for the LORD's help" (Psalm 27:14, NCV).
- "I am certain that God, who began the good work within you, will continue his work until it is finally finished on that day when Christ Jesus returns" (Philippians 1:6, NLT).

BREW IT!
Everyone is afraid at one time or another. Even the disciples were afraid in the midst of a storm at sea—though some in the group were professional fishermen and were used to sea storms. When you're afraid, give your fear to God and trust him to replace your fear with his boldness, confidence, and courage.

POUR IT!
Drink in the flavor from the following Scriptures: Psalm 27:13; Philippians 2:24; 1 John 2:28.

SAVOR IT!
Tell God you want to be a bold Christian, filled with his courage. Ask him to help you become all he wants you to be.

BREW IT!
Strive to build your reputation in a positive way, with God's help, every single day!

POUR IT!
Drink in the flavor from the following Scriptures: Proverbs 18:10; 20:15; 27:19.

SAVOR IT!
Ask God to help you guard your reputation and to show you anything in your life that could damage it.

GUARD YOUR REPUTATION

To many it would seem that professional basketball player Kobe Bryant had it all. At age twenty-six, he had already been a six-time All-Star starter with three NBA championships under his belt. He was the young-est NBA player to score 10,000 points, and he renewed his contract in July 2004 for $136.4 million with the Los Angeles Lakers. Many would say that Kobe is the most talented player in the NBA.

Even with all he has going for him—his talent, his money, his fans—he'll never have the respect of the general public he once had, due to the sex scandal he found himself battling a few years ago. His accuser, who claimed that Bryant raped her, finally dropped the charges after several months of legal battles. Kobe admitted to being unfaithful to his wife and having sex with his accuser, but he claimed it was consensual. Only Kobe, the accuser, and God know the true story. But Kobe risked a lot for a few moments of sexual indulgence.

You, too, have a lot going for you. Though you're not a pro ballplayer with the Lakers, God has gifted you in specific areas and has blessed you with special talent. Sometimes it may feel as though you have the world on a string, and everything is going your way. You passed the test you thought you'd failed. You got a date with the person you were hoping would ask you out. You unexpectedly got a raise at work. Life seems good. So good that you may be tempted to get a little careless and let down your guard.

Don't!

Determine not to do anything that will risk your reputation or harm the name of Christ. The Bible tells us that even if we gain the entire world but lose our soul, it's not worth it.

Take time to develop good character and a godly reputation. Use the gifts and abili-ties you have to bring glory to your heavenly Father, and ask him to help you guard your reputation with your life.

Though God will forgive a repentant heart, there are always consequences to sin. King David sinned against God by sleeping with Bathsheba, but he repented and received forgiveness. He was known as a "man after [God's] own heart" (Acts 13:22). Yet though he was forgiven, he still had to live with the consequences of his sin. He raised a dysfunctional family, complete with rebellion and murder from his sons.

Refuse to succumb to anything that will taint your reputation or hinder your relation-ship with Jesus Christ.

THE GREAT GIVEAWAY

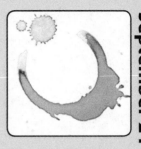

You probably heard about it. To start out the nineteenth season of Oprah's daytime talk show (September 9, 2004), each member of her studio audience received a new car. The total? Two hundred seventy-six automobiles. Can you imagine the excitement of being in the audience that day?

Besides giving away Pontiac G6 cars, Oprah also gave away a full college scholarship to a twenty-year-old homeless woman who had been living in and out of shelters. She then gave $130,000 to a couple who housed eight foster children so they could purchase and repair their home. "This year," she said, "no dream is too wild, no surprise too impossible to pull off."

The lucky people who received the cars also got the opportunity to customize them with heated leather seats, OnStar (a built-in wireless phone system), and XM Satellite Radio. Pontiac spent more than $7 million to supply the vehicles. Oprah said that she was so excited about presenting each member of her studio audience with a brand-new car, she couldn't sleep the night before.

There really is joy in giving! Sure, it's always fun to receive a gift, but there's something special about making someone else happy by giving. Even though receiving a new automobile, a college scholarship, or money to purchase a home is exciting, all those things are temporary. In fact, by the time this book is printed, many of the owners of those Pontiacs will have already traded them in for a newer model. The house will continue to need repair, and the college scholarship only lasts for four years.

The most valuable gifts to give and receive are the ones that have eternal value. Leading someone to Christ, inviting a friend to church, praying with someone who's hurting, giving a Bible to someone who doesn't own one. These gifts will last forever.

Have you given to someone recently? Or have you become so caught up in receiving that you've forgotten about the joy of making someone else happy? If you are in the habit of giving, what have you given? Are you making time to share the love of your life—Jesus Christ—with those who are closest to you?

You serve a God who loves to give good gifts to his children. Oprah says no dream is too wild. But that's not totally true. While she can make most dreams that require money come true, she can't give everlasting peace, joy that won't fade, or release from the guilt of sin.

For God, however, there really is no dream too big or too wild. In fact, he dreams bigger for you than you'd ever dare to imagine. And because he dreams big for you, he wants you to dream big as well.

BREW IT!
So go ahead. Think outside the box. Dream big and dare to give to those around you!

POUR IT!
Drink in the flavor from the following Scriptures: Proverbs 14:30; 28:27; 2 Corinthians 8:7.

SAVOR IT!
Ask God to help you experience the true joy of giving.

ORDINARY PEOPLE

Throughout history, God has used ordinary people to impact their world. Ordinary people. People with only one or two talents. People like you and me, who sometimes get angry and lonely and hate practicing the piano. And through these ordinary, everyday people, God has defeated armies, turned a small group of slaves into a great nation, split seas, healed the sick, and melted the hardened hearts of sinners.

All this and more through people who were willing to be used by him. That's the key to having an impact for God in the world. Are you willing? Would you dare to let your faith impact your world?

Daniel did. Moses did.

So did Abraham, Noah, Enoch, Abel, Sarah, Jacob, Joshua, and Jonah.

Well . . . Jonah is a different story. Yes, he told others about his faith, all right. But he sure wasn't excited about it. Do you remember the Old Testament story? Maybe we'd better take a quick peek.

Place: Nineveh. Population: approximately 120,000, with more people constantly arriving. The fastest-growing city of its time.

Problem: City with a bad rep. Quickly becoming more and more wicked.

Solution: Destroy the city. Hmmm. Sure would be a tragedy for 120,000 people to die without ever knowing they could have received forgiveness for their sins and lived a better life.

Better Solution: Have someone tell them about God.

Newly Recruited Spokesman: Jonah.

Complication: Jonah doesn't want to be the one to go.

Further Complication: God commands him to go. (Read this out loud: When God speaks, it makes sense to obey.)

What Happens: Jonah complains that Nineveh is too far and too wild. He's heard of their bad reputation and doesn't want to get involved. Jonah wants God to destroy the Ninevites.

Does it sound like someone needs an attitude check? God is in the business of loving and saving, and he's constantly recruiting us to be his hands and feet. When you think about all he has done for us, is it really too much to ask us simply to obey him when he gives us a job to do? Remember the devotional on September 11? *We* are his marketing plan.

He's counting on us to spread the gospel. Sometimes it'll be convenient, and other times it won't. But we need to remember it wasn't convenient for Christ to go to the Cross. He did it because he loves us. We, in turn, share the gospel with others because we love him.

TRYING TO RUN

Jonah decided to run from what God wanted him to do, so he went to a travel agent and bought a ticket for a cruise. Maybe he was thinking if he ran far enough away, sooner or later God would just forget the whole Nineveh thing.

This was no Carnival cruise line. Jonah set sail on a boat full of superstitious sailors. And instead of trying to share his faith with them, he went to the bottom of the ship to catch some z's. (All that running from God had worn him out.)

But God knew exactly where Jonah was. (He always knows were you are too. There's no such thing as hiding from God.) The Lord allowed a terrible storm to erupt at sea. It was such a nightmare that even those rough, macho sailors—professional seamen—were frightened.

They knew Jonah was a religious man. Maybe they saw him wearing his "See You at the Pole" shirt (see September 16 for the scoop on this important event) or noticed his Bible poking out of his backpack. So the sailors woke Jonah from his sleep and begged him to pray for their safety.

Pray for *them*? Jonah didn't feel like praying for anyone! His conscience bothered him too much. The ship continued to weave back and forth, back and forth, back and . . . You get the idea. Fifteen-foot waves emptied themselves on board. Frightening times.

Even though Jonah was acting like a jerk, he still had one thing going for him. He was honest. So he straightened his shoulders and fessed up. "I'm the reason for this storm," he volunteered.

Quiz time: How did the sailors respond?

a. They said, "Let's talk about your feelings of guilt."

b. They asked if Jonah knew how to jet ski.

c. They put their arms around him and said, "Ah, Jonah! Don't be so hard on yourself."

d. They tossed him overboard.

Answer: He was history as far as the sailors were concerned. They threw their new passenger right over the side of the ship!

It's never smart to try to run from God. Jonah was still running. He was desperately trying to avoid God's plan for his life. We don't always understand God's plan, but guess what? It's not our job to understand; our job is to obey. A mature Christian will learn to accept God's ways without understanding them.

BREW IT!
Instead of trying to figure God out, focus on getting to know his will for your life.

POUR IT!
Drink in the flavor from the following Scripture: Jonah 1:1-17.

SAVOR IT!
Ask God to mold you into his willing servant.

BREW IT!

Don't wait until the last minute to call on God for help. Develop a consistent, ongoing line of honest communication with your heavenly Father.

POUR IT!

Drink in the flavor from the following Scriptures:
Psalm 103:20; Jonah 2:1-10.

SAVOR IT!

Tell God you're available anytime to go anywhere and do anything he asks.

A WHALE OF A TALE

Jonah was fighting for his life in a raging sea with billowing, horrific waves, and God wasn't finished with him. The Lord sent a huge fish—about the size of a mammoth whale, which was probably the size of a football field . . . well, maybe not *quite* that big, but you get the picture—to swallow Jonah.

Our reluctant spokesman spent three days and three nights in his new home. Talk about boring—what can you do inside the belly of a fish? (1) Untangle the intestines, then measure them; (2) backstroke through the stomach juices; (3) taste the gastric acids; (4) chip off the ol' bone marrow; (5) make seaweed soup for breakfast; (6) alphabetize all the stuff a big fish eats—license plates, people, shoes, octopuses, school buses; (7) think.

Jonah chose the last option.

He thought.

And thought.

And thought some more.

He realized his back was against a wall. Check out what he says in Jonah 2:7: "As my life was slipping away, I remembered the LORD" (NLT).

Typical, huh? When we've lost all hope, then we turn to the Lord. Things would have been so much better if Jonah had just obeyed in the first place! But Jonah tried to do things his own way and ended up inside the digestive system of a giant fish.

When we try to do things without God's help, we're setting ourselves up for failure. It's dangerous for Christians to yank the control for their lives out of God's hands and do things their own way.

God is there for us when our back is against a wall, when we're out of options and we don't know where else to turn. But why wait until then? How much easier it would be if we'd depend on God constantly, listen to his voice, and obey him immediately.

THE UNEXPECTED

Jonah spent three days and three nights in the belly of a large fish.

Gag!

Literally.

God caused the fish to gag, and Jonah came out in its vomit. Not a pretty picture. But Jonah finally realized that he couldn't escape God, and this time he went straight to Nineveh and began preaching. He told the that people if they didn't turn from their wicked ways, the Lord would destroy their city in forty days.

Jonah still needed an attitude check, though, because when the people got interested enough to stop and listen, our reluctant spokesman secretly wished they'd continue on their merry way and die in sin.

But the people were intrigued. They never realized there was an all-powerful God who cared about how they lived. (Your friends will be intrigued too when you begin sharing your faith.) The Ninevites prayed, asked God to forgive their sins, turned from their wicked ways, and cleaned up their act. The king even gave his life to God, then ordered everyone else to do the same!

Jonah took his lousy attitude and waited underneath a tree outside the city gates, hoping, wishing, and pleading for God to burn down the city with fire from heaven. But God didn't. He didn't need to. The mission had been successful, and the citizens of Nineveh were now believers.

BREW IT!
Determine to show God, by your obedience, that you're always willing to fit into his plans.

POUR IT!
Drink in the flavor from the following Scripture: Jonah 3:1-10.

SAVOR IT!
Ask God to allow you to be instrumental in leading others to him.

So what did Jonah do? Praise God for using him? Nope. He threw a temper tantrum. "This is exactly what I thought you'd do, Lord, when I was in my own country and you first told me to come here. That's why I ran away to Tarshish. For I knew you were a gracious God, merciful, slow to get angry, and full of kindness; I knew how easily you could cancel your plans for destroying these people. Please kill me, Lord. I'd rather be dead than alive [when nothing I warned about happens]" (Jonah 4:2-3, TLB).

Whew! Jonah needed another attitude check, didn't he? What about you? Do you need a spiritual attitude check? Do you find yourself pouting when things aren't going your way? Remember, it's not *our* plan we should be focused on; it's *God's* plan. And though we don't always understand his ways, we can always trust him. He never makes mistakes. God always knows exactly what he's doing!

BREW IT!
Instead of praying about whether to witness, pray instead that God will send someone across your path. Pray for his boldness in sharing your faith.

POUR IT!
Drink in the flavor from the following Scripture: Jonah 4:1-11.

SAVOR IT!
Ask God to give you an opportunity this week to share your faith.

THE STORY CONTINUES

Jonah just continued to sit . . . outside . . . in the sun . . . underneath a shade tree . . . and sulk. Then a worm started chewing on the shade tree, and the tree withered. So Jonah began complaining about that! (Some people never learn.) Without the shade tree, he got a severe sunburn and was so miserable and physically sick he pleaded with God to let him die: "'Death is certainly better than living like this!' he exclaimed. Then God said to Jonah, 'Is it right for you to be angry because the plant died?' 'Yes,' Jonah retorted, 'even angry enough to die!'" (Jonah 4:8-9, NLT).

Maybe God should have granted his wish right then, but he continued to deal with his reluctant spokesman. There was still an important lesson for Jonah to learn. God wasn't finished with him yet.

God wanted to put things in perspective for Jonah, so he told it like it was. God pointed out that Jonah was feeling sorry for himself and asked why he shouldn't instead feel sorry for God's lost children in Nineveh. That pretty much hit Jonah right between the eyes. Yes, God *does* feel for his lost children. He's willing to go to great lengths to save them. His desire is that no one should perish and spend eternity apart from him.

Think about it: Your friends who don't know the Lord are dying spiritually. What could be more important than sharing God with them? What could possibly be as high a priority as delivering God's message of hope and salvation?

I like Isaiah's attitude: "Then I heard the Lord asking, 'Whom shall I send as a messenger to my people? Who will go?' And I said, 'Lord, I'll go! Send *me*'" (Isaiah 6:8, TLB).

Now *that's* an attitude God is pleased with!

So . . . will you tell?

God has made it clear: Anyone who doesn't know him personally is dying. Will you dare to share your faith with those around you?

Well, I'll pray about it, you may be thinking.

Why? Do you really need to spend time praying about something God has already told you to do? I don't think so.

PRAYING ABOUT IT

God has created each of us to do certain things well. He wants you to share your faith by using the gifts he's placed within you. In other words, he created you on purpose—just the way you are. If you're outgoing and love to be in front of people, he'll use that for his glory. If you don't like crowds and would much rather be with one or two close friends, he'll use that for his glory. The key is for you to use what he's blessed you with to spread his message to those around you.

So instead of praying about whether you should tell your friends about Christ, pray instead for God to help you:

- *Live your calling.* Do you enjoy having people over? planning parties? counseling others? working behind the scenes? being in the limelight? Use the skills and abilities he's given you to make an impact for him.
- *Live the light.* When Jesus Christ reigns in your life, you have the greatest gift in the entire world. Think about it: You walk hand in hand with the creator of the universe every day. You're on a first-name basis with God! That's powerful. Why keep it to yourself? Brag a little . . . let others know who you know.
- *Live your faith.* Your life is even more important than your words. You can talk about God all you want, but if your lifestyle doesn't match what you're saying, it won't do any good.

What attracts others to Christ? It's not really a church building or a fun, organized program. It's the people. Unbelievers see something different in the life of an on-fire Christian, and they want what that person has.

When a non-Christian is drawn to you, it will be because of your lifestyle. It will be because you're allowing the Holy Spirit to reflect Christ through you. When someone asks you about your faith, be ready to share your beliefs.

BREW IT!
Determine not to keep the gift of eternal life a secret. Pray for your non-Christian friends daily. Look for ways to show through your actions how much God cares about them.

POUR IT!
Drink in the flavor from the following Scriptures: Matthew 5:13-14; John 15:26-27; 2 Timothy 4:1-2.

SAVOR IT!
Ask God to help align your words and your actions so you'll be a positive witness for him.

BREW IT!
Have you set aside a specific time each day to talk to and listen to the Lord? If not, do it now.

POUR IT!
Drink in the flavor from the following Scriptures: Proverbs 15:8, 29; Acts 1:14.

SAVOR IT!
Ask God to teach you the sound of his voice.

LISTENING TO GOD

When you call your best friend on the phone, you first have to dial her number. After you've dialed the correct listing, you have to wait for an answer. It would be crazy to call her and then put the phone down. You have to wait until you hear, "Hello?" from her end.

That's pretty elementary.

So why do we miss the basics when we pray?

Think of prayer as "dialing God's number." If you just walk away after rambling on and on, it's like you're hanging up on him without giving him a chance to respond. And when you call on him, if you do all the talking, you won't be able to hear his reply.

But God never talks to me, you may be thinking. Yes, he really does. But it might be that you haven't yet learned the sound of his voice. When your best friend calls, you probably recognize her voice the first time she utters a syllable. You've talked with her so much, you know the sound of her voice. She doesn't even need to identify herself.

God wants it to be the same way with you. He wants you to be able to recognize his voice as soon as he begins speaking to you. He wants to help you become so confident in knowing the sound of his voice that you don't have to wonder, *Is that God? Is that me? Is that Satan trying to confuse me?*

You can learn the sound of God's voice by:

- *Talking to him frequently.* The more you talk with him, the closer you grow.
- *Listening to him.* The more you listen to him, the easier it will be to recognize his voice. So don't do all the talking. When you pray, make sure you pause, be still, and ask him to teach you the sound of his voice.
- *Reading his letter.* The more you read e-mails and notes from your friends, the better you know them. You don't only converse verbally with them, you communicate in other ways as well. It works the same way with your heavenly Father. Talk with him. Listen to him. And read his Holy Word. He'll speak to you through the Bible.

RULES, FINES, AND YACHTS

Following his wedding in 2004, Tiger Woods and his bride set out on his yacht for a cruise to San Juan. The fun ended abruptly, however, when he wasn't allowed to dock at port. Apparently, Tiger was unaware of a U.S. Department of Homeland Security regulation that requires boats to submit an arrival notice at least four days before entering a U.S. port. The coast guard detained Tiger and his new wife, Elin, and insisted they remain on board his 155-foot yacht, *Privacy*, after entering San Juan's port.

Tiger wasn't actually "driving" the yacht; he had hired a captain for that job. And even the captain said he didn't know that the regulations applied to Puerto Rico, a U.S. Caribbean territory. The skipper said he had stopped in San Juan to refuel. Immigration officials allowed *Privacy* to refuel, but they interviewed everyone aboard, including the newlyweds.

The Coast Guard could have fined Tiger as much as $32,500 for entering San Juan's port without giving prior notice. Because it was Tiger's first offense, though, the golf pro was simply issued a letter of warning.

Tiger and Elin were lucky, weren't they? Sadly, there will come a day when people's luck will run out. The Bible tells us that everyone will stand before God on the Day of Judgment. At that point, we won't be able to wish for luck. We won't be able to rationalize, make excuses, or plead to do things over. We'll either be welcomed into heaven—God's perfect Kingdom—to live with him forever, or we'll be banished to hell and will spend eternity separated from the Father.

That's why it's so important to get it right now. Tiger and his captain were able to say, "We didn't know the rule." We won't have that luxury at the time of judgment. God is working fast and furiously through his people and through modern technology so the entire world will know of his salvation.

Are you familiar with the *JESUS* film? It's being shown in some of the most remote villages on earth, and people are hearing, seeing, and understanding the plan of salvation. They're coming to Christ in great numbers. His message is getting out!

BREW IT!
Are you used to making excuses? Get out of that habit. Learn to take responsibility for your actions and determine to live as God calls you to live.

POUR IT!
Drink in the flavor from the following Scriptures: Jeremiah 25:31; Hebrews 6:1-2; 9:27.

SAVOR IT!
Ask God to help you take his commandments seriously.

BREW IT!
Do you recognize a miracle when you see one? Ask God to help you tune in to what he's doing in the lives of those around you.

POUR IT!
Drink in the flavor from the following Scriptures: John 2:1-11; 5:5-9; 6:5-14.

SAVOR IT!
Tell God you'd like to be involved in the miracle business of bringing lost souls to him.

FOUND!

It happened in Tokyo. A two-year-old boy was pulled out of his family's van after being trapped inside for four days. And he was alive!

An earthquake of 6.8 magnitude swept the van away in a mangle of boulders and earth on a Saturday. It wasn't until Tuesday that the van was spotted underneath a pile of hillside rubble. TV cameras filmed rescuers desperately digging through the mass to the sound of two-year-old Yuta's voice. When workers were finally able to pull the boy out of the wreckage, he was weak and covered in mud, but he was conscious. He was then airlifted by helicopter to a hospital for emergency treatment.

Thirty-two people died in Japan's earthquake in October 2004, and more than 440 aftershocks were recorded. One hundred thousand residents stayed in shelters, because they were afraid the aftershocks could trigger more landslides. Thousands more camped out in tents and cars.

Though Yuta's mother and sister didn't survive, the fact that he did is considered a miracle.

God is in the miracle business. When it seems all hope is lost, he has the ability to pull us through against insurmountable odds. He did it for Daniel. He did it for Shadrach, Meshach, and Abednego, and he continues to perform miracles today.

The Bible is a book of miracles. When Joshua commanded his army to blow their trumpets and the walls of Jericho crumbled, it was nothing short of a miracle. And when God used Moses to split the Red Sea, the children of Israel witnessed a miracle.

More than five thousand people had gathered to hear Jesus teach, but the hour was late, they were far from home, and they were hungry. When Jesus took a few slices of bread and a few fish and multiplied them to feed everyone with leftovers remaining, it was definitely a miracle.

When Jesus raised Lazarus from the dead, turned water into wine, made blind people see, and caused lame people to walk, he was performing miracles. When the creator of the universe was raised from the grave, made deaf people hear, and healed Peter's mother-in-law from a fever, he was demonstrating his miraculous power.

God is in the miracle business! But do you know the greatest miracle of all? The most exciting miracle in God's eyes is when one of his lost children is found. Every time someone repents of his sin, accepts Christ's forgiveness, and places his faith in God, it's a miracle. And all of heaven rejoices!

CELEBRATE!

Try to guess which of the following holidays in the month of October are real and which ones are fake. Write an *R* by those you think are real, and write an *F* by those you believe are fake.

___ Adopt-a-Shelter-Dog Month
___ National Children's Book Week
___ Pursuit of Happiness Week
___ National Bible Week
___ Celebrate Sun-Dried Tomatoes Month
___ Eat Better, Eat Together Month
___ National Cookie Month
___ National Crime Prevention Month
___ National Liver Awareness Month
___ National One-Hit Wonder Day
___ National Pork Month
___ World Smile Day
___ Be Bald and Be Free Day
___ National Roller Skating Month
___ National Good Neighbor Day
___ Dear Diary Day
___ National Sewing Month

Just imagine: People are actually celebrating these unique holidays this month! Some folks will try to find any reason in the world to celebrate. And, really, that's not such a bad idea. Have you celebrated your relationship with Christ recently?

BREW IT!
Do something special this week to celebrate your relationship with Christ and his free gift of salvation.

POUR IT!
Drink in the flavor from the following Scriptures: 1 Chronicles 16:27; Psalm 4:7; 21:6.

SAVOR IT!
Spend some time thanking God for his forgiveness of your sins.

Real: Adopt-a-Shelter-Dog Month; Celebrate Sun-Dried Tomatoes Month; Eat Better, Eat Together Month; National Cookie Month; National Liver Awareness Month; National Pork Month; Be Bald and Be Free Day; National Roller Skating Month.

BREW IT!
Meditate on the fact that when you walk with Jesus Christ, you're not walking with merely a friend; you're having fellowship with the King of kings!

POUR IT!
Drink in the flavor from the following Scriptures: Joshua 4:23-24; 1 Chronicles 16:29; Revelation 1:17.

SAVOR IT!
Ask the Lord to give you a healthy fear and awe of his almighty splendor and righteousness.

IS GOD ONLY YOUR FRIEND?

We often like to think of God as our best friend. But if he's simply our best friend, we don't know him in all his fullness. We're settling for less.

When the apostle John penned the book of Revelation, he described the glorified Christ appearing to him on the barren island of Patmos. John says he fell down at the Lord's feet as though he were dead. He temporarily lost all physical strength.

Yet John was the apostle who was most familiar with Christ when our Lord walked the earth in the flesh. Christ was extremely close to his twelve disciples, and he was even closer to a tiny group of three: Peter, James, and John. And out of those three, he was closest to John. At the Last Supper, John is described as leaning against the Lord. In other words, we can picture John tired and slumped over, with his head resting on Christ's shoulder. He felt close enough to Jesus to be this familiar with him.

But in Revelation, John doesn't rush to Christ and give him a big hug or slap him on the back. He falls down at the Lord's feet with all strength momentarily sapped from his human body.

What was the difference? When John walked with Christ on earth, he walked with God in human form. When the Lord appeared to him as he wrote the book of Revelation, he appeared in all his supernatural glory. He is no longer human, nor does he need to take on human characteristics.

Think about your own relationship with Christ. Do you respect and worship him as you should? Or do you simply think of him as your best friend with supernatural powers? Do you envision running up to Christ and jumping in his lap when you enter the Kingdom of Heaven? It may not be that way. You may be so overwhelmed by being in the presence of such perfection, such glory, and such God-ness that you may not be able to do much more than simply fall at his feet until he strengthens you to stand and breathe and live in his perfect paradise.

There's a danger in becoming too familiar with Christ. And by familiar, I'm not talking about growing close to him. God wants you to draw close to him. In fact, the apostle James tells us that if we'll draw close to God, God will draw close to us. But there's a difference between drawing intimately close to God and treating him casually. He is no human friend. He is our Savior, our Lord, and our all.

A FRIEND AND A WHOLE LOT MORE!

Do you have a healthy fear of God Almighty? Though he doesn't want you to be afraid to come to him, talk with him, and fellowship with him, he *does* deserve your respect and awe. When Christ spoke through a bright light to Saul on the road to Damascus, Saul fell to the ground. He couldn't stand to look at the light. How do you react when Jesus speaks to you?

When God spoke to Moses through the burning bush, Moses trembled and covered his eyes. He was in awe of the Lord God Almighty. Have you lost that holy awe of God? If you're simply approaching him as your friend, you'll miss out on an entire dimension of truth and blessings he wants to give you.

Yes, Jesus wants to be your friend. In fact, in John 15:14, Jesus tells the disciples they are his friends. But don't settle for a mere friendship with God when you can have so much more!

When you develop a healthy fear and awe of God, you'll learn things about his character that you can't learn any other way. We're told in Proverbs that "the fear of the LORD is the beginning of wisdom." Do you possess a healthy fear of God? When you open your Bible, is it with a holy expectation of what the Lord of lords will say to you through the printed words on the page? When you pray, do you realize what an amazing privilege you have of getting to converse with the One who raised the dead, healed blind people, and calmed storms?

Yes, Christ definitely wants to be your friend. But don't settle for a casual friendship with the King of kings! He desires to be so much more than just your friend.

BREW IT!
Does this change the way you think about Christ? Does it affect the way you approach him in prayer? We are to be in holy awe of almighty Jehovah—not simply on casual buddy terms.

POUR IT!
Drink in the flavor from the following Scriptures: Proverbs 9:10; Isaiah 66:2; Acts 7:32.

SAVOR IT!
Ask God to help you approach him in the respectful way he desires. Thank him for calling you his friend.

BREW IT!

When it's crunch time, and report cards will be out soon, it's common for many students to go the extra mile in trying to raise their grades. Are you willing to go the extra mile spiritually? What can you do to raise the bar in your relationship with Christ?

POUR IT!

Drink in the flavor from the following Scriptures: Isaiah 45:8; 1 Peter 2:2; 2 Peter 3:18.

SAVOR IT!

Ask God to help you discipline yourself so that you grow closer to him on a daily basis.

EXTRA EFFORT

Glenn was in my third-period English class. He was a big guy. He didn't seem to like school—or anyone in the human race, for that matter. He was tough. His nickname was Mallard. (He kind of waddled when he walked.) But he was proud of his nickname. He even wrote it on all of his homework assignments . . . well, the two that he actually turned in that year!

Many of the students in my third and fifth period English classes weren't doing well academically. Of course, I knew most of these high school juniors cared much more about the latest tunes in their iPods than they did about Henry David Thoreau, and more about last night's football scores than analyzing Emily Dickinson's poetry. But the reality was this: In five weeks, report cards would be issued, and if my students didn't get serious about their grades, many of them would fail.

So I came up with a fun plan to help them out. I created an extra study session that I called The Breakfast Club and announced that we'd meet every Friday morning for the next five weeks. (I always gave tests on Fridays.) I explained that during this time, we'd go over the same information we'd studied all week, but because they had made an effort to come and study with me an extra thirty minutes before school, they'd receive ten bonus points on the test that day. Not only that, but I'd provide all the doughnuts and juice they could down.

Sounded like a good deal, and students were showing their excitement. There was one catch, though. The Breakfast Club would begin promptly at 7:30 a.m., but the door to my classroom would lock at 7:29. So to be involved, students had to arrive *before* 7:29.

I knew Mallard was interested because he kept asking the same question every day: "Uh, what time is that breakfast club thing?" And I'd always respond, "Seven-thirty, Mallard. But you have to be here before 7:29 or you won't get in."

Our first Friday finally arrived, and students began arriving at 7:15. I had purchased about one hundred doughnuts, and I began writing dates and information on the board. By 7:28 the class was filled, and at 7:29 I locked my door.

TOO LATE

I began lecturing on the same information I had taught all week. Students were stuffing their faces with doughnuts and grinning from ear to ear. It was as if they finally realized there was hope. After all, I had told them if they came to The Breakfast Club for the next five weeks—and actually handed in their homework assignments—they'd probably pass. They were happy. I was happy.

Suddenly, we heard someone jiggle the doorknob, loudly. Knocking followed. Then pounding. Then the whole door started rattling on its hinges. No problem. We just increased our noise level to drown out the sounds outside the classroom. Whatever was going on in the hallway wasn't nearly as important as what we were doing. After all, we were eating doughnuts, downing juice, and getting ten extra points on the test that day.

I dismissed the students about five minutes before first period, and as I walked past the office, the principal caught my attention. "Susie, did you hear all that noise outside your classroom this morning?"

"Yes," I responded. "We didn't know what it was, and I didn't want to take the time to find out, so we just kept plugging away."

BREW IT!
Is it easy for you to be spiritually careless? Spiritual carelessness leads to spiritual disobedience.

POUR IT!
Drink in the flavor from the following Scriptures: Ephesians 5:6; 2 Timothy 3:2; Titus 1:16.

SAVOR IT!
Ask God to bring to your mind any area in your life in which you're disobeying him.

"It was Mallard," he said. "Glenn had come to The Breakfast Club but obviously arrived too late. When he realized he couldn't get in, he got angry and started screaming four-letter words. He tried to knock the door down—and when that didn't work, he tried to take the door off its hinges."

"Oh brother!" I said.

"I suspended him," Mr. Griffis said. Then he laughed slightly. "And you know? That's the first time in the history of our school that a student has been suspended for coming to school early to study!"

I laughed too. Until I got back to my classroom. By then I wasn't laughing anymore. I was angry. After all, I had created The Breakfast Club for students just like Mallard who needed a second chance with their grades. I didn't have to do that.

I had purchased the doughnuts and juice with my own money. And I had arrived an entire hour before school started, just to get everything ready. All Mallard had to do was simply obey the rule: Show up on time. And he didn't even do that! Now he was suspended and who knew if he'd ever pass? All because he was careless and didn't meet the club's expectations.

A few hours later, though, God began working in my thoughts. It's as if he wanted to remind me of the strong penalty disobedience brings. There's *always* a price to pay for being disobedient. The principle is found all through the Bible.

There's an interesting story in 1 Samuel 15. Quick synopsis: God had just given Saul and his men the strength to defeat an extremely wicked nation. Because of their evil ways, God wanted this nation and everything in it to be destroyed. He didn't want any trace of wickedness left. Everything meant everything. Even the sheep and cattle.

But Saul disobeyed God. He did not destroy all the sheep and cattle. He said, "Nah, let's keep the best cattle. And surely God wouldn't want us to waste the fattest sheep."

Hmmm. Would God really want Saul to destroy even the best animals? The more Saul rationalized, the more it made sense to disobey God's command.

We often think if something makes sense, it's okay. We love to rationalize, don't we? It's a dangerous temptation to try to make sense out of disobeying God! Maybe you've even heard yourself saying, "This makes sense, so let's do it!"

The issue isn't whether it makes sense. This issue is, are you obeying God? You see, God doesn't always make sense . . . at least not human sense. Here are a few examples of things God says that don't make sense to our earthly minds:

- The first will be last.
- The last will be first.
- Lose your life to find it.
- The greatest will be the least.
- Give away to receive.

BREW IT!

If you try hard enough, you can rationalize almost anything. Search long enough, and you'll find a religion or a belief system that condones all kinds of immoral behavior. God may not be present in that religion, but you can rationalize that your actions are okay simply because you've found others who support what you do. Don't fall for that!

POUR IT!

Drink in the flavor from the following Scriptures: Exodus 19:5; Deuteronomy 5:7; Joshua 1:7.

SAVOR IT!

Ask God to help you live in 100 percent obedience to him.

Saul and his men disobeyed God. What they did made a lot of sense, but they were still disobedient. In fact, because Saul thought his actions were so logical, he didn't even bother to hide all the animals they'd kept.

When the godly prophet Samuel found Saul, this is how Saul greeted him: "The LORD bless you! I have carried out the LORD's instructions!" (1 Samuel 15:13).

Saul had worked so hard to rationalize his wrong deeds that he had talked himself into believing it was okay. That's a dangerous trap to fall into! When God says "Do this," it's for a reason. We can rationalize all we want, but the bottom line is this: If we disobey God, we're living in sin.

HALFWAY ISN'T GOOD ENOUGH

Saul greeted the godly prophet Samuel with, "The LORD bless you! I have carried out the LORD's instructions!"

Typical, isn't it? We do something wrong and try to cover up by acting really positive, don't we?

I imagine the conversation between Samuel and Saul went something like this:

"You've carried out his commands? Then what's all this sheep bleating I'm hearing? And, Saul, I gotta tell you, man, I'm hearing a few hundred moos, too."

Saul cleared his throat—maybe even took a sip of Gatorade from his canteen—then defended himself. "Well . . . we spared the best of the sheep and cattle to sacrifice to the Lord. But we totally destroyed the rest!"

At that point, Samuel told Saul to put a lid on it (the Gatorade *and* his mouth) and give him a quick review of God's instructions. Then he gave Saul the bottom line: "You didn't obey God, Saul!"

Well, Saul didn't like that. (We don't like being told we've done it wrong either!) So he tried to make himself sound good.

"Yes, I did obey! I defeated this town and destroyed all these idols, and I did . . ."

The truth is, Saul had partially obeyed God. But halfway isn't good enough, is it? It's like brushing your teeth. From your very first trip to the dentist when you hear him say, "Brush your teeth at least twice a day," you know he means *all* your teeth. Can you imagine what he'd say during your next visit upon finding two cavities?

BREW IT!
Are you obeying God halfway? Or are you living in total obedience to him?

POUR IT!
Drink in the flavor from the following Scriptures: Joshua 22:5; Jeremiah 7:23.

SAVOR IT!
Seek God's forgiveness for any area in your life in which you've been disobedient.

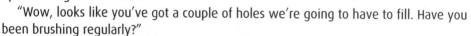

"Wow, looks like you've got a couple of holes we're going to have to fill. Have you been brushing regularly?"

You clear your throat and shift a little in that weird chair. "Well, yeah. Maybe not twice a day. And, okay, I don't always brush *all* of them."

"What do you mean you don't always brush all of them?"

"Well, I'm busy. I have band practice and stuff to do with my friends. So sometimes I rotate which teeth I brush. Last week, for instance, I brushed the top row of teeth on Monday and Wednesday, and the bottom row on Tuesday and Thursday."

"What about Friday, Saturday, and Sunday?" he asks.

"Hey! That's my weekend. Don't crowd me."

He'd probably tell you to find another dentist. Brushing *some* of your teeth just isn't good enough. It works the same way in your relationship with Christ. It's not enough to obey God a little. He wants to be Lord, and that requires 100 percent obedience.

BREW IT!
We cannot rationalize God's clear instructions, commands, or will. Sometimes his ways don't make sense to us. But it's not our responsibility to understand God's way. Our job is to simply obey his leading.

POUR IT!
Drink in the flavor from the following Scriptures: Psalm 103:17-18, 20; 119:17.

SAVOR IT!
Ask God to teach you true obedience.

IS IT REALLY THAT BAD?

Again, what Saul and his men had done made sense—to the human mind. It seemed reasonable to offer the best cattle and the fattest sheep as a sacrifice (offering) to God. But it was all done in disobedience! At this particular time God hadn't commanded a sacrifice; he'd commanded that everything be destroyed.

The godly prophet Samuel hit Saul with a real zinger: "Has the Lord as much pleasure in your burnt offerings and sacrifices as in your obedience? Obedience is far better than sacrifice. He is much more interested in your listening to him than in your offering the fat of rams to him" (1 Samuel 15:22, TLB).

Saul stammered around, shifting his weight while Samuel continued, "For rebellion is as bad as the sin of witchcraft, and stubbornness is as bad as worshiping idols" (verse 23).

Is it really that bad? Is disobeying God as bad as witchcraft? The Bible says it is!

"And now because you have rejected the word of Jehovah, he has rejected you from being king" (verse 23).

That got Saul's attention! When we realize what the consequences might be, we learn real fast, don't we? So he finally decided to come clean.

"I have sinned. . . . Yes, I have disobeyed your instructions and the command of the Lord, for I was afraid of the people and did what they demanded" (verse 24).

Well, it's one thing to come clean—it's another thing to blame our disobedience on those around us. But at least Saul was headed in the right direction. Samuel probably inserted a few powerful words on peer pressure. It *never* pays to follow the crowd when the crowd isn't following Christ!

Again, Saul's sin wasn't illogical. It wasn't that he couldn't make sense out of what he did. His sin was that he disobeyed God.

TRYING TO ERASE THE GUILT

Adam and Eve disobeyed God in the Garden of Eden. He specifically told them not to eat from a certain tree. They did, though, and they felt tremendous guilt. We humans have been disobeying and feeling guilty ever since. And it's when we wrestle with guilt that we do a million different things to try to erase it. We blame it on those around us (like Saul), or we say we didn't really understand in the first place. Some of us try to forget our sins by adding more sin on top of the wrong we've already done. Some hide—like Adam, who tried to cover himself with leaves.

Others go to even further extremes. I once read a magazine article about people who send money to the government because of a guilty conscience. It all started back in 1811 when the first guilty soul sent five dollars and an apology during the presidency of James Madison. Since that time, more than 79 million dollars has been sent in voluntarily to the U.S. government.

Since so much money has been voluntarily sent to the government over the years, the Treasury Department finally created a special fund for donations. The "Conscience Fund" includes money from people who say they once cheated the government and are trying to erase their guilt. Payments are often accompanied by confessions and are usually anonymous. Some people have cheated on their income taxes; others have recycled an uncanceled postage stamp. Others returning from overseas travels have slipped souvenirs past U.S. Customs Service officers without paying duty on them.

One former GI recently sent in $150 to pay for unauthorized items he had brought home after his discharge from the army way back in 1946! (Guilt has a way of staying with us, doesn't it?)

All of these people are trying to dissolve the guilt caused by disobedience. When we disobey God, it's a big deal. Throughout the Bible, we see that he consistently punishes the disobedient. Saul's kingdom was taken away because of it. Adam and Eve were cast out of the Garden because of it. You will not be the exception.

But wait a sec! you may be thinking. *What about forgiveness? Can't we seek God's forgiveness for our disobedience?* Absolutely! God will always forgive a repentant heart. But there are still consequences to sin. A murderer who becomes a Christian in prison is forgiven by God and will get to spend eternity in heaven, but he'll always regret his sinful actions. He may struggle with nightmares or flashbacks of taking someone's life, and he'll still serve his time in prison. He can be forgiven, but he'll still deal with the consequences of sin.

BREW IT!
Strive to obey God every single day.

POUR IT!
Drink in the flavor from the following Scriptures: Luke 11:28; John 14:15; 15:10.

SAVOR IT!
Ask God to help you obey all of his laws.

BREW IT!
God has made it clear that he's willing to wash clean your guilt and make you free!

POUR IT!
Drink in the flavor from the following Scriptures: Titus 3:5; Hebrews 10:22; 1 John 2:5.

SAVOR IT!
Thank God for his generosity and his desire to forgive all disobedience.

GOD IS FAITHFUL!

You don't have to pray about whether God meant what he said—even when it doesn't make sense to you. Many Christians spend a lot of time praying about things God has already made clear in his Word. Saul probably wrestled back and forth about whether he should destroy *everything*. But God had already given clear instructions, so there was no need for Saul to wonder about it.

Has God made it clear that he wants you to do certain things? If so, don't spend your time praying about whether to obey. Don't sit around trying to make it all make sense. Instead, ask Christ to strengthen you through the power of his Holy Spirit to consistently obey him, whether or not it makes sense.

You're human, therefore you're not perfect. It's just a fact that you're going to blow it from time to time. Simply meet God in prayer, confess your disobedience, and continue walking with him.

What should you pray for? Here are a few ideas:

1. *Forgiveness.* The same God who punishes the sin of disobedience is the same Father who forgives everyone who repents.

For proof positive that God wants to forgive your disobedience, sneak a peek at Hebrews 10:22. After you've read it, read it again. Notice the one-two-three approach in this passage that makes it really easy to understand. First, come to God with a sincere heart. Second, repent. Third, he promises to cleanse you from guilt!

Did you catch that last part of the promise? You don't have to beg God to take away the guilt. He's faithful. You can depend on him! He's already made plans to rid you of guilt and replace it with joy and forgiveness.

It's like telling your best friend that you want to treat her to a mocha latte after school. When she talks with you between classes, she doesn't need to spend that time begging you to take her for a mocha latte. You've already promised you would. All she has to do is come. Instead, she can focus her conversation on things you really need to talk about.

2. *Assurance that you're forgiven.* It doesn't matter how many times you've disobeyed God, or what's hiding in your past. *God will forgive!* And what's more, he even lets you share in his inheritance of eternal life. Copy Titus 3:5 on a note card and read it over and over again for assurance of your forgiveness and your eternal inheritance. Notice how generous God is in this passage:

He forgives. He forgets. He brings us out of past guilt and blesses us with freedom. He justifies us (*justification* means *just-as-if*-I'd never sinned). He gives us the inheritance of eternal life.

FALLING IN LOVE WITH OBEDIENCE

Yesterday we talked about praying for forgiveness and assurance that you're forgiven. It's also important that you pray for:

3. *The desire to obey.* God has the power to help us want to obey him. We must obey even when we don't feel like it, but he can give us the desire. Why not ask him for that desire?

David talks a lot about obedience in the longest Psalm recorded in the Bible—Psalm 119. Over and over again he writes that he loves to obey God. He loves God's commands, he loves fulfilling those commands, and he has literally fallen in love with obeying his heavenly Father.

Wow! What a difference it would make in our lives if we were truly in love with obeying the will of our Father! What kind of changes need to happen in your life for you to fall in love with obeying God? Are you willing to allow God to help you make those changes?

Even if you pray for the desire to obey, because you're human, there may still be times you don't want to obey. It's during those times that your solid commitment to God needs to win out over your desire. In other words, whether you feel like it or not, you simply decide ahead of time (like right now) to obey.

Think about Abraham, who had prayed for years that God would give him a son. God answered his prayer, then led Abraham to take Isaac to an altar of sacrifice. Abraham didn't *feel* like obeying. He certainly didn't want to sacrifice his only son, for whom he had longingly waited for years. But his commitment to God went beyond his feelings. He allowed his decision to obey to take priority over what he felt—and God rewarded his obedience by saving Isaac.

It can be the same with you. You can decide right now that you're going to live a life of obedience to God. Later, when you're tempted to disobey because you don't feel like obeying him, you can choose to live by your decision instead of your feelings.

BREW IT!
What do you base your actions on: feelings or commitment?

POUR IT!
Drink in the flavor from the following Scriptures: Psalm 119:67; Acts 5:29; Philippians 2:13.

SAVOR IT!
Ask God to help you fall in love with obeying him.

BREW IT!
Have you had a spiritual turning point in your life? Have you decided for yourself who Jesus is?

POUR IT!
Drink in the flavor from the following Scripture: John 1:23-40.

SAVOR IT!
Ask God to make your life eternally different as your Savior.

HE DECIDED FOR HIMSELF

Andrew was the first disciple chosen by Jesus. Yet he's never listed first in the Gospel accounts. His brother Peter is always listed first, and Andrew is second or further down the list.

Even before Jesus asked Andrew to be his disciple, Andrew was impressed with Christ. At that particular time in history, many people were expectantly looking for the Messiah.

There were rumors about Jesus. Some said he was the Messiah. Others said he was a prophet. Some hailed him as a healer. Many admitted he was an incredible teacher. And others said he was simply a really good person. Andrew had heard all the opinions, and he wanted to decide for himself.

You, too, may have heard a lot about Jesus. Maybe your parents have dedicated their lives to serving him. You might have friends who are convinced he's the Son of God. And you may have heard others say he's simply a historical figure and nothing more. At some point, you—like Andrew—will have to decide for yourself who Jesus is. Is he who he claims to be: the Messiah, the Son of God, the way to eternal life in heaven? Or was he merely a good person who did good things?

Andrew had heard that John the Baptist was baptizing people at the river, and he wanted to watch. Can you imagine his amazement when Jesus himself stepped into the water and asked John to baptize him? And then the really big surprise: As Jesus came up out of the water, the Holy Spirit in the form of a dove rested on him. God even spoke from the heavens, telling everyone that Jesus was indeed his Son!

The next time Andrew saw Jesus, he was so intrigued that he followed him at a close distance. You know that feeling when someone's following you? It was obvious—so obvious that Jesus finally turned around and asked Andrew what he wanted. Andrew said he'd like to talk with him. Christ was more than willing.

This was a spiritual turning point for Andrew. It was such a significant moment in his life that he even remembered the time of day it happened. We're told in John 1:39 that Andrew spent from approximately 4 p.m. till evening with Jesus. Those hours changed his life forever.

Are you willing to spend in-depth time with Jesus having intimate conversation? If you'll do that on a regular basis, your life will be changed forever!

THE DISCIPLE WHO SHARED

The conversation between Andrew and Jesus that afternoon was one that Andrew would always remember. It was during that conversation that Andrew realized Jesus truly was who he claimed to be. That afternoon, Andrew put his faith in Jesus Christ. And it was so significant, it became kind of frozen in time for him. It was as if Andrew was thinking, *I've found him! This is the Messiah. The whole world is looking for him, and I've found him. Look around. Soak in all the details of this moment. Remember everything about this conversation. Freeze this memory. Note the sounds of the insects buzzing nearby. Remember the grit of sand between my toes in these sandals. What time is it? Remember when this happened, because from this point on my life will be eternally different!*

Jesus loved Andrew's trusting and tender spirit. He noticed the friendliness of this young man and asked him to become his disciple. Andrew willingly accepted. He was the very first disciple chosen to follow Jesus.

Imagine how excited Andrew must have been. For years he had lived under the shadow of his brother, Peter. Andrew was used to being known as "Peter's brother." It seemed as though Peter had it all—popularity, physique, the cool factor. He could do just about anything he set his mind to. But Andrew? Well, Andrew was friendly, and that was about it. He was good one-on-one, but being center stage wasn't his talent. Peter, however, was right at home in the spotlight. In fact, he loved being center stage. But now Andrew had found the Messiah! He finally had something on his brother.

It would be easy to imagine Andrew thinking along those lines, but he didn't want to keep Jesus to himself. He loved his brother, and he knew Peter had abilities that he simply wasn't blessed with. I can imagine Andrew thinking, *Wow! If Jesus can use me—with the tiny bit of talent I have—imagine what he could do with my brother Peter!*

Andrew could have savored finally having something Peter didn't have. But Andrew was so excited about knowing Jesus personally, he wanted to share the good news! He immediately went to find his brother.

Are you excited about sharing your personal relationship with Christ with those around you? Or you do tend to keep your relationship with him private? Jesus loves it when you share him with others!

BREW IT!
Never think less of yourself for having only one or two talents. One- and two-talent disciples are indispensable to the Kingdom of God!

POUR IT!
Drink in the flavor from the following Scripture: John 1:1-18.

SAVOR IT!
Thank God for the gifts he's given you. Ask him to help you use those gifts to glorify him.

BREW IT!
Make time to discover what your God-given gifts are. No matter how many or how few you have, use them enthusiastically for him!

POUR IT!
Drink in the flavor from the following Scriptures: John 1:41-42; 6:8-11; 12:20-22.

SAVOR IT!
Commit your gifts to the Lord.

THE DISCIPLE WHO SMILED

Andrew found his brother Peter and brought him to Jesus. For the disciple who wasn't loaded with talent, Andrew was doing the most important thing in the world: He was bringing someone to Jesus! What would make Peter listen to his quiet brother? I can imagine Andrew smiling—because that's what he was good at—and excitedly telling Peter the news: "We have found the Messiah" (John 1:41).

He was direct. Confident. Unwavering in his faith. There was something about this bro that Peter respected and admired. Was it Andrew's integrity? Was it his smile? his friendliness? Perhaps it was his honesty. Peter listened to Andrew. He didn't make fun of him or question him—he believed him. And Andrew took his brother to meet Jesus.

Fast-forward a few chapters in Andrew's life. It was a hot, sticky day, and thousands had gathered to hear Jesus talk. The afternoon melted into evening, and Jesus was concerned about the people's need for food. Isn't it exciting that he cares about every need you have? He not only cares about which college you'll attend, whom you'll marry, and what career you'll have, but he also cares that you have enough to eat.

What was Andrew doing in the crowd of thousands? He was doing what he did best: He was smiling. He was being friendly. He was talking one-on-one with a youngster. And just as he had convinced his brother Peter to follow him to Jesus, he also convinced this little boy to go to Jesus.

There's not a lot of talk about Andrew in the Gospels. Peter is all over the pages, but Andrew is seldom mentioned. When he is mentioned, however (besides in lists of the disciples), he's always mentioned as bringing someone to Christ. What a way to be remembered!

First he brought his brother. Next he brought the boy with the loaves and fish. Then he brought some Greeks who were visiting Jerusalem. The Greeks had first approached Philip and asked him to take them to Jesus. This was quite a predicament for Philip. He knew God's chosen people were the Jews. Would Jesus even want to meet with Greeks? Not sure what to do, Philip sought Andrew. Friendly, smiling Andrew would know what to do. And sure enough, Andrew took the Greek visitors straight to Jesus.

Andrew doesn't dominate the Gospels as his brother Peter does, yet he played an important role in building the Kingdom of God. He wisely used what he had to bring glory to Christ. Refuse to compare yourself with another Christian who may have more talents than you do. God needs one-talent disciples. In fact, they're so important, that's exactly the kind of disciple Jesus first chose to follow him!

CAN YOU AFFORD IT?

It's fun to dream of owning a fast car, a luxury car, or a collector's car. But it'll take more than dreaming big to own any of the following cars:

- The Maybach, a luxury sedan from Mercedes-Benz: $300,000-plus.
- A sporty two-door Continental GT by Bentley: $149,000.
- Volkswagen's 12-cylinder Phaeton: $100,000.
- Volkswagen's V8 version of the Phaeton: $70,000.
- The Phantom by Rolls-Royce: $320,000.

It's obvious that only the wealthy can afford a car like the ones listed above. It would be impossible for someone on an average salary, let alone a college student with a part-time job, ever to have enough money to purchase one of these luxury cars. Fortunately, it's not imperative that any of us own a car of such quality. Most of us are mainly concerned with having a vehicle that's reliable—something we can depend on to get us safely from one place to another.

We can draw a couple of spiritual parallels from this car scenario.

- *Salvation is expensive.* It's much more expensive than a luxury car. In fact, it's the most expensive thing in the entire universe. It's so expensive, none of us can afford it—not even the affluent who have investments worth more than $10 million. But thankfully, because God loves us so incredibly much, he chose to pay the staggering price for us through the death of his Son, Jesus Christ.
- *Salvation is a gift.* Not only is forgiveness for sins so expensive that it cost Christ his life, it's being offered as a free gift to all who will receive Jesus as their Savior. And the best part? You don't have to have $10 million in investments, you don't have to put down a $50,000 deposit, and you don't have to wait four months. Salvation can be yours right now—no matter your status, your age, your position, your race, your past, or your size.
- *Salvation is a necessity.* Just as you need a dependable vehicle to get from one place to another, you need salvation to get from earth to heaven. The only dependable transportation is salvation through Jesus Christ. Buddha, Muhammad, a good life, or good deeds can't gain you entrance to heaven. The only way to spend eternity in paradise with God is through his Son, Jesus Christ. Without his salvation, you're lost.

BREW IT!
Don't take this precious, priceless gift of salvation for granted!

POUR IT!
Drink in the flavor from the following Scriptures: Psalm 9:14; Isaiah 25:9; Romans 1:16.

SAVOR IT!
If you've never accepted salvation from Christ, you can do so right now by praying the prayer included on February 21.

BREW IT!
Giving to someone who can't return the favor is exactly what Jesus did when he chose to die for your sins.

POUR IT!
Drink in the flavor from the following Scriptures: Psalm 68:5; Matthew 25:34-40; James 1:27.

SAVOR IT!
Ask God to show you what he wants you to give this coming Christmas season.

CHRISTMAS IN OCTOBER?

Yes, Christmas is still more than two months away, but it's not too early to start thinking about the incredible gift of giving. This year, why not give something that will truly make a difference? Consider giving to someone who can't give back.

Samaritan's Purse is a ministry that provides gifts to people in other countries who otherwise wouldn't receive a gift. Either by yourself or with the help of your family, youth group, Sunday school class, or close friends, you can give a gift this year that will make a huge difference in someone's life.

Here are a few gift suggestions:

• *Provide hot meals.* Whether it's Mom's home cooking or Christmas dinner at Grandma's, a hot meal demonstrates love because someone cared enough to prepare, cook, and serve the meal. From Central America to Southeast Asia, Samaritan's Purse operates a variety of feeding programs that include providing hot meals for street children and homeless senior adults. For only $7, you can provide a week's worth of meals and enable caring Christians to share Jesus Christ with people who are starving for his love.

• *Help a child learn to read and write.* Children in the world's poorest countries consider school a blessing, not a burden. They know that a good education is essential if they want to escape a life of backbreaking labor, scavenging, begging, or worse. Unfortunately, many parents can't afford school fees, textbooks, and other supplies. You can support schools, literacy programs, and other education projects that provide hope to the desperately poor and offer local believers an effective means of sharing the gospel. For $15 you can furnish a month of education for an eager student.

• *Give an orphan a month of loving care.* Each year thousands of orphaned, abandoned, and destitute children experience the Father's love through Christians who dare to give. For just $35, you can provide a month's worth of meals, lodging, health care, and education for an orphan.

• *Change the future of a disabled child.* Cerebral palsy, polio, congenital deformities, mental illness, blindness, deafness. In poor countries, life with such disabilities often means life without education, employment, dignity, or hope. Your gift of $20 can add to a larger gift that will help a disabled child receive surgery, therapy, medical devices, special education, or other life-changing assistance. A gift of $250 can help provide reconstructive surgery, a hearing aid, or braille resources, while giving a hurting child an opportunity to experience the transforming power of Christ. (If you'd like to participate with Samaritan's Purse, contact 1-800-353-5957 or visit www.samaritanspurse.org.)

ANOTHER ORDINARY DAY?

Remember the Old Testament story of David and Goliath? Goliath wasn't just tall; he was truly a giant! Here's a quick review: Goliath and the Philistine army were taunting God's people day after day after day. They challenged one of the Israelites to fight against Goliath, the Philistines' star player. He was huge, and God's people were frightened.

David probably wasn't old enough to serve in the army, but his brothers were there. And David had heard their stories of defeat. He couldn't understand why none of God's people were rising to the occasion. More baffling was the fact that God's people were allowing this giant to curse the one true God!

David wasn't frightened; he was angry. He approached King Saul and offered to take on the giant. Saul probably laughed at first, but when he realized David meant business, what did he have to lose? None of the other soldiers were brave enough to approach the giant. So Saul outfitted David with the best armor and equipment of the kingdom.

When David put it on, however, the armor outweighed him! He could barely move in that clunky stuff. So he took off the fancy armor and put down the expensive weapons. Then he grabbed his slingshot—the one he'd used for years to pass the time when he tended sheep—and headed toward the battlefield.

Of course, everyone laughed at David and mocked him when they saw him approaching. But David didn't care. He couldn't stand it that someone was cursing his God. He grabbed a few stones, placed one in his slingshot, and slung it toward Goliath. It hit the giant in just the right spot with just the right amount of force not only to knock him down, but to kill him!

Do you think it was a cool coincidence that David had just the right spin on that stone? Was it fate that the rock had exactly the right momentum? Could it have been luck that the stone hit Goliath in exactly the right spot?

No. It wasn't coincidence. Or fate. And it wasn't luck.

God had been preparing David his whole life for this moment! Day after day as he tended his father's sheep, hour after hour as he practiced hitting distant targets with his slingshot, God was working. He was preparing his young servant for this strategic moment in history.

Doesn't it make you wonder . . . thus far in your life, what has God been preparing you for? When you thought you were simply doing ordinary tasks without much meaning—cleaning your room, washing the car, taking out the trash, loading the dishwasher—could it be that God was working through those mundane tasks for a greater purpose?

BREW IT!
Never underestimate the power of the giant God you serve!

POUR IT!
Drink in the flavor from the following Scriptures: Jeremiah 29:11; Ephesians 1:19-20; 3:20.

SAVOR IT!
Ask God to use your ordinary days to bring him extraordinary glory.

BREW IT!
Don't expect to slay your giants on your own. You need the power of God to be victorious!

POUR IT!
Drink in the flavor from the following Scriptures: 2 Corinthians 4:8-9; James 1:2-4; 1 Peter 5:10-11.

SAVOR IT!
Identify the giant obstacles in your life and commit them to God.

GOT ANY GIANTS IN YOUR LIFE?

While David did the ordinary—tending sheep—God was dreaming big dreams for him. God was calling David to a purpose much larger than David ever would have imagined.

Guess what? It's the same with you. God always calls us to something bigger than ourselves. While we can only see directly in front of us, God sees the entire story. Continue to be faithful in the ordinary, daily routine of life and let God work behind the scenes to prepare you for something greater than you can even comprehend right now.

What kind of giants are *you* facing? Are there some mountains in your life that seem insurmountable? You can trust God!

Are you battling some issues you think you'll never overcome? Do you have people in your life who are mocking your faith and bullying you in your stand for Christ? You can trust God!

If God can empower a young man to slay a giant warrior, he'll do the same for you! He can give you the strength you need not only to face your giants but to overcome. God wants you to be victorious in him.

So what should you be doing right now?

- *Keep serving God.* David had heard the soldiers' reports about the giant who was cursing God and God's people. He didn't throw up his hands and give up. He didn't say, "Well, that's it! I don't see any way out of this mess. Might as well find something else to worship. Maybe my God isn't as big as I thought he was." No, he continued to serve God faithfully. He didn't waver in his commitment to his heavenly Father.

- *Make sure God is truly reigning in your life.* Have you given him control of *everything?* You need to be 100 percent surrendered to his authority if you want his power surging through you to slay a giant!

- *Give your giant to God.* David didn't enter the battlefield in his own strength. He sought the Lord's direction. He knew without a doubt that God was calling him to put an end to the giant who was cursing almighty, holy God. Have you given your giant to God? Have you admitted, "This is way bigger than I am, Father. I don't see any way out of this mess without a miracle from you. So I give this huge obstacle to you, and I'll respond in obedience to how you direct me."

WHOM DOES GOD CHOOSE?

Why do you suppose God chose a young man such as David to slay the giant Goliath? God had an entire army of soldiers to choose from. Certainly there were many warriors who had more experience, more strength, and a more professional battle strategy. Why choose David?

Out of all the people reading this book, whom will God choose to use? On whom will God place his hand of blessing? Whom will he raise up to do great and mighty things?

Well, what kind of person does God choose? Throughout the Bible, we see time after time that God chooses to use ordinary people to do extraordinary things. He's not looking for the one with all the ability. He's looking for the one with all the *availability*. So if you're willing to say, "Dear God, here I am. Use me. All that I am and all that I have are yours," you're exactly the one God will choose!

We often get all caught up in our abilities, don't we?

"Hey, I can sing, so God will surely use me!"

"I'm a strong athlete, therefore, I know God has plans for me!"

Or we get caught up in our lack of abilities. "If I were only thinner, smarter, more popular, or stronger, God would use me."

"If I could just play tennis like Adam. If I could be the leader that Brianne is. If I had the physique that Matt has . . . then I know God would use me."

It's not about your ability. It's not about your ability! *It's not about your ability!*

It's about your *availability*!

God doesn't care as much about your intellect, your athletic prowess, your leadership skills, your popularity, your musical gifts, or your other skills as he does about your availability. You see, he's simply looking for someone who's available. David was available! Though he was simply fulfilling the ordinary, routine, daily tasks of life (tending sheep), he was in love with God. He was committed to his calling, his direction, his plan. He was available!

God will definitely use committed Christians who are available. Isn't that exciting? Being used by God has absolutely nothing to do with your ability! You don't have to be good enough, popular enough, smart enough, tall enough, thin enough, anything enough. All you have to be is available!

BREW IT!
So how about it? Instead of being negative or critical about the things you can't do, why not simply let God know you're available to be used by him?

POUR IT!
Drink in the flavor from the following Scriptures: 1 Samuel 17:45-51; 18:14.

SAVOR IT!
Will you make yourself available to God right now? If so, ask him to use your life to bring glory to his Kingdom. Tell him you're willing to be used in whatever way he desires.

BREW IT!
Let this sink in: It's not about you! It's about God working through you.

POUR IT!
Drink in the flavor from the following Scriptures: 1 Samuel 17:14-16, 52-58.

SAVOR IT!
Ask God to help you stop focusing on yourself and what you can't do, and start focusing instead on him and all he can do.

IT'S NOT ABOUT ME

Whew! Knowing that you don't have to be good enough, strong enough, or smart enough to be used by God should take a tremendous amount of pressure off you.

You don't have to measure up. Or qualify.

There will be no auditions or callbacks.

If you're willing and available, *you're* the one God wants to use to do extraordinary things! Are you willing?

David was willing and available, and he had also placed his confidence in God's ability, not his own. Common sense would say, "I'm only a kid. How in the world can I approach this enemy giant? I don't have the battle experience. I don't have a fancy strategy. The armor doesn't even fit me!"

But when we're sold-out to God, we don't always operate on human common sense; we learn to live in his holy, supernatural sense that transcends our understanding. Yes, David was fully aware of his inability, but he chose not to focus on that. Instead, he zeroed in on *God's* ability! It was as if David was saying, "Hey, I'm fully aware of what I can't do. But I have full confidence in what my God *can* and *will* do!"

When you stop looking at your inability and start living with your eyes fixed on God's supernatural power, you'll realize anything is possible! He dreams bigger for you than you would ever dare to dream for yourself. His dreams for you are beyond your wildest imagination. So get the focus off of yourself and all you can't do, and start living your life based on what *he* can do!

Listen to what David said to King Saul when he questioned the boy's ability: "The LORD who delivered me from the paw of the lion and the paw of the bear will deliver me from the hand of this Philistine" (1 Samuel 17:37).

In other words, "Hey, Saul! It's not about my ability! It if was, we'd be in trouble. But the enemy is cursing God Almighty, and God wants to do something about it. He's simply looking for someone who's available—someone he can work through. Guess what? I'm available. I'm going to let him use me to defeat this giant. And because God has been faithful in the past, I know he'll be faithful now. I have full confidence in his supreme, all-powerful ability. It's not about me, King Saul! It's all about God simply working through me."

How can anyone argue with that?

GOD DREAMS BIGGER

Throughout history, God has chosen ordinary people—people who were committed and available—to do extraordinary things in his power. When Jeremiah was still a teenager, God called him to be a prophet—to speak out and tell others about him. Jeremiah was overwhelmed. Check out the conversation between the two of them: "The word of the LORD came to me, saying, 'Before I formed you in the womb I knew you, before you were born I set you apart; I appointed you as a prophet to the nations.' 'Ah, Sovereign LORD,' I said, 'I do not know how to speak; I am only a child' " (Jeremiah 1:4-6).

In other words, "I don't have the experience. Choose someone who has been to seminary, some-one who loves being in front of people, someone who's confident."

But again, God wasn't looking for the most tal-ented speaker. He wasn't interested in finding the national debate champion. He simply wanted some-one who was available. Jeremiah was available; therefore God chose him.

God was calling Jeremiah to something much big-ger than himself. And again, God will always call *you* to something bigger than yourself. If his dreams weren't bigger than you, you wouldn't need to depend on him; you'd be able to accom-plish the task by your own strength. God always has a bigger picture in mind. And by depending on his strength, his power, and his ability, you can accomplish the task he sets before you. *How?* Through his ability, not your own.

Let's keep eavesdropping on Jeremiah's conversation with God: " 'Don't say that,' [God] replied, 'for you will go wherever I send you and speak whatever I tell you to. And don't be afraid of the people, for I, the Lord, will be with you and see you through.' Then he touched my mouth and said, 'See, I have put my words in your mouth!' " (Jere-miah 1:7-9, TLB).

In other words, "Don't worry about what to say, Jerry! You just open your mouth, and I'll do the rest! I know you're not a great speaker, but I'm not looking for a great speaker. I'm simply looking for someone who's available, someone I can use, someone through whom I can speak. So trust me. I'll do the speaking. You just be available."

Again, I hope that takes a lot of pressure off you. You don't have to be "good enough" or "talented enough" to be used by God. You simply need to be available. And did you notice who God said we're not to fear? *The people!* Don't let the put-downs from those around you slow you down from doing God's work. Forget what your kid brother says about you. Don't listen to the critical remarks your older sister makes. The names you're been called? Forget about them! Fix your eyes and ears on God.

BREW IT!
Trust God to work in a mighty way through your availability.

POUR IT!
Drink in the flavor from the following Scriptures: Jeremiah 1:10; 17:7-8; 20:11-13.

SAVOR IT!
Ask God to remove all your fears regarding what people will say about you when you speak out for him.

BREW IT!
What are you learning in your journey with the Savior? Take note. Think it through. Pray about it. Share it with others.

POUR IT!
Drink in the flavor from the following Scriptures: Psalm 13:5; 25:2; 31:6.

SAVOR IT!
Tell God you don't want to miss anything he's trying to teach you as you walk with him.

WHO, ME?!

Another ordinary person who allowed God to do extraordinary things through his life was Moses. We know Moses felt insecure about what God was calling him to do, because he compared himself to his brother, Aaron, and begged God to use him instead. "He's a terrific speaker, Lord," Moses said. "And I-I-I get r-r-r-really nervous in front of people. So nervous that s-s-s-s-sometimes I st-st-st-stutter and can't speak clearly. Aaron's confident. Use him instead."

But God wasn't looking for the most qualified person. He was looking for someone who was available. And Moses was available. God wanted to free his people from the bondage of slavery they were in under Pharaoh, and he wanted to use Moses to accomplish his task.

Perhaps their conversation went something like this: "Whoa! God, this is way beyond me. I can't do it."

"I know you can't, Moses. But I can. I'm calling you to something bigger than yourself, something that's beyond your wildest dreams. Don't worry about your lack of ability, because that doesn't matter. I have all kinds of ability! And I want to pour my supernatural ability into you and raise you up to free my people."

Moses obeyed. It took a while, but the children of Israel finally escaped Pharaoh's rule, and Moses led them toward the Promised Land. They took a few wrong turns, and it ended up taking more than forty years. Moses never actually got to enter the Promised Land; he died before that. But he *did* get to see it from a distance and was amazed at God's provision all along the way.

Does it sometimes seem as though you're on a long journey filled with twists and turns? Do you tend to grow impatient, wishing God would hurry up and do what he wants to do in your life? God is never early, yet he's never late. His timing is perfect. If you'll keep your eyes fixed on him instead of on the road beneath your feet, you won't grow weary of the journey.

Though it took almost half a century for the children of Israel to reach the Promised Land, God was teaching them some important lessons. Sometimes where we're going isn't as important as the journey itself and what we learn along the way.

BUT IT'S SO ORDINARY!

Though their journey to the Promised Land was filled with miracles, it was also filled with frustration for the children of Israel and for Moses. You see, when God decides to use you, he needs 100 percent. He can't use you if you're only committed to him 50 percent or even 85 percent. He's looking for disciples who are 100 percent available.

Moses was almost there. He had given God his life, but he was clinging to the few material possessions he had. Mainly his walking stick—his rod.

"Moses, what do you hold in your hand?"

"Ah, it's nothing. Just my walking stick. Feels good to lean on it while we're trekking through the desert."

"I need all of you, Moses."

"You have all of me, God. I'm yours."

"I not only need all of your life; I need all of your things, too. Open your hand. Release the rod. Give it to me."

"Are you serious? It's nothing important. It's just an ordinary stick I found by the side of the road and whittled into a cane. It feels good to have it in my hand during this journey."

"Give me the rod, Moses."

You probably know the story. When Moses gave the rod to the Lord—when he released it and threw it down—it became a hissing snake! When God commanded Moses to pick it up, it became a rod again. God later had Moses do this miracle in front of Pharaoh so he would know God's power was with Moses. What God says to you may not always make sense to your feeble human mind. But he has proven himself to be faithful, and you can trust him.

BREW IT!
God wanted to show Moses that he could work through anything—even a stick of wood. But first Moses needed to give God control of everything.

POUR IT!
Drink in the flavor from the following Scriptures: Psalm 4:5; 9:10; 20:7.

SAVOR IT!
Ask God if there are any material items in your life that you are holding too tightly. Be willing to place them in his arms.

As humans, we tend to think in terms of time, space, and dimension. God isn't bound by those. He's always thinking outside the box. It's nothing at all for him to change a rod into a snake. He created both; he can do with them as he pleases. But here's what's exciting about this: If God can do miraculous wonders through an ordinary piece of wood . . . imagine what he'll do through a life that's totally dedicated to him! That ordinary stick of wood wasn't special on its own. But when God took control, it was suddenly transformed beyond what Moses could imagine.

In the same way, you're not much on your own. (None of us are.) But when you allow God to totally control your entire life, he'll do amazing things through you. If he can work through wood, he'll work through your life—if you're available!

BREW IT!
Are you willing to share what
you have?

POUR IT!
Drink in the flavor from
the following Scriptures:
Psalm 37:3; 40:4; 52:8.

SAVOR IT!
Tell God that you want him
to use what you have for
his glory.

YOU WANT *THIS*?

Think back to the little boy the disciple Andrew befriended on the day Christ spoke to thousands. (Flip back to the devotional on October 14 for a quick reminder.) We don't know the boy's name, but we can pretend we do. Let's call him Bobby. I imagine Bobby's mom had packed his lunch early in the day as he headed out with the crowd to hear Jesus speak.

It was hot. The day wore on. The crowd grew a little restless because they were hungry and far from food. Jesus called the disciples to him. "What are we going to do with all these hungry people?" he asked.

The disciples shifted their weight from foot to foot and wiped the sweat off their foreheads. "I don't know," one said.

"Me, neither," another added.

"Just counting the men only, there are at least five thousand!"

"So how will we feed them?" Jesus pressed. (Jesus already knew, because he knows everything, but he wanted to see if the disciples were on the same page as him.)

"We can't. It would take more than what all of us make in an entire year to feed this huge crowd."

"We don't know what to do, Jesus."

Can you believe it? The disciples are standing in the presence of the King of kings; the one who has made blind people see, made deaf peole hear, and calmed storms. Why didn't they simply say, "Jesus, you're the God of miracles. We trust you. Tell us what to do."

Perhaps it was because they were focused on the people around them instead of on Jesus Christ. When we start looking at how big the problem is instead of how big God is, our focus is completely off. Andrew, though, spoke up. Now remember, Andrew didn't have a ton of talent like his brother Peter. Andrew was good at being friendly and that was pretty much it.

But Andrew was using the one talent he had—he had found Bobby and made a friend. Bobby was so impressed with this friendly, smiling disciple that he even offered to share the lunch his mom had packed.

Andrew probably watched as Bobby excitedly pulled his lunch out of his back pocket. He'd been sitting on it all day. In the hot sun.

The bread was probably smashed and drenched with sweat, and the few small fish were probably stinky and very, very, very warm. I can imagine Andrew smiling and saying, "Hey, Bobby, I'll get back to you on that, okay?"

LITTLE IS MUCH IN GOD'S HANDS

Jesus called the twelve disciples up front and asked them how they would feed the crowd. While the other disciples were admitting they didn't have a clue, friendly Andrew spoke up.

"It's not much, Lord," he said, "but I didn't have much to offer you and you still chose me."

"What is it, Andrew?"

"Bobby. This kid I met. He has a few pieces of bread and some very small fish. He offered to share it with me. If he knew you wanted it, I'm sure he'd give it to you."

The other disciples were probably snickering. "A few pieces of soggy bread and some tiny fish?!"

"He's got to be kidding! What good is that going to do a crowd of this magnitude?"

Jesus said, "Bring the boy to me."

Andrew obeyed.

Bobby approached the King of kings and placed his lunch in the hands that created the universe. Bobby willingly gave Jesus all he had.

And he watched.

He watched in utter amazement as Jesus multiplied the bread and fish before his eyes. He couldn't believe it when everyone had eaten and twelve baskets of leftovers were gathered after the crowd had eaten until they were full.

Wow! Bobby must have thought. *If Jesus can do* that *with a few pieces of bread and some tiny fish, imagine what he could do with my life!*

Has the lightbulb gone on in your head? *If Jesus can do what he did with an ordinary stick of wood . . . if Jesus can do what he did with some bread and fish . . . what will he do with a* life *that's totally committed to him and available for his use?*

There's no limit! Do you get it? There is *no limit* to what God can do through your life. And it doesn't matter how much you have. Andrew had very little. Bobby didn't have much. Moses just had a stick. The issue isn't what you have. The issue is: Will you give what you have to the Lord?

BREW IT!
If you give all you have to him, you'll be amazed at how God will work through your ordinary life to accomplish extraordinary things.

POUR IT!
Drink in the flavor from the following Scriptures: Proverbs 3:5; 22:19; Isaiah 8:17.

SAVOR IT!
Thank God for wanting to use your life to accomplish great things for his Kingdom.

BREW IT!
Dare to quit thinking small. Pack your bags and move outta Smallville. Dare to dream big! You serve a giant of a God.

POUR IT!
Drink in the flavor from the following Scriptures: Psalm 56:3-4; 62:8.

SAVOR IT!
Ask God to give you his huge vision for your life. And when he does, accept it as truth.

GET OUTTA SMALLVILLE!

The Old Testament tells us that Abraham and Sarah had been married for years without having children, and they desperately wanted a son. When Abraham was one hundred years old and his wife, Sarah, was ninety, God told them he would bless them with a son. Abraham thought it was inconceivable. When Sarah heard the news, she laughed. Ridiculous! But guess who got the last laugh? God did. He blessed them with a son and commanded that they name him Isaac—which means "laughter"!

Why didn't Sarah take God at his word when he first announced he would give the couple a son? Perhaps she temporarily forgot that anything is possible with God. What often doesn't make sense to us as humans is completely clear with the Almighty.

God made another promise to Abraham. He led him outside his home and told him to look up at the sky. I can imagine their conversation went something like this: "What do you see in the sky, Abraham?"

"Stars. Lots of stars!"

"Get a good look, Abraham, because I'll answer your prayer for a son."

"What do stars have to do with my prayer for a son?"

"Abraham, you serve a giant of a God. Dream big! Don't you realize that I dream far bigger for you than you can even imagine? Why limit your request to one son? Abraham, quit thinking small. Get out of Smallville and dare to dream big! I'm going to bless you with more descendants than there are stars in the sky."

"What?!"

"That's right, Abraham. Not only will I bless you with a son, but the descendants I'll give you will outnumber even the stars! So get out of Smallville!"

And ordinary, elderly Abraham became the father of a great nation—the Israelites—because he was available for God to use him. And, of course, because he was totally committed to a God who specializes in making the impossible become reality.

Are you living in Smallville? Do you tend to box God into something small and compact that you can see and understand? God doesn't live in Smallville! And he doesn't want you to take up residence there, either. God cannot be contained. If you're afraid to dream big, you've become a citizen of Smallville. God always dreams bigger for you than you can imagine.

HAVE YOU FALLEN IN LOVE WITH GOD?

Think for a moment about the things you enjoy—the stuff that brings you pleasure. Your family? Friends, a car, sports, music, e-mail, your cell phone, books? Now think about the people you love. Family, friends, youth pastor, people you've met on mission trips?

Out of all the things that bring you pleasure, I hope your relationship with Christ tops the list. And out of all the people you love, I hope Christ is number one. Do you truly love God? Are you in love with your heavenly Father?

How do you fall in love with God? Similar to falling in love with a human, you need to:

- *Spend time with him.* The more time you spend with God, the better you get to know him. The more you know him, the more you love him.
- *Read and study his Holy Word.* Reading the Bible is important. But don't settle for simply reading it; determine to study it as well. Get to know the different books of the Bible. Discover how God's Word is relevant to your life right now.
- *Talk to him . . . a lot!* Prayer is your personal line of communication with the creator of the universe. Think about it: you can talk to God whenever you want! No call waiting, no caller ID, no forwarded calls, no roaming charges, and no busy signals. God's line is open for you 24/7. Are you taking advantage of it? Are you using this powerful avenue of prayer to get to know your Father better?

BREW IT!
Determine to fall in love with God. He's totally in love with you!

POUR IT!
Drink in the flavor from the following Scriptures: Psalm 37:4; Matthew 6:9-10; John 12:46.

SAVOR IT!
Ask God to help you fall more in love with him every day. And thank him for being in love with you.

BREW IT!
The disadvantage of giving a gift like this is that you can't see the reaction of the recipient. But the advantage is that you're giving as Jesus would give.

POUR IT!
Drink in the flavor from the following Scriptures: Isaiah 66:13; Zechariah 7:9-10; 1 Timothy 6:17-19.

SAVOR IT!
Ask God to help you earn some extra money before the Christmas season so you can help someone in need.

THINKING TOWARD CHRISTMAS

On October 16, you were challenged to begin praying about giving a different kind of Christmas gift this year—giving to someone who can't return the favor. Have you been praying about it? Here are a few more suggestions from Samaritan's Purse.

- *Keep a baby clean and dry.* Diapers may not be on your Christmas wish list, but they would be if you were a young mother in a refugee camp or a care-giver at a crowded orphanage. Clean diapers not only keep babies fresh and comfortable, they also prevent the spread of disease, instill dignity, and demonstrate how God provides for even our most humble needs. For $12 you can provide one hundred disposable diapers, a dozen cloth diapers, or other hygiene items.

- *Introduce girls and boys to God's Word.* "Jesus loves me, this I know, for the Bible tells me so." Many of us took the first steps on a journey of faith when we learned this simple truth in Sunday school. You can make sure children know what the Bible says about Jesus by providing Christian litera-ture and other materials to church and mission groups around the world. A gift of $18 can intro-duce a girl or boy to the Savior by providing weekly Bible lessons for an entire year.

- *Rescue a child from bondage and abuse.* Millions of children worldwide struggle to survive under the most desperate circumstances imag-inable. Victims of human traffickers, they are forced into virtual slavery as child soldiers, sweatshop laborers, field workers, menial servants, or worse. From South-east Asia to Africa to Latin America, Samaritan's Purse sponsors many Christ-centered programs to protect, rescue, and rehabilitate children from a life of bondage and abuse. For $200 you can provide one of these children with three months at a safe haven where he or she can begin a brand-new life. Or for $20 you can share in the cost of this program.

- *Feed a hungry infant for a week.* It's a familiar sight in famine-stricken villages and impoverished communities—an emaciated baby lying in her mother's arms, crying herself to sleep. These malnourished children often suffer from bone deformities, stunted growth, and other health problems. Christian workers care for the physical needs of babies and the spiritual needs of their families through this infant-feeding program. A gift of $9 can feed an infant for a week. (If you'd like to participate with Samaritan's Purse, contact 1-800-353-5957 or visit www.samaritanspurse.org.)

WHATEVER!

The apostle Paul didn't mince words in his letter to the Colossians. Let's take a peek at Colossians 3:17: "Whatever you do, whether in word or deed, do it all in the name of the Lord Jesus, giving thanks to God the Father through him."

That doesn't leave much room for questions, does it? "*Whatever* you do!" But just in case one of the Colossians had a question about what he meant, Paul extended the command: "Whatever you do, whether in *word* or *deed*." No one can question that, right? But again, just in case someone still didn't understand, Paul went a bit further: "Whatever you do, whether in word or deed, do it *all* in the name in the name of the Lord Jesus." In other words, glorify God in everything you say and do. In everything!

What does that mean? It means the music you listen to, the movies you watch, the way you dress, the way you do your homework, whether you clean your room, the e-mails you send, if you take out the trash or feed your pet, how you talk to your parents, the jokes you tell, the company you keep, the books you read, what you do in your spare time, what you choose to think about . . . in *everything* you do and say, let it be done to the glory of Christ.

Sometimes we forget, don't we? It might help if we quit saying, "Hi, how ya doin'?" to our friends and start saying, "Whatever!" That one word, *whatever*, would be a gentle way of saying, "Whatever you're doing and saying, are you making sure it's to God's glory?"

Try it for a few weeks. Grab a few of your closest friends and make a "whatever" pact with them. Every time you see each other, let your greeting be "Whatever!" instead of "Hi!"

BREW IT!
After you've tried the experiment for a few weeks, compare notes. What kind of changes do you need to make in your life to let your words and actions be glorifying to Christ?

POUR IT!
Drink in the flavor from the following Scriptures: Colossians 2:6-7; 3:12-17.

SAVOR IT!
Ask God to help you consciously move your actions and thoughts toward glorifying him.

BREW IT!
Don't try to hide unconfessed sin. Allow God to bring it to light.

POUR IT!
Drink in the flavor from the following Scriptures: Psalm 25:5; 26:3; 43:3.

SAVOR IT!
Ask God to use his Holy Spirit to make you sensitive to any unconfessed sin in your life.

BUT IT WAS SUCH A SMALL SCRATCH!

Federal aviation regulators are requiring airlines to inspect approximately one thousand Boeing 737s after potentially dangerous scratches were discovered in the skin of the jets. What caused the scratches? When many of the big planes were being repainted, some of the workers didn't use the metal tools properly, and a few scratches occurred. The scratches weaken the thin aluminum skin of the jets and result in cracking.

So far the scratches haven't caused any accidents, but if they're not repaired, the scratches could lead to cracks that in extreme cases could make jets burst open when flying at high altitudes. In 1988, the roof of an Aloha Airlines 737 peeled open at twenty-four thousand feet in the air. A flight attendant was literally blown outside of the aircraft. That particular accident was blamed on corrosion.

Who would think a small scratch could give birth to a crack? And who would imagine a small crack would grow and corrode into something big enough to cause extreme danger and even death?

Sin works in a similar pattern. When we get comfortable with something in our lives that shouldn't be there, eventually we start accepting other questionable things. We begin to wonder if sin is actually sin. We tend to think, *Everyone else is doing it! Could that really be wrong? Would God truly punish that? Maybe it's not really sin after all.*

Sometimes we rationalize, *No one saw me do that. No one knows what I fantasize about. No one suspects I'm struggling with this. And as long as no one knows, I can keep it hidden.*

Just as the scratches on the 737s may be hard to detect right now, they can't remain unnoticed forever. Time will cause the scratches to turn into cracks. And eventually, just like a crack in your car windshield, the crack on a 737 will spread.

As the cracks of unconfessed sin begin to multiply in our lives, we become a time bomb that will eventually explode in defeat. God uses his Holy Spirit as a "crack detector" in our lives to point out the scratches and corrosion that sin causes. When he brings a scratch, crack, or an area of corrosion to your attention, don't ignore his warning!

Listen to him. Thank him for showing you the crack. Seek his forgiveness and allow the Holy Spirit to mend what's wrong in your life before it leads to further damage.

GET STARTED ON YOUR CHRISTMAS SHOPPING

I hope you've been praying about how you (or you and your family and friends together) can provide someone less fortunate with a terrific Christmas this year. Samaritan's Purse, headed by evangelist Franklin Graham, ministers around the world to malnourished children, orphans, and the needy. Here are some more suggestions for gifts you can purchase through their ministry to touch someone in a third world country.

BREW IT!
Ask your family to pray together about how you can help someone less fortunate this Christmas season.

POUR IT!
Drink in the flavor from the following Scriptures: Psalm 57:1; 1 Corinthians 1:7-9; 15:54-55.

SAVOR IT!
Take a few minutes to thank God for the many blessings he's given you. Go ahead and name them one by one.

- *Supply a thirsty family with clean water.* The mighty Amazon River dominates the geography of South America, and the Mekong River stretches across much of Southeast Asia, yet clean, safe drinking water is in short supply in both places. The situation is the same in many developing countries, particularly in rural areas where rivers and lakes also serve for bathing, washing clothes, and watering livestock. Samaritan's Purse provides filters, wells, pumps, and water storage systems to impoverished families as a way to introduce them to the "living water" of Jesus Christ. A gift of $75 can provide a water filter for a family or cover the cost of a heavy-duty hand pump.

- *Provide emergency medicine.* You're probably familiar with the ER found in local hospitals, but you may not realize an "emergency room" in a war zone or at a disaster site has the same needs but not necessarily all the supplies. Samaritan's Purse has gone into some of the most difficult and dangerous places on the planet to care for the sick and injured. They often send bulk shipments of medicine and supplies, including a special one-ton health kit designed to meet the emergency needs of ten thousand people for three months. Each kit costs $6,000, which means $60 can provide essential medicines for one hundred people. Thousands of men, women, and children hear the gospel for the first time as teams provide emergency relief.

- *Give a family survival kit.* Families surviving a tribal war in the Congo, a hurricane in Grenada, or an earthquake in Iran take nothing for granted. On a cold, dark night, they welcome warm blankets and a lantern. In the struggles of the day, they appreciate a water bucket, a small stove, cooking pots, and even soap. For $45 you can enable Samaritan's Purse to assemble items like these into a kit to help a family survive a calamity. As they start life anew, they'll be pointed to safe refuge in God's unfailing love. (If you'd like to participate with Samaritan's Purse, contact 1-800-353-5957 or visit www.samaritanspurse.org.)

CELEBRATION TIME!

Try to guess which of the following holidays in the month of November are real and which ones are fake. Write an *R* by those you think are real, and write an *F* by those you believe are fake.

___ Cook Something Bold and Pungent Day
___ National Ample Time Day
___ Buy Nothing Day
___ National American Teddy Bear Day
___ Sisters' Day
___ National Night Out
___ Be an Angel Day
___ National Coupon Month
___ National Game and Puzzle Week
___ Swap Ideas Day
___ Pursuit of Happiness Week
___ National Men Make Dinner Day
___ Clean the Bathtub Day
___ Admit You're Happy Day
___ What Do You Love About America Day
___ Homemade Bread Day
___ National Tie Month
___ Clock Appreciation Week
___ Be Kind to Cheese Day
___ Kiss and Make Up Day
___ National Wheel Week

BREW IT!
You serve a God of joy! Are you enjoying your relationship with him?

POUR IT
Drink in the flavor from the following Scriptures: Psalm 119:73, 89-90; 125:1.

SAVOR IT!
Ask the Lord to help you enjoy your time with him.

Fake: Sisters' Day, National Night Out, Be an Angel Day, National Coupon Month, Swap Ideas Day, Clean the Bathtub Day, Admit You're Happy Day, National Tie Month, Clock Appreciation Week, Be Kind to Cheese Day, Kiss and Make Up Day, National Wheel Week.

BREW IT!
Remember, we are the church. Christ could easily point to us and say, "You're dead" if we're not growing in him.

POUR IT!
Drink in the flavor from the following Scriptures: John 14:15-19, 26; Revelation 3:1.

SAVOR IT!
Ask God to use his Holy Spirit to help you maintain a vibrant, growing relationship with him.

THE FIFTH LETTER

When the apostle John was exiled to the island of Patmos, he had a vision of Jesus Christ in all his glory. From that experience, he wrote the book of Revelation. The Lord gave him seven specific letters to send to the churches in Asia Minor. We looked at the first few letters on April 28-30, July 17-23, August 2-4, and August 19-21. Now we're ready to dive into the fifth letter. It was written to the church in Sardis.

The word *sardis* means "remnant." Sardis was a very wealthy city that seemed invincible until Cyrus—the Persian king who conquered Babylon—flattened this city in 549 BC.

Christ begins his letter to the church in Sardis by reminding them he's the one who sent the Holy Spirit into the world. In the Gospel of John, we read that Christ gathered his disciples together before he was crucified and told them that he wouldn't be around physically much longer. But he told them he would send his very Spirit to guide them into all truth.

If there was one thing the church in Sardis needed, it was the Holy Spirit. The same holds true today. Many churches in our nation are filled to capacity. They boast fancy methods, fun courses, and the latest technology. All that is fine and good if the Holy Spirit is in control—meaning that everything the church does points toward Jesus Christ.

Then Jesus says, "I know your deeds; you have a reputation of being alive, but you are dead" (Revelation 3:1). He was referring to people in the church who claim to be active in the Lord's work but who really aren't. You see, it takes more than simply going to church on Sunday morning to have a vibrant, growing relationship with our Savior. We also need to be serving and worshipping him twenty-four hours a day, seven days a week. If we're worshipping him only on Sunday mornings, chances are we're not growing; we're dead. We're simply going through the motions and doing what looks right on the outside.

WATCH OUT!

You may remember from Christ's letter to the church in Thyatira (see August 19–21) that though the Lord had much to correct them for, he *did* commend them for their service, faith, and patience. But here at Sardis, he just says, "You're dead."

We, too, need to be careful not to fall into the easy trap of being complacent because we're saved. God expects us to dedicate our lives to him and keep growing spiritually.

Christ tells the church in Sardis to "be watchful" or to "wake up!" This is the Lord's word of condemnation. When the people of Sardis weren't watchful, their city fell to invaders. It was located on top of a mountain. They only had one entrance into the city, and it was on the southern side. Sounds easy to defend, doesn't it? All they needed to do was place some guards by that one entrance!

But twice Sardis had been invaded by its enemies because the guard fell asleep on the job. You see, because the city was on top of a mountain, they felt secure. They believed no one would dare climb the mountain to attack them. They found out the hard way that they were wrong.

So, too, people in the church had fallen asleep spiritually. It was as if they were thinking, *We're on solid ground. We won't get knocked down. We're feeling good.* So when Jesus condemns them, it's with a warning. It's as though he's saying, "You church people should know better! Take a look at the history of your own city. That itself should tell you the results of resting in a false sense of security. Watch out!"

We need to be alert and remain watchful for the coming of our Savior. We don't know when Christ will return, but we know he's coming! We should live in expectancy so he won't find us spiritually asleep when he returns for his children.

BREW IT!
Make sure you have yielded everything to his control and are living a vibrant relationship with him.

POUR IT!
Drink in the flavor from the following Scriptures: Matthew 25:1-13; Revelation 3:2.

SAVOR IT!
Ask the Lord to keep you ready and watchful for his coming.

Jesus told a parable about the bridegroom coming for his bride. Ten bridesmaids anxiously awaited the bridegroom. (The bridegroom symbolizes Christ, and the bridesmaids symbolize the church—Christians.) Some of the bridesmaids ran out of oil for their lamps. They left to go get more oil, and the bridegroom came while they were away. Jesus ended this parable by saying, "Therefore keep watch, because you do not know the day or the hour" (Matthew 25:13). We need to be ready for his coming.

BREW IT!
Be ready! Actively prepare for Christ's return.

POUR IT!
Drink in the flavor from the following Scriptures: 1 Thessalonians 4:13–5:11.

SAVOR IT!
Ask God to show you any-thing specific you should be doing right now to be ready for his return.

JUST LIKE A THIEF

Jesus warned the church at Sardis to be ready for his return. It would be easy to be ready for Christ if we knew the exact day and hour, wouldn't it? If we knew he was coming back next Saturday, we'd have all our ducks in a row. We would seek forgiveness from those we've hurt. We'd make sure our tithes and offerings were paid. And we'd probably spend more time reading the Word and praying.

Since we don't know the exact day or hour of his return, we have to be *constantly* ready. Live as though he might return tonight.

Christ tells the Christians in Sardis that if they're not ready and watchful for his coming, his return will seem sudden—just like an unexpected thief. We don't plan to be robbed. A thief doesn't alert us a couple of days in advance, "I'll be in your neighborhood on Wednesday. Leave your front door unlocked, okay? I'll back the truck right up to the garage to make it easy to load that plasma TV you have in your living room."

It doesn't happen that way! The thief comes when we aren't expecting him, so wise home owners will invest in alarm systems and keep their doors locked for safety. The home owner wants to be prepared to avert the thief when he approaches. "Rats! They have an alarm system. Not gonna be able to crack that. And their doors are locked. Ah, might as well go find another house whose owners aren't so prepared."

In the same way, Christians want to prepare for Christ's coming. We should have the door to our hearts unlocked, have our Bible open, and be wear-ing a welcome sign through our actions. We want to be ready for his return. If we're not ready, Christ says his coming will seem unexpected to us. "Hey! I've had a really tough week with exams and work. I didn't think he'd come *this* week! I was planning on catching up on my Bible reading during Christmas break. But he came this morning, and he caught me totally off guard."

BACK TO THE BASICS

Christ tells the church in Sardis to remember what they first heard and were taught. What was that? It was the Word of God. They had strayed from biblical teaching and the message of the gospel, as many of us have today. Christ condemns them for this and tells them to repent.

Some churches today don't preach the Word of God. Their people hear positive messages full of feel-good advice, but when it comes to calling sin *sin*, truth isn't being taught.

Please be aware of what you choose to believe. The apostle John tells us in 1 John 4 and in 2 John to examine what we hear, and if it can't be backed up by Scripture, we shouldn't assume it's from God. Simply because a good person holds a microphone in his hand, stands on a church platform, and speaks positive words doesn't mean he's speaking God's truth.

There are leaders in the church today who hold huge conferences to decide what in the Bible is really true and what's not. Friends, that's dangerous ground! I know Christian professors at Christian universities who tell their students that the only thing they can count on for sure from the Bible is the resurrection of Christ.

Some students on Christian campuses are being told by their religion professors to forget everything they ever learned in Sunday school because it's all wrong. "During the course of this semester," they boast, "we'll teach you what's true."

BREW IT!
Decide, with God's help, not to involve yourself in sexual intimacy outside of marriage, underage drinking, lying, spreading gossip, and other activities that lead you away from an intimate relationship with him.

POUR IT!
Drink in the flavor from the following Scriptures: Luke 12:32; Galatians 5:19-21; Revelation 3:3-4.

SAVOR IT!
Ask God to help you not to stray from his Word.

They teach that the sayings of Isaiah, many of the promises of the Kingdom, and the teachings of Revelation are just allegorical. They're asking students to question the historicity of Job, Jonah, and the first few chapters of Genesis. There's absolutely nothing wrong with looking critically at aspects of our faith. But when we question God's very Word, we're wandering from the basics.

Christ, in his letter to the church in Sardis, tells us very clearly to get back to the basics—to lean on the gospel as dependable truth. If we don't, he says we'll be caught off guard by Jesus' return.

Christ continues by saying that he knows some Christians in Sardis *have* remained faithful. They hadn't given up the gospel message, they were living in watchful expectation of Christ's return, and they were actively involved in ministry.

It's always only a remnant of people who choose to follow Christ. It was that way in Sardis, it was that way when Jesus walked the earth, and it's still that way today. Perhaps that's why he refers to us as his "little flock." Christians who live holy lives empowered by God's Spirit have certainly always been in the minority. Choose to be one of the godly minority.

BREW IT!
Are you listening to what Jesus is saying?

POUR IT!
Drink in the flavor from the following Scriptures: Revelation 3:5-6; 13:8; 17:8.

SAVOR IT!
Ask the Lord to give you blessed assurance that your name is recorded in the Lamb's Book of Life.

HE WHO OVERCOMES

Christ encourages the Christians in Sardis who have remained faithful to continue in their faithfulness. There was only a remnant of faithful followers, but he promised to reward them. Christ said he'll call them worthy and clothe them in white garments. None of us can remain faithful on our own. We can overcome only through the blood of Christ and by the empowering of his Holy Spirit within us.

Christ then mentions that he will not "blot out" their names. Some Bible scholars believe that everyone's name is written in the Book of Life. If, however, someone never places his trust in Christ and doesn't live for him, that person's name is removed, or blotted out.

Other theologians believe that when you become a Christian, your name is *then* entered into the Book of Life. The important thing is simply to make sure your name is in heaven's book. How can you know for sure? If you've confessed your sins, accepted the Lord's forgiveness, placed your faith in him, and are living in a relationship with him, you're a Christian; your name is recorded in the Book of Life. You can know for sure. You don't have to wonder. God wants to give you his blessed assurance.

The Lord closes his letter to the church in Sardis by repeating what he's said in previous letters: "He that hath an ear, let him hear what the Spirit saith unto the churches" (Revelation 3:6, KJV).

Again, *we* are the church. The Christians are the body of Christ. And he tells us to listen carefully to what he's just said. That tells us the book of Revelation is certainly relevant to us right now! Not only were the Christians in Sardis expected to heed Jesus' words, but the same is expected of us today. We do not have the authority to declare that the Bible is untrue.

PLANNING FOR CHRISTMAS

On October 16, 28, and 31, I challenged you to ask God what you could do to make a difference this Christmas in the life of someone living in a third world country, someone less fortunate than yourself. Samaritan's Purse—a ministry organization headed by Franklin Graham—has several gifts that you alone or you and your friends and family could give. But if you don't do it soon, the gift won't arrive in time for Christmas.

Here are a few more options:

BREW IT!
Will you think and act outside the box this year by reaching out with a gift to those less fortunate?

POUR IT!
Drink in the flavor from the following Scripture: Matthew 25:31-46.

SAVOR IT!
Ask God to show you specifically what and to whom he would have you give this Christmas.

- *Transform a life with a wheelchair.* Samaritan's Purse has provided wheelchairs to thousands of disabled people in poverty-stricken regions of Latin America, Africa, and Asia. One young Mexican man, unable to walk since he was run over by a truck when he was eleven years old, had to be carried around in a plastic chair. At age twenty, he had no hope for the future. That changed when local believers delivered a wheelchair provided by Samaritan's Purse. Now he can go back to school, get a job, and make a fresh start in life. For only $75, you can supply a needy child or adult with a sturdy wheelchair, bringing hope, freedom, and dignity in the name of Jesus Christ.

- *Comfort an innocent victim of AIDS.* One chilling statistic sums up the tragedy of HIV/AIDS: 14 million orphans. Over the next decade, that number could exceed 50 million. Sadly, many of these children are infected with HIV at birth. Local believers in hard-hit areas of Africa and Asia are eager to help these suffering girls and boys, but often they're overwhelmed by the expense. For $35 a month, you can help loving Christians care for an AIDS orphan in a home filled with the peace and joy of Jesus Christ. You may only be able to provide care for one month; that's still priceless to an orphan suffering with AIDS.

- *Give food parcels.* When church workers deliver family-size parcels of food in impoverished communities, doors and hearts open up. Believers are encouraged, while nonbelievers are eager to learn more about the Christian faith. Monthly home visits provide regular opportunities to share the gospel. In poverty-stricken areas of Mozambique, Israel, Iraq, and other countries, Samaritan's Purse provides local ministry partners with the resources to reach out to needy families with food and other aid. For $35, you can furnish a malnourished family with a supplemental food parcel filled with rice, beans, flour, salt, cooking oil, and other items.

BREW IT!
God is a jealous God. He wants to be Lord, and he desires that you worship him and him alone.

POUR IT!
Drink in the flavor from the following Scriptures: Exodus 20:5; 34:14; Deuteronomy 4:24.

SAVOR IT!
Ask God to show you anything in your life that's contaminating your relationship with him.

BOWL GAME

Ready for the scoop on some cereal factoids? Seventy-two percent of people who eat breakfast eat only cereal in the morning. Ten percent of households across the nation eat cereal for other meals.

Cheerios was ranked the most popular cereal and boasted $288 million in sales last year. Frosted Flakes came in second with $242 million.

Imagine entering a restaurant to place your order with an employee who's wearing pajamas. That's the norm for Cereality Cereal Bar and Café. Think Starbucks and then translate that to cereal. You have your choice of several varieties of cereal and toppings. If you're a regular customer, you can even enter your ID number on a touch-screen computer and your regular order will come up automatically.

Customers get to create their own selections and mix different kinds of cereal. It's a cereal smorgasbord where the customer chooses everything!

Sounds like fun, doesn't it? Customers enter a casual atmosphere surrounded with pajama-clad servers and order whatever cereal concoction they come up with.

Unfortunately, many people view religion this way. They casually saunter through a bookstore, picking a book on Hinduism, a brochure on New Age thought, and something else on Buddhism, and then they grab a Bible on their way out. They assume religion, like cereal, can be mixed and matched to their convenience.

I'll take a tiny bit of Christianity, they think, *and add a touch of New Age, toss in some Wicca, and coat it with Islam.* They're oblivious to the fact that we can't create our own religion if we want to spend eternity in heaven.

Christianity is all about a relationship with Jesus Christ. And trying to mix other beliefs into a relationship with Christ doesn't work. Imagine returning from your honeymoon someday and saying to your spouse, "Honey, I love so many things about you! But I'm also attracted to some qualities I see in other people. So don't be surprised if I add these other people to our marriage. I think we can make it stronger by adding more participants."

Your spouse would think you're crazy! In essence, that's what we're doing when we try to bring pieces of other belief systems into our relationship with Christ. It doesn't work. It won't work. It will *never* work!

WHEN I GROW UP

A survey was conducted with 890 middle school students, ages eleven to thirteen. They were asked if they'd like to be president of the United States when they grew up. Only 43 percent said they'd want the job. Fifty-seven percent admitted they wouldn't be interested. The students said the most important issues facing the nation were:

- keeping the United States free from terrorists (30 percent).
- helping students become well educated (26 percent).
- making sure everyone gets good health care (16 percent).

So what do most kids want to do instead of becoming a future U.S. president? Sixty-six percent aspire to be entrepreneurs.

While those are wonderful aspirations, what would it take for students to say:

- "I want to be in full-time ministry when I grow up."
- "I want to learn an unwritten language and translate the Bible for a specific people group."
- "I'd like to be a nurse for AIDS orphans."
- "I want to help people in third world countries with agriculture."
- "I'd like to teach deaf students."
- "I want to make a positive difference in the inner city by running for mayor."
- "I want to be an attorney and offer my services for free to help the poor."
- "I'd like to be a physical therapist for the handicapped."

BREW IT!
Instead of creating your own plans and asking God to bless them, seek to be in the center of his perfect will.

POUR IT!
Drink in the flavor from the following Scriptures: Psalm 68:10; 112:9; 113:7.

SAVOR IT!
Ask God to show you where he wants you to go and what he wants you to do.

Why do we most often think of careers that will fatten our wallets and build our prestige instead of careers that can make a lifetime of difference? God may very well call you into a lucrative career. If he does, he's trusting you to remain faithful to him and support your local church and worldwide missions by making giving a priority.

But what if he has something else in mind for you? He's still going to trust you to make tithing a priority, to support your local church, and to give as he directs toward missions. But would you be willing to consider a future of giving to people who can't give back? Would you agree to pray about doing whatever God calls you to do?

BREW IT!
If God were to give you a teachability test, how would you rate?

POUR IT!
Drink in the flavor from the following Scriptures: Proverbs 16:1; 21:8; 22:12.

SAVOR IT!
Ask God to give you a teachable, flexible spirit.

THE FINAL I FAILED (PART 1)

BY BERNICE BROOKS

Finals week had arrived with all its stress. I had been up late cramming for an exam. Now, as I slumped in my seat, I felt like a spring that had been wound too tight. I had two tests back-to-back, and I was anxious to get through with them. At the same time I expected to be able to maintain my straight-A grade point average.

As I waited impatiently for the professor to arrive, a stranger walked up to the chalkboard and began to write. "Due to a conflict, your professor is unable to give you your test in this classroom. He's waiting for you in the gymnasium."

Oh great, I thought. *Now I have to walk clear across campus just to take this stupid exam.*

The entire class was scurrying out the door and rushing to the gym. No one wanted to be late for the final, and we weren't wasting time talking. The route to the gym took us past the hospital. There was a man stumbling around in front of it. I recognized him as the young blind man whose wife had just given birth to a baby in that hospital. He had been there before, but he must have become confused.

Oh, well, I told myself. *Someone will come along soon and help him. I just don't have time to stop now.* So I hurried along with the rest of the class on our way to take that final exam. As we continued down the sidewalk, a woman came rushing out of a nearby bookstore. She had a baby on one arm, a stack of books in the other, and a worried look on her face. The books fell onto the sidewalk, and the baby began to cry as she stopped to pick them up.

She should have left that kid at home, I thought. I dodged her as the class and I rushed along.

:::

We'll take a break in the story right here and finish it during tomorrow's devotional. But let's chat about something first, okay? How do you react when someone changes your plans at the last moment? Like the student in this story, do you become frustrated with those last-minute changes? Or are you flexible?

An unteachable spirit is hard to deal with. God needs disciples who are willing to be broken, reshaped, and molded into his holy image. That means we need to go with God's flow. When he tells us to change directions, we do it. When he decides to alter our plans, we comply.

THE FINAL I FAILED (PART 2)

BY BERNICE BROOKS

Just around the next corner someone had left a dog on a leash tied to a tree. He was a big, friendly mutt, and we had all seen him there before, but today he couldn't quite reach the pan of water left for him. He was straining at his leash and whining.

I thought, *What cruel pet owner would tie up a dog and not leave his water where he could reach it?* But I hurried on.

As we neared the gym, a car passed us and parked close to the door. I recognized the man who got out as one of the maintenance crew. I also noticed he left the lights on. "He's going to have a problem when he tries to start that car to go home tonight," the guy next to me said.

By now we were going in the doors of the gym. The maintenance man waved a greeting to us and disappeared down one of the halls. We found seats close to where our teacher waited.

The professor stood with his arms folded, looking at us. We looked back. The silence became uncomfortable. We all knew his tests were also teaching tools, and we wondered what he was up to. He motioned toward the door, and in walked the blind man, the young mother with her baby, a girl holding the big dog on a leash, and the maintenance man.

These people had been planted along the way in an effort to test whether or not the class had grasped the meaning behind [Jesus'] story of the man who fell among thieves.

We all failed.

BREW IT!
Actively look for people you can help, kind things you can do, and specific ways to share God's love.

POUR IT!
Drink in the flavor from the following Scripture: Luke 10:30-37.

SAVOR IT!
Ask God to help you develop the qualities of the Good Samaritan.

: : :

How would you have rated in the above final? In a sense, God gives us this kind of final every single day, doesn't he? If we call ourselves Christians, it means we live out his love and kindness in the line at the grocery store as well as in front of a crowd. It's much easier to have others compliment us for being a good Christian than it is to live it out by pushing a wheelchair, carrying groceries for an elderly person, or stopping to chat with a lonely child.

Live and act as though you're aware God is giving you a final exam each day of your life.

BREW IT!
God sees potential in you
even when you fail.

POUR IT!
Drink in the flavor from
the following Scriptures:
Matthew 16:18-19, 21-23;
26:69-74; Luke 22:61.

SAVOR IT!
Ask God to help you become
spiritually rock solid.

THE MULTITALENTED DISCIPLE

It seemed as though the apostle Peter could do it all! Someone had to be the leader among the twelve disciples, and Peter more or less grabbed the role. As a child, he was probably the one who swam the farthest on hot afternoons in the Sea of Galilee. And when the weather cooled and kids from the neighborhood decided to build a tree house, he probably climbed the highest and barked out the orders.

He dominated fishing expeditions as an adult, and he dominated the Gospels as a disciple. He was usually the first to speak and the first to act. He was impulsive, extroverted, extreme, and impatient. And he was also the disciple whom Jesus called "the Rock."

In fact, the Master said that he would build his very church on Peter. In other words, Jesus saw a lot of strength, giftedness, and potential in Peter. Though he wasn't the first disciple chosen to follow Christ, he's at the top of the list in all four Gospel accounts when the disciples are named. His brother Andrew was actually the first disciple selected by Christ, but Peter clearly outshined him.

Andrew was good one-on-one (see October 12–14 for more information on Andrew), but his brother Peter was great with many. He loved the spotlight. He was at home in front of a crowd. He had multiple talents . . . and he was "the Rock."

But the road to becoming the Rock wasn't easy. Shortly after Jesus named Peter the Rock, he said his response was from the devil. Jesus had begun to tell his disciples that he would be handed over to the authorities and killed, and Peter blurted out, "No way! We'll never let that happen to you." And Jesus said, "Get behind me, Satan!" Whoa! One minute a rock and the next minute the voice of Satan?

It would be a long road for Peter. When he proudly boasted at the Last Supper that he would never deny Jesus, the Lord calmly told him that by the time the rooster crowed the next morning, Peter would have already denied him—not once, but three times!

Sure enough, after Jesus was taken away, people noticed Peter hanging out by the fire to warm his hands and mentioned that he was one of Christ's disciples. Peter flatly denied it. It was brought up again, and Peter vehemently denied it. The third time it was mentioned, the Bible tells us Peter responded in anger and cursed.

Imagine how he must have felt when the rooster crowed and he turned around to see Jesus being led away. Imagine their eyes meeting and how terribly low Peter must have felt. *A rock?* he must have thought. *I'm sand, and I know it!*

FISH FRY ON THE BEACH

When Peter's eyes met the eyes of his Master—when he heard the rooster crow and realized he'd denied his Savior three times—something happened.

Something died that night: Peter's self-reliance. His confidence in himself. His arrogance. It all died that night. He realized he wasn't anywhere near being the rock that Christ needed him to be. He was merely a pebble, and he knew it.

But that night, when Peter saw himself as he really was, humility took root. He realized he could never become the rock the Lord envisioned him to be . . . unless he quit trying to accomplish it by his own strength. The only way *any* of us can live up to the potential the Master sees in us is by total surrender to him. Then through his power, his might, and his strength, we can do all things through him and become all he calls us to be.

After Christ rose from the dead, he appeared to all the disciples. Later he went to find Peter. Jesus knew exactly where he would be. He knows exactly where you and I are too, and he loves us enough to find us.

He found Peter by the beach. It was in the early morning hours, and Peter and some of the other disciples were fishing. When Jesus called out to them, Peter jumped out of the boat and ran to him. Later, after they fried some fish they'd caught, Jesus approached Peter. He wanted to reaffirm him—to let him know he still believed in him and saw great potential in him. Christ wanted Peter to know that he still dreamed big dreams for him and wanted to build his church on Peter's leadership.

As they shared breakfast, Jesus asked Peter if he loved him. Peter was probably a little saddened that Jesus had to ask him that question; yet in light of his three-time denial, he understood. "Yes, I do," Peter responded.

"Then feed my sheep," Jesus said.

They took a few more bites of fish and downed some coffee. And Jesus looked Peter in the eye and asked him again, "Peter, do you really love me?"

Again, Peter was probably saddened that the Lord had to ask twice. But he affirmed his love for his Savior. And Jesus responded by telling him to feed his sheep.

After they'd eaten a few more bites of fish and put out the fire, Jesus looked at Peter again and said, "Peter, are you even my friend?"

BREW IT!
How often do you declare your love for the Lord?

POUR IT!
Drink in the flavor from the following Scriptures: John 21:15-17; Philippians 4:13

SAVOR IT!
Have you told Christ recently how much you love him? Do it today.

BREW IT!
What are you doing to feed
Christ's sheep?

POUR IT!
Drink in the flavor from
the following Scripture:
1 Peter 5:1-6.

SAVOR IT!
Ask the Lord to show you specific ways you can care for and
serve those around you.

A PEBBLE BECOMES A ROCK

Peter was grieved that Jesus asked the question this
way. He responded that he was indeed Christ's friend.
We don't know everything that was in his heart, but
he might have said something like this: "Oh, Jesus!
I'm so sorry I denied you. You were right. You know
me better than I know myself. And you also know my
heart. You know that I've committed my life to you
and that my greatest desire is to do what you ask me
to do and to become all you want me to be.

"Sometimes I blow it, and when I blow it I usually
blow it big. I'm so sorry I failed you. But I still love
you. And you know that deep in my heart I truly want
to serve you, love you, follow you, and obey you.

"I'm not a rock yet, Jesus. But in your strength I can
become one. I'm giving up the confidence I used to
have in myself, and I'm placing everything in you. I
realize now that I can never be who and what you
call me to be of my own doing. It's only through total
surrender to your lordship that I'll ever be your rock.
Jesus, I want to be your rock. I give myself totally to
you. Take control. I surrender. Make me a rock, or
make me a mud pie. I don't care as long as I'm in the
center of your will."

And I can hear Jesus responding with a smile on his
face, "Yes! You get it. I forgive you. I reinstate you. I
still dream for you. Feed my sheep, Peter. Feed my
sheep!"

Are you thinking what I'm thinking? Jesus told him
he was going to be a rock—now he's telling him to go
feed sheep. What's the deal? Is he going to be a
shepherd, or will he be the rock the church is built on?

Actually, both. You see, to be a great leader, you need to be willing to be a servant.
Jesus refers to his children as his sheep. It was as if he was saying, "Peter, you say that
you love me. Prove it. Not by loving me—that's easy. But prove it by loving others. Love
and serve and care for the other people. That's a lot tougher than simply loving me,
isn't it, Peter? But if you *do* love me, if you're truly my friend, let it show by the way
you treat others."

A much older and wiser Peter penned two books of the New Testament: 1 and 2
Peter. And we can tell by what he says that the pebble was transformed into a rock-
solid Christian. He tells us to feed sheep—to care for one another—and to do it lovingly,
not grudgingly.

GRATEFUL? SHOW IT!

As you approach Thanksgiving, take some time to make a list of everyone you're thankful for. After you've completed your list, send an e-mail, make a phone call, or mail a note to each person on your list, explaining why you're grateful to have him or her in your life. Here are a few ideas of people you can begin with:

- your mom and dad
- a favorite teacher
- the worship leader at your church
- a grandparent
- a coach
- your pastor
- your brother(s)/sister(s)
- friends
- a Sunday school teacher
- an adult who's involved in your life (employer, piano teacher, discipleship leader, gymnastics instructor, etc.)
- an aunt
- a cousin
- someone you don't know personally who has made a positive impact on your life (a contemporary Christian artist, writer, evangelist, government official, etc.)
- an uncle
- someone who probably doesn't get much encouragement (school bus driver, mail carrier, librarian, school cafeteria worker, etc.)
- a neighbor

BREW IT!
As you show these people your gratitude, pray that God will remind them how much he loves each of them.

POUR IT!
Drink in the flavor from the following Scripture: Philippians 2:1-5.

SAVOR IT!
Ask God to help you consistently demonstrate an attitude of gratitude.

BREW IT!
Read this devotional a few more times and let it really sink in.

POUR IT!
Drink in the flavor from the following Scripture: John 17:1-10.

SAVOR IT!
Thank Jesus for praying for you.

CHRIST'S PRAYER FOR YOU (PART 1)

Guess what? The creator of the universe has been praying for *you*! Would you like to know what he's saying? I've paraphrased the prayer Jesus prayed in John 17. I'm using the pronouns *he* and *him* throughout as generic terms. Cross them out and use *she* and *her* if you want, and write your own name in the blanks provided.

Father, (insert your name) is my personal glory. I glow when I think of him. That's because I love him as if he were the only one in all the world to love. I believe in his potential. I see so much in his life. I'm excited about all you have in store for him.

Keep him close to you, Father. Help _____ to realize that you and I dream big dreams for him. I ask you to take extra good care of him. Those days when he feels like the whole world is against him and no one understands, let him sit in your lap—just like a child. Wrap your strong arms of love around him and wipe away his tears.

Sometimes, Father, he doesn't show his tears. Sometimes he does all his crying on the inside. Help him feel comfortable enough around you to act on what he's feeling.

He can be so hard on himself. There are times when he's his worst enemy—beating himself up over not meeting someone's expectations. Teach him that your expectations are what's truly important in life.

He's so much fun, Lord. I love laughing with _____. Sometimes we just talk about daily stuff—like his latest test scores, who's spreading rumors about him, and why he's trying to get so-and-so to notice him. And you know what? I love it! I'm glad he knows there's absolutely nothing too big or too small to pray about. I'm thrilled he knows that you and I care about everything!

CHRIST'S PRAYER FOR YOU (PART 2)

It's cool to be able to eavesdrop on Christ's prayer about you to God Almighty, isn't it! Ready to read the rest of his prayer to you? Let's continue.

I'm concerned about unity, Father. I want _____ to live in harmony and peace with those around him. Help him to get over this feeling of having to be right all the time. Help me teach him humility and genuine concern for others. I crave unity between my children. I want them to have the same kind of oneness that you and I have.

Keep him safe. Protect him. We'll walk by his side together, Father. We'll take each step he takes, and we'll feel everything he feels. The good and the bad. The laughter, the pain, the aloneness, the confusion, the joy. I want to experience all that with him.

I've told him a lot. I even wrote it all down for him in a personal collection of letters. I hope he listens. I'm going to keep talking to him— leading and guiding him—through my Spirit that I'll pour inside him and through my letters. I'm concerned that he hear and understand my voice. If he'll just read my letters, things will make sense. Help him do that, Father. And help him be consistent in getting to know us.

The world hates _____. They hate him because he doesn't really fit in. And I'm glad he's not fitting in, because he's really no more a part of this world than I am. But he has a hard time understanding that. Sometimes he wants to fit in—forgetting that his real home is with us and that it's far beyond his wildest imagination. I wish we could give him a little taste of heaven, Father.

But I know that's where faith comes in. Help me to increase his faith. I want nothing more than for him to become all we dream for him to be.

I'll be joining you soon. And together we'll work on getting his house ready. In my place, though, I'll leave my very own personality—my Spirit—full of every-thing I am, for his fulfillment and spiritual victory.

I love _____ so much, I'm giving my very life for his growth in holi-ness and truth and understanding. My life for _____. It's worth it, Father. We have a genuine treasure when we have _____.

BREW IT!
Read this devotional a few more times and let it really sink in.

POUR IT!
Drink in the flavor from the following Scripture: John 17:11-26.

SAVOR IT!
Thank God for loving you more than you'll ever comprehend.

BREW IT!
If you accept Jesus' payment, seek his forgiveness, and place your trust in him, you can be freed from an eternal death trap.

POUR IT!
Drink in the flavor from the following Scriptures: Micah 7:18; Zechariah 3:4; Romans 6:23.

SAVOR IT!
If you're still trapped in sin, consider praying the prayer of salvation found on February 21.

TRAPPED!

You may have heard the true story of Aron Ralston, who was pinned for six days by an eight-hundred-pound boulder in spring 2003. Aron was an experienced climber but still found himself trapped in Bluejohn Canyon in Utah. Surprisingly, he had his video camera with him and was able to record his thoughts and feelings during the entire ordeal.

He focused the camera on his forearm and wrist, then panned to where it disappeared in the skinny gap between a large boulder and the canyon wall. He pointed the camcorder to his grayish-blue hand and recorded the details: "What you're looking at here is my arm, going into the rock . . . and there it is—stuck. It's been without circulation for twenty-four hours. It's pretty well gone."

As much as he tried, Aron couldn't yank his arm free, and he couldn't budge the half-ton boulder holding it. Using a dull pocketknife, he tried sawing into the boulder, but it was useless. Then he tried stabbing the rock. Neither worked.

With his limited water supply running low, he was out of options. No one knew he was there. Knowing he was close to death, he did the only thing he could think of. As a last resort, he plunged his pocketknife into his wrist and began sawing through his flesh. *My only chance out of here is to amputate my wrist and hand,* he thought. Forcing himself to continue, he gradually moved the knife back and forth across his bone until he accomplished the amputation. Miraculously, he lived to write a book and even shared his story on national television.

Because no help was available, Aron had to take care of his tragedy himself. And while we rejoice that he can still climb and lives a normal life, it's terrible that he had to lose his hand in the process.

Each one of us is in a similar predicament. Because we were born with sin, we're trapped in its death hold. Aren't you grateful you don't have to take matters into your own hands and try to save yourself? God loves you so much that he sent help in the form of his only Son, Jesus Christ, to pull you out of the death trap.

The bottom line is that sin has to be paid for. You can pay for it yourself—the Bible calls this hell—or you can accept the fact that Jesus paid the price for you.

IT MAY LOOK LIKE A MUSHROOM . . .

A man drove his old pickup truck from Mexico to a southern Arizona junk pile to acquire a large heap of scrap metal. He planned to sell the metal for cash at the scrap metal recycler in Mexico. He didn't have much money, and jobs were scarce, so he was glad to be able to sell the metal and use the money to buy groceries for his family.

His old pickup rattled down the highway carrying an antique dental X-ray machine. Tiny steel balls fell from the machine onto the bed of his truck. These little steel balls were actually radioactive marbles rolling back and forth, but the driver didn't know it.

After he sold the metal, he hurried home, anxious to share his money with his family. Children from the village noticed the shiny, colored balls between the ribs of his truck bed and laughed in delight as they used them for game after game of marbles.

After a few weeks, however, many of the people in this Mexican village came down with a strange set of symptoms. Some were losing their hair. All were extremely tired, suffering rashes, and vomiting. Some people even died. Several months later, it was discovered they were suffering from severe radiation poisoning.

Those little balls looked so shiny. They were fun to play with. But they were deadly because they were radioactive.

Have you ever seen a toadstool? You probably know that toadstools are poisonous. But they look very similar to mushrooms, don't they? It would be sad to eat a toadstool and die . . . all the while thinking it was a mushroom.

Just because shiny little balls look pretty and are fun to play with doesn't mean they're not harmful. And a toadstool may look very much like a mushroom. You can call it a mushroom, tell everyone else it's a mushroom, and even serve it in a salad. But if it's really a toadstool, it can kill you!

It works the same way with sin. Most Christians aren't tempted by something ugly and evil, because it's obvious that's sin. Most Christians are tempted by sin that has been disguised as something cute, pretty, or fun. You may not be able to tell the difference on your own. That's why you need the discernment the Holy Spirit provides.

BREW IT!
Are there some things in your life that you've rationalized yourself into believing are harmless mushrooms or shiny marbles?

POUR IT!
Drink in the flavor from the following Scriptures: Genesis 4:7; Numbers 32:23; 1 Kings 3:9.

SAVOR IT!
Seek God's forgiveness for playing with sin instead of walking away from it.

BREW IT!
Are you trying to remove the stain of sin from your life? Or have you allowed the blood of Jesus to remove it for you?

POUR IT!
Drink in the flavor from the following Scriptures: Psalm 51:7; 103:9-12; Isaiah 1:18.

SAVOR IT!
Thank Jesus that his blood is powerful enough to remove the stain of your sins.

STAIN REMOVAL

Ever been stuck with a laundry problem you couldn't take care of? Here are some incredible remedies that have been proven to work.

- Problem: *You've washed your red shirt with a load of whites, and now everything's pink.* Solution: Rit Color Remover. This product removes dye that's been transferred to washable white fabrics. Get it at any fabric store or most grocery stores.
- Problem: *Pornography.* Solution: Jesus Christ. Throw away all printed porn (books, magazines, posters) you have in your home. Get a computer software program that acts as a filter (visit xxxchurch.com or covenanteyes.com). Set up accountability with a friend. Both of these Web sites offer software programs for you and an accountability partner; they will automatically e-mail your partner all the sites you access on your computer. Seek forgiveness from Christ and allow him to break your bondage.
- Problem: *Your wool sweater shrunk in the wash.* Solution: This isn't guaranteed, but it's worth a try. Soak the sweater for a few minutes in a bucket of water to which you've added a couple of capfuls of hair conditioner. The conditioner will loosen the fibers enough that you can lay the sweater on a dry towel and gently pull and stretch it back into shape. Allow to dry thoroughly.
- Problem: *Uncontrollable anger.* Solution: Jesus Christ promises there is victory in him. Confess to the Lord. Seek his guidance. When you feel an outburst of anger coming on, pray silently. Submit to his authority. Claim his peace.
- Problem: *Sin.* Solution: Soak completely in the blood of Jesus Christ. Only he can remove the stain of a sin-filled life. Confess, accept his forgiveness, and walk in obedience to him.

We often try different things to deal with the stain of sin, don't we? You may have tried alcohol to numb it, or drugs to make you forget it. Perhaps you've thrown yourself into doing good things and joined several clubs to try to counteract the stain. Or maybe you think listening to more Christian music or going to church more often will remove the stain of your sin.

None of these are viable options for sin's stain removal. There's only one proven remedy: Jesus Christ.

THE SIXTH LETTER

When the apostle John was exiled to the island of Patmos, he received a vision of Jesus Christ and wrote the book of Revelation. The Lord gave him seven specific letters to send to the churches in Asia Minor. We looked at the first five letters on April 28–30; July 17–23; August 2–4; August 19–21; and November 2–6. Now we're ready to dive into the sixth letter. It was written to the church in Philadelphia (no, not Pennsylvania).

Only two of the seven letters contain no criticism—this one and the letter to the church at Smyrna. Christ spoke no words of condemnation to the Philadelphian Christians, only words of praise. Perhaps one of the reasons the Lord thought so highly of the Philadelphian church was because they were actively involved in evangelism. The word *philadelphia* means "city of brotherly love." The city was a commercial center, so the church was strategically located to reach out to the many people traveling through. The members of this church had returned to the Word of God and were teaching it fervently while winning others to the Lord.

Christ begins his message to this church by reminding the Christians that he is holy. He was holy at birth. He was holy during his time on earth. He was holy when he died and was resurrected. And he is holy today. Then he reminds the church that he is true. The apostle John also recorded Christ saying this in his Gospel: "I am the way and the truth and the life" (John 14:6).

Christ says seven things to the church in Philadelphia:

BREW IT!
Are you taking advantage of the doors God opens for you?

POUR IT!
Drink in the flavor from the following Scriptures:
1 Thessalonians 5:12;
Hebrews 13:17;
Revelation 3:7-8.

SAVOR IT!
Ask the Lord to help you become involved in good works for his glory.

1. *"I know your deeds"* (Revelation 3:8). Jesus looks for fruit in the lives of Christians. While we're saved by faith, good works are a sign of maturity in our relationship with the Lord. There's something wrong with our faith if it doesn't produce any good works. Christ affirms the Philadelphians for being involved in so many good things. *How about you?* Do you claim to be a Christian without doing anything good for the Lord? Or are you a Christian who's also producing good fruit for others to see?
2. *"See, I have placed before you an open door that no one can shut"* (Revelation 3:8). Christ will give you opportunities to share your faith and witness to others. He will also open the door to your knowledge of his Word. He'll use his Holy Spirit to make the Bible come alive to you and to help you understand what you read and study.

BREW IT!
Do you "walk your talk"? Do your actions match your words?

POUR IT!
Drink in the flavor from the following Scriptures: John 4:24; Romans 9:6; Revelation 3:8-9.

SAVOR IT!
Ask God to point out anything in your life that doesn't match the definition of being a Christian, and commit that area to him.

DOING GOOD!

Christ says seven things to the church in Philadelphia:

1. *"I know your deeds."*
2. *"See, I have placed before you an open door that no one can shut."*
3. *"I know that you have little strength"* (Revelation 3:8). Christ is using "strength" to refer to power. *Dunamin* is the Greek word for power. (*Dunamin* is the root of our word *dynamite*.) The Lord is saying, "I see you have little power." This particular church in Philadelphia was simply a humble group of believers who didn't have large crowds, buildings, or programs.

We often get caught up in numbers. We like to boast about how large our church is or how many people were saved in our church this year. But more important than numbers is the teaching and preaching of the Word of God. If we remain true to that, God will work through us to save those in our midst, and he'll do the counting! We won't have to worry about numbers. He can move in powerful ways through small groups who are surrendered to him.

4. *"Yet you have kept my word"* (Revelation 3:8). In a time when there was so much pressure to believe other religions, this little group of believers held tightly to the gospel they had been taught. They didn't stray. They didn't succumb to questioning the authenticity of Jesus' life or teachings. They simply believed the Word, taught the Word, preached the Word, and lived the Word. Christ smiled at that and commended them for it.
5. *"And have not denied my name"* (Revelation 3:8). The Lord affirmed the Philadelphian Christians for believing in his deity. They believed Christ was exactly who he claimed to be. He wasn't just a teacher or prophet or healer; he was indeed the Messiah who had come to die for our sins. They remained faithful to him even under pressure.
6. *"I will make them come and fall down at your feet and acknowledge that I have loved you"* (Revelation 3:9). The remnant—or small section of Israel that was being saved—had left the synagogue at this time. Those who remained in the synagogue denied Christ and refused to believe that the Christians had God's approval. The apostle Paul tells us in Romans 9:6 that not all who are descended from Israel are really Israel. What does that mean? Throughout the Bible, we're told that Israel is God's chosen people. But Paul says that not everyone who claims to be following God is actually doing it. The true Israelite is the one who has turned to Christ for salvation and not to the synagogue laws. What about you? Spiritually speaking, are you who you claim to be?

WILL WE BE HERE OR NOT . . . ISN'T THE QUESTION

Christ says seven things to the church in Philadelphia:

1. *"I know your deeds."*
2. *"See, I have placed before you an open door that no one can shut."*
3. *"I know that you have little strength."*
4. *"Yet you have kept my word."*
5. *"And have not denied my name."*
6. *"I will make them come and fall down at your feet and acknowledge that I have loved you"* (Revelation 3:9). Christ is telling the church in Philadelphia that he will reveal to their enemies that he loves the Christians. Someday Christ will make every person in the entire world know that he dearly loves his church. Who is the church? You and me, the believers, those who have placed their trust in Christ and are living in a relationship with him. Someday the entire world will bow at Jesus' feet and confess that he truly was and is Lord. And when Jesus welcomes Christians into heaven, unbelievers will see how much he loves those who placed their faith in him.
7. *"Since you have kept my command to endure patiently, I will also keep you from the hour of trial that is going to come upon the whole world to test those who live on the earth"* (Revelation 3:10). Jesus affirms the church for patiently keeping his Word. Though there were many false religions in their city, and though they faced persecution, they endured and kept his Word alive.

Some Bible scholars think this verse is also saying that Christ will remove believers from the world just before the Great Tribulation. Other Bible scholars have a different interpretation—some think Christians will be present during part of the Great Tribulation, and others believe that Christians will experience the whole Tribulation. Each group of scholars can point to Scripture to support their view.

Instead of concerning ourselves with whether we'll be on earth during the Great Tribulation, let's pray for the Christians who are currently being persecuted, and let's make sure we stay faithful to the Lord. The apostle Paul reminds us in 1 Corinthians that God is faithful and will not let us be tempted beyond what we can handle with Christ's help. In other words, every temptation you face can be overcome in Christ's power. If Christians are on the earth during the Great Tribulation, we'll trust the Lord to strengthen us and to keep us from falling away.

BREW IT!
The real question isn't if you'll be here during the Great Tribulation. The real question is: Are you ready to meet Christ at any time—before tribulation, during tribulation, and after tribulation? Will you remain faithful to him?

POUR IT!
Drink in the flavor from the following Scriptures: 1 Corinthians 10:13; Jude 25; Revelation 3:9-10.

SAVOR IT!
Ask the Lord to give you his deep, settled peace concerning the future and the end times. Trust him.

BREW IT!

Just as wearing a team jacket proves you're part of a special group, does your lifestyle prove that you're a follower of Christ?

POUR IT!

Drink in the flavor from the following Scriptures: Luke 9:23; John 10:4; Revelation 3:11-13.

SAVOR IT!

Thank God that he's preparing your eternal home with him.

WEARING HIS NAME

Christ tells the church in Philadelphia that he'll come quickly—or suddenly (Revelation 3:11, KJV). We need to constantly be aware that he could return at any given moment, and we should live in daily expectancy. If you thought Jesus would return tomorrow, what difference would it make in your actions today? What would change?

Have you ever been part of a sports team? One of the best parts of being on a team is that you get to wear the special jacket. It's a symbol—identifying you as part of the team. It makes you feel good, special, included. Everyone who sees you wearing the team jacket knows that you're part of a specific, elite group. Christ begins wrapping up his letter to the church in Philadelphia by telling them that he'll write the name of God Almighty on the believers. In other words, he's going to put the name of his Father on your jacket! His name will be the one you wear for eternity.

Christ also says that he will write *his* new name upon us (see Revelation 3:12). In other words, there are aspects of who he is that we haven't discovered yet, because it will take all of eternity to get to know Christ. His new name is hidden right now. We won't know it until we reach heaven. And it will be our privilege to search out his character throughout eternity.

This letter to the church in Philadelphia ends the same way the other letters do—by telling those who have ears to listen to what the Holy Spirit says to these churches. Why? Because in a sense, *we* are those churches! Though these seven letters were written ages ago, the message in each one is relevant to us right now.

We, too, live in a world that's hostile to Christianity. We, too, face temptation and are up against false religions. So let's listen very carefully to what Christ says to them—to us—the church . . . his body of believers.

THINK ABOUT JESUS

Spend time today concentrating on the different names of Jesus:

Image of the invisible God
Indescribable gift
Jesus Christ our Lord
Jesus Christ our Savior
Jesus of Nazareth
Judge of the living and the dead
King of kings
King of the ages
Lamb of God
Light of life
Light of the World
Lord of glory
Lord of lords
Lord of peace
Lord of the harvest
Lord of the Sabbath
Master
Mediator of a new covenant
Merciful and faithful High Priest
Messenger of the covenant
Messiah
Morning star
Man of Sorrows
Physician
Prince of Peace
Ransom for all men
Refiner and Purifier
Resurrection and the Life
Righteous Judge
Righteous One
Rock of ages
Ruler of God's creation
Savior of the world
Shepherd and Overseer of your soul
Son of Man

BREW IT!
When Christ walked the earth, people had different ideas about who he was: teacher, prophet, good person, Savior. At one point he turned to the disciples and asked, "Who do you say that I am?" (Matthew 16:15). Have you answered that question?

POUR IT!
Drink in the flavor from the following Scriptures: Psalm 18:46; 25:5; 42:5.

SAVOR IT!
Thank the Lord for being all the things listed in today's devotional (and more).

CHRISTMAS IS JUST AROUND THE CORNER

Though you may still have the taste of turkey in your mouth from Thanksgiving, it's not too soon to think about Christmas. Before Christmas comes this year, let's take a peek at how the light of this special season can brighten our darkest days. One of the most enjoyable aspects of Christmas is the lights. We see them along neighborhood streets, in store windows, on trees. In just under one month, we'll experience the shortest day of the year—December 21—which also means it's the longest night.

Isn't it interesting that around the darkest time of the year, Christmas pierces through the darkness with light! This is when we celebrate the angels' dazzling light show in the sky. The shepherds who saw it were so amazed, they followed and found the Messiah. Light is a major theme in the Bible. The first recorded words from God Almighty are, "Let there be light!" (Genesis 1:3).

We're told in the Gospel of John that Christ came as a light to shine in our dark world. If we place our trust in him, we won't have to keep wandering in darkness. Everyone experiences some darkness; that's simply a part of life. We all have days when we just don't want to get out of bed or talk to people or face our responsibilities. But some dark days are much deeper than simply wanting to sleep a little longer or stay home for the day.

Over the next few days, let's take a peek at four kinds of dark days. We'll see how the light of the upcoming Christmas season can pierce through those dark times.

1. *We have dark days of disappointment.* In the book of Job we read that Job had hoped for happiness but instead faced trouble and darkness. Have there been times when you were expecting one thing and became disappointed when you got something else? I'm reminded of Jacob, who asked Rachel's dad, Laban, if he could marry her. Laban said they could get married after Jacob had worked for him seven years.

Jacob fulfilled his obligation. After the wedding, however, you can imagine his surprise (and disappointment) when he discovered his bride wasn't Rachel! It was her older sister, Leah. "Oh, did I forget to mention that it's customary around here for the older daughter to marry first?" asked Laban. "If you'll work seven more years for me, you can have Rachel, too."

You've probably felt deceived at times. You were promised one thing and instead got something completely different. When we're deeply disappointed, it feels as though we're walking through dark days. Good news: The light of Christ can pierce through the very darkest of days to give us hope, faith, and a renewed spirit.

BREW IT!
Will you allow God to turn your dark days into light?

POUR IT!
Drink in the flavor from the following Scriptures: Job 30:26; Psalm 27:1; John 12:46.

SAVOR IT!
Ask God to help you experience his light as the Christmas season approaches.

TURNING DARK DAYS INTO BRIGHT ONES

Can you imagine Mary's excitement when she learned that she'd be the mother of the Messiah—God's only Son? She would be the one to deliver the Savior of the world! She may have had high expectations about the birthplace and delivery. Surely she was disappointed when she learned she'd have to travel about ninety miles on a donkey during the last few days of her pregnancy, just to take part in a Roman census.

And then she had to deliver the Messiah in a cave amidst smelly animals. She had no friends or family present to help her deliver her first baby. She may have been disappointed, discouraged, and lonely. She probably felt as though she was walking through some dark days.

1. *We have dark days of disappointment.*
2. *We have dark days of distress.* Sometimes we feel overwhelmed. Our stress level rises to new heights, and we feel pressure from all sides. Undoubtedly, you've experienced days when you've felt stretched to the limit and wondered how and if you'd get it all done. King David wrote that he desperately cried for help and didn't get any (Psalm 22:1). Can you relate? Have you felt distress because it seems as though you're all alone? Remember: Christ is with you! He promised he'd never leave you, forsake you, or walk away from you. Let the light of his presence pierce through your dark days of distress.
3. *We have dark days of doubt.* You've probably experienced times when you didn't really know what was ahead. You've felt as though you were drifting, with your mind in a fog. We're told in John's Gospel that the one who walks in the dark doesn't know where he's going. Can you relate? Have you had days when you just couldn't see where you were headed? The light of Christmas—Jesus Christ himself—can illuminate your dark days of doubt.
4. *We have dark days of depression.* Research tells us that more people experience depression between Thanksgiving and Christmas than any other time of year. The prophet Jeremiah, author of Lamentations, wrote that he was depressed and thought of pain constantly. When you're depressed, you tend to think about it a lot. When you're in the middle of a dark day, all you're able to see is darkness! During days of depression you may feel as though your "get up and go" has "got up and gone."

When World War II began, Winston Churchill said, "The light has gone out in Europe." During dark days of depression, you feel as though the light has been extinguished from your life. Even David, who was known as a "man after [God's] own heart" experienced darkness, as described in Psalm 88:18.

But there's hope! Because even in the pit of depression, Christ is a light that shines brightly. His light expels the darkness!

BREW IT!
His light expels the darkness!

POUR IT!
Drink in the flavor from the following Scriptures: Lamentations 3:19-20; Psalm 88:18; John 12:35.

SAVOR IT!
Ask God to help you focus on his light instead of on the darkness around you.

BREW IT!
God is your hope . . . now
and forever!

POUR IT!
Drink in the flavor from
the following Scriptures:
2 Samuel 22:29; Jere-
miah 29:11; Psalm 23:4.

SAVOR IT!
Thank God for being willing to
strengthen you through disappointment and distress.

JESUS DISPELS THE DARKNESS

As you're reading this devotional today, you may be in one of three places: (1) You're headed into dark days, (2) you're experiencing dark days right now, or (3) you've just come out of dark days and are wondering where to turn.

How can Christ brighten your dark days?

1. *Jesus will encourage you when you're disappointed.* We're told in 2 Samuel 22 that the Lord is our light and can extinguish our darkness. When all we see is darkness, we tend to ask questions such as, "Does anyone care?" "Does anyone see me?" "Am I all alone?"

   God cares, and he sees! And he loves you enough that he sent his only Son into our sick, darkened world to be your light. This is what Christmas is all about—the light of Christ illuminating our dark, depraved world. The whole message of Christmas is God saying to his creation, "I'm with you!" Emmanuel—God is with us!

   Even in your darkest days . . . when that special relationship ended abruptly and without warning; a loved one died; you failed the exam you spent so much time preparing for; you didn't get that part-time job you'd been counting on; your parents got a divorce. In the middle of the darkness, God wants to remind you of his plan for your life. It's as if he's saying, "I dream big dreams for you, but sometimes I allow you to experience disappointment to get your attention." Let him remind you of his special purpose for you.

2. *Jesus will strengthen you when you're distressed.* Paul tells us in Philippians 4:13 that Christ will strengthen us. During days of distress, your Lord wants to infuse you with strength. Let him! Part of the Twenty-third Psalm reminds us that even when we walk through the deepest darkness—the shadow of death—we don't have to be fearful, because the Lord is with us.

There are 150 Psalms in the Bible, with one theme. Do you know what it is? *Life is tough, but God is good.* When you start thinking that life is good, but God is tough, you have the wrong perspective.

Are you allowing Christ to encourage you when you're walking through dark days ofdisappointment? Do you feel his strength when you're journeying through dark days of distress?

JESUS BRINGS CHANGE
How can Christ brighten your dark days?

1. *Jesus will encourage you when you're disappointed.*
2. *Jesus will strengthen you when you're distressed.*
3. *Jesus will guide you when you're doubtful.* He tells us that he is the Light of the World. If we follow him, we won't be stumbling around in darkness. He actually lights the path in front of us. When light illuminates our darkness, it chases doubts away.

   What are you worried about? What keeps you up at night? Let him guide you. Where will you go to find the right advice for your doubts? To his Holy Word. Jesus is the Light, and his Word is the Light. When you're experiencing dark days and battling doubts, go right to the Bible. Every situation you deal with is addressed in the Word of God. For everything you face in life, you can find direction and related principles in the Bible.

4. *Jesus will change you when you're depressed.* Christ doesn't want you to remain in a state of depression. He doesn't want you to continue living in days of darkness. When you allow him to fill you with his presence, he brings out the very best in you! Not only that, but he also helps you see the best in yourself and in others. When we allow the light of Christ to saturate our lives, the darkness disappears. Light and darkness can't coexist.

   Many people saw the star and the special lights in the sky that first Christmas. But the ones who actually chose to follow are called wise men. Will you be wise this coming Christmas? Don't settle for simply seeing the light. Experience the Light! Allow Christ to saturate, control, and energize your entire life.

BREW IT!
Let Christ extinguish the darkness of your dark days with his everlasting light.

POUR IT!
Drink in the flavor from the following Scriptures: Psalm 119:105; John 8:12; 1 John 2:8.

SAVOR IT!
Will you commit your darkness to Christ? Let him have it. Ask him to fill you completely with his light that can never be extinguished.

BREW IT!
Are you allowing Christ to be all these things in your life?

POUR IT!
Drink in the flavor from the following Scriptures:
2 Corinthians 4:6;
1 Thessalonians 5:5;
1 Peter 2:9.

SAVOR IT!
Thank Christ for who he is!

LET IT SOAK IN
Today . . . let who Jesus is totally sink into your mind, your heart, and your actions.

Son of the living God
Son of the Most High
Source of eternal salvation
Sure foundation
Teacher
The Amen
The atoning sacrifice for our sins
The Beginning and the End
The bright Morning Star
The First and the Last
The Gate
The Good Shepherd
The Living One
The Living Stone
The Lord our righteousness
The Most Holy
The One and Only
The radiance of God's glory
The rising of the sun (Dayspring)
The stone the builders rejected
The true Light
The true Vine
The Truth
The Way
The Word
True Bread from heaven
Wonderful Counselor
Word of God
Word of Life

CAN YOU SPOT THE FAKE?

Try to guess which of the following holidays in the month of December are real and which ones are fake. Write an *R* by those you think are real, and write an *F* by those you believe are fake.

____ National Grinch Day
____ National Whiner's Day
____ Cookie Cutter Week
____ Humbug Day
____ Homemade Bread Day
____ America Recycles Week
____ Sadie Hawkins Day
____ International Language Week
____ Be Kind to Your Colon Week
____ Tell Someone They're Doing a Good Job Week
____ Bathtub Party Day
____ International Shareware Day
____ No Salt Week
____ Babysitter Appreciation Day
____ Underdog Day
____ National Tie Month
____ National Resurrect Romance Week
____ National Spinal Cord Injury Awareness Month
____ National Personal Chef Days

BREW IT!
Just as there are false holidays listed here, there are also many false religions. Many claim to offer entrance to heaven, but there's actually only one way to heaven. That's through Jesus Christ, God's Son.

POUR IT!
Drink in the flavor from the following Scriptures: Psalm 25:5; Proverbs 16:13; John 14:6.

SAVOR IT!
Ask God to help you discern truth from falsehood.

Real: National Whiner's Day, Cookie Cutter Week, Humbug Day, International Language Week, Tell Someone They're Doing a Good Job Week, Bathtub Party Day, International Shareware Day, Underdog Day, National Tie Month.

BREW IT!
What God says will happen really does happen!

POUR IT!
Drink in the flavor from the following Scriptures: Isaiah 7:14; Jeremiah 31:31-34; Hosea 11:1.

SAVOR IT!
Thank God for giving you the most extravagant Christmas gift ever—his only Son, Jesus Christ.

CHRISTMAS COMES TRUE!

Prophecies concerning Christ's birth are recorded throughout the Bible. Every single one of those prophecies came true. You can count on God to keep his Word. Remember that as you begin preparing for Christmas this year. Let's take a look at just a few of those predictions about Jesus.

1. *The virgin birth.* Yes, it seemed impossible and ridiculous, yet the Old Testament prophet Isaiah predicted that the Messiah would be born of a virgin (see Isaiah 7:14). Several hundred years later, what Isaiah said actually came true (see Matthew 1:22-23).

2. *Little town of Bethlehem.* It was also predicted that the Messiah would be born in a small town called Bethlehem (see Micah 5:2). Everyone thought surely the Messiah would come from an important city and would arrive in style.

3. *Out of Egypt.* The Old Testament prophet Hosea predicted that the Messiah would come out of Egypt (see Hosea 11:1). We discover in Matthew 2:13-14 that prophecy came true when Joseph, Mary, and Jesus traveled to Egypt for safety, then later returned to Galilee.

4. *Rachel's weeping.* The Old Testament prophet Jeremiah predicted that there would be great weeping for children who were killed. Hundreds of years later, this came true when King Herod, in an attempt to murder Jesus, decided to kill every baby boy two years old and younger throughout Bethlehem and in nearby farms (see Matthew 2:16-18).

5. *He will be called a Nazarene.* That certainly didn't make sense. If the Messiah was actually born in Bethlehem and later came out of Egypt, how and why would he be called a Nazarene? In Matthew 2:19-23, we read that an angel appeared to Joseph in a dream and told him to go back to Israel because the ones who had tried to kill Jesus were now dead. Joseph and Mary returned from Egypt to Israel with Jesus. On their journey, however, they learned that the new king of Judea was Herod's son, Archelaus. In another dream, Joseph was warned not to go to Judea, so they went to Galilee and lived in Nazareth. This fulfilled the prediction that the Messiah would be a Nazarene.

6. *A New Covenant.* The prophet Jeremiah predicted that the Messiah would create a brand-new covenant for all who would come to him (see Jeremiah 31:31-34). It would no longer be necessary to sacrifice animals, and everyone who wanted forgiveness of sins could freely receive it from the Messiah.

People must have thought Jeremiah was crazy! They couldn't imagine receiving forgiveness for sins without offering a sacrifice. But with Christ's birth, life, and death, we realize that the prediction came true. We can truly celebrate Christmas this year with gratitude that Christ willingly became the sacrifice for our sins.

YOU CAN DEPEND ON GOD!

Have you ever wondered what God is really like? Yes, you've read about him in the Bible, and you may have heard a lot about him in Sunday school, Bible studies, youth group, church camp, or church. But what's he really like? Through Jesus' birth, we can make that discovery!

We can find out what God is like by taking a close look at the Christ child. First, through the birth of Jesus, we realize that God is faithful. Every single prediction concerning the Messiah and his birth came true.

We also discover that God is extremely trustworthy. He keeps his promises. He is true to his every word. Through Jesus, we see that God is a God of immeasurable love. A heavenly Father who would give his one and only Son to pay the price for the sins of all who accept him personifies love beyond description.

With the birth of Christ, we also witness the presence of God. Right here, right now, he is among us! What an honor to be able to spend Christmas—and every other day of the year—in the presence of the King of kings. God is present through his Son, Jesus.

By observing Christ's birth, we quickly learn that we serve a God who keeps his promises. This means every single thing that God said and continues to say is something you can stake your life on! You can count on him. He is faithful, dependable, and worthy of your trust.

What do you need to depend on God for this coming Christmas season? Are there some doubts you need to give him? Are you frightened about finances, relationships, or your future? This Christmas season, you can give every single one of those issues to your heavenly Father.

Do you need his direction? Want to feel his presence? Are you yearning to grow closer to him? Right now, as you approach the Christmas season, is the perfect time to depend on him for these needs.

Politicians often make promises they can't keep. Guy/girl relationships sometimes turn sour. Someone you assumed would be a friend for life suddenly backs off. It's tough to find someone truly dependable. But God wants you to know—beyond all doubt—that he is dependable. You can count on him. Everything he says he will do, he'll do!

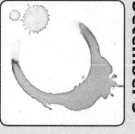

BREW IT!
God himself came to earth in the person of his Son, Jesus, to keep his promises. You can trust him.

POUR IT!
Drink in the flavor from the following Scriptures: Deuteronomy 7:9; 32:4; Psalm 25:10.

SAVOR IT!
Spend some time simply thanking God for being exactly who he says he is. Express your gratitude for being able to count on him.

BREW IT!
Whatever your need, God would love to give you a spiritual makeover this season so you can experience him in all his fullness.

POUR IT!
Drink in the flavor from the following Scriptures: Lamentations 3:23; Galatians 5:19-23.

SAVOR IT!
Ask God what he wants to do in your life this season.

A WHITE HOUSE CHRISTMAS

The White House is the most popular home in America. If you've seen the White House television specials, you have an idea of the extreme makeover it receives for the Christmas season. It's not done overnight. Almost a year of thought and planning goes into decking the halls of the White House. Nancy Clarke, the chief floral designer for the White House, and the first lady spend February, March, and April creating a theme; then they begin working out the logistics. Nancy uses a diagram to divide the White House rooms into smaller, more manageable areas before decorating begins.

A full-time crew of four, plus more than fifty volunteers, begins the process of decorating right after Thanksgiving. Each year a different theme is selected, and everything revolves around that specific theme. In 2004, an eighteen-foot noble fir stood in the middle of the Blue Room. This is where President Bush took most of his Christmas photos.

Approximately 350 of the ornaments on the Blue Room's Christmas tree were hand-painted by artists from every state in America. The volunteers who trim the tree use gold ribbon to divide it into four sections. When an ornament is hung, its location is recorded on a list. Then when artists visit Washington, they can easily find and view their work.

Onya Tolmasoff entered a contest sponsored by the Society of Decorative Painters. She paid ten dollars to purchase an ornament and was given general instructions to paint it with bright, rich colors and to use bold strokes. Her ornament was chosen by a committee from more than seven hundred entries. Onya was so honored that she flew from California just to see her ornament hung in the Blue Room.

Even more exciting than seeing an ornament you painted hanging in the White House will be seeing your name recorded in the Lamb's Book of Life at heaven's gates. But much like the White House receiving a makeover for Christmas, perhaps you're in need of a spiritual makeover this season.

Are you missing God's peace? He would love to replace your worry with his peace that passes all understanding. Are you feeling discontented? He'd love to fill you with his genuine joy.

GREATER PLANS

Ornaments get broken even at the White House. If an ornament falls to the floor, a volunteer immediately sweeps up the mess. There are always two extra bags of ornaments for each tree for situations like this. After the holidays, all the ornaments are stored in Riverdale, Maryland.

A lot goes into transforming the White House into a spectacular Christmas memory, doesn't it? It may seem incredible that plans begin a year in advance for the transformation, but there's someone who has been planning way longer than just one year for *your* transformation!

The Bible tells us in Psalm 139 that God saw you and knew you even before you were formed in your mother's womb. He's been making plans forever to grant you eternal life and to transform your sinful life into a holy life empowered by him. Do you realize that right now God is creating your eternal home in his perfect paradise in heaven? If it's hard for you to imagine all the glitz and glimmer of the beautifully decorated White House, you won't believe your eyes when you view your eternal home!

Your salvation and your heavenly home have been years in the works. God chose you not only to view this exquisite place called heaven, but to call it your forever home. Have you accepted his invitation?

Have you actually confessed that you're a sinner and asked him to forgive your sins? This Christmas, the most important thing you do won't involve expensive decorations and fancy ornaments. The most important thing you can do this Christmas season is to make sure you're right with God. If you've never asked Christ to be your personal Savior, pray the prayer found in the devotional on February 21.

BREW IT!
Make this Christmas your best ever by making sure Jesus is Lord of your life.

POUR IT!
Drink in the flavor from the following Scriptures: Psalm 100:5; 108:4; 115:1.

SAVOR IT!
Thank God for his faithfulness.

BREW IT!
Mary trusted God in spite of what others said about her.

POUR IT!
Drink in the flavor from the following Scriptures: Luke 2:19, 21, 39.

SAVOR IT!
Thank God for giving you his very Son.

MARIA
FICTION BY CHRISTINA TURNER

"I'll be back in just a second, honey," Joe said. Maria nodded. She felt sick. "It's almost over," she told herself.

Joe emerged from the truck stop, drinks in hand—a coffee to keep him awake and a 7-Up to settle her stomach. "Here, honey," he said, kissing her cheek.

"How much longer, Joe?"

Joe looked away. "A couple more hours, Maria. I'm sorry."

Maria smiled weakly. "That's okay," she whispered.

It had been a long drive, and a long nine months, for that matter. Maria remembered when she first found out that she was pregnant. God had promised to be with her, but sometimes it seemed like he was the only one.

Maria didn't know people could be so cruel. Rumors spread, people pointed and whispered, and there was nothing she could do about it. They would never believe her even if she told them what had really happened. School was impossible to deal with, so Maria quit and taught herself at home. Church was just as bad—people made their assumptions. No one could believe that Maria and Joe—such good kids from good families—would do such a thing.

But the worst was that her parents wouldn't even believe her. "After all we've done for you, Maria, you have to go and ruin your future like this!" her father exclaimed.

"But Dad, you don't understand . . ." she tried to explain.

But they refused to listen. If Maria was old enough to get pregnant, she was old enough to find somewhere else to live.

Joe sped up. Ten minutes passed, and the contractions were getting closer together. Lights from a city approached. Joe turned off. They drove through the sleepy town, but nothing seemed to be open. All they saw was an empty parking garage, so they turned in.

"Oh, Joe, this baby deserves better," Maria said.

"I know, honey, but there's nothing else. We'll just have to trust God."

They stopped the truck and spread the blanket out on the bed of the truck. "It's time, Joe," Maria said as she shrieked with pain.

"Okay, Maria, just push."

As she did, more questions raced through her panic-stricken mind. *Is it supposed to hurt this much? What if I do something wrong? What if I miscarry this child?* she thought in horror. *Oh, Lord, help. Help!*

At last she heard the baby crying and breathed a sigh of relief. As she looked at the baby, so perfect, tears filled her eyes. *Thank you, Lord!*

Joe put his arm around her as she held her child, and they prayed, "Oh, Father, we don't deserve this. You've given us so much. Thank you. Thank you for giving us your Son."

THERE'S STILL TIME!

Though Christmas is only a few weeks away, you still have time to gather your friends and family and get a special gift for people who are not as fortunate who live in a developing country. Here are a few more suggestions from the relief organization Samaritan's Purse.

- *Blankets.* A warm blanket is a blessing on a chilly night—especially for a child whose home was destroyed by war or disaster. A blanket to wrap up in provides protection from the cold and a welcome touch of comfort. For just $6, you can share a blanket with a child who needs to sleep in heavenly peace.

- *Musical toy lamb.* Ruth Bell Graham was inspired with the idea to hand out musical lambs to suffering children as part of Operation Christmas Child (a division of Samaritan's Purse). As children hug these cuddly lambs, the sweet music of "Jesus Loves Me" brings smiles to sad faces. Your gift of $4 will give a precious girl or boy a comforting reminder of the Lamb of God and his love.

- *Baby chicks.* Baby chicks are soft, cuddly, and fun to hold against your cheek. But as adorable as they are when they're little, they're even better when they grow up. Female chicks become hens that lay lots of nourishing eggs—plenty to eat with some left over to sell at the local market. Just $10 can provide a starter brood of twenty-four chicks that will grow into a fine flock of laying hens.

BREW IT!
What can you do without during the next couple of weeks (pizza, Cokes, movies) so you can give to someone less fortunate?

POUR IT!
Drink in the flavor from the following Scriptures: Matthew 5:3; Mark 12:41-44; 1 Peter 2:2.

SAVOR IT!
Ask God to give you a desire to help others this season.

- *Milk.* A cup of cold milk is as healthy as it is yummy. You can enjoy it even without knowing that it's good for your bones and teeth. The Bible tells us that "the pure milk" of God's Word is good for our souls as well. To make sure that poor children get both of these blessings, Samaritan's Purse provides milk to many orphanages, schools, and hospitals. For $3, you can provide a needy child with a week's supply of milk.

- *Dairy goat.* If you're looking for a gift that keeps on giving, a dairy goat can supply a poor family with four or more quarts of fresh milk a day. That's nearly a ton of milk, butter, and cheese each year! And a nanny goat can produce as many as three kids a year, enabling a family to start a small dairy to pay for essentials like medicine and schooling. As volunteers assist communities with the care of their flocks, they have many opportunities to talk about the Good Shepherd. Just $50 can purchase a dairy goat for a family.

BREW IT!
Would God have cast you in the Christmas scene?

POUR IT!
Drink in the flavor from the following Scriptures: Psalm 16:11; Psalm 23:4; Matthew 1:24.

SAVOR IT!
Ask God to help you develop a pure heart, a spirit of obedience, and deep faith in him as you prepare for Christmas this year.

THE CHRISTMAS CAST

Who else appears in the Christmas story? Let's take a look at the cast. The people we usually imagine surrounding the manger are Mary, Joseph, the shepherds, and the wise men. Even though our nativity scenes picture the wise men standing near baby Jesus, they weren't actually there at his birth. They traveled a long distance and didn't arrive until two or three years later.

Have you ever wondered why God chose the people he did for his "cast" on the very first Christmas? Let's take a peek at each person.

Cast of Characters

• *Mary.* She was a teenager from poor family. Why did God select her to be the mother of his only Son, when he could have chosen someone with more prestige, more prominence, more education, more wealth?

She had a pure heart. She also loved God with all her heart and desired to obey him no matter the cost. Mary listened when God spoke to her through an angel. She didn't say, "Maybe you're not familiar with the facts of life, but I'm a virgin! What you're telling me is impossible. Besides, I'm not even married. I don't want to be pregnant right now." She simply listened and believed. She asked how this would happen (see Luke 1:34), but she never doubted that God would accomplish it.

God is still looking for disciples with pure hearts who love him more than they love themselves. He has big plans for his children who will listen when he speaks and believe what he says. Will you allow God to develop these qualities in your life this Christmas season?

• *Joseph.* Perhaps God cast Joseph as Christ's earthly father because Joseph exercised extreme faith in God's plan even when it didn't make sense. The angel's message, which told him that Mary's child had been conceived through the Holy Spirit, must have seemed not only ridiculous but far-fetched and even impossible. Yet Joseph's faith remained solid. He knew he served a God of miracles. He realized the impossible was nothing at all for his God to accomplish.

Joseph easily could have broken off his engagement to Mary. The Jewish law stated that an unmarried pregnant woman could be stoned. Joseph could have put an end to something he didn't understand. But he trusted God. Even when God's plan failed to make sense, Joseph's faith remained strong.

THE REST OF THE CAST

Not only did God cast Mary and Joseph in the first Christmas scene, he also cast some other important roles. Let's take a quick peek at the others.

- *The shepherds.* These guys smelled! They hung out with dirty sheep, and they probably hadn't taken a bath in weeks. They were considered the lower class. They were social outcasts. Yet they were given an important role that first Christmas. Why? Could it have been their excitement? Our heavenly Father loves it when his children get excited about what he's doing.

  The shepherds were excited! They received the news of Jesus' birth with great joy. God knew that for the gospel to be spread, it would need to be shared with enthusiasm. The shepherds exhibited great anticipation when they learned the Messiah was near. They hurriedly set out to find him.

- *The wise men.* God knew the wise men would give their best to his Son. They couldn't make the trip quickly, but they were determined to find Jesus and give him their very best. It took them two or three years to reach Jesus. And when they saw him, they bowed in praise and worship. They brought expensive gifts and presented their very own treasures to the King of kings.

Do you give God your very best? Or have you fallen into the habit of giving him your leftovers? God gave you his very best when he sent his one and only Son to die for you. He desires that you, in turn, also give your best to him. The best of your time, your energy, and your enthusiasm.

This shouldn't be because you feel obligated. The Bible tells us that God loves a cheerful giver. You should give God your best because you love him, because you're grateful for what he's given you, and because he deserves nothing less than your best.

How can you give God your best this season? First, evaluate your life with his help. Ask him to show you areas where you're giving him second or third best. Seek his forgiveness and make the necessary changes. Next, establish some accountability with someone of the same sex whom you trust spiritually. Ask this person to meet with you on a regular basis and help you make sure you're continuing to give God your best instead of slipping back into leftovers.

BREW IT!
With God's help, live a life that would make him proud to choose you for the Christmas cast.

POUR IT!
Drink in the flavor from the following Scriptures: Psalm 143:1; Matthew 2:11; Luke 2:16-20.

SAVOR IT!
Pray for excitement in serving the Lord as you give him your very best this season.

BREW IT!
Do others see your dedication to Christ? Do you continue your journey with him even when the going gets tough?

POUR IT!
Drink in the flavor from the following Scripture: Matthew 2:1-12.

SAVOR IT!
Commit to serve the Lord with renewed dedication this year.

THE CAST'S RESPONSE TO CHRISTMAS

Now that we've taken a look at the cast and why they were chosen for the first Christmas, let's sneak a peek at how they responded to Jesus' birth. Our responses say a lot about us.

Mary. The earthly mother of Jesus responded to the first Christmas with *contemplation.* The Bible tells us she pondered a lot of things in her heart. She treasured what she had heard from the angel. She thought a lot. She reflected on and cherished all God was teaching her.

Mary had to travel about ninety miles with Joseph from Nazareth to Bethlehem so they could register for the government census. She had to be uncomfortable in those last couple of days during her pregnancy—especially riding on a donkey! But all along the way, she took mental snapshots and treasured everything in her heart. Like Mary, we need to take time to reflect quietly on what we see God doing in our lives.

Joseph. The earthly father of the Christ child responded to the first Christmas in *cooperation.* When an angel appeared to Joseph in a dream and instructed him to take Mary home as his wife, Joseph cooperated immediately. He didn't prolong his decision or procrastinate until he could figure out another plan. He simply did what God told him to do.

The Lord needs disciples who are ready and willing to follow his plan. Are you cooperative? Or do you tend to question and doubt when God's plan doesn't make sense to you? This Christmas, ask God to give you a teachable spirit. This might mean you need to be broken. Tell God you're willing to be broken and reshaped in his image so you can fully cooperate with his perfect plan.

The Shepherds. Men of this particular occupation were considered unreliable. They were social outcasts. In fact, their testimony wasn't even accepted in a court of law. Yet God chose shepherds—people others wouldn't believe—to play an important role in the first Christmas. Their response was *celebration,* They left their fields in great excitement and joy to find the Messiah. And once they found him, they celebrated! They believed. They placed their faith in him.

God wants his children to get excited about having a personal relationship with his Son. He wants us to celebrate. When you stop and consider that Christ paid the death penalty for your sins, that's worth celebrating! Get out the party hats.

The Wise Men. They so desperately desired a personal encounter with the Messiah, they were willing to make a two- or three-year journey to reach him. The wise men's response to the first Christmas was *dedication.* As soon as they saw the unusual star in the sky, they knew something significant had happened. They left in faith and followed the star that led them to Jesus. They dedicated their lives to him.

MAKE CHRISTMAS DIFFERENT THIS YEAR

Will this Christmas be different from last Christmas? Are you thinking this season will be the same ol' same ol'? Guess what? You get to choose! Christmas can be either a blessing or a burden. You can make this Christmas different from all your Christmases past simply by the way you respond to Jesus Christ. Your reaction to him can make this year fresh, different, and brand-new.

Do you realize almost everyone in the world missed the first Christmas? They didn't realize these significant events had even occurred. It's pretty hard to miss Christmas today, but did you know you can celebrate the date but still miss the real Christmas? Again, it all depends on your response to Christ this season.

Millions of people have become bored with Christmas. They say, "I've heard the Christmas story. I've hung the same ornaments for years. There's nothing different. It's all routine."

The true fulfillment of Christmas isn't found under the tree; it's found in an intimate, growing relationship with Jesus Christ. Here are four ways you can make Christmas different this year.

BREW IT!
Jesus came to be with you twenty-four hours a day, seven days a week. Now that's worth celebrating!

POUR IT!
Drink in the flavor from the following Scriptures: Psalm 23:4; 16:11; Proverbs 3:5-6.

SAVOR IT!
Tell Jesus right now that you will respond to him in obedience to make this Christmas different and better than past years.

1. Like Mary, determine to contemplate God's Word. Decide right now (before Christmas is actually here) not to get too busy with holiday activities and movies. Make specific time for his Word in your life. Think about the Christmas story. Read it in several different translations of the Bible. Turn off the TV and reflect on God's story.
2. Like Joseph, determine to cooperate with God's will. Even if his will doesn't make sense to you, decide right now that you'll live in total obedience to him. Before you even hear God speak to you, decide ahead of time that your answer is "Yes, Lord!"
3. Like the shepherds, determine to celebrate God's presence. Be excited about all he's doing in your life, and don't keep it a secret. Share with your friends what he's teaching you.
4. Like the wise men, determine to dedicate your best to God. If this doesn't include the spiritual dimensions of your life, you're not giving him your best. So think finances, relationships, and your spiritual commitment level.

BREW IT!
Make this Christmas your very best by giving these special gifts to your heavenly Father.

POUR IT!
Drink in the flavor from the following Scriptures: Psalm 36:5; 40:10; 57:3.

SAVOR IT!
Ask God to help you truly adore and worship him this season. Then watch your life take new direction.

YOUR CHRISTMAS GIFTS TO JESUS

You can actually give Christ some things this Christmas. How do you shop for the King of kings and Lord of lords? What does the creator of the universe want for Christmas?

1. *You can give him your time.* Instead of rushing through your week and waiting until Sunday to spend time with your heavenly Father, determine to spend quantity and quality time with Christ each day throughout the week. Strive to "pray without ceasing" (1 Thessalonians 5:16, NKJV). In other words, place yourself in a consistent attitude of prayer. Enjoy your time together. Take advantage of the fact that you get to meet with the God of the universe every single day!

2. *You can give him your treasures.* Instead of just contributing something in your church's offering plate from time to time, decide to give out of the depths of your heart. Commit to giving at least a 10 percent tithe of everything you earn. Even if all you earn comes from babysitting or a paper route, at least 10 percent is due him. He actually owns everything you have, but all he asks for is 10 percent. He deserves your very best. Give cheerfully from your heart.

3. *You can give him your talents.* Are you using your unique abilities to make yourself feel good, or will you use them to bring glory to the giver? Once you give God your time, treasures, and talents, your life will never be the same.

When the wise men left Jesus, God warned them to return home another way. Once you've truly been with Jesus—in genuine worship and adoration—your life takes a new direction!

HAPPY BIRTHDAY, JESUS!

The red-and-white-striped candy cane we've all grown to love has great meaning behind it. According to tradition, a choirmaster in 1670 was frustrated by fidgety kids at the living Nativity. He gave the children white sugar-candy sticks to keep them quiet. The candies were curved to look like shepherds' staffs in honor of the first Christmas.

Some people find additional meaning in the candy cane. They say the three small stripes represent the Father, the Son, and the Holy Spirit. The large red stripe is for the life of Christ that he willingly gave up for us. The candies are a double gift. They are sweet, sugary treats, and they are also symbols of Christmas. Think about their meaning as you enjoy candy canes this season.

While it's fun to think about Christmas favorites, strive to make Christ's birth your *very* favorite part of Christmas. Have you ever considered having a birthday party for Jesus? Several days before Christmas (like now!) would be good timing.

Invite your friends and ask them all to bring canned food and gifts that you can give to a homeless shelter or to a needy family in your neighborhood. Bake a birthday cake and take it to the shelter or the family as well. Decorate it with "Happy Birthday, Jesus," and when you present it, make sure you explain the reason for the season.

At your party, before you deliver the gifts and cake, celebrate Jesus' birthday with prayer and a special gift exchange. But instead of giving material presents to one another, exchange Scripture verses instead. Choose a different verse for each person; pick verses that you feel are especially appropriate to each individual at your party.

BREW IT!
Have fun this Christmas, but always keep the real reason for the season in mind. Determine to exalt the Lord this Christmas.

POUR IT!
Drink in the flavor from the following Scriptures: Exodus 15:2; 1 Chronicles 29:12; Psalm 30:1.

SAVOR IT!
Ask God to help you create some brand-new spiritual traditions this Christmas as you celebrate his Son's birthday.

CHRISTMAS: IT'S NOT ABOUT US

There's a story about two men, Frank and Thom, who decided to go sailing just a few days before Christmas. The plan was that they'd go on a little sailing trip while their wives went Christmas shopping. Unfortunately, a violent storm attacked their boat at sea. The mighty waves rocked the little sailboat back and forth across the water.

Finally, Frank and Thom were forced upon the shore of a small island. As they dragged themselves out of the boat and onto the shore, they suddenly realized they were under attack from the island's hostile natives. They dodged poisonous darts and desperately tried to push their sailboat back into the sea. As they stood waist-deep in freezing water, the storm still raging, Thom said to Frank, "This trip hasn't exactly gone the way we planned it, but it sure beats Christmas shopping, doesn't it?"

It's easy to get too busy this time of year and fall into the trap of thinking only of ourselves. But Christmas isn't about us. It's not about focusing on what we want to do or receive. It's about putting others first—especially Jesus Christ.

Four-year-old Chelsea had finished unwrapping all her presents when her mom asked, "Did you get everything you wanted for Christmas?"

Chelsea thought for a moment and finally answered. "No," she said. "But that's okay. It's not *my* birthday."

That little four-year-old was certainly on the right track, wasn't she? She may not have fully understood the meaning of Christmas, but she *did* know it was about something or someone much bigger than her. She realized that all the decorations, food, gifts, and glitz weren't because of her.

A pastor on the West Coast placed a sign in front of his church during the Christmas season that read, "Jesus is the reason for the season." He received a complaint from someone in the community who was offended by the message of the sign. She said, "I don't think the church should try to drag religion into every holiday."

Non-Christians may not understand the true meaning of Christmas, but as God's disciples, we not only understand, but we celebrate in gratitude to our King of kings. This season, try to think of ways you can show others that Christmas isn't about us; it's about Christ. It's okay to decorate and make cookies and enjoy shopping, but let everything you do revolve around giving glory to the Lord.

CAN YOU BELIEVE THEY ACTUALLY SAID THIS?

Check out the following actual quotes from well-known personalities:

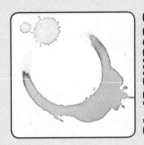

- "I've got a talent to act. No matter what any newspaper says about me, I am one of the most sensitive human beings on earth, and I know it." —Jean-Claude van Damme
- "I mean, it's unheard of for somebody to hit 70 home runs, so I'm like in awe of myself right now." —St. Louis Cardinals slugger Mark McGwire after finishing the baseball season with a two-homer day, giving him a record 70 for the year
- "Filipinos want beauty. I have to look beautiful so that the poor Filipinos will have a star to look at from their slums." —Imelda Marcos
- "I'm not conceited. Conceit is a fault, and I have no faults." —David Lee Roth
- "I'm not an egomaniac like a lot of people say. But I am the world's best dancer, that's for sure." —Michael Flatley
- "I never know how much of what I say is true." —Bette Midler
- "I do not like broccoli, and I haven't liked it since I was a little kid, and my mother made me eat it. Now I'm President of the United States and I'm not going to eat any more broccoli." —George Bush
- "When I sing, people shut up." —Barbra Streisand

The Bible tells us that someday we'll be asked to give an account of the words we used during our lifetime. That means we should be extremely selective when choosing our words. The book of James warns us against using our tongue carelessly. People can steer a giant ship with a small rudder and start a huge forest fire with a small spark, James writes, but no one has ever been able to tame the tongue.

When we don't think before we speak, our words can be harmful to those around us. We can break hearts, poison reputations, and give Christianity a bad name simply by the words we choose to use. This Christmas season, determine to use your words to affirm and encourage your friends and family. Let your speech be a wonderful gift to others. Use your words in a positive way to make a genuine difference in the lives of those around you.

BREW IT!
Think about the words you used today. Did they affirm others or hurt them? It's your choice to make a positive difference or a negative one. Choose the high road.

POUR IT!
Drink in the flavor from the following Scriptures: Proverbs 15:1; Romans 3:19; 14:12.

SAVOR IT!
Commit your speech to Jesus. Ask him to be in charge of your conversations.

BREW IT!
What would happen if you truly united in prayer with your friends, your family, and your youth group?

POUR IT!
Drink in the flavor from the following Scriptures: Acts 4:24; 19:8-12.

SAVOR IT!
Ask God to lead you out of Smallville forever.

LEAVING SMALLVILLE

On October 26, we took a peek at Abraham and Sarah. When they realized God's dreams for them were bigger than their own, they left their small ways of thinking and followed him in faith on a journey with an unknown destination. In a sense, they left Smallville for God's greater plan.

The apostle Paul also left Smallville. It happened like this: He was preaching in the city of Ephesus, but some people with small-minded ideas had crept into the city. Paul preached boldly in the synagogue each Sabbath day for three months. He explained the gospel in detail, and many people confessed their sins and accepted Christ as their personal Savior.

But some people from Smallville rejected Paul's message, and they even spoke against him. So the apostle Paul left and refused to preach to them again.

Hey, God will talk until he's blue in the face. He'll do whatever it takes to get your attention, but he won't force himself on you. So if you harden your heart and simply refuse to obey, there *will* come a time when he may leave you in Smallville. He may move his messengers elsewhere to deliver the gospel to those whose hearts are open.

Do you know what Paul did next? He left that area and began meeting instead at the lecture hall of a guy named Tyrannus. And he didn't limit his preaching to just the Sabbath. He preached every single day. Talk about revival! It was happening, and this went on for the next two years. God definitely blessed these services. It wasn't Smallville anymore.

Sometimes it's necessary to separate ourselves from unbelievers. Yes, God tells us to preach the gospel, and he wants us to share our faith with those around us. But if these people continue to live in Smallville (if they refuse to listen, begin speaking against you, or harden their hearts to the gospel), it may be time to turn your attention to those who *are* receptive to salvation. Jesus told his disciples if they entered a town that wasn't receptive to the gospel, they should shake the dust off their sandals and leave.

As Paul continued to lead a revival, God blessed him with special power, and he did amazing miracles. When Paul's clothing touched sick people, they were healed! And people testified about what God was doing in their lives. They united in prayer with one another. This is true revival. This is refusing to keep God in a box. This is refusing to live in Smallville.

Smallville is for small-minded people who refuse the gospel, have their own way of doing things, and fail to believe that God wants to do big and exciting things in their lives.

TRUE REVIVAL

The early Christians in Jerusalem often prayed together and united as a community. We're told in Acts 4:31 that after one prayer, the building where they were meeting shook! They were then filled with the Holy Spirit and they, too, preached boldly throughout their city.

Spectacular? Yes! The building where they were meeting shook. Wow! How would you react if you went to youth group this week, prayed, and your church started shaking? As exciting as that is, we can't focus on the spectacular. If we're looking for big, exciting signs that God is near, we're concentrating on the wrong thing. Our focus has to be on total obedience. God will do something spectacular if he chooses, but he may not. If you don't see something huge and dynamic, don't interpret it as a sign that God is not present. He often works in quiet, still ways in a believer's heart.

While all this exciting stuff was happening with the building shaking, take a look at what was quietly going on behind the scenes. We're told in Acts 4:32-35 that the Christians were of one heart and mind. They shared their material possessions with those in need. They had warm fellowship. They made sure no one in the church felt excluded. And there wasn't any poverty in this particular church, because the Christians who had extra land or houses sold them and gave the money to the believers in need.

Amazing, isn't it? We tend to want to see the spectacular. We yearn to watch a building shake, but we often don't discipline ourselves to the quiet, consistent, behind-the-scenes effort that's necessary for God to work in and through our lives.

BREW IT!
Want to experience true revival? Start praying for it!

POUR IT!
Drink in the flavor from the following Scriptures: Matthew 7:7; Acts 4:31-35.

SAVOR IT!
Ask the Lord to teach you to pray in his name—as he would pray.

We serve a God of miracles, and he wants to do miracles in our lives, such as empowering us to lead others to him. The Bible tells us that if we ask in his name, it will be given to us. But we have to remember that asking "in his name" means praying *as Jesus would pray.* It's not a ticket for free stuff.

Let's say your mom allows you to use her charge card to buy new clothes for a Christmas party. You shop in all your favorite stores and finally discover exactly what you want. Because you're signing your mom's name on the credit slip, you're probably careful to purchase something that she agrees with. You're buying in her name. When you pray in Jesus' name, you're praying as you truly believe he would pray to the Father.

GETTING READY FOR A MIRACLE

God did powerful miracles through Paul's ministry in Tyrannus's lecture hall. He also worked through the believers in Jerusalem. God wants to do miracles in our lives. How can we prepare for him to work in us? Let's get ready for a miracle!

1. *Get out of Smallville!* If you're doubting, confess that to God. Ask him to deepen your faith. Believe God and believe in his Holy Word.

2. *Admit your need.* God knows what you need, because he knows everything. But he still wants you to admit it to him. Remember the story of the blind man in the book of Mark? When Jesus asked what he wanted, the blind man unashamedly responded, "I'm blind! I want to see" (see Mark 10:51). He freely admitted his need to the Lord.

   We need to do that too. But we hesitate, don't we? Why? He already knows! He's not going to respond by wringing his hands and saying, "Oh, no! I hadn't counted on this! Now what?"

3. *Accept God's logic.* What God says and what he wants to do in your life may not make sense to you. In John's Gospel, we read an account of Jesus healing another blind man. The Lord's response here surely didn't seem logical. Jesus spat on the ground and made mud. Then he spread the mud on the man's eyes and told him to wash it off in the pool of Siloam. What kind of remedy is that for blindness? But God's logic rarely makes sense to humans: The last will be first; the first will be last; if you want to be great, be willing to serve; gain the whole world, lose it all; lose it all, you get everything; give away, and you'll get back.

4. *Obey him!* The mark of a mature Christian isn't understanding God's ways, it's accepting without understanding! The blind man did what Jesus told him to do, and he went where Jesus sent him. The result? He came back with 20/20 vision!

5. *Refuse to move back to Smallville!* Tell God you're finished putting him in a box. Be willing to dream big and trust him for all he wants to do in and through your life. Tell God you trust him even though you don't fully understand.

BREW IT!
Experiencing revival and miracles is not about seeking the spectacular. It is about total obedience.

POUR IT!
Drink in the flavor from the following Scriptures: Mark 10:46-52; John 9:1-11.

SAVOR IT!
Ask the Lord to prepare you for a miracle. What obstacles does he want to remove from your life? Are there specific things you need to give him? Tell him you're moving out of Smallville.

TURKEY, HAM, AND CHICKEN

With less than a week left before Christmas, many families will start grocery shopping to prepare for a big Christmas dinner. The most common foods served for Christmas dinner are turkey, ham, and chicken. Let's take a quick peek at some facts behind those top three choices.

- Turkeys originated in North and Central America, and evidence shows that they've been around for more than 10 million years.
- Ham from the left leg of a pig is more tender than the right leg. Here's why: A pig scratches himself with his right leg, which means he uses those muscles more often, so the meat will be tougher.
- The greatest number of yolks ever found in one chicken egg is nine.
- Domesticated turkeys (those that are farm raised) can't fly. Wild turkeys can fly for short distances at up to fifty-five miles per hour. Wild turkeys are also fast on the ground, running at speeds of up to twenty-five miles per hour.
- Chicago artist Dwight Kalb made a statue of Madonna from 180 pounds of ham.
- The heaviest turkey ever raised weighed in at eighty-six pounds—about the size of a large German shepherd.
- The Hormel Company in Austin, Minnesota, sold the first canned ham in 1926.
- A chicken will lay bigger eggs if you change the lighting in such a way as to make her think a day is twenty-eight hours long.
- Mature turkeys have approximately 3,500 feathers.
- Ninety percent of American households eat turkey on Thanksgiving Day. Only 50 percent eat turkey on Christmas.

BREW IT!
Determine to live a life above reproach. Let your actions and your lifestyle reflect the Lord Jesus.

POUR IT!
Drink in the flavor from the following Scriptures: Psalm 17:3; 91:1; Daniel 1:8.

SAVOR IT!
Ask God to shine through your actions and your reactions.

As interesting as that trivia may be, even more interesting would be trivia about you! Sure, your close friends and your family know all kinds of things about you, but what if your trivia facts were public knowledge? What if someone could enter your name on a search engine on the Internet and immediately receive all kinds of trivia about your personality? What would we read?

- Prone to outbursts of anger on the basketball court when fouled.
- Can run really fast—especially when discovered guilty.
- Very tender heart.
- Tame and approachable—especially to those who don't have many friends.
- Willing to sacrifice selfish desires for the needs of others.
- Stubborn and a little too tough.
- Often seen hanging out at church or youth group.
- Reads Bible often.

What kind of trivia are people passing around concerning you?

BREW IT!
Genuine Christ-given love
never gives up.

POUR IT!
Drink in the flavor from
the following Scriptures:
Psalm 130:7; 138:8;
1 Corinthians 13:6-7.

SAVOR IT!
Ask God to help you believe
the best of people.

MY FIANCÉE'S HAVING SOMEONE ELSE'S BABY (PART 1)

FICTION BY GREG ASIMAKOUPOULOS

Only a few weeks ago everything seemed perfect. I had just graduated from school with honors. My girlfriend and I got engaged the same day my father made me a full partner in his construction business! I was so excited—and definitely in love. Life seemed complete. Even my faith was at an all-time high.

Now I feel as if my life is ending. What seemed like the ideal dream has become an unending nightmare. It all started when my fiancée met me after work one Friday. She looked as if something was bothering her, but I couldn't get her to talk about it. My imagination was running wild. *Didn't she love me anymore? Did she want to call off the wedding? Did she have cancer? Was she dying? Had her father abused her?*

We went to Baskin-Robbins for dessert. Finally she whispered the words I hadn't dared to think: "I'm pregnant." Then she burst into tears.

I was stunned. "You? Pregnant? But we haven't even—"

A wave of nausea hit me as I realized the horrible truth. Because it wasn't me, it had to be someone else. "Who is he?" I forced myself to ask. She looked down.

"You wouldn't understand. I just want you to know I love you, and I still want to be your wife."

"If you loved me, you wouldn't be in the condition you're in," I snapped. But I knew I still loved her with all my heart and that was why I hurt so much.

I was too shocked to say anything the rest of the evening. Although I've never been very emotional, I cried myself to sleep. I woke up the next morning angry and full of questions. *How could she do this to me? Hadn't we promised to save ourselves for each other? Didn't she believe in the standard God has set for relationships? Was she thumbing her nose at our faith?*

:::

We'll continue the story tomorrow, but let's chat for a few seconds. How would you feel if someone you loved and trusted shared such shocking news with you? How would you respond? Would your trust in that person be destroyed, or would you somehow be able to continue believing in him or her?

MY FIANCÉE'S HAVING SOMEONE ELSE'S BABY (PART 2)

FICTION BY GREG ASIMAKOUPOULOS

"I've made arrangements to leave town for a while," she said a couple of days later as I was closing shop. "I think it's best for you and me and our families. I'll be staying at my cousin's place upstate." I must have been frowning, because she added, "Don't worry, my love. I'll be in good hands." She handed me a piece of paper with the phone number where I could reach her. Then she turned and left.

What should I do now? I loved her so much, despite my anger. Yet my trust in her had been destroyed. Still, the thought of walking away from the girl of my dreams left me more confused. The shame and embarrassment of being pregnant and unmarried in our small town would be unbearable for her. She'd be the target of endless harassment. On the other hand, if I stood by her and pretended the child was mine, it would destroy my reputation, which was something I didn't think I could risk losing to cover her selfish mistake.

My gut feeling was to break off the engagement and try to forget what had happened, but I cared too much for her to make an ugly scene. Maybe I could tell our friends we'd called off the wedding—that it was my idea to break up and that she had to get out of town to escape the pain of the decision. I want to do what's right. *Should I stay with her regardless of what others think? Or should I quietly break off the engagement and just go on with my life?*

(For the rest of the story, read Matthew 1:20-25.)

BREW IT!
Spend some time thinking about what Mary and Joseph experienced to be obedient to God.

POUR IT!
Drink in the flavor from the following Scriptures: Luke 1:46-50; 2:6-20.

SAVOR IT!
Thank God for loving you so much that he provided a way for you to spend eternity with him through his Son, Jesus.

BREW IT!
Strive to make your Christmas truly revolve around Christ this year. Let all you do be in honor of him.

POUR IT!
Drink in the flavor from the following Scriptures: Psalm 34:3; 99:5-9; 118:28.

SAVOR IT!
Thank God for all he's taught you during the past year.

MY CHRISTMAS LETTER TO JESUS
Highlights of my life this past year . . .

- Passed algebra, but barely. I think Dr. Smith has it in for me. He keeps talking about X equaling something else, and I don't think he gets it that X is totally unimportant. After all, it's almost at the end of the alphabet. It's like Dr. Smith is totally oblivious to the other letters. Once I substituted L for X (because hey, everyone adores Larry the Cucumber from Veggie Tales), and he marked it as wrong and suggested I get a tutor. Gimme a break!

- I realized the bucket hat fad is over. With that knowledge, I tossed my fifteen-dollar khaki-colored two-year-old head-friend in the trash. A friend said I should have taken it to Goodwill. But if bucket hats aren't in anymore, why would we want to see anyone wear them? I don't get it.

- Got more involved at church. Joined a small group. Started reading the Bible every day and really enjoy it.

- Tried a new shade of hair dye. Now I know why it's called dye—'cause after you put it on your hair, that's what you want to do—die! What was supposed to be Beautiful Brown Blessing came out like burnt fudge. I took a pic and sent it to Guinness World Records, positive no one's hair could have ever looked as pathetic as mine. They responded that I'd have to get a lot more creative—or desperate—to set a world record with my hair. Who knew people have had mice breeding in their hair?

- Found out that you, Jesus, want to be much more than my best friend. More than someone I rush to when I forget to study for my history test. More than someone who catches my tears when nothing goes my way. I learned you want to be my Savior, my God, my energizer, my reason for living, and my empowerment to live a holy life.

Merry Christmas, Jesus! Please help me demonstrate my love for you with my lifestyle.

AN INVITATION FROM THE KING

You are cordially invited to . . .
celebrate Christmas forever!

GUEST OF HONOR
Jesus Christ

DATE
December 25

TIME
Now. And please don't be late,
or you'll miss out on all the fun.

PLACE
In your heart. Jesus will meet you there.
You'll hear him knock.

ATTIRE
Come as you are. Grubbies are okay because
he'll be washing your clothes anyway. He said
something about new white robes and crowns
for everyone who stays till the end.

TICKETS
Admission is free. He's already paid for everyone. He
says you wouldn't have been able to afford it—it cost
him everything he had!

REFRESHMENTS
Bread and a way-cool drink he calls "living water."
This will be followed by a supper that
promises to be out of this world.

BREW IT!
The only way to truly celebrate Christ's birth is to be
a part of his family. If you've
never made that commit-
ment, consider praying
the prayer given on
December 25.

POUR IT!
Drink in the flavor from
the following Scriptures:
Exodus 15:2; 2 Samuel 22:3-7;
1 Chronicles 16:23.

SAVOR IT!
Thank God for making it possible for you to experience
eternal life.

GIFT SUGGESTIONS
Your heart. He already has everything else.
(He's very generous in return; just wait till you see what he has for you!)

ENTERTAINMENT
Joy, peace, truth, light, life, love, real happiness, communion with God, forgiveness,
miracles, healing, power, eternity in paradise, and much more.

RSVP
Very important! He must know in advance so he can reserve a spot
for you at the table. Also, he's keeping a list of his friends for future reference.
He calls it the Lamb's Book of Life.

BREW IT!
If you haven't responded to God's invitation to join his family, right now would be a great time to do it!

POUR IT!
Drink in the flavor from the following Scriptures: John 1:12; Romans 8:17; Galatians 3:29.

SAVOR IT!
If you'd like to join God's family, pray the prayer given on December 25.

CHRISTMAS CARD FROM GOD

Hi, Princess! (If you're a guy, you have permission to grab a pen. Scratch through princess every time it appears and replace with prince.)

You are my Princess. You're probably thinking, Wow! I've never gotten a Christmas card from the King before. While this is the first Christmas card I've sent you through a devotional book, I actually sent you another one—a much more important one—a couple of thousand years ago.

I sent you my very own Son. He left the royalty of my perfect Kingdom and arrived in a dirt-filled, musty cave filled with animals and dung and cobwebs and mice. From the moment his tiny lungs delivered his first cry to the cry he delivered from the cross, he has been furiously, intently, and passionately in love with you.

He's working on your eternal home right now—personalizing it just for you. We can't wait to welcome you with open arms into the Kingdom.

Have you responded to our invitation yet? Merry Christmas, Princess!

GOD'S CHRISTMAS GIFT

Wow, God!

I never thought of Jesus Christ as an actual Christmas card. This is really cool—getting a card from you in human form. I want to accept your invitation to celebrate Christmas forever. I want my name recorded in your Lamb's Book of Life.

I realize your gift of eternal life is free . . . yet I also know that grace isn't cheap. To live with you forever will cost me everything. I'm ready to make that commitment now.

Will you forgive me for being so selfish? I confess I'm a sinner, and I'm so sorry I've broken your heart. From this point on, I want to live for you.

I give you my life and every detail in my life. I give you my will, my future, my relationships, my free time, my entertainment, my talents, my desires. Thank you for this incredible gift of forgiveness and grace. Thanks for loving me more than I can comprehend.

Help me to fall in love with you more and more every day of my life. And empower me to live fully, completely, and wholly for you.

Merry Christmas, Jesus!

BREW IT!
What God can do with a life that's committed 100 percent to him is beyond words!

POUR IT!
Drink in the flavor from the following Scriptures: Psalm 145:1; Isaiah 24:15; 25:1.

SAVOR IT!
Tell God you're excited about your future with him.

BREW IT!
Are you spiritually hot, cold, or lukewarm?

POUR IT!
Drink in the flavor from the following Scriptures: Matthew 7:5; 22:37-38; Revelation 3:14-16.

SAVOR IT!
Ask God to help you serve him with great fervor.

THE LAST LETTER

Throughout this devotional book, we've taken a glance at the seven letters the apostle John sent to the churches in Asia Minor (now known as Turkey). These letters were dictated to him by the Lord when John was exiled on the rocky, barren island of Patmos. It was there that John received the revelation of the glorified Christ and wrote the book of Revelation—the last book of the Bible.

For the next few days, we'll take a peek at John's last letter, the one he wrote to the church in Laodicea. (If you'd like to refresh your memory on the first few letters, flip back to April 28–30 and July 17–23.)

Some Bible scholars refer to Laodicea as "the city of compromise." It contained great wealth and commerce, and it was a center of Greek culture. It was also a place of science and literature. The Laodiceans boasted about their excellent medical school. Jupiter—or Zeus—was the object of worship in Laodicea.

In his letter to the Laodiceans, Christ identifies himself as the "Amen." This is the only place in the Bible where *Amen* is used as a proper name. He goes on to describe himself as the only faithful and true witness. In other words, Jesus alone is the one who will reveal all and tell all.

Most of the letters to the seven churches contain both affirmations and condemnations (although we noted that Christ had only encouragement for the churches at Smyrna and Philadelphia). But Christ has no words of affirmation for the church in Laodicea. Everything he says to them is condemning.

Do you wonder what God will say to you someday as you stand before his throne? Determine now to live a life that's pleasing to your heavenly Father.

Jesus told the Laodiceans they were being lukewarm, and they understood exactly what he meant. As a matter of fact, they had been drinking lukewarm water for years. The Phrygian mountains near Laodicea are extremely high. Even in June, there's often still an abundance of snow on their peaks. The Laodiceans built an aqueduct to bring that ice-cold water down from the mountains. But by the time it reached Laodicea, it was lukewarm.

Another water source was steaming hot springs in the valley where the Lycus River meets the Maeander River. But when this water was routed up to Laodicea, it was no longer hot; it had become lukewarm. So when Jesus told the Laodiceans they were neither hot nor cold but merely lukewarm, they knew exactly what he was talking about.

Churches that have departed from genuine faith in God and his Word can quickly go from hot to lukewarm. They may not be cold yet, but they're right in the middle. This is a dangerous place to be in your relationship with Christ. It can easily lead to hypocrisy and even a falling away from the Lord.

IT'S NOT ABOUT MONEY

Laodicea was a rich city full of material goods. The citizens were wealthy and in need of nothing. They believed that money was the answer to everything. Does that sound familiar? Do you tend to think that most of your problems would be solved if you could just get your hands on a few hundred dollars?

The Christians in Laodicea thought they were rich, but the Lord told them they were wretched, miserable, poor, blind, and naked. This church was worse off than the other six churches that received letters, because it was spiritually poverty stricken. There was no evidence of God's grace, evangelism, or growth in the church. And yet the people themselves failed to notice!

We can become so comfortable in our surroundings that we assume we're okay with God when we've actually fallen asleep spiritually. If you're spiritually lukewarm, you're sleeping through your relationship with Christ. Allow the Holy Spirit to wake you up through God's Word and your prayer life.

Christ told the Christians in this church to anoint their eyes with salve so they could see again. They were spiritually blind, but they weren't incurable. The salve refers to the Holy Spirit, who opens the eyes of Christians and helps us recognize where we are spiritually. Jesus then told the Laodiceans to be zealous, or earnest. In other words, he wanted them to be hot, to get on fire spiritually.

This is exactly what God desires for you as well. He doesn't want you to remain in a lukewarm state, and he doesn't want you to abandon the faith and grow cold. He wants you to be zealous—spiritually on fire for him. He'd love you to be enthused, vibrant, and living out your faith day to day.

Because of the culture we live in, we tend to think we can fix everything with money. The Laodiceans couldn't do it, and neither can we. When we stop and realize that someday nothing else will matter except where we stand with Christ, it puts a proper perspective on money, doesn't it? Think about it: Someday, when the earth has decayed and you're standing in front of Christ, will it matter how much you had in the bank? Do you think he'll be impressed with the fact that you had a plasma TV? No. The only thing that really counts is an in-depth, growing relationship with him.

BREW IT!
Have you fallen asleep spiritually without realizing it?

POUR IT!
Drink in the flavor from the following Scriptures: Psalm 23:3; Hebrews 12:13; Revelation 3:17-19.

SAVOR IT!
Ask the Lord to use his Holy Spirit to wake you up spiritually and to open your eyes to all that he wants to bring to your attention.

BREW IT!
Have you answered the Lord's knock? Or, like the church in Laodicea, have you hardened your heart and ears to his knock?

POUR IT!
Drink in the flavor from the following Scriptures: Deuteronomy 11:18; 1 Kings 8:39; Revelation 3:20.

SAVOR IT!
Invite Christ's involvement in every single area of your life. Joyfully invite him to make your heart his home.

KNOCK, KNOCK

You probably laughed at lots of knock-knock jokes when you were a child. Remember how fun it was to try to figure out the answer to "Who's there?" before the punch line hit? Well, Jesus himself has a knock-knock for you, but it's no joke. As the apostle John wraps up his final letter to the church in Laodicea, Jesus tells the believers that he's standing at the door and knocking. While we tend to think of this verse in evangelistic terms (Christ knocking at the door of the sinner's heart and waiting to be invited inside), it was actually written to the *church.*

Isn't it interesting that Christ would say he's on the *outside* of their hearts wanting to come *inside*? We tend to assume those in the church are Christians. But it's possible to go to church all our lives and either never hear a sermon on repentance or never listen when repentance is preached. You see, Jesus desperately wants to live inside your heart, and he'll move heaven and earth to get your attention. But he will *not* force his way into your life. He won't crash down the door. He waits for you to open it, and when you do, he comes inside and you have fellowship with him and with God Almighty.

He tells us we'll have supper with him and he'll have supper with us. In other words, when we have a genuine relationship with him, we're able to come to his table. A lot can happen around the dinner table! And a lot happens at the Lord's table. When we approach, we're extremely aware of our past sins and ashamed of mistakes we've made. But we're also incredibly grateful for the fact that God has chosen to forgive and forget! We're in awe that he would choose to pay such a high price through the death of his Son simply to save us, to have supper with us, and to spend eternity with us. God is totally in love with you!

GOT EARS?

The apostle John concludes Christ's letter to the church in Laodicea by reminding the Christians that God promises we will sit with him on his throne if we stay faithful to him. In other words, keep your eyes fixed on the prize. And as Christians, we're in line for the ultimate prize: eternity with God Almighty! Can you imagine sitting with Christ in heaven forever? It's as if Jesus is saying that if we'll open our hearts to him, he'll open his Kingdom to us.

Deep down, that's exactly what you want. You want to know beyond a doubt that you'll spend eternity in God's perfect paradise. You want to be certain that your sins have been forgiven and there's no record of your guilt. Almighty God is big enough to give you the assurance that you'll go to heaven, and he's also faithful enough to wipe your slate completely blank and hold no record of your sins.

That's what God will do. Your responsibility is to confess your sin, accept Christ as your Lord, live in obedience to him, and remain faithful—no matter what the cost. If you do that, and the Holy Spirit can empower you to make this possible, you'll be considered an overcomer. Jesus will welcome you into his paradise to sit with him on his throne throughout eternity.

So be faithful. Stay true. Keep your eyes fixed not on what's happening around you, but on Christ himself. Jesus understands that you're going through troubled times. He knows about pressure and intimidation and insecurity. He's not oblivious to the daily issues you struggle with. But he wants to equip you with the power to overcome!

Jesus advises all who have ears to listen.

Got ears? Then listen to his message.

Who's speaking? The Holy Spirit.

To whom is he speaking? The church.

Who's the church? You are. I am. The church is the body of Christ, the believers who trust in him and live in obedience to him.

BREW IT!
Are you focused on Christ and the prize of heaven? Or do you tend to become wrapped up in what's happening around you?

OUR IT!
Drink in the flavor from the following Scriptures: Joshua 22:5; John 5:24; Revelation 3:21.

SAVOR IT!
Ask God to give you ears that are attuned to his Spirit.

BREW IT!
What place does God really have in your life?

POUR IT!
Drink in the flavor from the following Scriptures:Leviticus 19:2; Joshua 24:14; Job 28:28.

SAVOR IT!
Tell God you are giving him ultimate control and authority over your entire life.

MORE THAN A MASCOT

Do you sing your school's fight song or spirit song as you cheer on your team? Your school may even have a mascot—someone in a costume to represent the team—or a specific symbol that represents your athletes. Perhaps you wear sweatshirts with your mascot emblazoned on the front or you sell bumper stickers advertising your mascot to the community. The mascot is an important part of school spirit, but it's merely representative of something greater—the team itself.

To the church in Laodicea, Christ had pretty much been reduced to simply being their mascot. These people were happy to attend church each week, talk about their mascot, sing about their mascot, and brag about their mascot, but they failed to realized that Jesus is no mascot! He's to be our Master!

Jesus isn't simply representative of a holy life. Jesus *is* holiness. He doesn't want to be reduced to an object hanging from the mirror in our car, plastered on a bumper sticker, or worn on a shirt. He wants to be Lord of our lives. That's what he was asking of the Laodiceans, and that's what he's asking of you.

A human king may be content ruling just one country, but God isn't a human king. Because he created the entire world, he deserves to rule the entire world. And he doesn't want to settle for less in your life, either. He won't settle for being Lord of your relationships but not your finances. If you're going to call him Lord, he has to be Lord of all!

Got ears? Still listening? Remain tuned in to what his Holy Spirit is saying to you. Don't reduce your relationship with Christ to a habit, a mascot, or a feel-good song. Let him rule your entire life with his authority.

Worship him.
Adore him.
Submit to him.
Follow him intimately.
Imitate him.
Spend eternity with him.

A REALLY, REALLY WEIRD HOUSE

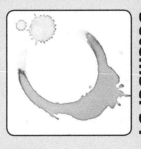

Back in the 1800s, the Winchester rifle was used in the Wild West by more outlaws, lawmen, and cowboys than any other rifle. Because of this, the Winchester family made a huge fortune. Mrs. Sarah Winchester didn't have a relationship with Christ, and she consulted mediums and psychics to discuss her future.

One day a psychic told her that because her family's rifles had killed many people, they had brought a curse that would haunt her for the rest of her life. This really frightened Mrs. Winchester, and she was determined to escape the curse.

She came up with a plan. She hired several construction workers to turn her San Jose, California, farmhouse into a mansion. She paid men to work on her house every single day until she died in 1922. Her plan was to confuse the ghosts of those killed by her husband's rifles by rearranging the house.

She had the builders make doors that opened into walls. They constructed staircases that led absolutely nowhere. Because of the constant building, this house going nowhere ended up with thirteen bathrooms, forty-seven fireplaces, forty staircases, fifty-two skylights, ten thousand windows, and two thousand doorways.

Just as passages in that really weird house went nowhere, you probably have some friends who feel as though their lives are going nowhere. And because they don't have a genuine, growing relationship with Jesus Christ, they'll continue climbing staircases that end abruptly and opening doors that lead to closed walls.

Your friends may feel as though they're constantly trying new things to fill the void inside—but getting nowhere. Maybe they're tired of noise from the "construction" of the world offering false hope and fake promises.

If you know Jesus Christ, you have the answer your friends are desperately searching for! They probably don't realize that what they need is a relationship with Christ, but you know it. Each one of us was created with a "God-sized hole" in our hearts that he, and only he, can fill.

Instead of letting your friends roam aimlessly in an existence that doesn't make sense, be willing to share your personal faith in Christ with them. Invite them to church, youth group, and Bible study. Ask them to read this book with you. Pray for your friends. The only way they'll enter heaven is through a personal relationship with Christ. So go ahead. Be a human Bible to them.

BREW IT!
May your friends read your actions as imitations of Christ himself.

POUR IT!
Drink in the flavor from the following Scriptures: Acts 4:12; Romans 1:16; 2 Corinthians 6:2.

SAVOR IT!
Ask God to help you be a bold witness to those who don't have a relationship with him.

Check out these other One Year Devos:

The One Year Devos for Teens

The One Year Devos for Teens 2

The One Year Devos for Sports Fans

CP0121